Brexit:
The Establishment
Civil War

Brexit:
The Establishment
Civil War

Josh Hamilton

Winchester, UK
Washington, USA

JOHN HUNT PUBLISHING

First published by Zero Books, 2021
Zero Books is an imprint of John Hunt Publishing Ltd., No. 3 East St., Alresford,
Hampshire SO24 9EE, UK
office@jhpbooks.com
www.johnhuntpublishing.com
www.zero-books.net

For distributor details and how to order please visit the 'Ordering' section on our website.

Text copyright: Josh Hamilton 2020

ISBN: 978 1 78904 490 4
978 1 78904 491 1 (ebook)
Library of Congress Control Number: 2019955249

A CIP catalogue record for this book is available from the British Library.

Design: Stuart Davies

UK: Printed and bound by CPI Group (UK) Ltd, Croydon, CR0 4YY
Printed in North America by CPI GPS partners

We operate a distinctive and ethical publishing philosophy in
all areas of our business, from our global network of authors to
production and worldwide distribution.

Contents

Contents

Part 1

The Data

1. Data, Data Everywhere

With big data comes big responsibilities.
Kate Crawford

27 January 2015, Twitter HQ: Twitter executives are preparing to unveil a set of tools for advertisers. This array of new tools will allow users to be targeted based on specific criteria, such as their postcode or geographical location. The new features even enable advertisers to target users based on specific accounts they may follow, websites they have visited (by tracking cookies), or even by TV shows they discuss on the platform.

Now, this may seem like a fairly standard development, why wouldn't Twitter want advertisers to get products in front of the most receptive consumers? Surely this helps us out as consumers too, allowing us to see the most relevant adverts to us – perhaps we will find the perfect birthday present or a deal on a product we had been looking at. But these tools were not developed with advertisers trying to sell us a holiday or a new Margherita maker. They were designed and created with political parties and campaigners in mind, Twitter made that abundantly clear in their blog post announcing the new services:

> The key benefit of geo-targeting is that it enables advertisers, or in this case political parties, the ability to reach users in specific regions, metropolitan areas and now postcodes... It brings real precision to online advertising and the ability to connect with and win people over at a local level...In battleground constituencies where the race to win a seat is likely to be close, targeting by postcode could prove to be a highly useful tool as part of any party's digital capability.

It was an incredibly significant acknowledgement of the way in which politics had truly entered the digital realm. One hundred days out from the 2015 General Election, Twitter had relented and joined Facebook in willingly courting political parties to use their platform to spread their message.

The 2015 election was the first British election to see the impact of targeted adverts. A leaked invoice from Facebook from November 2014 revealed that the Conservatives spent a staggering £114,956 in a single month. That equates to more than what 95 per cent of the British population bring home in an entire year. Why would the Conservatives need to spend so much money on a glorified chatroom?

The transition to the digital world was a natural progression for politics in the twenty-first century. By 2014, roughly 26 million of the British electorate were daily users of Facebook, the social media giant boasted that 89 per cent of ads reached the intended audience – far superior to the industry average of 40 per cent.

By the time the Brexit referendum came around, these practices had been honed by both the social networks and the advertisers. The referendum campaign illustrated with stark clarity the inherent problems of the growing power of big data analytics and the sheer amount of personal data that can be accessed through social media. The new tools were only given power by the data we offer up willingly and the more data they hoover up and campaigns they run, the smarter these tools will become. Data feeds these advertising tools and the tech giants amass more and more of it every day.

There is an unfathomable amount of data online. Facebook, Twitter, and the like hold more information on each and every one of us than most of us can possibly imagine and that information is being auctioned off daily to the highest bidder. This information, applied and analysed correctly, can wield unimaginable power. Whether willingly or unwillingly, we've handed over that power to the giants of Silicon Valley, so it is crucial that we understand exactly who is wielding that power and what it is capable of.

How Much Do They Know?

A survey of British consumers conducted by ComRes Global found that more than half (57 per cent) of the 2093 people polled worry about how much personal data they have shared online. Do you really know how much of your data is held online? Let's try a little experiment.

- Do you know how many companies hold information about you?
- Do you remember every single website you have ever signed up to?
- Did you take the time to read every single term and condition that you ever agreed to?
- Or take note of exactly who has your data and what exactly they know about you?

A total of 46 per cent of consumers in the UK say they do not feel they know how much data is available about them online. The reality is that most, if not all of us, are underestimating just how much of our personal information is available online. If you walked up to someone in the street in the early 1990s and told them that in the near future they would happily exchange all their personal information, their location, their likes and dislikes, and their daily habits, simply to be able to use some online services for free, they would probably have called you crazy. I can't imagine that they would so willingly forgo their privacy for such services. It has happened so gradually that we have all become complicit without a second thought.

This is the model for the digital economy that we created. Early on, we had to decide between paying for services with cash or with data. We chose data. Perhaps because it felt cheaper or easier or because it seemed impossible that this data could be analysed, weaponized, and monetized in the way it can be now. But for a handful of people, no one truly understood how this data could be used, at least not in the early days of the internet. It would have been almost inconceivable to imagine the impact the internet has had on our society 25 years ago. Even the most optimistic (or pessimistic) futurist would have had trouble conceptualizing the ways in which social media and technology has so rapidly permeated every single aspect of our lives.

Take Facebook, for example, based on your personal data they can tell how susceptible you are to their advertising, regulating your dosage to find the optimal level of advertiser content to maximize your number of clicks. They partner with firms who can monitor what you do in the real world, to see if those adverts translated into purchases offline, and even track your every movement. Nobody on the planet knows your location at every second of the day (not even your Mum), but if you leave your location services enabled on your phone, dozens of corporations will track every step.

You can take a look at the number of apps that access your location on your phone right now. If you're on Android:

1. Open the Settings app.
2. Press Apps or Application Manager (this varies depending on what device you are using).
3. Press Permissions or App Permissions. (If you can't find App Permissions, you may need to select an App or press Privacy and Safety followed by App Permissions.)
4. From here you can see what apps have what permissions on your phone and turn them on or off if you want to.

If you're on IOS:
1. Launch the Settings app.
2. Press Privacy.

3. From here you can see what permissions individual apps have on your phone and enable or disable them.

Just take a second to think, do Snapchat or Facebook really need to know your location at all times?

This information isn't exactly safe, either; in 2013, Facebook announced that the information of 6 million users had been leaked. When you are unaware of what data has been gathered on you and who holds it, it is impossible to ensure it is secure. Not only are we giving up our privacy to private companies that we interact with directly, but it is also available for third parties to bid on or access illegally.

Even if you have managed to avoid Facebook altogether, you aren't safe from companies attempting to gather data on you too. They have already been on the receiving end of multiple class-action lawsuits alleging that the firm has been profiling non-users without their consent. In one case they were accused of using face templates to scan pictures with faces that haven't been tagged, who may never have used the social network in their lives, and creating a 'digital biometric template' to build photographic profiles and match them to other data they have gathered through profiles of your friends.

Do yourself a favour, right now (or maybe after you read this book and recommend it to everyone you know), go and check how many apps have access to your data on Facebook.

1. On your computer or in the mobile app, tap the drop-down menu on the top-right side of Facebook.
2. Select Settings.
3. Select the Apps option. This is on the left side of the page on the desktop version. On mobile, simply scroll down the settings page.

Surprised yet? Not only do they store data on those with

accounts, they store data on people without a Facebook account – it is a global surveillance program in all but name, operated by a privately-owned company and enabled by us as a species.

They are tracking where you are, which applications you have installed, when you use them, and what you use them for. They have access to your webcam and microphone at any time, your contacts, your emails, your calendar, your call history, the messages you send and receive, the files you download, the games you play, your photos and videos, your music, your search history, your browsing history, even what radio stations you listen to.

The EU General Data Protection Regulation (GDPR) that came into effect in 2018 has put much more onus on companies to be transparent about what data they are collecting and why they are storing it, so post-GDPR there may be more accountability required on Facebook's part. Unfortunately, to curb the reach of this global juggernaut may be difficult or almost impossible at this point. Corporations have become almost as powerful as nation-states, especially the behemoths in Silicon Valley. The lack of regulation in the tech industry, the fast-moving nature of the business, and the potential lobbying powers emanating from California mean that taking on Facebook or Twitter, even for governments, can be incredibly complex and tiresome. The British parliament has been unsuccessful in summoning Mark Zuckerberg to testify to them, despite numerous attempts.

Maximillian Schrems

In the absence of accountable governments, Max Schrems, a 31-year-old Austrian lawyer, became one of many individual campaigners who have pitted themselves against the global juggernaut. Schrems began his anti-Facebook crusade back in 2011, he was making the case that Facebook had become a monopoly that needed to be restricted. As part of the campaign, he requested that Facebook show him all the data they were holding on him. He received a staggering 1200-page document encompassing everything he had ever clicked, liked, or commented on, and every single private message he had ever sent. He immediately filed 22 complaints claiming Facebook was breaking EU data protection laws.

From the very beginning, Schrems fought an uphill battle, struggling to find law firms to represent him in the fight against Facebook and dealing with a non-cooperative Irish Data Protection Commissioner (who routinely refused to return phone calls and described his case against Facebook as 'frivolous and vexatious'). He eventually had the Safe Harbour mechanism through which many companies transfer data across the Atlantic struck down as not providing adequate protection. He maintains that the decision didn't go far enough to protect our personal data and is continuing his fight using the new GDPR to file suits worth billions of Euros against giant institutions like Apple, Netflix, Spotify, Google, and Facebook.

Facebook has been singled out by world governments, and their gross negligence over data misuse in the Cambridge Analytica case has proven investigations necessary. However, just because they are the largest social network does not mean they are the only ones hoovering up the personal data of millions.

Facebook is simply an example, they are but one company (albeit a particularly large one). Yet, they seem to have become the scapegoat for governments of the world who are suddenly waking up to the power of personal data. Mark Zuckerberg has been dragged in front of Congress in America, the European Parliament, and has refused requests to appear before the UK parliamentary investigation into fake news. But for what? He may head one of the most prominent websites on the planet, collecting data from billions of people, but he isn't the only one. Twitter, Instagram, Snapchat, Microsoft, and countless others are all guilty of the same crimes. Yet there is one company that comes far and above every other in terms of just how much data they choose to store about you.

Enter Google.

Google

Google doesn't just track your web searches; it tracks your browsing via software installed on over 10 million websites. They own Gmail, Maps, Android, and YouTube, and much more. You may be one of the millions who use Chrome as their browser and you're probably signed in on the browser with your Google account.

They track your location, your search history, your YouTube history, your download history, and even build a profile of you for advertisers. If you want to, you can see the size of the data file that Google has on you at this very moment! Go to google.com/takeout and you can download the entire archive of data that Google currently holds on you.

Cirrus Insight, a CRM firm who developed an app to integrate Gmail and Salesforce, ran an estimate on how much data Google holds on everyone and everything, not just personal data, but every tiny piece of information that they possess. They calculated that Google holds somewhere in the range of 10-15 exabytes of data. An exabyte is equivalent to 1 million terabytes, which is 2024 gigabytes. The average laptop (much like the one I wrote much of this book on) has 500gb of hard drive storage, so Google currently holds the equivalent of 30 million laptops worth of data on all of us. This number is only going to increase, we continue to create exponentially more data with no signs of slowing. If you recorded all human communication from the evolution of humanity until 2003, you'd need roughly 5 billion gigabytes to store it all in. Those are rookie numbers, now we create that much data every 48 hours.

Google and several other INFO are also tracking your movements across different web pages and apps. Facebook, DoubleClick, and Google Analytics are present on over 60 per

hungry algorithms trying to sell us a product or a politician. When testifying in front of the Department for Culture Media and Sport (DCMS) committee, former Cambridge Analytica executive Brittany Kaiser told MPs:

> Corporations like Google, Facebook, Amazon, all of these large companies, are making tens or hundreds of billions of dollars off of monetising people's data...I've been telling companies and governments for years that data is probably your most valuable asset. Individuals should be able to monetise their own data – that's their own human value – not to be exploited.

This industrial-scale data hoarding is only the beginning of the story I want to tell here. Datasets are bought, sold, leaked, and stolen every minute. You are the product. The entire digital economy is a front for the shady world of data trading. Underneath the surface of free services, e-commerce sites, and the rest of the visible digital economy, lies a world where information about potential customers is sold off to the highest bidder.

> Consumers expect a connected experience. That means you have to understand their offline and online presence, buying behaviours, and interests. Acxiom offers the industry's most comprehensive data and models, and we can help you choose the most relevant and effective audiences to drive better marketing results both offline and online.

This is a line from the Acxiom website. They are a third-party data vendor whose sources include publicly available property transaction records, auto warranty and service records, consumer-reported product registrations, surveys, census neighbourhood statistics, and retailers. It provides:

- Age and gender
- Address and whether you rent or own your property
- Your choice of car
- Financial data like income bracket, credit history etc.
- Purchase data, including the types of products purchased, and frequency
- Interests and hobbies

It is now standard practice for advertisers to have access to these sorts of datasets to understand their target audience when launching a new advertising or marketing campaign. Your personal data is driving the modern economy.

The data market in the UK is growing rapidly, in 2016 its estimated net worth was some £700 million, rising to £900 billion in 2017 and it is projected to hit £1.1 billion by the end of 2018 – making it the second-largest data market in the world (behind the United States) and the largest in Europe.

And this is just the legal data market, there are untold amounts of personal data available for purchase illegally. Top10VPN, a technology website, investigated the average sales prices of specific items of personal data on three of the biggest dark web marketplaces, Dream, Point, and Wall Street Market. A PayPal account goes for around £280, banking log-in information can go for more than £150, Stolen eBay details will fetch about £26, whilst an Apple log-in is worth £11. Your entire life from JustEat or Deliveroo, to your Netflix account, your airline accounts, bank details, online shopping account, could be bought for just £820.

Click, Click, Click

To get an understanding of how powerful this type of advertising can be, we need to first get a basic grasp of how companies like Facebook use our personal data to sell us a product.

On any given social media platform, we will usually give our name, age, email address, and begin to follow a handful of pages or profiles of people or things we are interested in. From there we can instantly begin to be categorized into different groups that will be targeted by advertisers. Every single click is valuable to them, as David Sumpter writes in Outnumbered:

> We are clicking our personalities into Facebook, hour after hour, day after day. Smileys, thumbs up, 'likes', frowns, and hearts. We are telling Facebook who we are and what we think. We are revealing ourselves to a social media site in a level of detail that we usually reserve only for our closest friends.

A GlobalWebIndex report conducted at the end of 2016 estimated that on average around the world, users spent 2 hours per day using social networks and messaging apps. Facebook has us categorized using millions of points of data to sort us into 100 of thousands of different lists auctioned off to advertisers. Some of the names of the groups are quite amusing attempts by Facebook's algorithm to quantify in a word or phrase a specific cocktail of likes, hobbies, and interests, that could contain thousands of pieces of data, such as 'Toast', 'Platypus', and 'Neck'. We are, as Cathy O'Neil, author of Weapons of Math Destruction, puts it, being 'ranked, categorized, and scored'. Data released by Facebook has shown that they can guess when we are falling in and out of love, predict a depression diagnosis with over 70 per cent accuracy, and assess your psychological make-up more accurately than your friends, your family, or, given enough data, even your partner.

This dedication to craft from Facebook is far from fruitless; when they measured adverts and messages tailored to their assessment of our personality, such as our level of extraversion, they garnered 40 per cent more clicks and 50 per cent more purchases than randomly assigned adverts.

We could each easily quantify and sort our friends based on

a handful of traits or hobbies. Of course, we could define our closest friends in far more detail than the many acquaintances we have in our day-to-day lives, perhaps in 20, 30, 40, or even more different categories or dimensions, perhaps with hundreds of points of data. This is the absolute maximum that our brains can handle, it is inconceivable for us to visualize the 1000-dimension understanding of us that Facebook amasses by analysing our every action or inaction. They go to incredible lengths to discover what sort of adverts will draw us in, where they should be placed, and how they should look, even ignoring an advert supplies them with the knowledge that this advert at this time in this style did not work, every action or inaction teaches them something about us, and unlike us, they never forget, absolutely everything is catalogued, measured, and quantified.

'Facebook can learn almost anything about you by using artificial intelligence to analyze your behaviour,' Peter Eckersley, a chief computer scientist at the Electronic Frontier Foundation (a digital rights non-profit) told the New York Times. 'That knowledge turns out to be perfect both for advertising and propaganda.' Using their current methodology they can take 1 million different 'like' categories, chosen by 100,000 people, and reduce that to a few hundred dimensions in less than a second. Each click is a stroke of a brush on a vast canvass depicting our patterns of online behaviour right down to our subconscious, the Facebook algorithm captures everything and churns it out into useable and marketable data.

If you think that these companies would not pay attention to detail at this level you are sadly mistaken. Google cycled through A/B testing of 41 different shades of blue for part of their Gmail service – they have access to this data to help inform their decisions, why wouldn't they use it?

You can easily see what groups Facebook has placed you in:

1.   Log in to Facebook

2. Click on the drop-down menu in the top right-hand corner
3. Click settings
4. Click ads in the left-hand menu

From there you can see a list of your interests categorized by headings like People, Hobbies, and Activities, News, and Entertainment; lists of advertisers or businesses who have targeted you, uploaded a set of data matched with data from your Facebook profile to advertise to you, whose website or app you have visited; and there you can change your advert preferences. Under the Information section, you'll be able to see your categories. Facebook knew I was coming up to the end of my phone contract, my travel habits, and which categories I was highly engaged in.

Every company has unique ways in which they are able to collate data on each of us. Amazon collates data on your reading habits from your Kindle, analysing which phrases you highlight, which pages you skip, and whether you read straight through or jump around looking for information. All of this gets fed into which books get recommended for you next.

There may be a part of your brain that is currently saying, wait, isn't this just a more advanced version of how advertising has always worked? Haven't companies always altered their decisions based on past results of advertising campaigns and built up knowledge of what their customer base (or voter base) wants to hear? The only difference here is that we have computers to help store and process the data that informs these decisions.

Weapons of Math Destruction

The dangers of this type of technology come from failing to understand its potential fallbacks and risk of exploitation. Whilst it may seem reasonable to allow advertisers to simply target anyone based on characteristics that have been identified by the

Facebook algorithm, there are serious drawbacks and ethical conundrums. As well as using this information to target users based on needs, they can use the data available via Facebook to target people's deepest fears and dreams. In the book Weapons of Math Destruction, Cathy O'Neil details the way in which for-profit colleges in America exploited these weaknesses to sell students from a poorer background a degree worth little more than a high school diploma at wildly inflated prices by promising a way out of their problems.

Corinthian College in California was found guilty of lying about job placement rates, wildly overcharging students ($68,000 for a bachelor's degree that costs $10,000 in other parts of the country and fraudulently using military seals in online advertising). They were accused of targeting individuals who were labelled as 'isolated', 'impatient', 'low self-esteem', who are 'stuck' and 'unable to see and plan well for the future'. Money is poured into exploiting people's most vulnerable points; in the Corinthian University marketing team, there were 30 people with a $20,000,000 budget generating $600,000,000 in revenue. The recruiting team at ITT Tech in Indiana stayed motivated by admiring the picture of a dental patient with the caption 'find out where the pain is' in their offices.

Search Google for any personal problem or question and you'll quickly find yourself with adverts offering solutions. You will quickly see adverts for miracle cures, pay-day loans, or Vote Leave, all offering quick (often expensive) solutions to your every problem, be that the lack of employment options, poor career prospects, or a fear of never leaving the town you were born in. People will happily play on any psychological defect you have to sell you a product or idea. One Wall Street Journal study found that the top 50 internet sites, like Yahoo and MSN, on average install 64 cookies and trackers to your web browser. Eli Pariser, author of The Filter Bubble, decried the parasitic nature of these practices:

Search for a word like 'depression' on Dictionary.com, and the site installs up to 223 tracking cookies and beacons on your computer so that other Web sites can target you with antidepressants. Share an article about cooking on ABC News, and you may be chased around the Web by ads for Teflon-coated pots. Open – even for an instant – a page listing signs that your spouse may be cheating and prepare to be haunted with DNA paternity-test ads. The new Internet doesn't just know you're a dog; it knows your breed and wants to sell you a bowl of premium kibble.

One of the issues is that we are often more honest with our Google search bar than we are with people in the real world. 'Google won't judge us, Google is our friend', we all tell ourselves. Google is merely an algorithm and is trusted to answer our deepest and stupidest questions. But the reality is that Google is judging us more than any of our friends are likely to do, on an infinitely larger scale. People generally revealed the fears and worries when searching in Google, looking for fixes to their deepest insecurities and problems. Is there anything you wouldn't ask Google?

As well as targeting you through these categories, location, or age, Facebook can use a technique known as creating 'lookalike audiences'. This particular piece of tech can be incredibly powerful when applied correctly. By assessing the traits and likes/dislikes of individuals who they have already seduced through their advertising it can create lists of those who share those traits but have not yet fallen prey of advertising algorithms, such as 'big spending'. Murka, who develop casino games, used Facebook's data to target users who would be considered 'high-value players' who were ranked as 'most likely to make in-app purchases'.

This is big business for Facebook; selling access to your newsfeed and Facebook's targeting of you made them $40 million in 2017 rising to $55 million in 2018. The bad publicity suffered by Facebook in the wake of Brexit and Trump has not hurt their bottom line at all.

The very nature of politics means during an election you simply need to change the votes – in a bipartisan issue or a straight binary referendum – of 5 to 10 per cent of the population. A majority of people will know which way they will vote in a given referendum or election long before they vote, the key to winning is to capture the hearts and minds of the swing voters. We've been analysed, categorized, sorted, packaged, and sold off as a product for advertisers to pick off a shelf. Our worst traits and uncertainties are exploited for profit. All the while the all-devouring algorithms learn more and more as we pour more and more fuel onto this wildfire. With so much data available online, it was only a matter of time before people tried to utilize it for something more sinister and consequential than to sell us some weight loss pills or our next holiday.

2. How Social Media Drives Polarization

Maybe nobody cares about the truth anymore, as some have started to worry. Maybe political allegiance has replaced basic reasoning skills. Maybe we've all become trapped in echo chambers of our own making.

In 2012, Megan Phelps-Roper, accompanied by her younger sister, stepped out of the front door of their family home for the final time, knowing they were unlikely to ever set foot inside again or even talk to those they had left inside. They had both left the Westboro Baptist Church, an evangelical oddity of a church, famous for their picketing of soldiers' funerals and condemnation of everyone not subscribed to their ideology as bound for hell. Megan had begun to see cracks in their doctrines after engaging with people on Twitter and having genuine conversations with the people that her family had vilified. She did something not all of us would be capable of, she escaped from a cult.

How difficult do you think it would be to deprogram yourself and escape from a cult? You might reason that you could never fall foul of that way of thinking, to fall for such obvious lies. But what if we were all stuck inside our own little cults? Ones we built ourselves with a little help from Facebook and Twitter. Would we even notice? And how easy would it be to escape if we did?

C Thi Nguyen, an assistant professor of philosophy at Utah Valley University, has grown particularly concerned that the echo chambers we all inhabit have become more difficult to escape from than a cult. He is particularly worried about the way intellectual and social communities no longer share the same basic foundational facts, that they don't share a basic 'ground truth' from which they can all work. It isn't even that we share the same facts and draw different interpretations, we don't even share the same basic facts and it is destroying political discourse, both online and in the real world.

Jaron Lanier, the man who coined the phrase virtual reality, labelled social media firms as 'behaviour modification empires', suggesting that these technologies are changing the very way in which we as individuals and as a society behave and interact. Mark Zuckerberg famously described the worldview of himself and of the Silicon Valley disruptors as 'Move fast and break things. Unless you are breaking stuff, you are not moving fast enough.' Have we moved too fast? Is it really possible that these harmless little apps could be changing our very nature?

You Push the Button and We'll Do the Rest

We have already looked at how algorithms have been used to understand our behaviour and best sell us a product, but that is just one side of the analysis that is undertaken on each of us as individuals. It is crucial for Facebook or any other social platform to monitor your actions in order to understand how to sell you their products. The better they understand you, the more successful they are in cultivating sales or interactions for advertisers, and the more likely advertisers are to utilize their platform. So what does any algorithm require if it is trying to find patterns? Data, the more the better.

Let's say I found a social media platform called Blurt, where people are encouraged to blurt out everything that comes to mind. After a while, I start to get a little success and notoriety as users drift away from Twitter and Facebook in search of something more organic or original. How would I maximize data collection? The key is to find ways to keep people hooked into the platform for longer and longer periods of time, the more addictive the better. It makes sense to focus a lot of thought, energy, and capital into this side of the platform; it is hardly surprising that Facebook and its peers did the same.

They are designed to give us exactly what we want to see, or what we have told companies that we want through clicks and likes. The equations that produce your Twitter and Instagram feeds amass the entirety of our history on that platform, whatever data they have gathered about us from other websites or third parties' data vendors, the vast wells of content that are constantly being pumped out by users and creators. This is collated into a perfect cocktail of curated content designed to never let our eyes slip from the screen, lest we miss something.

This doesn't necessarily mean that we will always be fed content we agree with, just the content that engages us the most (whether that be through adoration or outrage). These platforms are simply designed to give us what they have found to be engaging to us, what truly captures our attention.

Let's take the Facebook newsfeed as an example. Many years ago (if you can remember back to the earlier days of Facebook), the newsfeed simply showed us what had been posted by friends of ours and pages we liked in chronological order. But that meant that people missed out on content or updates unless they were on Facebook every waking second of the day or spent hours scrolling through their newsfeed. Those of us with lots of friends and who followed numerous pages were always missing out on some of the highlights of the day. It was punishing those of us who used the platform most. It also meant that we were likely to miss the most engaging content if we weren't making constant use of the platform. That is unless we sought out the pages we liked of our own accord.

To counter this problem, Facebook decided we needed to see the most engaging things, those with the most comments, reactions, likes etc so that we never missed out on the biggest happenings of the day. They also made use of the well of data they were collating on each of us, continuously updating the algorithm that pumped out tailored content, refining its ability to keep us engrossed in the stream of memes, photos, articles, hot takes, or videos. It was designed to make us constantly crave the next little piece of information to stave off our boredom.

Please Like Me

The 'like' button, first introduced in 2009, tapped into our brains in ways that were never initially intended. By receiving a like on any social network we get a little fleeting burst of dopamine, which Facebook discovered made us more likely to return and scroll further down the newsfeed. This wasn't necessarily as sinister as it sounds, social media firms are simply competing for our time and attention, it seems only natural that they would try to find the best way to do that within the confines of the law. Sugar is addictive and causes major health problems, but there is no law against using sugar in food products.

Adam Alter, author of Irresistible: The Rise of Addictive Technology and the Business of Keeping Us Hooked, spoke to Vice about the issue: 'I don't think social media companies are trying to make "addictive" platforms, per se. But since they're all competing for our (limited) time and attention, they've always been focused on making the most engaging experience possible.'

Sean Parker, immortalized by Justin Timberlake in the film The Social Network, told a crowd at an event in Philadelphia that by triggering dopamine use to encourage users to stay on your platform, 'you're exploiting a vulnerability of human psychology'.

The founding president of Facebook and creator of Napster was incredibly upfront about the way in which Facebook was hooking you into their platform. It was a biological hack that they were happy to take advantage of.

Dopamine was discovered in 1957 and is created in various parts of the brain. It is critical in all sorts of brain activities, including thinking, moving, sleeping, mood, attention, and motivation. It's a huge part of the biological reward system in the brain and plays a major role in pleasure and addiction. Dopamine can be released by eating, exercising, listening to music, even simply spending time in the sun, or alternatively, by seeing a little like notification pop up on our phones. In Silicon Valley, dopamine is viewed as a sort of secret ingredient that can make an app 'sticky' i.e. potentially profitable. Ramsay Brown, a 28-year-old co-founder of Dopamine Labs, a start-up that claims to be able to significantly increase the rate at which you use any running, diet, or game application, describes the molecule as 'the sex, drugs and rock'n'roll molecule'.

Ever been scrolling through Twitter or Instagram and suddenly zoned back into the room? You have no idea how long you were scrolling for, or if you were even fully acknowledging what you were looking at. Maybe you've almost missed your bus stop (I know I'm guilty of that one). You've just been sucked out of your little digital world and thrown back into reality. You've probably just experienced a thing called a flow state similar to the one experienced by writers, musicians, athletes. DropBox has even launched a Flow State Academy aimed at educating people on using flow state. We all experience it to an extent in our daily lives when doing a task or hobby we do on a routine basis – anything from washing the dishes to painting a landscape. It's commonly known in the sporting world as being 'in the zone' and social media platforms induce the same sort of mindset in us. A paper published by Mauri et al in 2011 argued that Facebook induced its own unique 'core flow state', one MIT anthropologist Natasha Schüll calls 'the machine zone'.

The pull of social media has been compared to the pull of a slot machine. A former Google design ethicist and the co-founder of the Center for Humane Technology, Tristan Harris, believes that it is not simply about the understanding that these companies build of our behaviour, it is about understanding how our minds work at a chemical level. The machine zone is all about rhythm. It's essentially a dopamine feedback loop. Imagine you're sitting at a slot machine, you pull a lever and something will happen, you'll rarely have the same outcome twice in a row. Sometimes you'll win, sometimes you won't, but we are drawn into and stuck inside this loop. It's not even about winning, Natasha Schüll discovered that most people playing a slot machine are aware they aren't going to make any money, for them 'it's about getting in the zone'.

Vegas actually moved away from the lever model to slot machines that simply involve pushing a button, making the cycle even easier. When we scroll on through our Instagram or Facebook feeds we are inciting the same feedback look in our brains, scrolling for that next little dopamine hit. Facebook actually cites the invention of the scroll wheel for the computer mouse as a major turning point for it as a company where people were easily able to scroll through the newsfeed with very little conscious effort.

In an episode of the podcast 99 Percent Invisible with Roman Mars, Schüll described a state of mind that gamblers she interviewed fell into whilst they played, where everything seems to fall away: 'A sense of monetary value, time, space, even a sense of self is annihilated in the extreme form of this zone that you enter.'

The feedback loop that induces this state of flow is engaged as soon as you open one of your favourite apps, every article, photo, or comment feeds the loop, taking you deeper and deeper. This loop cannot be truly satisfied and is often only broken by an outside interruption, or perhaps a notification from another app. Any dopamine inducing drug overruns the neural pathways connected to rewards centres to the pre-frontal cortex, which is used by the brain to rein in impulses. The more the drug is used, the more difficult it becomes to stop.

Facebooks algorithm is designed to provide an infinite curated stream of content based on our history of use on the social network. It is powerful, but as with all machines, far from perfect. Some pieces of content may engage us, some may not, there is no distinct pattern to it. This, in fact, makes it even more addictive. BF Skinner, an American psychologist, found that the best way to reinforce behavioural patterns in rats was to reward them randomly. This technique has been used for decades by the producers of slot machines and has been inadvertently mimicked by social media sites.

Make Sure You Choose the Right Filter

These platforms drew us in, harvested our data, and addicted us to their streams of attention sucking content. Their desire to keep us hooked on their platform had unintended consequences, rather than making us more connected than ever, they herded us into groups. Fed an increasingly concentrated diet of our own decisions was never going to be healthy, but as Facebook became the biggest platform in the world for sharing news, new problems began to emerge. We've always read media that conformed to our interests, that is hardly something new. People who consider themselves right wing will have likely read the Mail or the Telegraph for years, self-selecting our media diet is not simply a feature of social media.

During the referendum, the phrase 'Westminster Bubble' was thrown about a lot by those on the Leave campaign. Insinuating that those inside the bubble didn't understand what was going on in the country outside of the capital. In a way, we are all stuck in our own little bubble wherever we live. It's difficult to escape it without a conscious effort to go out of our way to engage with people from all walks of life and understand how people outside of our immediate surroundings feel and what they believe.

With so much of our time consumed by social media, we have slid into our own digital filter bubbles. The very nature of click-driven algorithms has filtered out opinions and ideas that will not elicit a reaction from us. The idea of the filter bubble was initially articulated by Eli Pariser in his book Filter Bubbles. He saw the internet as a form of one-way mirror, that reflected your own interests back at you, tailored by algorithmic observers to give you exactly what you want. He described this as a filter bubble, 'a unique universe of information for each of us... which fundamentally alters the way we encounter ideas and information'.

Unfortunately for us, there are a number of side effects of these filter bubbles, none of which can be easily untangled. No one's Facebook or Instagram feed will ever look identical, not even close, there are so many factors at play bathed in an almost infinite pool of content that the chances of the top three posts in two friends' newsfeeds are identical are infinitesimally tiny. Even your Google searches are personalized to you. Google uses 57 different signals to tailor your search results, including your location, which web browser you are using, and the make of the computer being used. Thus your search results could be vastly different from your friend, simply based on your previous history on Google. Pariser gave an example where two users searched for British Petroleum, one saw news relating to investment, the other saw news of a recent oil spill. Try it right now, you could search for Greece, Apple, Farming, anything simple seems to show the starkest variations in results.

Google's CEO from 2001-2011, Eric Schmidt, warned that in the future every single piece of content could be individually tailored, down to articles and videos. He believes that very soon: 'It will be very hard for people to watch or consume something that has not in some sense been tailored for them.'

This has already been seen in an early form in the Brexit referendum, micro-targeted Facebook adverts were disseminated amongst specifically chosen groups, only to be seen by them. We will look at Facebook dark adverts in detail later on.

The Google news algorithm gives higher priority to news providers based on their size, traffic, and whether they cover the most topical issues. Even your search engine can shape your worldview in the way it ranks the results it provides to you. The top result on any given Google search gets clicked on one in every three searches, whilst the top two results account for more than 50 per cent of the clicks. Think about that, Google decide what answers you are getting based on metrics you don't understand and that no one really knows apart from the engineers at Google. They have the ability to shape the way in which entire populations understand almost any given issue – how many questions are met with the response 'Google it' in your everyday life?

It isn't just Google. Take SkyScanner, a flights comparison site that aggregates flight prices from across the web, their results vary dependent on similar metrics to Google. My girlfriend and I recently booked a trip looking at SkyScanner whilst we talked over Skype. We were seeing slightly different flight pricings on almost every search, with some not appearing at all – even when we were browsing in incognito mode.

Pariser warned that these filters were creating 'a kind of invisible autopropaganda, indoctrinating us with our own ideas'. In a political realm, this kind of 'filtering out' of opinions can be incredibly damaging. In the book 'The End of Absence', Michael Harris lamented that this becomes incredibly damaging to truly learning about and understanding our world. 'Personalization – the glorification of your own taste, your own opinion – can be deadly to real learning.'

We become utterly oblivious to the opinions of those outside of our own filter bubble. We are gluttonously consuming our personally curated news diets, with very little incentive to do otherwise. Filter bubbles wall us off from opinions that we may not agree with, we choose with our clicks, just as we do with everything online. It's easy and pleasurable for us to swim around in these little filter bubbles, it makes us feel safe in our own ideas and opinions. They can become like our own little digital safe spaces. They amplify an effect called cognitive dissonance, where we tend to favour information that conforms to our personal world view. When we consume a news diet made up primarily of sources with whom we share an ideological outlook, we interact positively with these sources, choosing them over others, meaning we see increasingly more of the same types of news story from the same handful of news outlets. As a result, our beliefs are being constantly reinforced building our own little impenetrable bubble.

Even more problematic is the fact that Facebook's algorithm isn't concerned with how factually accurate an article was, or how much we needed our own worldview to be challenged, it was only worried about what was going to draw us in.

Bias search rankings can have a very tangible real-world impact. A Princeton University study by Jacob N. Shapiro found that biased search results could sway the preferences of undecided voters by 20 per cent or more and that the search ranking bias can easily be hidden so there is so suspicion of manipulation at all. This is similar to a phenomenon called the Fox News Effect. It was estimated that the biased coverage by Fox News during the 2000 presidential election was enough to change almost 11,000 votes. The state of Florida swung the entire US election, coming down to some 537 votes in the state.

We're becoming increasingly entrenched in our filter bubbles and it has begun to affect the very roots of our democracy. As Pariser writes, 'Democracy requires citizens to see things from one another's point of view, but instead we're more and more enclosed in our own bubbles. Democracy requires a reliance on shared facts; instead, we're being offered parallel but separate universes.'

This is the exact phenomenon that C Thi Nguyen detailed is his essay arguing that algorithms and filter bubbles had constructed intellectual and digital cages that are more difficult to escape from than a cult itself. To get a better understanding of how this works, Nguyen divides the issue into two specific strands, echo chambers and epistemic bubbles. Both serve to reinforce the beliefs of the individual (and more broadly of a specific community), but in completely different ways.

Epistemic Bubbles

An epistemic bubble is the circle of people we surround ourselves with, it's the little corner of society that we experience in our day-to-day lives. It's generally filled with interactions with people we feel comfortable around, that share our world view and are on similar tracks in life. Obviously, conflict with other opinions, ideas, and outlooks are there if we seek them out, but we tend to naturally seek the company of those with whom we can agree and predict the reactions of. It almost inevitably feeds the individual a false sense of self-confidence in their own beliefs and the social acceptability/acceptance of these beliefs.

This can happen either consciously or unconsciously; either we choose not to hear outside opinions that challenge our worldview because we actively refuse to let them into our lives or we subconsciously surround ourselves with people whom we agree with on a majority of topics.

You're probably thinking to yourself right now, 'Well I don't do that, I can safely say I'm not guilty of this!' Think about it. Now, really think about it. What major issues do you really disagree with your friends on, especially your close friends? Brexit? Taxing the rich? Immigration? Tuition fees? Climate change?

It is possible that if we encounter people with whom we disagree, we struggle to form social ties with them due to fear of conflict. That's not to say it is impossible to avoid these pitfalls and have a more varied set of friends, it's not beyond any of us – Nigel Farage happens to be friends with George Galloway; George H.W. Bush and Bill Clinton have struck up quite a bromance since they both left 1600 Pennsylvania Avenue, and Frank Field (formerly Labour and then independent) and Nicholas Soames (Conservative) had an unlikely friendship that stretched across the benches in the Commons.

Echo Chambers

An echo chamber, on the other hand, describes the phenomenon whereby people tend to only expose themselves to media and discussion that reinforces their own beliefs, such as within private Facebook groups. Michela del Vicario, the co-author of a study about the effect of online misinformation on the Brexit vote, described echo chambers as 'closed environments, inside of which users are not reached by contrasting information'. The world view of the group is simply repeated, absorbed, and regurgitated, no one challenges anything, lest they be cast out by the group.

Not only does this cycle reinforce their own beliefs, it also creates a fear of the 'other side' and actively discredits the views and opinions of those on the opposite side of an issue or political divide as stupid, dangerous, or simply deranged. They label outsiders as untrustworthy, corrupt, or naïve in order to reject their world view without due consideration. Almost everyone is guilty of this.

In his essay, Nguyen uses the right-wing Talk Radio host Rush Limbaugh and his supporters to illustrate how echo chambers work. Limbaugh discredits all contrary opinions as being part of the liberal media establishment and thus already invalid, his supporters are still exposed to these voices but this only seems to serve to further reinforce the voices from inside the echo chamber.

There is a theory that more exposure to the views of the 'other side' reduces political polarization. Take us out of our self-selected groups, force us to be exposed to opinions we don't like, disagree with, or don't want to hear, and we'll start to become more reasonable and less extreme. The problem is, data shows us that often this isn't the way it works. In the paper, "Escape the Echo Chamber", Nguyen writes,

'Perversely, exposure to outsiders with contrary views can thus increase echo-chamber members' confidence in their insider sources, and hence their attachment to their worldview. The philosopher Endre Begby calls this effect "evidential pre-emption". What's happening is a kind of intellectual judo, in which the power and enthusiasm of contrary voices are turned against those contrary voices through a carefully rigged internal structure of belief.'

In the UK there is a similar cult following of Nigel Farage, who repeatedly labels the BBC as utterly biased despite countless appearances on BBC programming (he has appeared on Question Time alone 33 times, despite not being a member of a political party from 2016 to the beginning of 2019). Farage dismisses all challenging lines of questioning, valid or invalid, as proof of the BBC bias and portrays himself as a martyr for the forgotten and ignored. The Leave campaign was built on the idea of sticking it to the liberal establishment, any warnings about Brexit became 'Project Fear', a desperate attempt by the establishment to scare people into voting to remain. In the eyes of Farage and his cult following, he is the last defence holding back the oncoming tide, the soldier they chose to stick it to the establishment. Every major TV appearance is greeted with a complete divide in the reactions – either you believe Farage has stuck it to the liberal elites, or you see him as a terrifying demagogue stirring up racism and hatred for his own personal gain, there is no middle ground here.

Christopher Bail at Duke University conducted an experiment where Democrats and Republicans were asked to follow a bot on Twitter that would retweet content from the opposite side of the political spectrum to try to measure whether this could make their views less extreme. The results actually showed that Republicans became more extreme when exposed to Democratic views, whilst the Democrats showed no change in their views.

The Talk Radio/Fox News Conservative echo chamber that Rush Limbaugh inhabits has been around for decades. It was a concerted effort by Republicans to build these media bubbles back in the late 90s that began this deliberate polarization of the political debate. When the internet blew up and Reddit, Facebook, and Twitter came crashing into our daily lives, online meme culture – ironic, humorous, or exaggerated caricatures of opposing political opinions – spread like wildfire across the interconnected world we inhabit. The digital echo chambers we have constructed through Facebook groups, subreddits, and 'Twitter-spheres' mean we are never more than 15 seconds from seeing the latest sliver of news or opinion to reinforce our own beliefs, echo our own thoughts, or parody the 'other side'.

Filter bubbles, epistemic bubbles, and echo chambers have existed in different forms in society for millennia, but the algorithms that make up social networks have super-charged these phenomena. We're all playing guinea pigs for a brand-new epoch of political campaigning.

Jordan Peterson believes that social media is not so much an echo chamber as it is an amplifier. He argues that social media connects us in ways that we can't quite even grasp – for example, if we befriend 1000 people on Facebook, we're just two steps away from one billion different people. That is a crazy level of connection to the rest of the planet. It is very difficult for us to appreciate the impact that this is having on society. What we say online today is transmitted faster, heard by more people, and amplified more than any speech in the history of the world. Would we be fools to think that this may not have had any noticeable impact on culture, society, politics, and political discourse?

In his book Outnumbered, David Sumpter outlines his critique of the filter bubble theory, suggesting that it is far too simplistic and that even in our modern world it is impossible to insulate ourselves from outside opinions. We are all presented with the views of the 'other side', with the vast majority of people who consume news online following outlets from all sides of the spectrum. He does, however, fail to consider two key points in this issue. Firstly, the way in which algorithms are built means that we become less and less exposed to the types of articles and pieces of content that we tend to disagree with. I could follow every single news site in existence, but that does not mean the coverage I will see in my newsfeed is completely balanced. All it takes is a few clicks on The Sun or the Daily Mail and that begins to colour the sort of content I will see, thus beginning the vicious downward cycle towards extremism. It doesn't matter how many left-wing news sites I follow, if I only click on articles from the Express, that is all I am likely to see.

Secondly, he fails to consider what impact being presented with articles from the 'other side' might have. He reasons that exposure to ideas of the other side means our brains will give them equal weight. We will look into the psychological reasons why this isn't the case in the next chapter, but for now, we simply need to consider how echo chambers work. In our example of Rush Limbaugh, he exposes listeners to the crazy ideas of the left to further entrench his own ideas. By portraying them as insane, or stereotyping their positions, he is able to further discredit the other side through the exposure of their ideas.

Steve Bannon and Andrew Breitbart bought into the idea that politics is downstream from culture, so to change politics you had to change the culture. Where does 90 per cent of modern culture preside? In the digital world. On Facebook, YouTube, Twitter (and now Instagram). To change the culture, and therefore politics, you have to wage war on the digital battlegrounds and that is exactly what happened on both sides of the Atlantic.

Down the YouTube Rabbit Hole

YouTube, also owned by Google, has become a huge part of politics and modern media. YouTube news shows, vlogs, documentaries, podcasts, live streams, have all become a major part of the political and media landscape over the past few years. Almost every major TV and news network posts clips and interviews on YouTube. But YouTube is not neutral, it suffers from the same flaws that all modern media seem to suffer from, its business model is click and ad-revenue driven. Zeynep Tufekci, a sociology scholar, argues that YouTube is driving the extremism and polarization that we see in society and politics today (willingly or unwillingly).

Try watching any political video on YouTube and see where 'autoplay' takes you. Go on, give it a go right now! Try a Nigel Farage interview and you may find yourself being recommended Tommy Robinson videos, watch a few interviews with Bernie Sanders and you might be faced with Hillary Clinton/Seth Rich conspiracy videos, watch a clip from Jacob Rees-Mogg on LBC and soon you'll find Britain First in your up-next queue. This isn't confined to the political world, try watching a video on vegetarianism and vegan videos start appearing, check out a few videos on running and you'll soon see videos on running ultra-marathons, watch any conspiracy video and you might find yourself tumbling down the flat-earth rabbit hole.

Why is this? YouTube designs its algorithm for clicks, much like every other social network or technology company. Their business model is based on clicks, that is their goal above all else. So when you task some software engineers with designing some algorithms to produce the most clicks, it learns which types of recommended videos will optimize the bounce rate (how likely you are to click on another video). The most powerful 'click bait', in this case, is extremism and controversy. The most effective method for the algorithm to seduce the most viewers to watch another offering is by providing something intriguing, captivating, or just triggering – i.e. something more extreme than what they are currently viewing.

The 'autoplay' feature has made this effect even more prominent, users need not even click, YouTube will automatically cycle through one recommended video after another, leaving the user with no say in where the rabbit hole goes. This was not a nefarious or malicious design, it was simply designed to maximize profits – if another video plays automatically, another advert is likely played, and YouTube reaps another little drop of revenue, another view on their platform, and may even another click as users choose to override the 'autoplay'.

Zeynep Tufekci believes we are witnessing:

> the computational exploitation of a natural human desire: to look 'behind the curtain,' to dig deeper into something that engages us. As we click and click, we are carried along by the exciting sensation of uncovering more secrets and deeper truths. YouTube leads viewers down a rabbit hole of extremism, while Google racks up the ad sales.

Tufekci points out the same flaw we identified earlier about the Facebook algorithm, it 'is not optimising for what is truthful, or balanced, or healthy for democracy'.

As the referendum campaign heated up, so did the online discourse. The other side of the click-driven algorithms was exploited. Interactions on social media were increased by curating content that we agreed with, things that confirmed our worldview. However, we were also incited to comment or react to content that was controversial, things that sparked outrage drew us in, even just a headline or a comment. Just like with YouTube, the Facebook algorithm discovered that controversy and extremism drove interactions, putting the most controversial items at the top of our newsfeed.

Trevor's Axiom

South Park may be a cartoonish, poorly drawn parody of society, but more often than not they manage to make some fantastic insights into culture and society. The season 20 finale introduced me to an idea called 'Trevor's Axiom'.

Trevor's Axiom is a well-known equation in online trolling, it's a way in which one person can create a massive reaction on the internet. Person A trolls Person B, but it's not about Person B. Person A is trying to push buttons to try to get a reaction from hundreds, eventually creating Person C, whose over-reaction and self-righteousness will elicit a reaction from Persons D through F who weren't trolls but can't help but rip on Person C. Their reactions lead to outraged Persons G through N and it keeps going creating massive energy. It's like the fission reaction that leads to a fusion explosion all bringing out the worst in humanity.

This is one of the best explanations I found to help me understand how trolls and extremism can infect the online political conversation, bubbling over into the real world.

Extreme abuse is never meant to simply harm the individual at which it is aimed, rather the trolls are trying to elicit a controversial reaction from someone jumping to the defence of the victim. The goal is to start a chain reaction of responses that stokes the stereotypes that both sides have built up of the other in any given argument, to further reinforce the echo chamber and perpetuate the myth that the 'other side' is completely crazy, delusional, and out of touch with reality. Former High Court Judge at the Supreme Court of Trinidad and Tobago, and later president of the twin islands, Anthony Carmona put it rather eloquently when he said: 'Social media websites are no longer performing an envisaged function of creating a positive communication link among friends, family and professionals. It is a veritable battleground, where insults fly from the human quiver, damaging lives, destroying self-esteem and a person's sense of self-worth.'

Trevor's Axiom is partially based on concepts of bullying, whereby one individual can successfully divide societies and groups up as defenders or attackers of a victim. This can happen in prisons, school-yards, offices, and now is happening more and more in the digital space. David Graeber, author of Bullshit Jobs: A Theory, explains it like this:

> Just as a woman, confronted by an abusive man who may well be twice her size, cannot afford to engage in a 'fair fight,' but must seize the opportune moment to inflict as much damage as possible on the man who's been abusing her – since she cannot leave him in a position to retaliate – so too must the schoolyard bullying victim respond with disproportionate force, not to disable the opponent, in this case, but to deliver a blow so decisive that it makes the antagonist hesitate to engage again.

So how much of this can we map onto our online discourse? Reactions in online discourse have become so strong that any attack on the ideas of one side is automatically refuted as an attack on the very roots and identity of that group or individual, that anyone not with them must be against them. Log in and find any political discussion on Facebook or Twitter with enough engagement and arguments often descend rapidly into hurling insults vaguely based on the tribal identity of one side or the other. You're either a 'butthurt Remoaner' who can't accept democracy or a 'racist Leaver' who doesn't understand what they voted for. People become emotionally triggered by controversial content. We're all guilty of it, I know I am prone to becoming emotionally triggered when I see Boris Johnson discussing the 'technological solutions' to the Irish border issue.

Being triggered is a term used on social media to describe a violent emotional reaction to a piece of content. This may be a post about Trump's latest sexist comments, an article about how the EU is legislating on how straight a banana should be or how immigrants are cheating the welfare system, or simply just a provocative piece of content designed to push your buttons. How often have you seen online discussions descend rapidly into hurling insults at one another until someone plays the Nazi card? It's easy to vilify someone on social media. We know very little about them, perhaps we can see a Union Jack in the profile picture, so they must be a racist Brexit voter. The echo chambers that have reinforced our beliefs about 'the other side' makes it very easy for us to place anyone who disagrees with us in that 'other' category and treat them with the contempt and resentment with which we would treat an enemy on the battlefield. We barely see them as human anymore, just some words and pictures on a screen at which we can vent our anger.

When we are confronted with something controversial that 'triggers' us online we often lash out in response. We find it much easier to be abusive sat in front of a computer screen than we do when we are forced to confront someone in real life. When we are interacting online we don't have the societal pressure to be polite or conform to social norms.

As we drew closer and closer to polling day and tensions ramped up higher and higher, we were more and more prone to being triggered. Every little comment against your side feels like an attack on your very identity and so every issue becomes a battle between Leave and Remain, Democrat or Republican, Labour or Conservative, and it is destroying our political conversation. Graeber purports that by being 'triggered' we could actually become the perfect victim for bullies (or in this case for trolls).

The ideal victim is not absolutely passive. No, the ideal victim is one who fights back in some way but does so ineffectively, by flailing about, say, or screaming or crying, threatening to tell their mother, pretending they're going to fight and then trying to run away. Doing so is precisely what makes it possible to create a moral drama in which the audience can tell itself the bully must be, in some sense, in the right.

This moral drama is played out a million times a day across

Twitter, Facebook, and Reddit. As drama ramps up in an election or referendum and the stakes seem to get higher and higher, the fires of outrage are stoked higher and higher. The more consequential the election feels or is, the more open we as a society become to these vicious cycles that are destroying our political conversation and undermining our very system of government. Worst of all bad actors have demonstrably attempted to exploit these weaknesses.

The IRA

The clock strikes 9pm. On a cold spring night in Moscow, a tired huddle of people emerge silently from the 'Business Centre' at 55 Savushkina Street. They'll be back at 9am tomorrow for another 12-hour shift, as they are every day of the week. This is the headquarters of Russia's 'troll army', a remarkably efficient misinformation factory dubbed the Internet Research Agency (IRA). The four-storey building is divided into a newsroom, bloggers and social media workers, and even an images department tasked with crafting gigabytes of spicy memes.

The hoard of paid bloggers work relentlessly to flood the internet with propaganda and messaging dictated to them through their daily briefings. They are employed without a contract, they simply sign a non-disclosure agreement and are forbidden from discussing their work with friends or family. Trolls are discouraged from talking to their fellow keyboard mercenaries and cameras watch their every move. Fines can be imposed for the tiniest infractions; arriving just a few minutes late or not hitting the required quota of posts in a day will cost you. These can hurt when you're earning £520 a month.

Social media workers and bloggers operate in rooms of roughly 20 people, headed and overseen by three editors, who would review posts at random and enforce fines if language had been copied and pasted or was not ideologically consistent with the desired messages. The goal is to create a 'circle of lies' where trolls spread, repeat, and enforce the messages being deployed by state media through comments, link sharing, and memes. All in service of what one former troll described as 'Make Russia Great Again'. They worked in groups of three, one would post a link or leave a comment and the other two responded with links to articles or provocative memes.

Marat, a former IRA troll, told The Guardian that he saw the real-world impact of the misinformation campaign first hand.

'The scariest thing is when you talk to your friends and they are repeating the same things you saw in the technical tasks, and you realise that all this is having an effect.'

Another former employee, Vitaly Bespov, detailed how, back in 2012 during the Russian annexation of the Crimea, he would be asked to rewrite news reports from other outlets changing the language to a more pro-Russia tone. For example, the word 'annexation' became 'reunification', the Ukrainian government would be described as fascist, and 'separatists' in the east of Ukraine were always portrayed in a positive light. Russia has been attempting to drive public opinion within Russia and outside since 2012 using social media.

After the 2016 presidential election, Facebook announced that the IRA reached 126 million US citizens during the election campaign through posts and adverts. Twitter also revealed that 50,000 Russian-linked automated accounts were able to drive interactions with 1.4 million users. During and after 2016 pundits were suggesting that fake news was part of what led the Trump charge. However, new information revealed by Facebook suggests that there was a far more subtle digital campaign taking place. Facebook admitted to congressional investigators that it had sold ads to a Russian company attempting to influence voters. Facebook accounts with alleged Russian ties bought around $150,000 in political ads aimed at American voters during key periods of the 2016 presidential campaign. Around 470 accounts associated with around 3000 ads were connected and according to Alex Stamos, Facebook's chief security officer, they were 'likely operated out of Russia'. The vast majority of these ads did not specifically reference any party, candidate, or even the election itself, rather they were designed to amplify 'hot-button social and political issues, such as LGBT rights, race, immigration and gun rights'.

Many of the ads in question ran before the primaries had concluded and many experts have dismissed the minimal spend of $150,000. It pales in comparison to the $55 million spent by one of Hillary Clinton's primary digital firms and the $90 million spent by Donald Trump through his main digital adviser, Brad Parscale.

The New York Times (in conjunction with FireEye) has recently revealed that on Twitter (and on Facebook) thousands of suspected Russian-linked accounts used the platforms to spread anti-Clinton messages and promote leaked material. Many of these were bots which, according to FireEye researchers, put out identical messages seconds apart in the exact alphabetical order of their made-up names. For example, on election day, they found that one group of Twitter bots sent out the hashtag #WarAgainstDemocrats more than 1700 times. There is even evidence of Russian attempts to influence the conversation on issues that are seemingly unrelated to politics. Thousands of tweets from Russian-linked accounts have been uncovered that were attempting to sow online discord over GM foods. Renée DiResta, a specialist in disinformation who has advised the US Congress, has argued that the anti-GM messages are part of a web of disinformation intended to discredit accepted science: 'Undermining a nation's trust in its health services, scientific experts and research institutions is an effective way to destabilise a society.'

DiResta amassed around 241,000 tweets and retweets from the Twitter-sphere about GMO over 60 days. More than 100,000 accounts were part of the discussion, but the ten most prolific were almost undoubtedly bots, given how rapidly they were tweeting.

Just how effective they were in swinging the election is another question. Robert Mueller released his long-awaited report into Russian meddling in the US election in April 2018. In the report, he accused the Russian government of having 'interfered in the 2016 presidential election in sweeping and systematic fashion'. Unfortunately, there were no studies being conducted on the effect that propaganda of this kind can have on an election, that is until the 2018 Alabama Senate race.

The 2018 Alabama Senate race was never going to be boring, especially when a study was approved to test the influence of micro-targeted digital propaganda on a voting population. Then Roy Moore and Donald Trump got involved.

David Goldstein, a US electoral expert and consultant, became intrigued by the tactics that were used by the Trump and Brexit campaigns to win against the odds. 'It is so rare and so hard in politics to pull an upset. They are few and far between,' he told Planet Money. Yet somehow, one company pulled off two upsets in the space of 6 months. Cambridge Analytica. We'll get to the company itself a little later, but here I want to examine some of the tactics they used to try to swing the election and assess whether there is any demonstrable impact on the results of elections.

Goldstein believes that this is comparable to an arms race, with Democrats in America or Remainers in the UK falling far behind. Initially, the Alabama Senate race to replace Jeff Sessions (who was named as Attorney General by President Trump) didn't seem like one that Democrats could win. They hadn't had a senator there in over 25 years. But Goldstein simply had to prove that their methods could be demonstrably proven to have impacted on voting patterns.

He picked three districts to test on and three control districts and assembled a team of individuals to pump out a constant stream of content. He actually found that amateur levels of graphics production worked best, it feels more organic and fits with the types of adverts you might expect to see on social media.

They produced content for both sides, designed to discourage Republicans from voting or to encourage Democrats to get to the polls. When a user clicked on one of his adverts, they would be taken to a personally curated website, in the case of Democrats it was designed to uplift them and make them feel positive about voting for their candidate. For moderate Republicans, he sent them to a page filled with news stories about how other Republicans are planning to write in other candidates and for conservative Republicans they were sent to a page filled with content on how terrible Roy Moore was as a candidate. None of the stories were 'fake news', it was all real and accurate content from around the world. He was hoping to help construct a fake view of the world from real stories, encouraging the creation of a digital echo chamber.

Everything went live just 10 days before election day, research told him that is the most effective time to launch this sort of digital campaign. In a tight election race, you might only need to change the opinion of one or two people out of every 100 and with Roy Moore, who was accused of sexual assault by 8 women (several of whom were under age), running for the Republican Party, the stage was set with controversy and a much tighter race than would normally be expected. To Goldstein's shock, he found that the most engaged group was conservative Republicans. Engagement is one thing, but did the experiment have any real impact on voter turnout or voting behaviour? Democrats targeted with his adverts and websites turned out at a rate 4 per cent higher than the control group of Democrats, more than the margin of victory in tight elections. Moderate Republicans turned out 2.5 per cent less than the control group and conservative Republicans at a 4.4 per cent lower rate than those who didn't see Goldstein's adverts. Roy Moore lost the election to the Democrat Doug Jones by 1.5 per cent of the vote, just over 20,000 votes across the state. Goldstein estimated that he was able to affect roughly 8-9000 votes. There are far too many variables to verify whether he was able to have any impact, perhaps Doug Jones held some big rallies in the test districts and drove up Democratic turnout.

Obviously, it is very difficult to draw causation with correlation, but at this point, the idea that you could swing an election with digital advertising is far from wild speculation. There exists demonstrable evidence of digital campaigning affecting real-world elections. Goldstein spent just $87,000, not exactly a huge sum in US politics (consider that each campaign was allowed to spend £7 million during the Brexit campaign). How much impact do you think you could have with more resources and more data?

Social Media Takeover

The toxic nature of social media is quite clearly not solely due to the paid trolls. The very nature of social media breeds an ever-polarizing political conversation. We already looked at how social media can trap us in our own echo chambers and epistemic bubbles, but now I want to explore just how damaging the quality and tone of our online discourse can be.

Jay Van Bayvel recently conducted a study on the types of tweets that tend to go viral. His findings revealed that the more emotionally stacked the language is, the more likely the tweet is to elicit a reaction. Words like blame, shame, or hate were particularly effective. One theory is that this sort of language is a subconscious way for us to signal which tribal group we belong to – are we Leave or Remain, Labour or Conservative, Republican or Democrat? In the attention economies of Twitter and Facebook, only the most outrageous content will elicit reactions and only the most extreme views will gain us the approval of our group. This drives political polarization by pushing influencers and those seeking approval or attention further and further to the extremes in order to gain approval or notoriety.

The 10-year study on Twitter conducted by Van Bayvel found that false stories were seen on average by thousands more users than objectively true news articles. This exact phenomenon was taken advantage of by a handful of Macedonian teenagers who abused the gullibility of the entire US electorate to make thousands of dollars in ad revenue on fake news websites.

Veles in Macedonia once supplied porcelain to the whole of Yugoslavia, but its primary export now is 'junk news'. This quiet riverside town was home to more than 100 websites tracked down by US investigators producing mostly pro-Trump news. But the partisan slant of the news was irrelevant, either side of an issue was alright, the goal was generating clicks regardless of the validity of a story. It just so happened that pro-Trump or anti-Clinton headlines had the most viral potential. Mikhail, who ran one of the numerous fake news factories, told CNN: 'At 22, I was earning more than someone [in Macedonia] will ever earn in his entire life.' He claimed to have earned something in the range of $2500 a day, a fortune compared to the average $426 monthly wage in Macedonia. This revenue wasn't provided by bad actors, billionaires, or governments trying to spread misinformation. It was just Google AdSense revenue, that anyone with a home address and a website can earn from impressions and clicks on any website they own. It doesn't matter how these visitors arrived at the website, whether the stories were accurate or the headlines misleading, all they needed was your clicks to monetize their 'junk news'. Advertisers didn't care because they were getting clicks, Google didn't care because it was feeding money and data into their AdSense programme, and most people who visited these sites didn't care because what they read was confirming biases they already held.

Even Tumblr wasn't safe from the influence of trolls, some posed as black activists on Tumblr to generate hundreds of thousands of interactions driven by anti-Hillary, pro-Bernie Sanders content that focused on racial and wealth injustice and inequality. Researcher Jonathan Albright told BuzzFeed News that: 'The evidence we've collected shows a highly engaged and far-reaching Tumblr propaganda-op targeting mostly teenage and twenty-something African Americans. This appears to have been part of an ongoing campaign since early 2015.'

The Russian-linked Tumblr accounts operated under remarkably similar usernames to a list of confirmed IRA Twitter accounts and even promoted suspected IRA-linked accounts across platforms. For example, the 4mysquad Tumblr posted a screenshot of a tweet from the @4mysquad Twitter account and invited people to 'support me on #twitter'. The Twitter account's bio also contained a link to the 4mysquad Tumblr page, and they both used the same profile image. It was one of the more successful accounts, racking up numerous posts that each generated hundreds of thousands of notes on Tumblr.

Australian journalist Chris Zappone was highly critical of who he called the techno-libertarian social media overlords in Silicon Valley. He argued in his book, The Age, that social media had become the weak link in Western democracy, the opening through which Russia, and thus anyone with sufficient resources, could sow discord and unrest from afar. In an article for the New York Observer entitled 'Social Media Is Helping Putin Kill Our Democracy', John R. Schindler reasoned that: 'Social media made Moscow's clandestine work much easier and more profitable, they are now disseminated so quickly, and through so many fronts, trolls, and bots, that Western governments are severely challenged to even keep up with these weaponized lies, much less push back.'

Zeynep Tufekci warned in a piece in Wired that we are living through 'the (democracy-poisoning) golden age of free speech'. The freedom we all have to say, publish, and post anything we want on social media almost instantaneously is the ultimate expression of free speech, but this speech is not part of a dialogue. It is simply being used to perpetually promote self-selecting tribalism, where people express increasingly extreme and partisan viewpoints for two primary reasons. Firstly, to gain and keep the approval of those within their tribe by signalling to them that they are part of the in-group through the support of specific positions or ideas, such as the condemnation of the EU or taxing the rich and seizing the means of production. Secondly, echo chambers tend to encourage groupthink, where no one forms their own opinions within a community because the community has already decided. Want to know what to think of the leading issue of the day, simply log in to Twitter and see what the rest of your 'side' believe.

Brexit Bots

This might all seem irrelevant to you. Who cares if Russia tried to influence the US election? Well, there was a concerted, albeit less intensive, effort to influence the online conversation surrounding Brexit. In November 2017, Theresa May gave a speech at the Lord Mayor's banquet, in which she accused Russia of attempting to meddle in elections around the world. She declared: 'I have a very simple message for Russia. We know what you are doing. And you will not succeed. Because you underestimate the resilience of our democracies, the enduring attraction of free and open societies, and the commitment of Western nations to the alliances that bind us.'

For a woman frequently accused of failing to answer questions and being far too vague, these words were not minced. Meanwhile, the parliamentary probe into 'fake news' asked both Facebook and Twitter to hand over information on Russian-linked advertising that may have been targeted at influencing voters in the Brexit referendum. Damian Collins, the Conservative Party MP, wrote to Mark Zuckerberg asking for details on the Russian-linked adverts and accounts, including how much money was spent on ads, how many times they were viewed and which Facebook users were targeted.

The Computational Propaganda Project has been producing research surrounding the use of bots in election campaigns around the world and they have penned several reports on 'Brexit bots'. In a study of 1.5 million tweets from 5 June to 12 June 2016, they found 54 per cent were pro-Leave, 20 per cent were pro-Remain and 26 per cent were neutral. From over 313,000 accounts sampled, a third of the tweets – half a million – came from less than 1 per cent of the accounts – those that are automated accounts. Researchers noted that roughly 45 per cent of Twitter activity in Russia is managed by highly automated accounts and the geo-location of the tweets that could be tracked came overwhelmingly from outside the UK. They used a handful of hashtags that included things like #EUref, #BrexitInOut, #BritainInOut, and #BrexitOrNot to secure maximum impact.

'The family of hashtags associated with the argument for leaving the EU dominated, while less than one per cent of sampled accounts generated almost a third of all the messages.'

Bots can be used to stir controversy and manipulate conversations online by using hashtags to drive specific discussions up the agenda that will gaslight and trigger outrage. Similar to the way in which trolls can be used to drive engagement through Trevor's Axiom, bots using hashtags can drive controversial topics further up the agenda, manipulate what the public perceives to be the most talked-about or controversial issues on Twitter, and disrupt commentators' perception of the focus of online discussion. The conversation will blow up as exponentially more people are sucked into arguments and discussions online. This generates a political discourse that serves to polarize both politics and society.

Edinburgh University researchers identified 419 Twitter accounts operating from the Russian Internet Research Agency (IRA) attempting to influence UK politics as a part of 2752 accounts suspended by Twitter in the US following the US election and revelations about the IRA. If you don't think such a small number of accounts can even begin to have an influence on a national political conversation, you are wrong.

One of the accounts identified as a part of the research posted a picture claiming that a woman walking past in a headscarf was a Muslim woman simply ignoring the victims of the March 2017 terror attack on Westminster Bridge that left 50 people injured and 4 dead. That claim was then rehashed by the Mail Online and the Sun, much to the enjoyment of the troll.

He tweeted: 'Wow...I'm on the Daily Mail front page! Thank you British libs! You're making me famous.'

Then just a day later, he tweeted on the topic again: 'I'm on The Sun! Thank you again, British libs! Now I'm even more famous!'

He was literally thanking the mainstream press for running with his propaganda, in public, with no consequence or retraction from the paper. The troll, known as @SouthLoneStar, churned out buckets of anti-EU and anti-Muslim rhetoric:

'I hope UK after #BrexitVote will start to clean their land from muslim invasion!'

'UK voted to leave future European Caliphate! #BrexitVote.'

Bots aren't all-powerful, they lack the ability to interact properly or act like real people and thus are fairly limited in their capacity to influence online conversations. However, when used correctly they can be successful in driving hot-button issues up the agenda.

The polarization of the two major political parties on both sides of the Atlantic is not solely due to this digital influence, there is obviously a multitude of factors including the natural ebb and flow of political polarization, the growing wealth gap, and the impact of immigration. But this digital propaganda campaign has exacerbated the situation, though the extent to which remains immeasurable.

Bots can be hard to trace and are becoming ever-more realistic as technology improves and machine learning allows them to better mimic human behaviour online and evade detection. Ben Nimmo, a senior fellow in information defence at the Digital Forensic Research Lab at the Atlantic Council in Washington, believes that bots are incredibly useful for helping to bring ideas from the fringes of society into the mainstream through a combination of hashtags, memes, spamming, fake news, and blog links. He believes these bots are becoming more influential as more and more people realize their power: 'People have woken up to the idea that bots equal influence.'

Theresa May even acknowledged that Russia was attempting to use digital misinformation campaigns to influence Western politics. She alleged that the Russian government was 'planting fake stories' to 'sow discord in the West'. A former IRA troll told the Mail on Sunday that they were working on social media to influence the online conversation around the Brexit vote:

'We were active on social media, including Twitter, mainly posting on contentious topics obsessing the Brits.'

Whether Russian or otherwise, these bots and trolls are having an influence on our political conversation. By provoking an already polarized culture they can magnify their message a thousand times over. Through posts and articles crafted to incite outrage, they found their way to the top of our news feeds and into our collective psyche.

Our own then prime minister acknowledged and routinely condemned Russian interference in Western politics and their foreign policy as a whole. Theresa May singled out fake news and misinformation as one of their key tactics but failed to move any further with the issue. Why not? If Russia is capable of interfering in elections, and it is theoretically and demonstrably possible to influence elections with digital campaigning, then what is to stop political forces from inside and outside our democracy pouring money into digital campaigning techniques that are harmful to democracy and society? Eric Schmidt described the internet as 'the first thing that humanity has built that humanity doesn't understand, the largest experiment in anarchy that we have ever had'. It's a brand-new world, with more power than any technological revolution that has come before. It's changing politics and we have to understand how it is vulnerable to weaponization by bad actors to the detriment of us all.

Social media lured us in and drove us apart. It built little cultural bubbles and helped push us in more and more extreme directions. Algorithms that sorted us into groups curated a personalized diet of our own choices, cementing us in our little digital communities. We did what humans have done for millions of years, we divided into tribes. Trolls and bots were used to stoke fires and hone in on controversial issues all the while our political discourse descended into shouting and screaming at one another across cyberspace. Is it so hard to believe that this all spilt out into the real world? It didn't radicalize the country, just poured gasoline on already flammable issues.

3. The (Conscience) Free Press

DON'T GO OUTSIDE! It's full of *queers, blacks and crime*! Oh if only Diana was here! They're all the same, the Daily Mail, every day; ASBOs, Muslims, speed camera, speed camera, ASBOs, Muslims, speed cameras...
Russell Howard

Number 10 and the Press

As midnight approached on New Year's Eve 1999, Prime Minister Tony Blair was apoplectic. A group of journalists due to attend celebrations at the Millennium Dome found themselves stranded at a London underground station. He turned to his former flatmate Lord 'Charlie' Falconer begging,

'Please, please, dear God, please tell me you didn't have the media coming here by tube from Stratford just like ordinary members of the public.' Falconer was quick to point out to his boss that this was 'more democratic', but Blair swiftly fired back:

'Democratic? What fool thought that? They're the media, for Christ's sake. They write about the people, they don't want to be treated like them.'

After a moment, Falconer looked across at Blair and asked (perhaps with a hint of sarcasm):

'Well, what did you want us to do, get them all a stretch limo?'

The PM saw no irony in the question. He retorted: 'Yes, Charlie, with the boy or girl of their choice and as much champagne as they can drink.'

News UK holds The Sun and Times titles and is owned by infamous media mogul Rupert Murdoch. As they got into power in 1997, Blair and his team took some advice from Australian Prime Minister Paul Keating on how to deal with Murdoch:

'You can do deals with him, without ever saying a deal is done. But the only thing he cares about is his business and the only language he respects is strength.'

Lawrence Price wrote in Where Powers Lies: Prime Ministers v the Media: 'Blair and his team believed they had achieved exactly that. A deal had been done, although with nothing in writing. If Murdoch were left to pursue his business interests in peace he would give Labour a fair wind.'

If the prime minister is meant to be the most powerful person in the country, why are they constantly bowing and cosying up to press barons like Rupert Murdoch? He and Murdoch have become good friends since he came to power. After he resigned in 2007 Blair was named Godfather to one of Murdoch's children, baptized on the banks of the River Jordan.

Blair wasn't the first prime minister to identify the need to keep Rupert Murdoch onside. Thatcher also courted Rupert Murdoch, at a Sunday lunch at Chequers, the British PM's country residence, in January 1981. She allowed Murdoch to purchase The Times and the Sunday Times (giving him control of almost 40 per cent of the British press) by ensuring his bid would not be referred to the Monopolies and Mergers Commission. In return Thatcher would get a friendlier reception from his media empire; she was trailing in the polls and fighting a recession she had inherited. Lord Mandelson accused the Conservatives of striking a similar informal deal with Murdoch in the lead up to the 2010 election when The Sun announced their support for the Tories. Gordon Brown's wife quite controversially threw a birthday party for Rupert Murdoch's then-wife at Chequers; the wife of a press baron having her party at a massive state-funded residence seems completely normal don't you think? My birthday is actually being planned there by Boris Johnson's nephew for next year.

Cameron and Osborne were fond of Rupert Murdoch, meeting the media baron himself, or other News UK executives, on numerous occasions whilst the two of them occupied Downing Street. The austerity happy duo (and later May and Hammond) racked up 10 meetings between them in the space of a year from 2015-2016 with News UK execs, seven with BBC executives, and four with the son of a former KGB agent, Evgeny Lebedev, who owns the Independent and the London Evening Standard (for whom Osborne is now Chief Editor).

In total, the report by the Media Reform Commission detailed 20 meetings with senior executives at News Corp and senior government ministers, including seven with Murdoch himself. Theresa May even found time during a one-night whistle-stop trip to New York in September 2016. During the Leveson inquiry, Murdoch revealed that he had met the PM seven times since he was elected – five of these had never been acknowledged by Downing Street before that. He also told the inquiry that Cameron had gone 'out of his way to impress' him by interrupting a family holiday and flying out by private jet to meet Murdoch on his daughter's yacht on the Greek island of Santorini. He did add that he didn't ask any favours of the Prime Minister and that these meetings were simply 'all part of the democratic process'.

When Theresa May first strode into Downing Street it was crucial to get the press onside. Rather than court Murdoch, May chose to endear herself to the readers of another pro-Brexit paper. She hosted Daily Mail editor Paul Dacre at a private dinner in Number 10 less than 6 months into her tenure as PM. She had meetings with several other newspaper editors, including John Witherow of The Times, and Chris Evans of the Daily Telegraph, but Dacre was the only member of the press that was afforded hospitality by May in 2016. She subsequently hired the Mail's political editor, James Slack, as her spokesman in February 2017. She also attended a dinner with the Daily Mail Group with Lord Rothermere and Geordie Greig, editor of the Mail on Sunday.

Cameron had tried to convince Dacre to tone down the Mail's anti-Europe rhetoric, inviting him to Downing Street for a private meeting. When that failed, the PM approached Lord

Rothermere to attempt to persuade him to sack Dacre as editor (who was said to be 'incandescent' with rage when he found out after the referendum result). So perhaps May has been attempting to repair the relationship with the paper, given their influence upon the Conservative voter base.

N.B. The list doesn't include meetings between government ministers or officials and staff at Murdoch's papers.

This relationship between Number 10 and the press has been a part of establishment politics for decades. Now, this is hardly a profound point, it is well known that the political elite has rubbed shoulders with each other for decades, operating on an 'I'll rub your back if you rub mine' sort of arrangement. This is just one of the many reasons that people became wary of both the press and the establishment.

It is this mistrust that allowed alternative media to flourish and for 'fake news' to become such a salient form of spreading misinformation. If the mainstream media cannot be trusted or there are reasons to be wary of their motivations, they may have to portray events a certain way or promote a specific topic of news, such as the anti-Brexit BBC publishing warnings of economic damage during the referendum. The ability to dismiss specific news sources as illegitimate gave social media the space to trap us all in digital echo chambers.

Mediacracy

Wielders of power have known for quite a while that the press is crucial to swaying and influencing public opinion. Tony Blair understood the importance of the press in successfully governing a country. But the relationship between Downing Street and the press has existed for decades.

Without the press, there is no link between the politicians and the citizenry (though social media has changed this somewhat, traditional politicians still rely on the press). Theresa May was hardly the technology-savvy modern PM that Cameron tried so hard to be. Regardless of the impact of new media and social media, the mainstream media are still crucial to controlling narratives and framing the debates that politicians want to have.

The press cannot thrive without access to politicians, that is the most direct line to help understand decisions and plans that the government is making and putting forward. Thus they are afforded access, or at least the most desirable are, those who ask the right questions, don't corner politicians, or offer up the friendliest coverage. It can quickly become an exclusive club, politicians wielding their power to control the narrative to ruthless effect. We call this rule of the media class a mediacracy.

The press need politicians and government officials to provide statements, information, updates etc. in order to fill their day. Journalists with no information won't be in a job for very long, especially in the modern attention economy. Politicians need the press just as much as the press need them, they need an outlet through which to make announcements and statements that create the appearance that they are working hard for the people to make the country a better place.

One of the purest examples of a mediacracy is the Japanese system of press clubs or 'Lisha Kurabu'. The nationwide network of press clubs comprises some 800 journalists who, through their exclusive membership, enjoy exclusive access to politicians, government departments, political parties, and even the royal family.

Journalists who exist in this world have very little reason to challenge the system that has benefitted them. Their entire career, their life, their livelihood is based upon their success within the system, why on earth would they try to tear down their world along with a system that has benefitted them? When faced with the possibility of losing everything, people will quickly fall into line, sacrifice personal integrity and journalistic principles they may have held earlier in their careers. That isn't to say people will consciously abandon their morals or belief systems to actively prop up a corrupted mediacracy. It could be and often is far more complicated than that. It could mean dropping a particularly controversial question or refusing to confront politicians on topics they would rather avoid in order to ensure you can get the next interview. Journalism is based on access, so one might reason that it makes no sense to be particularly forceful over an issue when it could lose you all access to that politician. You could reason that this is not logical, some access is better than no access, so it is better to avoid asking the toughest questions so that you can continue to ask questions at all.

Put yourself in the shoes of an aspiring journalist; you've just been asked to do a major interview with a cabinet member when you hear rumours that they have been fiddling expenses and have lied to parliament about it when questioned. However, you know that confronting the minister over this issue could mean you are never assigned an interview with them again, that you might get a reputation for not pulling punches, and lose the rapport you have built up with the ruling party over the past few years of covering them for your paper. Should you stick to your guns and ask the tough questions? Or do you offer up the softballs to preserve your access to the party, improve your career prospects, and ensure you are granted further interviews?

Channel 4 have opted to go hard at the government and, as a result, Theresa May refused them an interview for the first time in almost 30 years at the 2018 Conservative Party Conference. Whether this affects their position as a news outlet is debatable, but if they are unable to get interviews with top politicians, they will lose viewers to outlets that do.

Who Owns the Press?

The five men in control of the British press are Rupert Murdoch, Jonathon Harmsworth, Richard Desmond, and the Barclay twins. According to a 2015 report by the Media Reform

Coalition, 'Who Owns the UK Media?', three companies (Sun and Times owner News UK, Daily Mail publisher DMGT, and Daily Mirror owner Trinity Mirror) control 71 per cent of the national newspaper market and 90 per cent of the daily circulation. The national newspapers are owned by just eight different companies, four of which account for 80 per cent of all copies sold. Similarly, the report found that six major regional newspaper groups own 81 per cent of local newspapers, claiming that this ongoing media consolidation has created regional 'news deserts', where professional journalists have been pushed out by cuts and closures resulting in local monopolies or duopolies.

The 85-year-old Barclay twins' press holdings own The Telegraph and the Sunday Telegraph, famed for claims such as 'More than 700 offences are being committed by EU migrants every week'. In 2013, Sir David and Sir Frederick Barclay were named the richest people in the British media with a £2.3 billion fortune. The brothers own their own Channel Island and run much of their business through tax havens like Bermuda to minimise tax liabilities to HMRC. On the morning of the referendum result, Nigel Farage and Aaron Banks had breakfast with Sir Frederick Barclay at the Ritz to celebrate their successful liberation of Britain. Barclay had been a big supporter of Brexit and of UKIP; such a politically opinionated owner doesn't seem compatible with a free and independent press.

Rupert Murdoch through News Corporation owns The Times, Sunday Times, The Sun, and the Sun on Sunday (as well as Fox News in America). Journalist Anthony Hilton wrote a column in the Evening Standard describing a conversation he once had with the media mogul: 'I once asked Rupert Murdoch why he was so opposed to the European Union. "That's easy," he replied. 'When I go into Downing Street they do what I say; when I go to Brussels they take no notice.'

Murdoch's influence can hardly be seen as a positive in politics, a study from 2011 found that those who watched

Murdoch's Fox News channel were less knowledgeable about current events even than those who watched no news at all. Meaning it has essentially become a misinformation platform. I think you'd be hard-pressed to say that titles like The Sun or The Mail in the UK are vastly different.

Lord Viscount Rothermere IV is the owner of Daily Mail and General Trust plc (DMGT) who hold the Daily Mail and the Mail on Sunday titles. He inherited the trust in 1998 when his father died. He appeared third on the Sunday Times Rich List 'media top 20' in 2012, with an estimated fortune of £760 million. He is said to try to protect the 'independence' of his editors and feels that the paper reflects the views of its readership, 'the values of Middle England'. In September 2013, the Mail published an article titled 'the man who hated Britain' about Ralph Miliband. The paper didn't back down to criticism of the piece, but did apologize for their use of a picture of Ralph Miliband's tombstone with the pun 'grave socialist'.

DMGT has been, since 1995, through Rothermere Continuation Ltd, registered in Bermuda but run from Jersey. Rothermere Continuation Ltd is owned by an unknown trust administered in Jersey for the benefit of Rothermere and his family; it holds all the voting shares in DMGT and receives over £10 million in annual dividends. This set-up was likely suggested or arranged by John Hemingway, DMGT non-executive, company director, and retired lawyer who advises the rich and powerful on 'structuring and management of their family resources'.

The current Lord Rothermere was born in Hammersmith and went to school in Scotland, but inherited a 'non-domicile' tax status from his father in France. As a result, the income for DMGT passes through Bermuda and Jersey and is only taxed on its remittance to the UK. Private Eye covered the story, quoting the words of one of Britain's most senior tax accountants, 'to all intents and purposes for your well-advised truly wealthy [non-dom] this is a complete exemption for investment income and gains'.

In 2008, HMRC was set to investigate whether Lord Rothermere had surrendered his non-dom status given his 240-acre grounds in Wilshire upon which sits his family home. That is until then HMRC tax boss Dave Hartnett intervened and had the investigation pulled. This allowed Rothermere to borrow money against the offshore held DMGT shares, rather than bring his offshore wealth into Britain and having to pay full income tax on it, just as he did to expand his east and west wings at his Wiltshire residence in 2006. Many of Rothermere's investments are owned and run through a complex web of offshore structures from Jersey to Geneva and the Caribbean and Bermuda that enable the most 'tax-efficient' financial arrangement.

The Daily Mail also relegated its coverage of the Paradise Papers, one of the biggest financial leaks this century, to the tenth page where it also took aim at Corbyn for speaking out about the Queen's tax affairs. The Paradise Papers was a leak of 13.4 million files, mostly concerning a firm named Appleby, who help structure and manage offshore accounting across the Caribbean and Pacific. You might also have expected the Mail to raise a fuss when the government scrapped the non-dom tax loophole that Viscount Rothermere had long enjoyed the benefits of, but there was no protest.

Paul Dacre was a passionate Eurosceptic and had always felt that Cameron had failed to acknowledge the help his paper provided in giving Cameron his majority in 2015. The Sun editor, Tony Gallagher, branded Cameron's renegotiation deal with the EU prior to the referendum a 'steaming pile of manure' and ended up in a face-to-face row with the prime minister himself.

Reach plc (formerly known as Trinity Mirror), owned by billionaire Richard Desmond, holds the Daily Express, the Sunday Express, the Daily Mirror, the Sunday Mirror, Sunday People, Daily Star, and Daily Star Sunday. The Daily Express has become famous for its doggedly anti-EU rhetoric, such as '75 per cent of new jobs go to EU migrants'. The Express later corrected this, but the Press Gazette considers the Daily Express as 'very misleading' and so does the Independent Press Standards Organisation (IPSO). More than 25 misleading anti-EU headlines from the Express resulted in a complaint to IPSO – though it is not a state-backed regulator and has essentially no power to compel the press to be more factually accurate.

Let's Talk About Six Baby

The healthy functioning of both a government and society is largely aided by a free, honest, and independent press. The fourth estate has essentially six different roles in which it contributes to the running of politics, culture, and society. The press have been responsible for the lack of quality debate in British politics for quite a while and the Brexit campaign displayed in all its glory both the state of our press and our political conversation. No-one was willing to discuss the trade-offs or the pros vs cons of the EU – you were either for or against the EU with no room for nuance. Jeremy Corbyn was heavily criticized by the Stronger In campaign for his declaration that he felt the EU was about a seven out of ten, good but not perfect.

The campaign was conducted in broad, colourful, almost childlike terms. Leave wasn't an alternative economic or political model, it was a blank canvas which people could project their hopes, aspirations and frustrations onto...It was a fantasy land of universal expectation.
Ian Dunt

In a functioning democracy the press fulfils six roles:

1. Informative Role – to keep citizens up to date with what is going on in parliament
2. Educative Role – to explain what these events entail

3. Platform Role – to give a stage to various groups in society
4. Publicity Role – to enable politicians, campaigners, anyone with anything of note to access the public
5. Adversarial Role – to hold to account and challenge the government
6. Advocacy Role – to promote ideas from every side of society

In all these roles it is of vital importance that the press remains as impartial as possible. Any paper that begins to drift too far towards one corner of the political spectrum is immediately failing to present journalism that is impartial and truly informative. I will not sit here and pretend that unbiased journalism is actually possible, even down to a philosophical level, it is almost impossible to present something without some sort of bias. But much of the British press have long ago abandoned the concept of impartiality, instead choosing idle and damaging partisanship as the way forward. Writer John le Carre said of the British press: 'In the last 15 or 20 years, I've watched the British press simply go to hell. There seems to be no limit, no depths to which the tabloids won't sink. I don't know who these people are but they're little pigs.'

UN High Commissioner for Human Rights Zeid Ra'ad Al Hussein accused the UK press of conducting 'decades of sustained and unrestrained anti-foreigner abuse, misinformation and distortion' following a particularly inflammatory article in The Sun in which Katie Hopkins compared migrants and refugees fleeing the war in Syria to cockroaches (a description used by the Nazis and the Rwandans to justify mass genocides). His criticism was not confined to The Sun, he was critical of the unaccountable tabloid press relentlessly vilifying migrants:

'To give just one glimpse of the scale of the problem, back in 2003 the Daily Express ran 22 negative front pages stories about asylum seekers and refugees in a single 31-day period.'

The papers utterly failed in their role of the fourth estate during the referendum campaign (their failures were evident long before and have been evident since, but we'll stick to the referendum). Take their constant vilification of immigration from the EU as an example. If you were to believe the papers then you'd think we have little to no immigration from outside the EU. In fact, EU migration has not exceeded non-EU migration since 1991. Net migration from inside the EU peaked at 184,000 in 2015 but was topped by net non-EU migration even that year at 189,000. Net non-EU migration peaked at 266,000 in 2004. It cannot be denied that the numbers of both EU and non-EU migrants arriving on British soil year on year have increased over the past 30 years, but what is constantly under-discussed is the role of immigrants in society and what leaving the EU would mean for immigration.

Our current levels of immigration provide several things to Britain that are rarely discussed in these sorts of debates. Too often the argument is solely presented as how much immigrants make our society better and more diverse, without tangibly understanding how and why. We need immigration to plug employment gaps, especially within the NHS, because there are severe staff shortages – leaving the EU will not fix this. In 2013 nearly one-third of new London nurses were recruited from abroad, mainly from Africa and Eastern Europe according to the RCN. At the same time, NHS London scrapped almost one-quarter of their training spots. The campaign group Migration Watch has argued that a drop in EU migrants would only lead to an even larger rise in non-EU migrants. 'UK businesses will no longer be obliged to advertise jobs in the UK and there will be no cap on numbers entering for work, thus enabling employers to scour the world for the cheapest staff they can find.'

There has been a proposed minimum salary for skilled migrants hoping to enter the UK at £30,000, but this seems unlikely to be adhered to in the case of staffing shortages in the

NHS, where most nurses are paid below this threshold. There have also been government proposals to introduce uncapped 1-year low-skilled visas. Countries like India have also been insistent that higher visa quotas would be a central part of any post-Brexit trade deal.

To address our immigration issue, we need to encourage more people to study medicine and nursing (or whatever field we deem to need new recruits). Instead, our current government has failed to give NHS staff a pay rise, cut student nursing bursaries, pushed through a hugely unpopular junior doctors contract, and has cut staff numbers in the NHS leaving the current crop of NHS workers under-staffed, underworked, and looking to get out of the profession. But this is not discussed in the papers.

Migrants are net contributors to our economy. From 2001-2011, EU migrants made a net contribution of £20 billion to the economy. They arrive fully educated and ready to contribute taxes to the economy, no need to spend 15-18 years educating them in the state system (a saving of £6.8 billion in education spending and contributing £8.5 billion in 'pure' public goods like research or defence), caring for them on the NHS, or provide them with all the public services we all take advantage of before we become tax-paying citizens. Instead, all that is ever mentioned are the fraction of cases of benefit fraud, or of people arriving in Britain simply to take benefits.

The vilification of migrants as drains on the economy uses a trick known as forced perspective. Just as camera angles were used to make the hobbits in Lord of the Rings look smaller, so too does this focus on migrants draining our economy mean we ignore any benefits they bestow upon our society and fail to see other drains on government resources. Research published in 2014 by the UCL Centre for Research and Analysis of Migration also found that EU migrants were 43 per cent less likely than natives to receive state benefits or tax credits, 7 per cent less likely to live in social housing, and had a far higher likelihood of having a university degree (62 per cent compared to 24 per cent of British natives).

Take the issue of tax evasion and benefit fraud. Which is more costly to the British government? Tax evasion costs the UK some £34 billion per year according to an HMRC estimate, compared to the £2 billion estimated benefit fraud bill (1.2 per cent of the entire welfare budget and less than half of the total unclaimed benefits). It should be noted that other estimates put the tax evasion bill much higher; Tax Research UK estimated that the tax gap in 2014/15 was around £122 billion.

The DWP employs over 4000 staff to deal with benefit fraud, compared to around 1000 people employed at HMRC to deal with tax evasion. HMRC's own figures suggest that every £1 spent would bring £97 back to the taxman, but it is almost unheard of to see the tabloids slamming companies who use offshore tax structures to avoid paying into the country that they sell their goods in. Instead, they vilify the immigrants as the cheats and fraudsters.

The Citizens' Rights Directive, or Free Movement Directive, outlines the rights of free movement within the EEA (European Economic Area), that's the (current) 28 EU member states, Iceland, Norway, and Liechtenstein. It gives citizens of these nations the right of free movement and residence across the area as long as they are not an undue burden on the country of residence. The right of residence becomes permanent after 5 years and the rights are extended to close family members who are not EEA citizens.

The treaty states that:

Citizenship of the Union confers on every citizen of the Union a primary and individual right to move and reside freely within the territory of the Member States, subject to the limitations and conditions laid down in the Treaty and to the measures adopted to give it effect.

To be covered by the European right of free movement, the individual needs to exercise one of the four treaty rights:

1. working as an employee (this includes looking for work for a reasonable amount of time)
2. working as a self-employed person
3. studying
4. being self-sufficient or retired

The Citizens' Rights Directive outlines that individuals should not 'become an unreasonable burden on the social assistance system of the host member state during an initial period of residence.' Anyone is permitted to stay for up to 3 months, at which point they must satisfy one of the conditions listed above to allow them to stay in the country beyond that period. They may be asked to register with the authorities to confirm the legality of their residence.

For example, in Belgium, if an individual is no longer working, self-employed, studying, or if they no longer have 'sufficient resources' and become an 'unreasonable burden' on the social system, they can be asked to leave. They won't be physically thrown out or deported, but they stop receiving any social benefits or welfare. In 2014, residence permits of 2042 EU citizens (and their family members) living in Belgium were rescinded by the Belgian authorities. That number fell to 1700 in 2015. In 2007, Belgium even amended the legislation to be more considerate of personal circumstances, the nature of their employment, and the number of dependents in the family. The idea was to help counter 'social tourism' that can place a strain on a country's welfare system. The Belgian Immigration Office's Geert de Vulder remarked: 'If they don't contribute by themselves to the social system or they never have contributed to the Belgian social system, they only get benefits from it, then we will withdraw the residence permit.'

Yet again, this was never mentioned by the papers, or during the immigration conversation surrounding Brexit.

Bureaucracy Gone Mad

In October 2011 the Daily Mail published a story that was echoed by the Express and the Telegraph detailing how 'EU bureaucrats have banned children under 8 from blowing up balloons because they might hurt themselves'. In reality, it was a draft directive that was to be proposed that suggested that unsupervised use by young children could be dangerous. It was simply a Commission recommendation, not a new law to be contended with.

In a way they invented Project Fear, bombarding the British public with a stream of consciousness rabble about the encroaching European super-state that meant we all had to eat straight bananas and would be bowing to Supreme Leader Junker before long.

This style of anti-EU 'straight banana' journalism was actually invented by a young Boris Johnson. During his time at the Daily Telegraph as a correspondent for Brussels from 1989-94 he pioneered this type of 'bureaucrats gone mad', 'what on earth will they do next' journalism about the EU. He is heralded by some as the man who put the spice into European reporting; not through hard-hitting journalism and solid investigative work, but with a long list of fabrications and exaggerations. Ian Dunt commented that 'By the time Johnson was finished, Brussels reporting had turned into a journalistic genre...a daily diet of half-true stories about faceless bureaucrats and rigid conformity stilting British ingenuity.'

Johnson is proud of his record as well, not seeing it as something to be ashamed of at all. He reminisced about his time reporting from the continent, remarking on his excitement at gaining notoriety by nobly crusading against Brussels by shamelessly painting them as wasteful, corrupt architects of stifling red-tape and ridiculous, business impeding regulations:

Everything I wrote from Brussels, I found was sort of chucking these rocks over the garden wall and I listened to this amazing crash from the greenhouse next door over in England as everything I wrote from Brussels had this amazing, explosive effect on the Tory party, and it really gave me this I suppose rather weird sense of power.

The British press has been pumping out wads of anti-Brussels rhetoric for decades. In 2003 the Daily Mail labelled a draft EU constitution as a 'blueprint for tyranny' and then in 2011 they warned readers that Germany was turning Europe into a 'Fourth Reich'. The Express have become famous for their almost parody-of-themselves style of headlines that include 'EU brainwash our children', 'Now EU Wants to Ban our Kettles' and 'Get Britain out of the EU'.

As a part of his submission to the Leveson Inquiry in 2011, former spin doctor Alastair Campbell critiqued the tabloids' habit of blowing tales of Brussels bureaucracy wildly out of proportion. He wrote:

At various times, readers of UK papers may have read that 'Europe' or 'Brussels' or the 'EU super-state' has banned, or is intending to ban kilts, curries, mushy peas, paper rounds, Caerphilly cheese, charity shops, bulldogs, bent sausages and cucumbers, the British Army, lollipop ladies, British loaves, British-made lavatories, the passport crest, lorry drivers who wear glasses and many more.

Media coverage of the entire referendum campaign was labelled as 'acrimonious and divisive' and dominated by 'overwhelmingly negative' stories. The study conducted by researchers at King's College London (KCL) incorporated a study of 15,000 online articles published across 20 different digital outlets.

The KCL study found that immigration was by far the most

negatively discussed issue, framed on 'almost entirely negative' terms. Immigration coverage rose faster up the news agenda than anything else, with coverage tripling as the 10-week campaign rose to a pinnacle. The report notes that the press did very little to correct or balance the nature of immigration-related stories, negative stories or outright lies told by politicians like Ian Duncan Smith or Michael Gove were 'covered copiously and prominently in the press'.

Immigration came to be the base issue through which almost everything could be viewed – Dominic Cummings and Vote Leave saw immigration and the economy and the NHS as one big package to roll out together. In the final 4 weeks of the referendum a full half of all articles that mentioned the economy also mentioned immigration. The papers published more front pages on immigration than anything else, with the Daily Express, the Daily Mail and the Daily Telegraph accounting for 60 per cent of those front pages.

Words like 'floodgates', 'wave', 'flocking', and 'swarming' dominated media depiction of the immigration issue. These words evoke a primal animalistic force almost like the force of nature coming to get you, you'll simply be swept away in the tides of migrants that are coming to take everything you hold dear. From 15 April until 23 July 'Project Fear' appeared 739 times in articles that appeared online, 250 of those in the last fortnight of the campaign, whilst 'scaremongering' was mentioned in 737 individual articles discussing Brexit.

When asked about the way in which the Mail has covered the hordes of migrants arriving on our shores over the past several decades, Mail Online publisher Martin Clarke denied that they had played a part in stoking fears surrounding immigration. He told The Guardian: 'We've reported people's very legitimate fears over immigration. We don't stoke the fears. The fears are there.'

According to the KCL study we looked at earlier examining the language used as a part of the coverage of the Brexit referendum, the Brexit vote was the 'most divisive, hostile, negative and fear-provoking of the twenty-first century' that was 'encouraged and inflamed by a highly partisan national media'.

One of the aspects of the referendum that most shocked David Cameron were the actions and attitude of the press. One minister was quoted as saying: 'What genuinely surprised Number 10 was not that the Mail, The Sun, and the Express were supporting leave, but that the tone of the criticism was so venomous.' Cameron had never had to fight an election campaign with so much of the press pitted against him. He had been aligned with the prevailing attitude of the press in the 2010 and 2015 general elections and during the AV and Scottish Independence referendums. This was the first time that the right-wing echo chamber was not available for hire and it derailed the In campaign every time they thought they had scored a major victory.

Pro-Leave papers outnumbered pro-Remain rivals four-fold in terms of readership and the number of anti-EU stories they were able to pump out. After the referendum, one of Cameron's inner circle lamented the hostility of the press: 'It pains me to say it, but if the Mail, Sun and the Telegraph had been for 'In' we'd have romped home.'

Brussels is hidden from everyday view; it's an incredibly complex machine whose process is obscure and poorly understood by the vast majority of people. On the morning the referendum result was declared, some of the most Googled questions in Britain were 'What does it mean to Leave the EU?' and 'What is the EU?' Because of the lack of understanding and its removal from the forefront of the lives of most Britons, Brussels can easily be scapegoated and vilified with little or no consequences. As author Ian Dunt puts it: 'It becomes easy for politicians and the press to blame Brussels for everything because no-one sees it doing anything.'

The tabloid scare stories about the EU became so bad that the EU founded a blog called 'Euromyths' in order to debunk the claims of the British press. Not only are many of the 'Brussels gone mad' type stories either exaggerated or largely falsified, but many of the real regulations also hail from an even higher regulatory body than the EU. A full 33 per cent of EU regulation and certification comes from international trade bodies like the UN, the OECD (Organisation for Economic Cooperation and Development), the International Maritime Organisation, and the International Labour Organisation. A further 28 per cent of EU regulation is in relation to 'veterinary and physio-sanitary matters' of which a huge majority is handed down from higher trade bodies like the WTO (World Trade Organisation). This is again entirely ignored by our press. A 2013 tabloid scare which took aim at EU bodies removing the Union flag from packets of meat was deemed as another of Brussels' crazy schemes. The Telegraph subheading read: 'The Union Jack flag and Scottish saltire could disappear from packs of supermarket poultry, pork and lamb under "crazy" proposals by the European Commission'; the Express ran with the headline 'Fury at EU plan to ban Union Flag from British meat packs' whilst the Daily Mail went with 'Now EU wants to ban Union flag from being displayed on meat reared in Britain.'

Only in the last lines of each of these articles do they quote an EU spokesperson who debunks the fears, explaining that the rules surrounding country of origin labelling would not affect the use of flags as long as they were not misleading and that DEFRA (The Department for Environment, Food and Rural Affairs) had misinformed industry leaders. What is more, Brussels simply rubber-stamped these rules from the Codex Alimentarius, which is a tome of internationally recognized standards and codes for food production and distribution, which in turn was based on the WTO's international agreement on rules of origin. The British press has chosen sensationalism to sell papers and demonize the EU for decades and our understanding has suffered almost immeasurably as a result. Leaving the EU would not absolve us from these regulations at all, we would still be forced to abide by all the rules of international trade that we are bound to within the EU. International standardization is a consequence of globalization, isolationism will not protect us from the way in which the whole world currently trades.

The British tabloids have killed truth, nuance, facts, complexity, and journalism. Now they are finally beginning to suffer the consequences

Print Journalism is Dying

Print journalism is dying. That's not to say it is dead, useless, or should be discounted as a crucial cog in the press machine, but the emergence of new digital media has coincided with the waning influence of the traditional press and played a major role in political upsets around the world. Now there is nothing wrong with a wealthy businessman choosing to purchase a newspaper. Large news institutions are difficult to set up; you require resources, capital, and perseverance. To run a successful paper, you also have to be ruthless, business savvy, and understand your audience. It is no easy feat, especially in the modern media landscape, but it will not be long before long-established media institutions begin to die as a result of digital transformation.

In 2015, for every £100 newspapers lost in print revenue, newspapers only gained £3 in digital revenue. More than 200 local newspapers have closed since 2005. Google and Facebook control more than 60 per cent of the UK digital ad market, with as much as 90 per cent of all new online ad spend going to the two giants. The Daily Mail saw shares drop by a full quarter in November 2017 when it was announced that DMGT, which also owns the Metro, recorded a £112 million loss for 2017, down from a £202 million profit in 2016. Print advertising sales fell 5 per cent, whilst digital ad revenue rose 18 per cent – though it would be difficult to claim that mailonline.com is a source of great journalism. A number of firms have stopped advertising with the paper in the past 18 months including Lego, Paperchase, and The Body Shop. Lego decided to ditch the paper after a public campaign asking big companies to stop advertising with newspapers accused of promoting 'hatred, discrimination and demonisation'.

The Mail has seen its circulation fall significantly since 2016, sales dropped 11 per cent in the year to February 2018, whilst the Mail on Sunday saw a 13 per cent decline. They are not alone either, The Sun and the Sun on Sunday saw their circulations fall by 8 per cent and 9.2 per cent respectively, the Daily Telegraph readership fell 18 per cent, The Express by 7.5 per cent, and the Daily Star by 11 per cent. The worst affected titles were The Daily Mirror and The Sunday Mirror, with sales tumbling by 19 per cent and 20 per cent. The Sun and the Daily Mail have now fallen behind the Metro as the most widely read print paper in Britain.

One of the last bastions of print investigative journalism in the UK is The Guardian/Observer. It is the only British paper that consistently and routinely launches far-reaching, in-depth investigations that have been consequential to British and world politics over the past decade. They played a central part in the Panama and Paradise Papers leaks, the Edward Snowdon leaks, and most recently, Carole Cadwalladr has been on a one-woman crusade to uncover the shady links and data misuse by Leave.EU, Vote Leave, Cambridge Analytica, and AggregateIQ, producing what could be some of the most crucial pieces of investigative journalism in twenty-first century Britain. (Without Carole's work I would never have been able to write this book, but let's not get ahead of ourselves.)

That isn't to say there aren't other fantastic digital outlets doing crucial media work; OpenDemocracy, DesmogUK, Source Material, and Buzzfeed Politics UK have been critical to peeling back the layers of mystery surrounding the Brexit vote. Private

Eye has been given a new lease of life as people have craved for objective, often witty, journalism in a barren press landscape. Ian Hislop and his team are selling more copies than they have in years – 2016 saw their circulation hit a 55-year peak and the Christmas 2016 issue sold more copies than any other issue in Eye history.

Despite some of the great work still being done, trust in the British media is the lowest in Europe. Our press has ranked thirty-third out of 33 European nations for the last 4 years consecutively. In 2017, just 23 per cent of the public said that they have trust in what the media says. That's not just the EU, that is within Europe, including countries like Albania and Malta. It's a truly stunning indictment of the state of the British press.

Don't Trust the Papers

Think of the press as a great keyboard on which the government can play.

Joseph Goebbels

Mistrust in the mainstream media has been fuelled by allegations of bias and the spread of 'fake news'. Reuters Institute Digital News Report 2017 found that just over 40 per cent of people in the UK agreed with the statement, 'I think you can trust news most of the time', a shockingly low figure for a developed Western nation with a free press. We should, however, be thankful that the problem isn't quite as bad as in the US – given the level of madness in America and in Brexit you may have missed or forgotten the incident where President Trump launched a series of bizarre personal attacks over Twitter aimed at CNN and 'Morning Joe' hosts Mika Brzezinski and Joe Scarborough. He tweeted: 'Crazy Joe Scarborough and dumb as a rock Mika are not bad people, but their low rated show is dominated by their NBC bosses. Too bad!'

He followed this up with an edited professional-wrestling

video of him tackling a man with the CNN logo superimposed on his face. It might seem trivial to mention this, but it is a great example of the way Trump (and to an extent our politicians) can get away with disparaging the media because they are biased; even defenders of the free press can't help but accept that critics of the media have a genuine point. I'm alarmed by the attack on the press, but CNN is far from the world's greatest news channel – they don't have a single investigative reporter on staff. It is basically a 24/7 political theatre, where pundits and guests compete to get the best zing in that fits in 280 characters or a 30-second soundbite.

Members of our government have repeatedly accused the press of being overly critical of the Brexit process; Andrea Leadsom famously asked the BBC if the media could be a little more patriotic about Brexit. We should be thankful for the integrity of democracy and our political system that they haven't directly attacked the press in the way Trump has.

There have also been accusations that certain members of the right-wing press, most notably Daily Mail editor Paul Dacre, have received preferential treatment and were courted by Theresa May's government to help them sell the Conservative message. It was revealed in March 2017 that Theresa May had hosted Dacre at 10 Downing Street several months into her reign as prime minister, which triggered further allegations that the Daily Mail was simply a mouth-piece for the Conservative Party. Running headlines like 'Crush the Saboteurs' and 'Enemies Of The People' in full-throated support of Brexit and Theresa May's distaste for democratic debate did little to quell or combat these allegations.

These sorts of headlines hardly seem like reasonable responses from an independent press, especially one that spent months campaigning for British courts making British decisions. The judges who declared parliament should have a vote on the Brexit deal were labelled treasonous for dictating that parliament should be sovereign. This definitely seems like the response of a reasonable and well-balanced news outlet.

The anti-Corbyn bias and almost unwavering support of the Conservative Party amongst the right-wing papers, combined with the level of mistrust in the media, have spawned an explosion in independent media over the past few years. Outlets like The Canary, Evolve Politics, Novara Media, and Another Angry Voice have sprung up to provide a counter-narrative to the establishment media. They have not yet come to dominate our news landscape, despite their best efforts, though they are making serious inroads into the influence of the right-wing media. There are also still traditionally centrist and left-wing outlets running in the mainstream press, but it is the right wing, and particularly the tabloids, that have the widest reach and thus the biggest impact on our political landscape and conversation.

This isn't just in print either, traditional outlets have made a somewhat successful jump to digitally-driven journalism and media, although some have had to resort to paywalls or asking for donations/subscriptions in order to compete in such a media-rich environment. This transformation towards digital media is just another iteration of the disruption that tech and the internet have caused across every industry. Look at what Uber did to transport, what Amazon did to retail, what Fintech start-ups are doing to financial institutions, what Airbnb did to hostel and hotel bookings, the list goes on.

In our drive to find truth where mainstream media has left gaps, we have been left open to being fooled or manipulated, especially if we don't do our due diligence. We have to find new ways of ensuring that people know who can be trusted as honest arbiters of information. Back in 1996, just as the internet was starting to grow beyond the very fringes of society and technology, Nicholas Negroponte predicted that the digital revolution would create a 'cottage industry of information and entertainment providers'. That is what we see now, a mass of public and privately funded news and content providers pumping out hours of exactly what we want to hear or read, their business model relies on our clicks and engagement. Our commitment to the truth is rarely as prominent as our own biases, so whilst the truth is most important to a free and functioning press, it may not be what we really crave – we want to remain in our echo chambers.

Net Neutrality has levelled the playing field in terms of our access to information, but now we have to rely on our critical thinking skills, not just the press regulator. Unfortunately, the press is largely unaccountable, no major outlet has signed up to a state-backed regulator. In fact, the only outlets who have signed up to a state-backed regulator are sites like the Canary, Evolve Politics, and Left Foot Forward (a left-wing blog) through the independent regulator IMPRESS. Ironically, these outlets are often criticized by those in the mainstream press for being nothing but fake news and lefty nonsense, despite IMPRESS being the only press regulator in Britain to have complied with the results of the Leveson Inquiry into press practices. It's fantastic to see a media revolution attempting to improve the quality of journalism in the UK, it's a testament to the human desire to seek out truth. Yet, these outlets cannot be relied upon to produce the kind of investigative journalism that we need in a democracy. In an interview with Vice, Ian Hislop explained that:

What you can't get online is that dedication to journalism which is very expensive and requires a lot of time. People investigate things and nothing happens – you don't get a story and people say, 'Well, that's a waste of money.' It isn't, it's part of the next story that will be any good. Online is much better at opinion and 'bleugh'.

Within news and media, traditional outlets have managed to stay competitive in the market, and whilst disrupting independent blogs have started to gain more and more traction online, their imprint on the entire population is still rather small. According to 2017 research done by NewsWorks.org, print journalism still reaches one in every two adults each week, whilst online, UK news brands have driven 940 million social media interactions in the last month, including 817 million interactions on Facebook and 110 million interactions on Twitter. Despite the meteoric rise of blogging and alternative media, news brands still reach 97 per cent of all millennials and have significantly more interactions online than even Buzzfeed can garner. The influence and reach of mainstream papers has been reduced in the past few years, and trust has been eroded, the MSM still play a huge part in our political conversation. Sun editor Tony Gallagher texted The Guardian team about an hour after the final result of the Brexit referendum was revealed, 'So much for the waning power of the print media.' Despite trust in their content waning rapidly, the mainstream tabloid press has had a hugely detrimental impact on our understanding of Europe (and politics as a whole) and on the quality of our political conversation.

And we haven't even mentioned the biggest broadcaster in Britain.

The Beeb

The BBC, supposedly impartial, is criticized heavily by both left and right alike for their coverage. The BBC is often chided for simply reporting what the other has said instead of challenging the factual nature of statements made by either side. They are too liberal, PC, and anti-Brexit for the right wing, whilst simultaneously being too anti-Corbyn, Labour, and socialist for the left wing. Andrea Leadsom famously asked the BBC if the media could be a little more patriotic about Brexit after they challenged her support for Brexit during an interview.

In reality, the BBC are pro-establishment. They are famously anti-Brexit and yet seemed incredibly reluctant to report on the shadier and murkier dealings that have been unearthed about the Leave campaign groups (we will get to that, don't worry). Carole Cadwalladr, backed by an entire corner of Twitter, has been focusing in on the role of Russian interference, data misuse, and dark money in Brexit, and has lambasted the BBC relentlessly over their coverage of the entire Vote Leave and Leave.EU investigations. For example, when an audience member brought up the charges against Vote Leave in a Question Time episode in November 2019, host Fiona Bruce wrongly claimed that they had been cleared of all charges. When the Electoral Commission report that stated Vote Leave had broken the law was first released, the BBC was accused of simply repeating the Vote Leave claim that no-one at the Electoral Commission had attempted to contact them without stating that it was a lie.

For their coverage during the referendum, the BBC endured almost universal criticism. Craig Oliver, David Cameron's former director of communications, believed that they had fundamentally misunderstood their role during the referendum. The BBC tactic seemed to be to attempt to give equal air time to Remain and Leave groups, with little to no semblance of fact-checking. Oliver was particularly put out when, on the day that Mark Carney, Governor of the Bank of England, delivered the Bank's prediction that the British economy would be plunged into recession if Britain were to vote to leave the EU, he tuned in to see that the news was being dominated by senior Tory figures bashing the Bank and accusing one of the largest banking institutions in Europe of 'startling dishonesty'. Tim Shipman, in his book 'All Out War', explained that Oliver 'believed the national broadcaster had confused its traditional responsibility to be impartial with the need during an election campaign to be balanced'.

A source in Number 10 was quoted at the time as saying 'they seemed...to be obsessed by providing a fifty-fifty balance'. Rather than trying to identify who was being more factually accurate, or to provide criticism, the BBC seemed to simply report what each side was saying rather than providing any form of scrutiny. Perhaps out of fear of accusations of bias (though they came flooding in anyway).

A member of the Stronger In board told Shipman that they grew increasingly concerned with this pattern of broadcasting: 'They got obsessed about having to have equal billing on every side of the argument. You'd have the IMF, then you'd have a crackpot economist, or you'd have a FTSE 100 CEO and then someone who makes a couple of prams in Sheffield.' A senior Downing Street source cited similar qualms they had with the BBC: 'You'd have ten Nobel-Prize winning economists who were given equal weight to Penny Mordaunt.'

Lucy Thomas, deputy director at Stronger In (and a former BBC journalist who reported from Brussels), felt the BBC had an issue becoming the fact-checker that was needed in a campaign full of falsehoods. 'There was no independent arbiter of truth. Nobody was able to rule whether what a campaign said was fact or fiction. Broadcasters usually do more of a job of that. It just became tit for tat, and nobody was really any the wiser.'

The BBC pushed back on criticism of their referendum broadcast coverage, claiming that issues like the £350 million for the NHS and Turkey joining the EU had been frequently and repeatedly challenged and debunked. A BBC explainer video on their website that declared the chances of Turkey joining the EU were incredibly small was welcomed by Leave as it meant they had successfully put Turkey in the public consciousness as an issue to be addressed. The truthfulness of the coverage wasn't relevant in Vote Leave's eyes – it simply needed to be discussed and remain part of the debate. (We'll look at why it is difficult to dislodge ideas from our heads in the next chapter and examine why that means the ability to drive the direction of the political conversation is of such importance.) A BBC source said, 'They didn't mind that we were taking apart their spurious claims, they were just delighted to get that agenda discussed.'

After the referendum one of David Cameron's closest aides scalded the BBC for their performance, even going as far as to say they had failed the country. 'They fucked up the referendum because of this weird obsession they had with misunderstanding what impartiality actually means. For two elections in a row they have had a demonstrable impact in a negative way. The solution is very clear: you don't report things that are palpably untrue.'

John Humphreys of the Today programme often lets pro-Brexit guests ramble on unchallenged, whilst heavily criticizing pro-EU arguments or anyone attempting to criticize Brexit. Andrew Neil called Carole Cadwalladr a 'mad cat woman' because of her relentless pursuit of the truth surrounding pro-Brexit funding and suffered no consequences. Debates on the BBC have descended into an almost CNN-like political theatre, where entertainment (and thus clicks) drive the news agenda. Author of the book 'Punch and Judy Politics', Ayesha Hazarika, told The Guardian:

all of a sudden they have to do this box-ticking balance, which leads to false equivalence. On their flagship news shows, the debate is sometimes so polarised and dumbed down. It's almost like the BBC has decided to bypass quite a lot of the sensible people in the middle because they're not exciting enough, and what you get instead is a cartoon punch-up between the most extreme views.

Part of the issue is the revolving door between the BBC and government, it is a part of the Mediacracy that we discussed earlier in the chapter. Robbie Gibb, the former head of BBC Westminster who ran Daily and Sunday Politics, The Andrew Marr Show, This Week and Radio 4's Westminster Hour, walked straight out of Broadcasting House and into Number 10 as Theresa May's director of communications, whilst Rona Fairhead quit her position in the BBC Trust to become an unpaid minister of state at the Department for International Trade.

An April 2016 report from Media Tenor revealed that a stunning 7 per cent of BBC coverage of the EU was positive and 45 per cent negative – in fact, Vladimir Putin, Chinese President Xi Jinping, and Syrian strongman Bashar al-Assad all received a higher portion of positive coverage than the EU. Rather than simply focusing on the referendum campaign, this study looked at the style and topic of coverage from 2001 to 2016. During that time, the EU accounted for some 1.5 per cent of flagship stories on the News at 10. The quality of reporting may have risen and been more positive as the campaign continued, but the British population have two qualities refined by years of EU bashing in the tabloids. They are fundamentally Eurosceptic and fail to understand Europe – just as many people fail to understand exactly how Europe works. By the time the campaign came around, there was essentially nothing that could be done to re-educate the public after years of unchallenged misinformation. The author of the study concluded that 'reporting about the advantages of EU membership has come too late and will not convince a public that has been accustomed to EU bashing'. They were right.

Obviously, many of these criticisms are being taken straight from the mouths of those who lost the referendum. Vote Leave had little to say about BBC coverage in the aftermath and why would they, they broke the bank, they hit the jackpot. You're unlikely to see thieves on the morning news complaining that the bank security system made a bank heist too easy. One BBC political reporter confessed after the result, 'It makes me feel queasy that we gave Vote Leave such an easy ride.'

Brexiteers were also heavily critical of the BBC, both before and after the referendum. In an interview on the Andrew Marr Show just before the 2019 European Elections, Farage accused the BBC of being 'ludicrous' and 'in denial'. Though their complaints aren't always based in reality, an Express article from April 2019 cites a 2005 Times report to prove BBC pro-EU bias. Interestingly, according to a YouGov poll in February 2018, more than a quarter of British people believe the BBC hold an anti-Brexit bias, topped only by their belief that The Guardian is anti-Brexit. That equates to just over half of Brexiteers.

It would be foolish to suggest that providing satisfactory coverage of Brexit for everybody would be easy (or even achievable at all). The very way in which the debate was framed meant that the BBC could not rely on traditional methods of coverage, it was unable to draw on its experience of covering decades of general election campaigns. In an article in Prospect Magazine, Matt Damazer lamented the difficulty of the BBC's task:

> The core issues have turned out to be more about values and identity than anything factual, so the trusty 'opinion from over here, opinion from over there, hard information over here' formula can't be relied on to work. The debate goes round and round, on and on, with even the criterion of democratic legitimacy in dispute. What did the last vote mean, and was it final or might we need another? This is not the stuff of general elections, where we all know and accept the ground rules...It is more complex than anything I can recall.

In his article, Damazer cites numerous examples of where two opposing points of view are presented, such as an EU ambassador citing security concerns were the UK no longer willing to accept the jurisdiction of the ECJ, which was promptly dismissed as 'twaddle' by a Conservative spokesperson. There is no scrutiny, the Tory spokesperson is not asked to explain why it is 'twaddle' and the EU ambassador cannot rebut these criticisms. This leads to what Damazer calls anaemic journalism:

'there to signal balance and fairness but in doing so avoiding anything that looks like independent scrutiny or judgment. The public is left with "six of one and half a dozen of the other" and the show rolls on.'

Perhaps we should use a slightly less toxic and partisan issue than Brexit to illustrate this point. Take the coverage of the Syrian bombings and alleged use of chemical weapons by Assad on his own people as an example (I did say only slightly less toxic).

The legality and the justifications given by the UK government for the recent airstrikes in Syria have been questioned on both sides of the Atlantic. Nearly every mainstream outlet unequivocally pushed the line that the chemical attacks that provoked the response from the UK, US, and France were perpetrated by Assad on his own people as a part of his oppressive and dictatorial regime. The BBC then released an article condemning 'The online activists pushing conspiracy theories' for daring to question the legitimacy of reports of the use of chemical weapons – despite their own admission of 'the uncertainty about what happened in Douma'.

Mainstream outlets in the US were also quick to condemn anyone who criticized the chemical attack narrative that drove the airstrikes in Syria. Yet numerous journalists who are on the ground in Syria questioned whether there was any chemical attack at all.

Robert Fisk, an award-winning journalist for The Independent, was one of the first to visit the site of the alleged chemical attacks and reported with great scepticism over whether these attacks had taken place at all. The seven-time Press Awards Foreign Journalist of the Year spoke to doctors and civilians on the ground and found that people depicted in the video of the alleged gas attack: 'were overcome not by gas but by oxygen starvation in the rubbish-filled tunnels and basements in which they lived, on a night of wind and heavy shelling that stirred up a dust storm'.

Fisk went on to discuss the claims by the US and France that they have evidence that chemical attacks took place.

'There are the many people I talked to amid the ruins of the town who said they had "never believed in" gas stories – which were usually put about, they claimed, by the armed Islamist groups.'

Independent journalists like Carla Ortiz, Pearson Sharpe, and Lee Camp have all openly dismissed (or at least expressed serious doubt over) the chemical attacks narrative pushed by mainstream media outlets. Part of the story is built on the idea that Assad has used chemical weapons against his own people before – both in 2013 and 2017 – although the UN was never able to accurately assign blame to the Assad regime for these attacks. There have been unsubstantiated theories floated that they were committed by rebel forces in the past, to draw Western intervention against the Syrian leader, or simply as false flag attacks that facilitate Western intervention in Syria.

Several days after the Syria bombing, the BBC published an article entitled 'Syria war: The online activists pushing conspiracy theories'. The language used in the BBC article to describe anyone not towing the mainstream line is rather shocking, they declare that:

'They've seized on a theory being floated by Russian officials and state-owned media outlets that the attacks were "staged" or were a "false flag" operation, carried out by jihadist groups or spies in order to put the blame on the Assad government and provide a justification for Western intervention.'

The uncertainty surrounding the alleged use of chemical weapons made the BBC condemnation of anyone daring to question their narrative rather bewildering. Even more bewildering now that we know that the OPCW has declared that there were no chemical weapons used during the incident used to justify the last round of bombing. There are several possible explanations for this current BBC campaign to counter online narratives that contradict the mainstream narrative of the Syrian chemical weapons attack:

1. The BBC are becoming increasingly concerned about the power of independent digital media. Having seen the power that it held at the last election, especially its influence over younger generations, they are making a concerted effort to discredit this reporting as they watch an entire generation turn away from traditional outlets (at the cost of their TV licence funding) towards independent reporting. They could be reacting to the generally 'left wing' and pro-Corbyn stances of online media outlets in an attempt to push the political conversation back to the 'centre' and away from dangerous socialist ideas.

2. The BBC, in an effort to protect their pro-war 'establishment' stance, is attempting to promptly crush all anti-interventionist voices that are popping up around the internet. Pro-war establishment narratives need to be propped up in order to ensure public support for further intervention in Syria.

3. They are genuinely concerned about the Syrian people suffering under the rule of Assad and about misinformation and 'junk news' being spread online and are doing everything they can to ensure the truth rises to the top of the pile. Humanitarian assistance for the people of Syria is paramount to their motives and supporting their cause is crucial to fostering peace and prosperity in the Middle East.

After the troubles that have come from intervention in Afghanistan and Iraq, it is natural that the public be wary of more intervention in the Middle East. They were openly lied to by the UK and US administrations, as well as the media at large, when there was no substantial evidence of Weapons of

Mass Destruction in Iraq, in order to push for intervention in Iraq. After a more than decade-long conflict things are no better in Iraq, arguably worse with the emergence of IS in the past few years.

In 2018, it was revealed that the BBC ran a half-century campaign in conjunction with MI5 from 1930–mid-1990s to prevent 'left-wing' journalists from rising too high in the BBC. Is it really out of the question to hold doubts over their motives in trying to discredit and demonize all alternative voices and narratives? MediaReform.org examined the amount of discussion time given to Labour and Conservative backing papers during the 2017 election campaign on the BBC morning segment. Conservative Papers had a 69 per cent excess of mentions, and Labour Papers had a 26 per cent deficit of mentions based on fair time rules.

Despite their failings, the BBC are frequently considered to be one of the most trusted outlets in Britain. They seem to be suffering from a desire to not offend any side of an argument, lest they be seen as biased. This has led to a loss of scrutiny that is crucial to good journalism. Their presentation of the Brexit debate illustrates perfectly how the quality of political debate has been sullied over time. Any criticism is seen as bias, any questions are seen as not believing in Britain, whilst failure to ask questions is seen as weakness, establishment bias, or implicit support for the fringe opinions of society.

The media is an integral part of the British establishment; its owners share the same underlying assumptions and mantras. Journalists and politicians alike obsessively critique and attack the behaviour of those at the bottom of society. They fail to hold the government to account, debase the quality of our national debate, and reinforce the ideas of the British establishment. The British press primed us to be anti-Europe and when the time came we were unable to engage with the Brexit debate on anything other than the most child-like, simplistic, binary, us vs them level. Worst of all, human nature, tribalism, and our tendency to cling to what we believe makes it increasingly difficult to bring us back from our hyper-partisan stances and embrace a little nuance and complexity.

4. Our Divided Society

Deep-seated inequalities continue to cast long jagged shadows over the map of England.

Alex Niven

We've learnt how technology has helped advertisers and political campaigners alike to understand us and how social media is exacerbating societal divisions. We've also looked at how the press has helped exacerbate anti-immigrant and anti-EU sentiment and exploited fears and divides that were already embedded in British society. The EU referendum uncovered many of the underlying divisions and social cleavages in British society.

In my last chapter, I was heavily critical of the press and their demonization of both immigration and the EU. I pointed out the positive financial contribution immigrants make to the EU, the opportunities that the EU has afforded Britain, and the administrative costs of customs checks and trade negotiations that the EU provides. On the whole, I believe that the EU and immigration have been a net positive for our country and society, but that is not to say that immigration levels should remain untouched or unchanged. What I will gladly oppose every hour of the day is the disgusting 'hostile environment' policy that had led to the Windrush scandal and the utterly unforgivable deportation of British citizens. That does not mean immigration should not be discussed. In this chapter, I will lay out what I believe to be the major dividing lines of British politics and the forces that led to the anti-establishment backlash.

Immigration is always a touchy topic to discuss. It can often lead to allegations of racism and can be grossly over-simplified. A detailed discussion of the topic is difficult and asks us to confront issues that we may not have considered or may find uncomfortable to think about. Consider the effect of mass immigration on feelings of community and national unity, how much we value national borders, do we want to prioritize national citizens over EU and non-EU immigrants, or whether we as a country are comfortable with our current levels of immigration. I have often heard the argument used that we shouldn't discuss immigration in these ways because it ignores the human reality of the people who come to live and work in the UK. Discussing immigration in these terms encourages and acts as a dog-whistle to genuine racists and bigots. I believe that is fundamentally wrong. You cannot shut down discussion in order to prevent it sliding too far to the extreme. Should we never discuss nationalization of water or energy companies in case the Communists take over and put the entire economy under state control? Should we never discuss speed limits on roads out of fear that motorways will become 30mph zones?

The human story of immigrants and immigration is often incredibly inspiring. People willing to uproot and move to another country for the promise of opportunity. They may leave amidst war, famine, disease, or all three, traverse continents and oceans in search of a better life, oft knowing they may never return to the land of their ancestors. This is never a decision that will be taken lightly, thousands of people have died crossing the Mediterranean since 2013 desperately searching for a better life. It's a moral blight we won't quickly forget. I don't believe that we should let people drown as they flee bombs we are dropping just because they are from some 'shithole countries'. Immigration can be explored in isolation of this and I believe there is a way to discuss immigration without sliding into racism. We should never treat people like numbers. That is the first step to dehumanizing anyone. However, that doesn't mean we can't have a rational and full discussion about the impact that EU membership and mass immigration have on the country.

The Road to Somewhere

The short book Folk Opposition released in 2010 is an eerily prophetic lament to the loss of a sense of shared community and the rise of neo-liberalism. Author Alex Niven explores what he believes was the re-emergence of a ruling class: 'modern politics has come to resemble the pre-Labour movement Whig/Tory divide of the eighteenth and nineteenth centuries, with two parties representing different divisions of a sizeable wealthy class'.

Niven argues that the ascension of David Cameron to the heights of Downing Street revealed the deep divides in British politics, between the general populace and the establishment. The new establishment is a combination of businessmen, bankers, estate agents, new money from entertainment and leisure industries, the media, advertising, and the traditional old money establishment of the aristocracy, small landowners, and farmers. Released in 2010, Niven argued that the current establishment has, over the past 40 years, successfully diminished the role of the general populace in politics, shrunk their representation, and allowed the neo-liberal ideology of Thatcher to occupy the political mainstream. He warns of the exorbitant inequalities in the UK, those which were further exacerbated as the coalition government enacted sweeping cuts to the welfare state, deepening the divides in British society, and pushing those at the bottom even further down the ladder: 'In our own country there is an underworld of suffering lurking beneath a surface world of consumerist fantasy and lifestyle myths.'

Niven correctly predicted that this divide would cause a (then unforeseen) backlash against the current establishment. The country was split down the middle as a previously silent majority made their voices heard. 'The Road to Somewhere' by David Goodhart successfully identified what I believe to be the new emerging divisions in British society and politics. He splits the UK into two tribes, the Somewheres and the Anywheres (with a few inbetweeners stuck in the middle). This might seem reductive and Goodhart readily admits that the simplified aspect allows us to understand broad voting trends whilst conceding that no one individual is a perfect representative of either category.

He defines the typical Anywhere broadly as:

1. Feeling comfortable about the modern world
2. Having a loose and open idea of national identity
3. Putting liberty before security in the civil liberties debate

And the typical Somewhere as:

1. Feeling uncomfortable with the modern world
2. Having a more 'fellow citizens first' view of national identity
3. Being prepared to sacrifice liberty for security

Electorally, both groups can include a broad coalition of voters – Goodhart estimates that some 50 per cent of the British population can be categorized as Somewheres, 25 per cent as Anywheres and 25 per cent as Inbetweeners. The Somewheres make up who Trump described as the 'forgotten people', those left behind by the modern world ruled by affluent and mobile Anywheres. It may seem simplistic to reduce the British population to just two groups and some inbetweeners, but technically that is how the First Past The Post electoral system often divides the country, between Labour and Conservative (with a small portion of inbetweeners voting Lib Dem). What we are witnessing with Brexit is the unveiling of the new split in British politics, it's driving the divisions within both Labour and the Conservatives over Brexit policy. This divide is not a new phenomenon, it has been growing since Thatcher redefined the political landscape, going unrecognized and unaddressed by the Anywheres who occupy government. Before we get too deep into the ideology of the Anywhere establishment, I think it is important to explore the divides that separate the Somewheres from the Anywheres.

The major dividing lines between the two tribes of Britain are where you live, your type of education, and your attitude towards the modern world. Those who feel they belong to their neighbourhood have a stronger attachment to their national identity. A total of 42 per cent of UKIP voters and 62 per cent of Plaid Cymru voters live within 15 minutes of where they grew up, compared to 25 per cent of Greens or 30 per cent of Liberal Democrats. A large part of this depends on whether you left school and took a job in your home town or whether you took yourself off to university.

Before I go any further, I want to make it clear that I am not here to disparage those who have not gone to university. It is an educational path designed for some but not all. Throughout the 1990s and 2000s, successive governments oversaw a huge transformation of educational norms and that has made an unforeseen contribution to the division of Britain. In 1992 the Conservative government abolished the two-tier higher education system, designating the 35 polytechnics as universities and essentially pushing a university education as the single most desirable form of higher education. Tony Blair pushed even further with this transformation, advocating for a US-style mass higher education system. In a 1999 speech, Blair proposed what may have seemed an outlandish target of 50 per cent of each age group attending university. Yet by 2017 it was estimated that 49 per cent of people would attend university before the age of 30, compared to just 14 per cent in 1984. John McTerna, the former New Labour Adviser, once commented that: 'New Labour rhetoric was always on the side of change and mobility. But it was off-putting to many people. We were in effect saying to many people especially in the north: stay with your community and fail, or move.'

To the Anywheres in government, it is only natural that one should attend university. A total of 90 per cent of the 2010 parliament had a university education (94 per cent of newly elected MPs), though this number dropped slightly in 2017 to 84 per cent. The 2017 election was also the first time in history in which Labour elected a higher percentage of graduates (84 per cent) than the Conservative Party (83 per cent). Though Conservative MPs are still far more likely to be privately educated, with 48 per cent having attended a private school (private education in Britain costs over £16,000 per year on average) compared to 17 per cent of Labour MPs and 14 per cent of Liberal Democrats. Most MPs are part of a select group of 1 per cent of the population who attend Oxford or Cambridge. A total of 75 per cent of the 2017 parliament went to one of these two universities. McTerna astutely pointed out that, 'In Britain it is, increasingly, university or bust.' In 'The Road to Somewhere', Goodhart is particularly critical of this policy, questioning whether it made any sense at all to push for mass university education without considering our need for tradesmen: 'Where were all the sub-graduate technicians and engineers going to come from? And how were the 50 per cent not taking the approved route supposed to feel about their place in the world?'

Having been told all their lives that the way to make a success of your life was to move away and attend university, more than half of each age cohort is left to contemplate life without university. There has been a significant deviation in the rhetoric about good jobs (i.e. graduate jobs) and more basic jobs, ones that don't require a degree but still offer some form of career opportunity. The decline of career opportunities without higher education has not been addressed by any of the main political parties in a meaningful way. Not attending university is sometimes seen as less socially acceptable, something you choose as a last resort or if you're not cognitively capable of handling a university education. How should we deal with a society when half of every age group are told they were not worthy of the most desired path on the way to a brighter future? One of the problems is that we simply don't acknowledge it. The university educated Anywheres who have run the country for decades have no idea what it is like to fall at that hurdle. It's just a natural progression, you finish school and then go to uni. What else would you do? Goodhart writes,

'While the expansion of higher education has certainly created new opportunities for many people it has also exacerbated the fault line in British society that this book is about – those that leave and those that stay.'

A lot of people, until globalization arrived, had access to a well-paid unionized manufacturing job without the need for a university degree. In-work training has declined and apprenticeship schemes are few and far between. Employers have been willing to pay to train a young employee for decades, it was accepted as a necessary cost. With Freedom of Movement employers can hitch a 'free ride on the training systems of other European countries'. Why go to the costly expense of training someone who may leave your firm inside a year or two? It makes more financial sense to import trained workers from Europe. There has also been a fiscal incentive for governments to push university attendance as mandatory. Higher education has become big business and more students means a larger university sector to tax. Today, universities generate around £95 billion for the economy annually. The Conservatives have begun to sell off billions in student debt at below-market value to make the government accounting look more effective.

Our world view is substantially influenced by our experience (or lack thereof) at university. Those who leave home to attend university in another city, or perhaps even another country, become immersed in a culture that celebrates the idea of finding a new home, one where you belong. You're coming together with a whole bunch of people who have left home at the same time, to forge a new identity and find your place in the world. It's only natural that such an experience is going to be crucial in forging your outlook on the world as you learn more about it and take your first steps away from home. University is a fast track to the Anywhere class. A total of 90 per cent of academics voted to remain in the EU. It helps to shape an elite that is insider based, tight-knit, and distant from much of society. The higher education industry has profited greatly from the influx of foreign students (who pay much higher fees) since the New Labour years. The 24 Russell Group universities are vocal opponents of immigration restriction and heavily promote the import of foreign students. They have ideological and financial incentives to back remaining in the EU and the cocoon of university helps to perpetuate this. University drops you right into a cacophony of people who think they are going to change the world, you're exposed to new ideas, new foods, new ways of looking at the world, new drugs, new people, and new music. Almost everything about going to university in Britain pushes you away from the Somewheres of the world and transforms you into an Anywhere. Safe and comfortable in the modern world.

Immigration and the Changing World

In the 1960s, academic Marshall McLuhan predicted the coming age of electronic communication would result in the breakdown of established societal structures and identities and return us to a form of tribal politics.[1] He described this interconnected world as 'the global village'. It's an idea that has been celebrated by technologists, dataists, and the Silicon Valley overlords. It is the purest form of Anywhere-ism, we don't need to belong anywhere because we are all citizens of the global village. Over the past 30 years, British society has undergone a massive period of liberalization. There is now widespread acceptance of issues many thought to be unacceptable 30 years ago, including homosexuality, sex before marriage, and inter-racial relations.

However, attitudes to other liberal issues such as immigration, European integration, welfare, and national identity have barely shifted at all. Goodhart makes the case that: 'Since the turn of the century western politics has had to make room for a set of voices pre-occupied with national borders and pace of change, appealing to people who feel displaced by a more open, ethnically fluid, graduate-favouring economy and society, designed by and for the new elites.'

As Freedom of Movement blossomed in Europe and borders became more porous, the benefits of this policy were sung and championed as a triumph of post-war Europe. Yet, in the midst of celebrating the removal of walls and borders within Europe, there was very little discussion of what this actually meant for the integrity of the individual nation-state. It provokes some difficult questions. What is a nation without borders? Is national pride wrong? How much should we value those who stay put, who choose not to leave their home towns for personal or financial reasons?

Living as a good citizen of the earth may have seemed an easy thing to do a few years ago, but thanks to the wonders of modern society we are now endlessly confronted with the consequences of every action. I'm not decrying suffering that is caused by modern capitalism, just trying to make note of its inexhaustive assault on the brain. Every action has an unintended consequence to consider in a world where it feels we have less and less time. This quote from 'How Britain Works' by Stig Abell sums it up beautifully:

Sip a coffee: who grew it, processed it, stuck it in a curiously semi-recyclable cup? Put it on the table: who made the table, who felled the tree, who designed the blade that cut it, who mined the metal that made the alloy that made the blade? Modern life is an Escher-like series of interconnected structures, dizzyingly and uninventable complex. And getting more complex every day.

A 2011 YouGov poll asked respondents to state whether they agreed or disagreed with the statement, 'Britain has changed in recent times, it sometimes feels like a foreign country and this makes me feel uncomfortable'. A total of 62 per cent agreed, though just 16 per cent of graduates agreed strongly, compared with 41 per cent of non-graduates. Polling inaccuracies aside, that's not a number we can easily ignore. A 2014 Ipsos MORI poll found that just over 60 per cent of people agreed with the statement, 'People led happier lives in the old days when they had fewer problems to cope with'. This yearning for the days of old is a lightning rod for criticism of Brexiteers, their apparent wish to move backwards. It is seen by most Anywheres as a form of xenophobic nostalgia, a desire to re-tread the paths of history to when the rich white men ruled the world and there weren't so many brown faces on the street.

These feelings are often dismissed out of hand. By doing so we exhibit the stereotypical sneering latte-drinking liberal elite that many Brexiteers seem to harbour so much hatred for. The thoughts and apprehensions held by half the population cannot be ignored or dismissed. People are concerned about the rapidly changing world, that's not stupid or irrational, just a consequence of the uncertainty of our times and grievances that have not been addressed. The British National Party (BNP) and UKIP spoke to a more overt and genuinely racist streak of those who hold these views, but this is not a small minority. The reality is that more than half of the British population feel uncomfortable and at times completely out of whack with the modern world. Is that so wrong? If you're unable to acknowledge the rate at which our culture, politics, society, and technology are changing, then I would urge you to think again. For those of us who were born into the tech-drenched modern world, it still seems overwhelming. Put your feet in the shoes of someone who was born 10, 20, maybe 40 years before you. Jamie Bartlett describes the trials of the twenty-first century citizen attempting to make sense of politics and meaning as a muddled cacophony of disparate thoughts and concepts:

> The modern citizen is expected to sift through an insane torrent of competing facts, networks, friend requests, claims, blogs, data, propaganda, misinformation, investigative journalism, charts, different charts, commentary and reportage. Social media platforms give you an endless, rapid flow of dissonant ideas and arguments, one after the other, without obvious order or sense of progression.[2]

The world is vastly more interdependent than it was when we entered the EU. Organizations like NATO, the WTO, and the Basel financial regulators club mean that countries all around the world have traded sovereignty for international trade and co-operation. Without this, the modern world as we know it wouldn't exist in its vastly globalized and interconnected form. Despite this, the liberal 'Anywhere' outlook that has commanded politics for the past 30 years is now experiencing a major backlash. The trend of international free trade agreements continued unabetted until the stalled TTIP talks (Transatlantic Trade and Investment Partnership). TTIP would have allowed corporations to sue elected governments. Trade agreements like NAFTA (North American Free Trade Agreement) and TPP (Trans-Pacific Partnership) have become unpopular, either because of their acceleration of globalization or as a symptom of the corporatization outsourcing culture of neo-liberalism. The global backlash against free trade and open borders has begun and Western democracies are feeling the heat of a far-right power surge, rising on a tide or opposition of globalization and free trade.

Goodhart argues that the EU's 'inability to reform freedom

of movement has led directly to Brexit'. The idea that national citizens should get preferential treatment is still highly popular across the EU, but because it is one of the four founding principles (the freedom of movement of goods, labour, capital, and services) it remains unbreakable. This is why David Cameron was unable to achieve a renegotiation of freedom of movement, or get much traction or flexibility with his proposed emergency brake on immigration. As the EU has pushed for greater integration, Somewheres have become more 'attached to national social contracts as more open, knowledge-based economies increased economic uncertainty for the less well off'. Despite widespread support for moderate nationalism, even in the most liberal states, the EU has resisted reforming Freedom of Movement and thus given birth to more extreme, far-right parties across the EU.

Since 2000, the level of mass immigration to the UK has been largely ignored by the Anywheres in parliament. The consensus amongst the Establishment has consistently been that immigration brings many benefits and should be welcomed. This has been the argument made by the political classes and has ignored the consistent polling that indicates 75 per cent of British people want immigration reduced. The Conservative pledge since 2010 was to reduce net immigration into the tens of thousands, but that is all but impossible within the EU. As we discussed in the previous chapter, non-EU immigration could have been reduced, but that would still have left it well above the 100,000 target. It should also be noted that whilst comments that immigration alone is putting a strain on public services are ill-founded, anxiety about immigration levels has closely tracked the increase in immigration since 2000.

Large-scale immigration is unpopular almost everywhere. This is not to say it isn't welcome, necessary, or even required at the time. The press has vilified immigration as a concept and the Leave campaigns were all too happy to take advantage of this underlying prejudice. Yet the binary nature of this debate has meant that a significant majority of the British population, many of whom have genuine concerns about the level of immigration, have been ignored, just as those who have genuine concerns about the EU have been dismissed as racist. A Delta/Channel 4 poll found that in 2018, 70 per cent of British people still believed that a reduction in immigration was necessary. The British population are generally welcoming of immigration, despite the rhetoric that the entire Leave vote was just a xenophobic backlash. Many people are simply concerned about the high levels of immigration that we have seen post-2000. In 2019 an Ipsos MORI poll for the BBC found that only 26 per cent of people thought immigration had had a generally negative impact on the UK (down from 64 per cent in 2011), compared to 48 per cent who felt it was positive (up from 19 per cent in 2011). A study of six European countries by Ettore Recchi of Sciences Po in Paris revealed that British people tend to be better connected internationally based on travel, friends, and contacts and living abroad, both in Europe and around the rest of the world.

Obviously, that doesn't discount that there are genuine racists living in our society. Goodhart estimates that these people make up some 5-7 per cent of the British population, pointing to the nearly 1 million votes the BNP won in the 2009 European Elections. Are we to believe that some 52 per cent of the population is racist and simply voted to get the immigrants out? Or is it possible that many of these voters simply took an opportunity to finally rectify a situation that they felt had been slowly slipping out of control? Did they take the opportunity to make a statement against what they had been told for decades was the reason for their problems? Immigrants and the European Union. Many majority Leave areas were former industrial centres or seaside towns with lower than average levels of immigration. The feeling that the national conversation is forgetting or ignoring them drives the sense of helplessness or abandonment by the political elites. That the Anywheres who run the country do not listen to their concerns.

Britain's immigrant and minority population has grown to 12 million (20 per cent across the UK and 25 per cent in England). This has happened against the majority consensus. So whilst British people are friendly and welcoming to immigrants, and have happily absorbed for decades, successive waves of immigration and the number of people arriving in Britain since the expansion of the EU to include Eastern Europe, have been difficult for a lot of people to accept.

A majority of British voters also feel that there has been a lack of integration from recent migrants. YouGov polling from October 2016 found that 58 per cent of people thought newcomers were not integrating well (79 per cent of Leave voters compared to 38 per cent of Remainers). Though it must be noted that people are often hostile to legislation that promotes integration as such. It is a difficult feeling to remedy. Integration is another touchy topic. It's easy to confuse the desire for better integration with a dislike of diversity or other cultures. It is also crucial to note that it would be wrong to blame anyone specifically on the question of integration. Neither long-term citizens or residents, nor the immigrants themselves are to blame here. However, we should be concerned by the segregation that still goes on, even in the supposedly integrated and multicultural haven of London. A survey run by the Social Integration Commission found that London, despite its massive diversity, is actually the least integrated region in the UK relative to its minority population. A 2013 YouGov poll found that 26 per cent of Londoners were uncomfortable with the number of ethnic minority people in their neighbourhood (the highest rate in the entire UK). In an essay on Brexit for the New York Review of Books, author Zadie Smith, famous for her true to life depiction of London in her novels, wrote: 'The painful truth is that fences are being raised everywhere in London. Around school districts, around neighbourhoods, around lives.'

A total of 90 per cent of Londoners do say that they think different races and cultures get on well together and only 60 per cent of Londoners think immigration is too high, 10 per cent below the rest of the UK. Yet that is still an astoundingly high figure for what is supposedly one of the most diverse and multicultural cities in the world.

In the book The Authoritarian Dynamic, Karen Stenner found that humans have a predisposition to 'become intolerant when one's values or security or in-group feel under threat. Rapid change in a neighbourhood can trigger this feeling of threat to the moral order.' Talking about our differences is the surest way to cause the secretly intolerant to think more radically. Thus paradoxically, celebrating diversity makes us more intolerant. It is the discussion of community, of similar traits and values that brings us together.

When UKIP elections expert Chris Bruni-Lowe commissioned a poll of 10,000 undecided voters in November 2015, he found that controlling the UK's border and 'setting our own immigration policy' was the single largest reason that people gave that might convince them to vote to leave with 38 per cent (saving money came in second with 18 per cent). Whilst voters are generally welcoming of immigrants, they resent their inability to control levels of immigration. In a world in which many Somewheres increasingly feel out of place, under threat and as if they have no say in the running of the country, is it any wonder that 'Take Back Control' was such an effective campaign message?

During the campaign, it began to dawn on members of the Stronger In campaign group that they needed a response to the immigration attacks coming from Vote Leave and Leave.EU. Peter Mandelson wrote a memo on 13 June commenting that: 'The problem is that we – political mainstream/Remain – appear not (yet) to be listening on immigration.' He wanted Cameron to address people's fears on immigration and their concerns about its perceived impact on public services[3]. Mandelson proposed the following:

- New migration funds to be allocated to local authorities for public services with higher levels of EU migration
- A new law to prevent wages being undercut by EU migration
- Discussion at the EU level to implement further measures against welfare migration and economic migration
- Agreement with France and Germany to examine the management of the Free Movement of Labour and a push to introduce legislation in these areas
- Invitation for cross-party talks on immigration issues to develop solutions on protecting communities
- An affordable housing programme for those who had lived in the UK for a certain number of years

David Cameron's director of communications, Craig Oliver, urged Cameron to give it serious consideration, but he ultimately decided against it, feeling it could actually help the Leave campaign. This plan set forward by Mandelson also proves that there were meaningful steps that the government could have taken to address concerns over the impact of immigration, the government chose not to. Cameron also refused to say he would veto Turkey's membership as he feared it would inflame relations with Turkey, who are a vital Counter-Terrorism partner for the UK and Europe. Remain found it incredibly difficult to get people to believe that immigration was not causing the strains on public services that people thought it was. Ryan Coetzee emailed the senior staff at Stronger In during the campaign commenting that he could not persuade them of the benefits of immigration: 'They don't believe facts that contradict their feelings, although they are impressed by the benefits deal that the PM made.'[4] It was also always going to be difficult for a Tory administration who imposed the austerity cuts that led people to believe public services were strained because of immigration to admit that they have caused the strain on public services.

Populism vs Neo-Liberalism

The story of Brexit and Trump has been painted by some as the rise of populism in the West. Whilst populism itself can be difficult to define as a whole, it is not difficult to argue that Brexit and Trump were both populist movements (as too were Bernie Sanders and Jeremy Corbyn). Goodhart reasons that the source of mainstream populism (i.e. Brexit, Trump, other right-wing Nationalist parties across Europe) is a rally against the political institutions who for too long paid insufficient attention to 'the importance of stability and secure borders, the priority of national citizens' rights before universal rights, the need for narrative and recognition for those who do not easily thrive in more education-driven economies'.

For all their lies, emotional rhetoric, and easy solutions, populists give voice to grievances that are real – they wouldn't get very far if they weren't tapping into something that was in the minds of a sizeable portion of voters. These concerns, as we've discussed, were not addressed by the Anywhere establishment, only by the tabloids. The official establishment line has been, for several decades, that immigration is good and that immigrants are and have been through history, incredibly beneficial to Britain. That's hardly a lie. This line, however, fails to address people's concerns about the level of immigration. There has been no sensible discussion on immigration and Freedom of Movement and we have all suffered for it. The failure to articulate what seems like a reasonable position on immigration has driven people towards more and more extreme views. This is not a situation easily remedied whilst inside the EU. Politicians have been reluctant to admit this or confront the issue. Anywheres tend to welcome open borders and the issue stayed off the agenda. Thus we have seen the rise of anti-EU parties, first in the BNP, then in UKIP, and now in the mainstream Conservative Party. In Folk Opposition, Alex Niven warned of the consequences of allowing populism to become the driving force of British politics. The failure of mainstream politicians to confront the concerns of the majority of the British public, of the disaffected and the forgotten, has led us directly to the point we are in now, where nostalgia-driven populism dominates our politics: 'As the example of America teaches us, full-blown irrationalism and a cult of popular militarism are the obvious dangers resulting from a culture that allows its politics to become a hive of superficial populism and sentimental folksiness.'

Niven also warned of a backlash against the neo-liberal establishment consensus, noting that 'a gathering feeling of populist anger at the scarcely-articulated injustices of neo-liberalism might easily tip over into something very ugly indeed'.

The backlash we are seeing now is against the triumph of neo-liberalism on both sides of the Atlantic to consume the public and private spheres. Before we go any further I want to spend a little time describing what exactly I mean by neo-liberalism. It's a term that has been overused and so broadly applied that it has become almost meaningless, so I feel it is important to define it properly. Since the late 1970s, British politics has largely been dominated by neo-liberalism, whereby the left of British politics won the social argument and the right won the economic argument. Attitudes to liberal ideas such as gay marriage flourished alongside an ever-growing consensus on free-market economics. Thatcher and Reagan both believed in Milton Friedman's philosophy that modern society had become too dependent on the state. They sought to shrink the public sector and privatize public services as far as was possible, all whilst lowering trade barriers and taxes on the rich. Thatcher described Friedman as an 'intellectual freedom fighter'. Since then, three waves of neo-liberalism have seen the state rolled further and further back and increasingly privatized. The first wave was Thatcher, followed by second-wave neo-liberalism in the form of Blair and Brown with New Labour, and the third wave of Cameron and Osborne.

Thatcher sparked 'the Big Bang' in the City of London by deregulating financial institutions and upgrading the City to electronic trading. Rules on foreign ownership were abolished, retail banks merged with previously cautious investment banks (who were no longer playing with their own money) and capital controls were eliminated, meaning capital could flow in and out of the country unrestricted. In 2010, Nigel Lawson, chancellor to Mrs Thatcher, admitted that the 2007 financial meltdown was an unintended consequence of the 'Big Bang'. Before Thatcher's intervention, every single member of the stock exchange was a British-owned firm and within a year 25 per cent were foreign-owned. Capital controls can be useful for a national government, they can help prevent finance from controlling the will of governments by threatening to withdraw their cash. Without capital controls, money could begin to flow out of the country at the sight of an unpopular policy, perhaps leading to a catastrophic wave of capital flight. It was estimated that in 8 years following the introduction of a wealth tax in France in 1998, they lost $125 billion because of capital flight. In 2009 there was a steep rise in the number of company directorships relocating to tax havens like Jersey and Guernsey following Gordon Brown's tax increase on the wealthy. And in the 6 months prior to June 2016, the UK saw somewhere in the range of £77 billion leave the UK, compared to £2 billion in the previous 6 months. The wealthiest of Britain (and around the globe) have the luxury of being able to move their money around without hindrance. They will not be bound by the confines of Britain in the case of a catastrophe, they will offshore their wealth and wait for more favourable conditions. There was no better example of the growing power of the financial sector in Britain as when investors were able to force Britain off of the European Exchange Rate Mechanism. In

1992 speculators began to sell off British assets and sterling in an attempt to push Britain out of the system. They forced the Bank of England to spend £15 billion attempting to shore up the pound as they sold off currency reserves. In the end, the BoE was unsuccessful and some in the city made billions in the process. George Soros alone made $1 billion at Britain's expense.

People may have believed that Tony Blair offered new hope and an ideological alternative to the ideas of Thatcherism, but New Labour offered little real change. They sold themselves wholesale to the Thatcherite, neo-liberal ideology. Blair hosted Thatcher in a secret meeting in Downing Street within 2 weeks of his election in May 1997. Blair and Brown believed that the only way they could help Labour regain power was to become more of what had become the accepted norm in Establishment circles. It was that, or face the hostilities of the press. They welcomed free trade, free markets, privatization, and lower taxes on the rich. Privatization over the past 30 years has been incredibly costly to the British taxpayer. A total of 75 per cent of Britain's railways are now foreign-owned. Since British Rail was sold off in 1995, commuters have seen a 20 per cent real-terms rise in fares, costing an average of £5 billion per year. The cost of a ticket from London to Manchester has ballooned 238 per cent, from £50 to £169, three times the rate of inflation during that period. In 2018, a monthly ticket for Chelmsford in Essex to London cost £381, compared to £66 in France, £65 in Italy, or £118 in Germany for an equivalent commute. Research suggests that UK households would save £75 a year if water and sewage services were renationalized. One-third of money spent on water bills currently goes to banks and investors (at an average of £1.8 billion per year in dividends) as well as the 19 bosses paying themselves over £1 million a year. Corporate Watch also found that households could save £250 a year if energy, water, and rail were renationalized.

The pace of outright privatization did not slow. Instead,

under the third wave of neo-liberalism it picked up pace. George Osborne oversaw the largest sale of publicly owned assets in British history since Thatcher sold £21 billion worth of shares in British Airways, the British Airports Authority, British Petroleum, Rolls-Royce, and the Royal Ordnance Factories. In all, it was estimated that 2016 alone saw the sale of British assets worth £60 billion. The student loans book fetched an estimated £12 billion, whilst Kings Cross raked in £360 million. He sold the government share in RBS, Network Rail, and we haven't even mentioned the NHS. Private ambulances cost the taxpayer £60 million annually, part of the £9.2 billion now spent every year on services delivered by the private sector. All of this despite the fact that a majority of the British public back nationalization to bring these industries back into public ownership. A total of 53 per cent of people believe that the energy grid should be nationalized, 59 per cent back water nationalization, 60 per cent back bringing railways back into public hands, and 65 per cent believe we should have a publicly owned Royal Mail. Yet the march of privatization continues on unabetted. This fire sale and the crippling sweep of public sector cuts were not used to balance the budget. It paid for corporate and top-rate tax cuts that have blown the national debt to £2.2 trillion. The neo-liberal ideology has permeated every part of the British establishment. The civil service proposed the benefits cuts that David Cameron implemented under Tony Blair[5].

Since the 1970s, both sides of the political spectrum have converged in this narrow expression of the Overton Window. The Overton Window is a concept named after Joseph P. Overton, former vice president of the right-wing Think Tank Mackinac Centre for Public Policy, and describes the spectrum of what is considered to be politically possible or acceptable at a given time. The right wing of Britain and America have successfully dragged the Overton Window to the right, to a place where policies considered centrist in Europe are depicted as 'far-left lunacy' in Britain. The convergence of the Overton Window and the lack of alternatives to the accepted status quo is what leads cries of 'they're all the same' or 'what's the point in voting?'.

This is the ideology that Brexit campaigners attempted to rally the people against. This is what they define as the 'liberal elite' when what they really mean is the neo-liberal elite. The dismissive way in which they discuss people's concerns about immigration or the changing world is the sneering liberal attitude that they rally against. Much of the post-Brexit discussion between Remainers about how the poorest regions could possibly have voted to make themselves worse off is misguided. The decision by ordinary people to take an economic hit in exchange for something greater, for sovereignty or control of their borders, was seen as pointless or downright stupid. How could they be so stupid as to willingly make themselves poorer? What is the difference between less well-off people who voted to leave the EU and are willing to accept material and economic loss? Both of these examples are sacrificing short-term economics for a principled or moral choice. You may cry the idea that we may be worse off in the short term was not discussed by the Brexit campaign; after all, they said that we would be better off as an independent, free-trading country. But I think it is naïve to believe that the public believed them wholesale. There were obvious risks to leaving, they were well publicized by the Remain campaign, but people chose to leave despite those risks. Many Remain politicians and activists have missed two major points here, that the victims of austerity had nothing else to lose and that they were willing to make their voices heard in exchange for economic uncertainty. To this day, I still see very few examples of politicians, activists, or the electorate trying to understand why the other side voted the way they did. To Remain voters, staying in the EU was the obvious choice. Why would we choose to reject our European neighbours? To Brexiteers, it seemed a simple choice. Why would we lose our closest trading partner simply because we no longer wish to be part of their political project?

There was no admission that the EU has major flaws, just vague platitudes about how it needs reform. From the other side, Brexiteers seem determined to vilify the EU and everything associated with it as the work of the devil. We can't influence EU rules if we choose to leave the Single Market or European Union. We can negotiate, but ultimately, once outside the EU, we will have as much influence as Canada, Japan, or Norway in the internal trading rules of the EU, which we will have to abide by if we want to trade with them. We can't fully control immigration from within the EU, for some people that is a serious problem. There are no easy answers here. Around 3 million people who didn't vote in the 2015 General Election voted in the 2016 referendum. Three million more people felt that this was the moment to have their voices heard. That should speak volumes. Three million people feel so unrepresented by the options on display at a general election that they don't vote, and yet when it came to Brexit they were inspired to give their vote. Neo-liberalism has left vast swathes of the British population disenfranchised, sliding ever closer to poverty, and feeling out of place in a rapidly changing world. It is these divisions that were understood and exploited by the Leave campaign. It was not simply racists vs non-racists, or the educated vs the uneducated masses. Desperation blew from the Brexit vote like steam from a kettle left too long on the hob. Desperation induced not just by immigration anxiety and a feeling of losing their place and meaning in the world, but from the economic anxiety forced upon the country by austerity.

Trimming the Magic Money Tree

For the first time in decades, the upcoming generation is going to be worse off than their parents. This is not because or despite Brexit. Wages and social mobility have stagnated comparative to the cost of living and the housing market. Britain's millennials earned £8000 less during their twenties than their predecessors and they may well be the first to earn less than the previous generation over the course of their entire lifetime. The poorest 50 per cent of Britain holds 9 per cent of the wealth whilst the richest 10 per cent own 45 per cent, CEO pay has almost doubled over the past decade, and the Social Metrics Commission has estimated that more than 14 million people now live in poverty in Britain. This has been exacerbated by the brutal policy of austerity imposed by the Conservative and coalition governments since 2010. By 2021, if current spending projections continue, there will have been a £37 billion drop in annual funding for working-age social security since 2010, despite the rising cost of living. Spending on PIP (Personal Independence Payments) and ESA (Employment and Support Allowance) alone has already been cut by £5 billion since the beginning of the decade and a UK poverty measurement published by the Social Metrics Commission in 2018 found that more than half of families living below the breadline contained at least one person with a disability. Tax credits have been cut by £4.6 billion, universal credit by £3.6 billion, child benefit by £3.4 billion, disability benefits by £2.8 billion, and housing benefits by £2.3 billion.

Austerity has bitten hard, there can be no doubts that it has had a crippling effect on a huge portion of the population. A University College London report found that cuts in health and social care spending could be linked to an estimated 45,000 additional deaths between 2010 and 2014, though the report notes that there could be many other explanations for a rising death rate. The 2016 BSA survey showed us that 71 per cent of people believe that immigration increases pressure on schools and 63 per cent believe it puts a strain on the NHS. The UK is one of the most unequal countries in Europe, home to the richest area in Northern Europe, Inner London, and nine out of ten poorest including West Wales, Tees Valley, Northern Ireland, and

Durham. The gap between the richest and poorest regions in the UK is also the highest in Europe in terms of disposable income. Outside of London, only the South-East of England has a higher GDP per capita than the EU-15 average and only 27 per cent of the country live in regions wealthier than the UK average. The Resolution Foundation predicted that between 2015 and 2020 we are set to have experienced 19 successive quarters of real-terms disposable income decline. It also estimated that in the same period, the poorest one-third of households would end up £715 worse off annually compared to the richest third who are set to be £185 better off. Real wages have been growing on average since 2013, but by June 2016, only London and the South-East had returned to the pre-crisis peak of GDP per person. Roughly half of the UK population had no increase in take-home pay from 2005 to 2016. In 2019, the New Economics Foundation calculated that British people were still, on average, £128 per year worse off than they were in 2008. We have endured the longest period of wage stagnation since the middle of the nineteenth century.

Thiemo Fetzer, Associate Professor in Economics at Warwick, argued that these cuts were used to fuel anti-Brussels sentiment, convincing people that it was Brussels and immigrants that had taken their money and put a strain on their public services. Fetzer told the Huffington Post that welfare reforms 'activated existing economic grievances'. He found that aggregate real government spending on welfare and social protection decreased by around 16 per cent per person across the country, but the effects in the worst-hit areas were far more damaging, with social security spending falling by up to 46 per cent. Blackpool lost a staggering £914 per person in real terms, compared to the City of London which lost £177.

'In other words, by curtailing the welfare state, austerity has likely activated a broad range of existing economic grievances that have developed over a long period...In circumstances where austerity operates, and people's benefits are being cut, it's very easy to scapegoat immigrants and people become more receptive to an anti-immigrant message.'

In regions of the UK that suffered the average levels of cuts or 'austerity shock', UKIP vote shares were up 3.6 per cent in the 2014 European elections and 11.6 per cent in the last round of local elections before the referendum. The study estimated that support for Leave may have been up to 9.5 per cent higher than it would have been without the harsh effects of austerity. Let's take a more specific policy example. The 'bedroom tax' is a penalty imposed upon anyone receiving housing benefits who has a spare or unoccupied bedroom in their house. In 2016 this was even extended to cover elderly people and those on state pensions, to much criticism. Households who were victims of this penalty were more likely to fall behind on rent, think that their vote is 'unlikely to make a difference' and that 'public officials do not care' about them, and were more likely to vote UKIP. Globalization, a headline neo-liberal Anywhere policy, and trade integration with lower-wage economies has severely damaged British manufacturing and appears to have driven voters towards UKIP and Vote Leave. This effect has also been witnessed in America where trade deals like NAFTA have seen many manufacturers move operations from places like Michigan or Wisconsin to Mexico. Global Competition and Brexit, a research paper from Italo Colantone and Piero Stanig at Bocconi University, found that whilst there is a link between loss of industry to lower-wage economies and an increased likelihood to vote to leave the EU, there is no correlation between migration levels and voting to leave the EU. In fact, areas with higher levels of migration, most notably London, seem to have been more likely to vote to remain. Globalization puts an enormous strain on the welfare state as industries die out faster than workers can retrain or be replaced by new generations. When the Conservatives made the decision to butcher the social safety net post-2010, the victims of globalization were suddenly faced with the economic reality of their former livelihood being automated or shipped off halfway around the world. A fairly robust welfare state had held back this economic misery for almost 2 decades, but no more.

Economic distress can often be correlated with increased vote shares for right-wing or populist parties. For example, redundancies amongst 'low-skilled' native Swedes were shown to be responsible for a 31 per cent increase in vote share that the Sweden Democrats experienced at the last election. That number was even larger in areas with higher numbers of 'low-skilled' immigrants. According to British Election Survey data, around 80 per cent of Leave voters believed that leaving the EU would lead to a lowering of immigration levels. There are significant correlations between a decreasing share of employment in agriculture, manufacturing, mining, and construction in any given region over the past 30 years and a higher proportion of Leave voters in that area. Similar correlations have also been shown between lower levels of overall employment, higher income inequality, higher poverty rates, and the vote to leave the EU. UKIP support in the 2015 election and for Leave in the referendum was markedly higher in areas with lower real wage growth over the past 2 decades. This is the coming home to roost of the successive waves of neo-liberal policies that Britain has pursued over the past 4 decades. In a UN Special Rapporteur on extreme poverty and human rights, Professor Philip Alston described the rollout of Universal Credit (the UK's new benefits system) as 'a punitive, mean-spirited, and callous approach' which could be easily reversed by the government: 'If a new minister was interested, if a new Government were interested, the harshness could be changed overnight and for very little money.'

There are an estimated 14 million people living in poverty in the UK, with 1.5 million classed as destitute, unable to afford basic essentials. Alston also warned that it is those in poverty who will bear the biggest brunt of Brexit. This is not simply because Brexit is an impossible dream that could never have been successful; of course there was a scenario in which Brexit could have been dealt with sensibly and eventually led to Britain's separation from the European Union with little to no economic damage. Europe has very real problems. The Euro has expanded rapidly to include countries with a wide variety of different economic ills, each of which would have previously implemented their own monetary policy in order to deal with their own national economic issues. Under the Euro, to truly succeed, they will need to bring about further and further political integration in order to make a success of the single currency. Britain's potential loss of independence is a legitimate fear and exit from the European Union is not a completely irrational and stupid decision perpetrated by a horde of uneducated racists determined to take Britain out at all costs (though I am not saying those people don't exist).

In his fantastic assessment of the colliding worlds of democracy and technology Jamie Bartlett warns that we are slipping unabetted into the realms of a 'barbell economy'. A barbell economy describes a situation where the middle class is squeezed leaving a hollowed-out middle – jobs are either low pay or high pay and high skilled (like a software engineer). Symptoms of a barbell economy include 'a shrinking tax base, growing levels of crime, depression, addiction and infant mortality, lower life expectancy and poorer health'[6]. It's difficult to argue that we are not already experiencing these symptoms in Britain. Bartlett argues that technology is already squeezing the middle and pushing wealth into the hands of fewer and fewer powerful people: 'In addition to favouring more skilled workers, digital technology also increases the financial returns to capital owners over Labour.'[7] To him, a healthy and affluent middle class is the key to functioning democracy. He points to San Francisco as an example of the approaching barbell economy. It's a city of two halves, the tech workers bused in from their suburbs earning $100,000 and upwards and the service industry workers who struggle to provide them with other services in a city they can barely afford. It's a nineteenth-century, tech-driven Downton Abbey or Upstairs Downstairs. The rapid growth of productivity (largely due to technological advances) was not accompanied by similar wage growth and more and more profits ended up in the hands of CEOs and shareholders. From 1973 to 2011, productivity in the UK increased by 80 per cent whilst the median wage increased by just 10 per cent[8]. Since then wealth has only grown more concentrated, half of the world's population own less than the eight richest men (and four of them are founders of technology companies).[9] Bartlett is concerned that without action we will continue to slide into a world run by a handful of tech billionaires:

'The dystopia we should fear is not robots with all the jobs, but a barbell-shaped economy where socially progressive tech millionaires live in gated communities well away from the masses who they either fear, patronise or detest.'[10]

Ed Conway, Sky Economics Editor, sharply pointed out that falling wages cannot be the sole cause of Brexit. Right-wing populists in the FPO in Austria and the Sweden Democrats have been very successful in their respective countries despite healthy wage growth. These correlations do give us an indication that austerity and rising inequality in the UK were more responsible for driving up the likelihood of any particular region to vote to leave than the level of immigration to the local area. However, these studies are missing a key element in their understanding of the Brexit vote. It would be all too simple to say, 'it's just the poor people who hate immigrants'. Whilst many people can become resentful of the treatment of immigrants compared to British nationals, we must recognize that what we are ignoring is 'a sense of the dislocation – as much psychological as income-related – created by the shift from an industrial to a knowledge-based economy. This has left many Somewhere people in the bottom half of the income and education spectrum feeling demoralised and disrespected.'

Racism cannot be equivocally correlated with economic hardship. In America, where the cause of the Trump vote has been attributed to underlying racism, there has been little to suggest that there is a connection between the two. In a map devised by data analyst Seth Stephens-Davidson that used racially charged searches to predict the electoral success of Obama, areas of the country where higher levels of racist searches took place were less likely to vote for Barack Obama for president. No other indicator, such as gun ownership, church attendance, or education levels give this indicator which is estimated at about a 4 per cent handicap at a national level[11]. The study was actually rejected by five different academic journals in 2012 who refused to believe that America harboured so much hidden racism. There was zero correlation between the monthly membership rate of the racist and white nationalist online forum Stormfront and the level of unemployment. Nor was there even an increase of searches for Stormfront in areas disproportionately affected by the recession.

Andrew Marr recognized that the constant rhetoric of meritocracy (which Britain is decidedly not) means that 'those who are not at the top – struggling in the middle, or poor and powerless at the bottom – are supposed to understand that this is not their misfortune but what they, too, deserve'. The idea that we live in a meritocracy is laughable, it's insulting to anyone who watches the sheer incompetence with which modern politics is conducted. These are not the actions of those at the pinnacle of a meritocracy. It was not wrong to believe that Britain could prosper outside of the European Union, but that the current neo-liberal regime has no desire to make Brexit work for the majority of the country. It will work for the very richest. Politicians recognized the deep divisions in British society and saw them as an opportunity to escape from the EU red tape that has prevented them from lowering environmental standards, abolishing workers' rights, and further privatizing what remains of our public assets. It is impossible to say whether the referendum result would have been any different if the Conservatives had not made the decision to implement austerity, but idle speculation gets us nowhere useful. The campaigners for Brexit have little more than a superficial desire to respond to the grievances of ordinary people, simply to exploit them. How many times have we heard that austerity is over? And yet here we are watching the Conservatives repeatedly lie and lie and lie about new money for the NHS whilst they continue to implement cuts. It's about appearing to help the people whilst they stealthily privatize and auction off the British state to the highest investor. They used the 2008 crash to exploit the British people and they will use the Brexit fallout to do the same.

Feelings Don't Care About Your Facts

They broke the news, took the truth and made it fluid...Sound-tracked by a chorus of you don't know what you're doing.
Arctic Monkeys

Unfortunately for us, it isn't just our divided society that we have to worry about. The psychological make-up of our minds makes it very easy to divide us up into tribes and our stubbornness makes reconciliation almost impossible. Bartlett describes the new division of Western politics as 're-tribalisation'. Technology offered us up a world of connections and we clustered closer together. As we have re-tribalized we have lost a sense of shared truth or belief. The Oxford Dictionary named their word of 2016 as 'post-truth'. It is hard to imagine a word or phrase that better encapsulates the year 2016 and the rollercoaster ride that it took us on. Truth and lies became meaningless as tribal politics split the country down the middle (or 52/48 – it's a ratio that has become a joke online for political junkies after the ratio keeps popping up in polls). I use the word lie because they lied. It's not a half-truth, or an alternative fact, that they misspoke or misunderstood, it is that they lied. The unwillingness of the media to call out politicians for lying is a massive contributor to the divisions in our society. When you can argue with basic ground truths then there is no way we can operate as a society in a political debate. In Chapter 2 we looked at how C Thi Nguyen was concerned that we as a society no longer share basic ground truth. Obviously, facts can be interpreted in a number of different ways depending on the amount of information you have or the context that said facts operate within. But in my mind, there is a certain set of facts and truths that we have to begin with before we can have a good faith argument or debate about how to best proceed with any given policy, idea, or negotiating strategy.

Let's take an example so you understand exactly what I mean here. In December 2018, Theresa Villiers, former secretary of state for Northern Ireland, appeared on Sky News to discuss the Irish border issue. During the interview, she claimed that: 'There is no reason why we have to change our border arrangements in the event of a Brexit because they've been broadly consistent in the 100 years since the creation of Ireland as a separate state.'

Perhaps she missed the 30 years where smaller roads were blockaded, bridges were destroyed, and British Army surveillance points were peppered along the border. This is a lie. It cannot be anything else except operating in bad faith. Anyone who lived along the border during this time will attest to it. This isn't twisting the truth, it is unadulterated lying. How can that be acceptable? To make matters worse the BBC didn't challenge her on the ludicrous statement.

The defining post-truth moment for many people during the referendum campaign was the bus. The Brexit bus. The big red elephant that toured the country. In almost every communication put out by Vote Leave they repeated and repeated their claim that £350 million per week is being sent to the EU and we could spend that on the NHS instead. It was the Vote Leave counter to George Osborne's economic doom and gloom narrative that included the warning that Brexit could cost every household £4300 annually. By making a grand provocative statement, you can set the frame of the debate. It doesn't matter what was being discussed before, as soon as you say something outrageous, your detractors and opponents are forced to address it, you'll be plastered over social media and the front pages, replayed, quoted, and discussed on every news show and in every living room and coffee shop in the country. Lynton Crosby, the election campaign magnate and leader of the last two Conservative general election campaigns, calls it the 'dead cat' strategy. If you slam a dead cat down on the dinner table, people will be forced to talk about nothing else. You couldn't exactly go back to your conversation about a birthday party you were at last weekend once someone decided they would decorate the table with a dead cat. Was the £350 million per week claim a lie? Full Fact, the independent Fact-checking organization, explained: 'The closest – not perfect – analogy is that £350 million is like the amount a supermarket till displays before the discounts are applied. You never pay it and you never owe it. The number is just one step towards the final bill.'

There are three figures that could be used to describe the UK contribution to the EU: £19 billion is the gross figure, £15 billion is the gross figure minus the rebate negotiated by Margaret Thatcher (which never actually leaves the British treasury), or £11 billion, the net figure which deducts money spent by the EU in Britain on things like regional funds and farming subsidies[12]. So we pay £11 billion for access to the world's largest internal market, tariff-free, where they pay and provide all outside customs checks and trade negotiation and administration, the right to live, work, and travel for free across the entire Eurozone, as well as membership of groups like the European Space

Agency, Euratom, and co-operation on security and terrorism. The EU costs us just 2 per cent of public spending each year and the Confederation of British Industry has estimated that EU membership is worth £3000 a year to every British family – a return of nearly £10 for each £1 we pay in. Whether you think that the contribution is worth it is an entirely different matter. Much like in American politics in 2016, the truth was becoming much less important to political discourse. Politics had always been about emotion and feeling, or the country would be run by boring technocrats, but this was a true departure from the need to use facts or reality to win a political campaign. Vote Leave's team were happy to use the £350 billion figure because it's simple, easily repeated, and holds a grain of truth. It's also a not so subtle use of statistical manipulation. Politicians use this kind of statistical manipulation all the time to support their arguments. Theresa May consistently claimed in PMQs that the current Conservative government was putting more money into the NHS than ever before and treating more patients than ever before. If you look purely at these figures, she is correct. Where it becomes statistical manipulation is when you consider that when you adjust for inflation the numbers start to look considerably different, then when you consider the growing population you begin to see that these numbers are heavily contextual, inflation-adjusted per person we are spending much less than we used to, but you cannot call her a liar because her statistics are technically accurate.

Lies are irresponsible when you are running a country and you have to deal with real people's lives. To continually tell people that the Irish border has become unnecessarily politicized as a major issue cannot be condemned enough. Northern Ireland has benefitted massively from the tentative peace that exists in the country, no one wants to return to the days of the troubles and a hard border. It is abundantly clear that the Northern Irish public fears the consequences of a hard border. Any border posts would become targets for dissidents and, as is often the case, violence would inevitably breed violence. Any camera or physical infrastructure would be targeted and would quickly have to be monitored or abandoned. Once it was monitored, any officers monitoring the post would become a target. It isn't inconceivable to suggest that some backbench Tories might then call for army officers to be deployed at intervals along the border to prevent more attacks on cameras and checkpoints. Before you know it, we once again have British troops fighting in Northern Ireland and a country just beginning to emerge with renewed verve from 40 years of violence would be plunged 20 years into the past again.

That's not to say we should cave in to those threatening violence. The border as it existed during the Troubles is inconceivable for those who live in the numerous towns right on the border, farmers and workers who make multiple daily crossings, and those who rely on utterly frictionless cross-border trade. The fact that the peace in Northern Ireland is being threatened by some MPs because of their unwillingness to accept that the border is a major and almost impassable issue is either willful ignorance or utter disregard for the issues at hand. Jacob Rees-Mogg embarked upon a trip to the Irish border, spoke to numerous people who live along the border and had grown increasingly concerned about the possibility that a border may be imposed. Yet after what should have been a sobering confrontation with reality, Mogg and the ERG have put forward proposals involving drones, tagging citizens, still pushed their line about 'technological solutions', all whilst ignoring the fact that any border infrastructure is essentially untenable for at least half the population of Northern Ireland. Unfortunately, the Irish border is but one example. Andrew Bridgen appeared on Sky News and purported that he, as an Englishman, was entitled to an Irish passport. To make such a brazen, false, baseless claim on national TV is reprehensible – either he is utterly detached from reality or he believes he can get away with just flat out lying. Whatever the case may be, it is not behaviour that should be acceptable for a public representative. Rory Stewart was on BBC radio just hours after Theresa May's 500-page draft deal was released claiming that 80 per cent of the British public backed the deal. Based on nothing. Absolutely nothing. When pushed for the source of the figures he said he was using the figure to illustrate how he thought the British public would feel about the deal, despite not even having had the time to read it himself. If that is the only prerequisite for being able to quote statistics then I shall declare at least 93 per cent of people reading this book will love this book and will buy two copies.

It's become an increasingly problematic symptom of a country with no accountability. Unless there is some recourse at the ballot box, with the public, and with the press, we cannot expect to move forward as a country. Months after Boris Johnson and David Davis left the cabinet as two of the most influential Brexiteers, they continued to spout the line that they could have negotiated a better deal. Davis was the Brexit secretary. During his time in the post, he was rarely present at negotiations, insulted the EU, and seemed to have no desire to understand the situation at hand. If you were to count the hours he spent in 2018 negotiating with the EU (before he left the post), he wouldn't even qualify under the current Conservative Party definition of being employed – which requires you to work at least one hour per week. He was in arguably the most powerful position (aside from the prime minister) to influence the government's negotiating strategy; he wasn't able to achieve any goals he set out, before walking away claiming he could have done better. It would be quite easy to say, in the immortal words of Theresa May, that nothing has changed, that politicians and the press have always lied and always will. This is true, although perhaps it is more accurate to say that people have always lied to get what they want – it's an unfortunate characteristic of humanity that is unlikely to disappear any time soon. Our divided society means we now accept this from politicians of 'our side' in order to win the battle. Lying has become normalized and we need to get a firm grasp on the truth if we are going to move beyond Brexit.

People have always believed politicians lie and filter the truth to suit their own agenda. But it seems that the idea of taking responsibility for one's statements or actions has become increasingly less common in recent years. The most confounding facet of the Donald Trump presidential campaign was his ability to brush off crisis after crisis, scandal after scandal. He managed to say and do things that would be considered career suicide for most politicians – including some things you've definitely since forgotten about. He suggested women who have abortions should be punished, he paid off a porn-star whom he slept with to silence her, he mocked a disabled reporter, he began his campaign saying, 'They're bringing drugs. They're bringing crime. They're rapists. And some, I assume, are good people.' Yet, despite all this he was able to keep barrelling forwards on the campaign trail all the way to the White House, lurching from scandal to scandal with little to no acknowledgement of any wrongdoing. By apologizing he would have been acknowledging that he had done wrong. The post-truth world may seem scary, it is. But Nguyen, whose paper on echo chambers and cults we looked at in Chapter 2, argues that this is not as tragic as it seems. That these echo chambers are only reinforced by the trust structures that they build up. People aren't so much rejecting the truth, they still seek truth and facts, they simply differ upon who to trust as the arbiter of facts. We all rely on a variety of people, whom we trust to know better than us. Doctors, lawyers, accountants, mechanics, builders, and we have to trust someone to regulate whether these people are qualified to perform said tasks. We have a network of trust that holds together the foundation of society, trust that underpins our everyday interactions. Our current relationship with the truth isn't going to break society, but I still think we're in for a bumpy ride. There's a fear that the Remain vs Leave dividing line will endure at the centre of British Politics. It is, however, just as possible that we will fragment into sub-cultures. Marshall McLuhan told Playboy Magazine in 1969 that the current interconnected world would lead to a violent fracturing of society: 'As man is tribally metamorphosed by the electric media, we all become Chicken Littles, scurrying around frantically in search of our former identities, and in the process unleash tremendous violence.'[13]

We've always been tribal, but the connectivity of the internet has opened us up to more and more specific tribes, connecting us with people all around the world. McLuhan may have successfully predicted the violent fracturing of society, but he didn't predict that political parties would leverage these divisions in the way that they have. The fragmentation of our society was ironically brought about by the very technology designed to bring about the 'Global Village'. Bartlett writes: 'Silicon Valley, in its optimistic quest for a global village of total information and connectivity, has inadvertently let tribalism back out of the cage that modern representative democracy built for it.'[14]

The impact of big political moments tends to be to unite splinter groups and smaller movements across a specific political dividing line. In First Past The Post (FPTP) electoral systems, like the UK, with a quasi-two party system, the hot topic of each election cycle can become that dividing line. President Trump is already preparing to frame the 2020 election cycle, he wants to make the dividing line about borders. He is painting the Democrats as the party of open borders and is successfully causing them to confront the wide variety of opinions amongst Democrats about just how open the border should be. Should they decriminalize border crossings? Are illegal immigrants entitled to the same rights as American citizens? And whilst they argue amongst themselves, Trump can jump on any statement that proves that they are the party of open borders. This effect is exaggerated when political polarization becomes more prominent. Both parties in the UK are undergoing serious turmoil as they wrestle with the new Somewhere vs Anywhere, Leave vs Remain divide. Conservatives and Labour party MPs have left their respective parties citing issues over Brexit and the Liberal Democrats have been happy to mop up some of the seats. We might yet see both parties split if Brexit and Europe remain at the centre of British politics.

You really could make the case that nothing has changed, that new technology has simply given us more exposure to the lies of politicians and the press. The democratization of information on the internet has given us instant access to the world's most powerful fact-checker. In days gone by, unless we knew better, we were forced to take a person or newspaper at their word, but Google has given us the power to find out the answer to almost any question in a matter of seconds by simply typing a few short phrases into a phone. Yet, in spite of this newly acquired access to information, there seems to be something new about the relationship we all have with the truth. The lines between facts, figures, truth, and opinion have become severely blurred.

Our Broken Brains

In 1954 Marian Keech developed a psychic link with a god-like alien. The alien told her the world would end before the sun rose on 21 December 1954 and Marian gathered a group of followers together to wait for a spaceship that would come to rescue them from the approaching apocalypse. They sat late into the night, but the alien stood them up. In Black Box Thinking, author Matthew Syed recounts the tale of Leon Festinger, a researcher who had infiltrated the group. He watched on as their momentary sadness at the failure of Marian's prediction turned to jubilation; thankfully their faith had saved the world from destruction and God had given the earth a second chance.[15] Festinger explained the mental gymnastics our brains will take to save face: 'When we are confronted with evidence that challenges our deeply held beliefs we are more likely to reframe the evidence than we are to alter our beliefs. We simply invent new reasons, new justifications, new explanations. Sometimes we ignore evidence altogether.'[16]

We as humans like to believe that we learn from our mistakes, that we accept when we have been wrong in life and make our decisions based on rationality. Unfortunately, that's not exactly true. We lie to ourselves. We ignore the truth for our own pride. We struggle to accept information that means we have to admit that we were fooled or made the wrong decision, we cling to our ideas and ignore facts that challenge that. Some of this is conscious, but a lot of it is subconscious. In the case of Marian Keech, her followers had a strong incentive for her to truly be the prophet she claimed to be. They doubled down on their beliefs, lest they admit they had been fooled.

Even worse news for us is the fact that the more evidence we are shown in opposition to our own view, the more we fight against it. Festinger writes that 'cognitive dissonance is a deeply ingrained human trait'. It's as natural to us as walking, it's part of the human experience. In Black Box Thinking, Syed cites examples where prosecutors in the US challenged cases where DNA testing had overturned previous convictions. In one case the prosecutor alleged the convicted prisoner to have been a Chimera, where a single person has two different blood types because of the death of a twin in the womb. There are 30 such cases in recorded medical history. There exists a 249-page transcript of an interview where prosecutor Michael McGrath defends his original conviction after DNA evidence proved the convicted prisoner innocent. It includes a passage where he suggested that perhaps the 8-year-old girl had been sexually active with someone else.[17] We are deeply unconsciously motivated to believe that we were right in our past actions. Syed concluded that 'DNA evidence is strong, but not as strong as the desire to protect one's self-esteem.'[18] In The Fairy Tales of Hermann Hesse, Hesse paints us a picture of a man confident in his view of the world, 'He had very few doubts, and when the facts contradicted his views on life, he shut his eyes in disapproval.' We may think of ourselves as better than this, but we're all guilty of ignoring things that contradict with our reality.

The smarter we are, and the more routine it becomes, the better our mind is at performing the intellectual jumps to rationalize our past decisions. Tony Blair's reaction to the lack of WMDs (Weapons of Mass Destruction this time not the Weapons of Math Destruction I mentioned earlier, they're dangerous in anatomically different ways) in Iraq is a perfect case study. At first, the absence of WMDs proved that they were well hidden, strengthening his conviction that they would be found. A year later he told the House of Commons Liaison Committee that they may have been removed, hidden, or destroyed. When he eventually accepted that Saddam had no WMDs, he rationalized that it was right to remove him anyway, telling the Labour Party Conference, 'The world is a better place with Saddam in prison.'[19]

It is, as Syed puts it, 'a process of self-deception'. The human mind is a wonderful but untrustworthy memory bank, we are not overly rational beings, we are impulsive, we hang onto hunches and first impressions, we reject evidence we don't like, we get stuck inside epistemic bubbles and echo chambers, develop a deep hatred for other human beings based on minor differences. Thankfully, we're all guilty of at least something there, it's part of being human and living in twenty-first century society. But that doesn't mean we can't all aspire to be better and at least consider the idea that we may not each have all the answers.

Luckily for us, if we have to sacrifice a lot to become a part of a group (say the ridicule of your friends or peers for identifying as Leave or Remain) then we have to convince ourselves that our choice has been worth the sacrifice. If we've already argued in favour of one side, we hold on to that to protect our self-esteem. We are more likely to believe news stories that agree with our view of the world and are more likely to take in this information. We become prisoners of our own ideas, often unable to see beyond what we believe. Marijuana, for example, remains controversial and is often vilified regardless of the potential medical applications. Extracts from the marijuana plants have been shown to kill or reduce the size of cancer cells, reduce the severity and frequency of seizures, and treat inflammation, and yet it is still considered a dangerous drug on par with cocaine by millions of people. The more we cling to truth, the more we defend it, lest we as humans admit we were wrong. In the book Homo Deus by Yuval Noah Harari on the future of humanity, he writes: 'The more sacrifices we make for an imaginary story, the more tenaciously we hold on to it because we desperately want to give meaning to these sacrifices and suffering we have caused.'

How many Brexiteers will forever refuse to admit they were conned? How many Remainers refuse to acknowledge that Cameron lied about the immediate consequences of the vote on the UK? Humans are fundamentally flawed creatures, we won't simply admit we were wrong because of pride or insecurities or any number of psychological defects that we all carry. I am not perfect either, far from it, I simply want to point out the problems we all have with the motivations for our actions in the hope that we can understand each other a little better. In his book Brexit: What the Hell Happens Now?, Ian Dunt lays out the issue that we have in confronting the realities of Brexit and the EU: 'For the right, it is a tyranny in waiting, a crude Bonapartist force taking control of Europe. For the left it is a beacon of internationalism, support for which is considered a test of progressive values. Both views are hopelessly misguided.'

The EU is a complex, nuanced, contradictory experiment in

transnational governance and co-operation. It cannot be simply considered good or bad.

'For everything that is sensible about it, there is something absurd. For everything regrettable about it there is something to be commended.'

The idea that Brexit will be a success and that Britain will get through it based on the 'Blitz spirit' is one that cannot be challenged until we are presented with reality. Economic forecasting is only so accurate and can never foresee the events of the real world, we have lost faith in experts and won't accept the reality of what Brexit really means until it slaps us across the face. There will be no sunny uplands, at least not for the foreseeable future, yet that cannot be proven and thus Brexiteers cling to the idea. Just as some Remainer campaigners refuse to acknowledge that the EU has major flaws and is not the answer to all our country's ills. It is as Goebbels puts it:

> The lie can be maintained only for such time as the State can shield the people from the political, economic and/or military consequences of the lie. It thus becomes vitally important for the State to use all of its powers to repress dissent, for the truth is the mortal enemy of the lie, and thus by extension, the truth is the greatest enemy of the State.

Similarly, the lie that the EU is perfect will also eventually come crashing down. Even in what I believe to be the most ideal scenario for the UK, where we remain in the EU and attempt to deal with the issues that drove the Brexit vote; reduce the impact of immigration on public services and give a voice to those who feel they have been left behind by the modern world, we still cannot ignore the major grievances that a huge portion of the UK has with the EU. Freedom of movement will not be reformed, save for a major ideological change in the upper echelons of the EU, and thus these grievances will remain. The divisions that have been uncovered in British society will not simply be forgotten. Those who still want to leave the EU may feel even more disaffected, that their vote has been ignored and that their voices count for even less. Those who believe otherwise are being naïve. We have opened this pandora's box and there is no way to close it again. Worst of all the more evidence we are shown to the contrary, the more we fight against it.

Why Fact-Checking Doesn't Work

Unfortunately for us, the problem is deeper than simply fact-checking and critically thinking our way to a better place. Human psychology means that truths can be difficult to accept when they challenge our worldview and fact-checking can be ineffective once lies are in the public sphere of information. The act of simply hearing a false statement can, after a few days, leave us thinking that that statement is true, thus altering our very perception of reality. This is known as the 'Illusion of Truth'. The 'Illusion of Truth' principle indicates that people are far more likely to remember false statements as true. This is believed to be because of a phenomenon known as 'implicit memory' whereby something we have seen before is likely to seem more plausible, simply because we are more familiar with it.

A study done in 1997 by psychologist Graham Davey aimed to examine the negative effects of the sensationalism in news programming. This was long before the 24-hour news cycle or the outrage culture that exists today. He found that negative (often exaggerated) stories increased anxiety and worry amongst test subjects. Furthermore, in the book Applied Social Psychology, studies were shown to indicate that 'heavier viewers of the local news are more likely to experience fear and be concerned about crime rates in their community than lighter viewers'. More recently, a research team headed by Lisa Fazio of Vanderbilt University tested how the 'Illusion of Truth' effect interacts with our prior knowledge. They found that repetition made us more likely to believe untrue statements, somewhat vindicating the Joseph Goebbels quote: 'If you tell a lie big enough and keep repeating it, people will eventually come to believe it.' (I have already discussed Goebbels once and I am often reluctant to invoke such a character as a way to explain propaganda techniques. It's a slippery slope to accusing someone of being a Nazi, but as masters of propaganda, I believe that the Nazis, and more specifically Goebbels, make an excellent case study.) The team at Vanderbilt University discovered that the truthfulness of a statement was the biggest influence on whether we believe it, so perhaps all is not lost for humanity yet. These theories were initially developed during studies on traditional media, but it is difficult to discount their applicability to social media. Now we are all plugged into the news and streams of digital propaganda almost without respite. Just logged onto Facebook to message your friend about going for a drink? You might find yourself faced with videos of cops shooting seemingly innocent people, an article on the latest Brexit betrayal, or a picture of dead children in Yemen. We are all immersed in a world that never sleeps, just a click of the button away from the very best and worst of humanity at every second of every day.

The dreams of the sunny post-Brexit uplands remain untouched because any attempt to explain the political reality is dismissed as Anywhere attempts to maintain the neo-liberal status quo. The Liberal Democrat policy is pure Anywhere-ism, they want to simply revoke Article 50, cancel the whole endeavour, and move on as a country. As Bulgarian political scientist Ivan Krastev writes about how we now inhabit a political world 'in which populists are becoming openly anti-liberal and elites are becoming secretly anti-democratic'.

Resolving this crisis of truth should be as simple as discovering the truth and then telling everyone? The truth will always find a way, people naturally gravitate towards truthfulness, honesty, and the search for knowledge. That's how it works...Right? If only that were true. Lies are incredibly difficult to deal with. Journalists sometimes find it difficult to identify lies. They use the word untruth, misleading statement, or an alternative fact. News is becoming theatrical and guests are often chosen for drama and spectacle rather than the quality of their commentary. Virality is more important than utility because, as we have already seen, conflict drives clicks. The media is not well equipped to handle this sort of situation. They are excellent at normalizing crazy ideas because they fail to convey when something is truly insane. If you invite someone on your show to contribute their opinion, often it is courtesy to give them a fair hearing of their ideas, which can quite easily give the impression that any two sides of a given argument are equal. Look at the climate change debate. There is a 99 per cent consensus on the issue amongst scientists in the field, yet climate change deniers are often invited on major news networks or given space in newspaper columns to express their opinions as if there is still a debate on the issue.

The Our Future Our Choice campaigner Femi has frequently encountered accusations of being a sneering liberal elitist, despite his desire to get people to understand the consequences of leaving the European Union. An exchange he had with Richard Madeley acts as a microcosm of the debate that is still being played out daily across the country. Discussing the withdrawal agreement negotiated by Theresa May and whether that constitutes leaving the EU on Good Morning Britain, here is a brief snippet of what was said:

Madeley: 'You think it takes us out of the EU, but the majority of people who want to leave don't agree with you. Sorry, that's the maths.'
Femi: 'Is it a good deal? No. I'd agree it's a bad deal. But, does it take us out the EU? 100 per cent'
Madeley: 'Well a lot of people say it's not 100 per cent. Just

saying it doesn't make it so.'

Femi: 'Law says it makes it so. As in I literally studied EU law. We would be out of the European Union. It is literally an exit deal.'

Madeley: 'Go tell that to someone who wants to leave.'

Femi is correct. We would no longer be a part of the EU. We would remain in the customs union, because that removes mountains of bureaucracy and protects us from extra tariffs, creating our own customs checks and arrangements that would cost our economy billions of pounds annually, without even considering the cost of actually hiring extra customs officials and implementing checks at every border post coming in and out of the UK. Madeley is confusing what people feel about the Withdrawal Agreement with reality and in doing so, sums up the issue with our entire debate; almost no one has any clue what they are talking about. The consequences are unclear because there is essentially no historical precedent for what we are attempting to do, and anyone trying to discuss the facts and trade-offs is dismissed as being a 'remoaner', not believing in Britain, or simply being contemptuous of democracy. He is trying to make a point about understanding what we are doing and is swiftly accused of dismissing the Leave voters as idiots. We've lost sight of the very reasons that we wanted to leave or remain in the European Union. Just like the prosecutors in 'Black Box Thinking', we've become slaves to our past decisions. It's a problem that inhabits our very culture now, remarks made decades ago are suddenly relevant, the purity and blame culture that exists now makes it more difficult for politicians or individuals to change their thinking and evolve – once you've chosen your side that is it, you have to stick with your hand – willingly or unwillingly.

The media struggled to deal with Brexit and the prospect of a no-deal Brexit. They were unable to tackle the issues that should have been on the agenda, in an attempt to provide parity of coverage they often presented two differing opinions as being equal. This is partially due to the complexity of the EU, it is an incredibly vast body of institutions that few people truly understand. The EU relationship with the UK covers so many areas it is difficult to begin to explain quite how vast the reach is. We are part of a standardized EU-wide set of regulations on almost everything: agriculture, safety standards, advertising, data protection, policing and anti-terror campaigns, healthcare, and human rights. We were told by David Davis and Liam Fox that untangling all of these relationships could be easy, but the trade deal would easily be negotiated to give us everything we wanted, everything we had and more, without anyone being asked to explain how we could possibly achieve a better deal than we had at the time.

Journalists didn't have enough knowledge of different EU institutions and treaties to question politicians in depth and when pushed they simply repeated their soundbites or accused them of bias. Complexity was rejected, by journalists and politicians alike (we'll see later how ambiguity was a deliberate strategy deployed by Dominic Cummings). We had Single Market access that connected us with one-third of the world. We have a veto that would prevent us from being subject to the will of other EU countries without full consent and support. Immigration restrictions were available, we have our own currency, no commitment to ever closer union and 10 per cent of members of the European Parliament (three times the average EU representation). We had a budget rebate and no commitment to another EU country bailout. The EU is far from perfect, but we were in a strong position. It's certainly possible if Brexit goes ahead and we remain out of Europe, that we could prosper in the long run, but just as easily we could still be considerably poorer. Long-term economic forecasting can be incredibly tricky and unreliable, especially when natural disasters, political upsets, and technological advancements are unpredictable and often unforeseeable. Every single person lied when they said it would be easy to craft us a better deal and every single Brexiteer has crumbled thus far in an attempt to deliver what they simply call, 'the will of the people'.

In Fahrenheit 451, Ray Bradbury tells the story of a fireman whose job was not to put out fires but to burn books instead. In this world, books were forbidden, lest they incite madness. His world is much more like our own than we may consider, where, as he puts it, 'The word intellectual became the swear word it deserved to be.' The very idea of expertise has been all but decimated when it comes to Brexit. There is no trust in any organization, bias or unbiased. Michael Gove, now somewhat infamously, 'launched an all-out attack on the Enlightenment in the name of atavistic nationalism'[20]. During the campaign in a Sky News interview, he said: 'I think the people in this country have had enough of experts with organisations from acronyms saying that they know what is best and getting it consistently wrong.'

It's a strain of anti-intellectualism that populist causes often spring on, offering the idea that big problems have simple solutions. It's no coincidence that Trump's solution to every problem had three words, 'drain the swamp', 'lock her up', 'build the wall', 'troll the libs' (liberals). Issac Asimov, the famed science fiction writer, once said: 'Anti-intellectualism has been a constant thread winding its way through our political and cultural life, nurtured by the false notion that democracy means that "my ignorance is just as good as your knowledge".'

The world is complicated, we are forced to defer to those who know more than us. Would you self-diagnose and treat a medical condition? Would you try to fix your plumbing or electric yourself? Would you represent yourself in court? I know Google means DIY is easier than ever, but I like to think most of us would call a professional if we were in over our heads. It's naïve to think that vast, complex problems can have simple, intuitive answers. But politicians are frequently elected offering simplistic solutions for large and complex problems. (You may be tempted to say I am engaging in exactly the same form of simplification here but I'm trying to illustrate a point here not claim that untangling 40 years of political and economic integration would be easy.) Things are rarely as black and white as they appear and, as we have discussed, the EU is an incredibly complex amalgamation of countries and institutions, so deeply intertwined with the nations of Europe, that to truly understand the implications of leaving could take years of study. That isn't to say that the British public doesn't have a right to choose whether they stay as a part of the EU, but it means that very few people truly understood the trade-offs involved with leaving or remaining. It's something we have to take into account when considering how to respond to the vote.

The problems with putting such a complex issue to a binary referendum meant that there was no middle ground. To win an election campaign you have to double down, only promote the positives of your side and the negatives of the other. To admit a flaw in your position is a weakness that cannot be tolerated, lest the opposing side jumps on it as indecision. This isn't just partisanship or utter cynicism, it's human nature. We tune out things we don't want to hear and treat them with more scepticism when we do hear them. We find new ways to explain our earlier actions as correct and the longer we hold those beliefs the harder they are for us to let go of and politics amplifies it all. Spinsanity founder Brendan Nyhan told Vox:

When people are confronted with facts it doesn't often change their beliefs. It is psychologically difficult for us just to say we were wrong and to accept that. As humans, we are naturally sceptical to any piece of information that challenges that particular belief. This effect is amplified when we are discussing political figures – you become more likely to reject them if they are not aligned with your political beliefs.

Fact-checking rarely works. The amount of mental gymnastics that our brains will perform to prevent us from being confronted with reality is quite remarkable (some people will write entire books to justify the conclusion that their mind has come to). People don't like to hear things that challenge the way they see the world and the longer we have held these beliefs the more likely we are to reject anything that may prove us wrong. Over half of Republicans in a Knowledge Networks poll from 2003 hadn't noticed that there had been no weapons of mass destruction found in Iraq. The article is biased, it's just Remainer propaganda, it's funded by George Soros, or it is just 'Project Fear'.

Project Fear became synonymous with any warning of potential negative consequences of Brexit. George Osborne and Stronger In threw every economic warning they could at the public hoping something would stick. But nothing would. Osborne declared that house prices would fall by 18 per cent if Britain left the EU and claimed that property investors were inserting 'Brexit clauses' that could mean a huge loss of investment within days of a vote to leave the EU. They warned a Brexit vote may cause an immediate recession and even threatened what some dubbed a 'punishment budget' claiming that, 'There would have to be increases in tax and cuts in public spending to fill the black hole.' President Obama, during a visit to the UK, told the British public that they would be at the 'back of the queue' for a free trade agreement if they were to leave the UK. This was quickly dismissed as Cameron putting words in Obama's mouth as an American would use the word 'line', not the very British 'queue'. The treasury told the public that each household would be £4300 worse off, whilst the Organisation for Economic Co-operation and Development predicted a 3 per cent drop off in GDP growth compared to remaining in the European

Union, leaving us 1 per cent weaker overall. But nothing they could say seemed to cut through. As humans, we are looking for that easy way to dismiss evidence and the words 'Project Fear' provided just that. A way to discount it and forget it. We are more likely to forget things that challenge how we see the world.

The press did their best to help normalize the use of the phrase 'Project Fear' and sensationalize whatever they could. After a speech on 9 May 2015 where Cameron credited the EU with maintaining peace in Europe since 1945, Britain Stronger In Europe showed a film where four WW2 vets spoke about how they didn't want to see all the unity and progress they fought for undone. The next day the papers led with claims that the PM was claiming that Brexit would lead to World War 3. The Daily Mail led with 'EU VOTE: NOW PM WARNS OF WAR AND GENOCIDE', whilst The Times ran with 'Brexit will raise the risk of world war, PM claims'. He said: 'Can we be so sure that peace and stability on our continent are assured beyond any shadow of a doubt? Is that a risk worth taking? I would never be so rash as to make that assumption.'[21] The problem with warnings from groups like the IMF or the Bank of England was, as Labour MP Phil Wilson put it, 'It was just elites talking to elites, saying it's in your best interest to do this, and people weren't listening...Many voters thought, "What's the IMF? What's that got to do with my life? What's the OECD? What's that got to do with me? It wasn't something that was real for them in their communities."'[22]

Immigration-focused adverts had much more cut through during the campaign than 'Project Fear'. One week before the referendum, 45 per cent believed that a vote to remain would mean Turkey gaining fast-track entry to the EU and its people allowed entry to Britain through the free movement of people. A total of 47 per cent of people believed the Brexit Bus claim that we send the EU £350 million every week, yet just 17 per cent believed the claim by George Osborne that UK households would be £4300 worse off annually. Regardless of which side of the issue voters lay on, they were equally likely to believe their decision would be better for the economy over a 20-year period. Though even some Brexiteers conceded that it was likely the economy would take a short-term hit. Right up to the day of the vote, Brexiteers held immigration as their most important issue. Remainers, on the other hand, valued the economy above all else, with immigration coming in fourth behind trade and jobs. Just 18 per cent of people felt their personal finances would suffer, compared to 31 per cent who thought the general economy would weaken. A total of 59 per cent of British Election Survey respondents viewed the Remain campaign as being about fear, whereas just 43 per cent said the same of the Leave campaign

We are defined in modern Britain by divisions. The divisions between what we believe and reality, the Somewheres and Anywheres, Leavers and Remainers, university graduates vs non-graduates. A majority of the population has been uncomfortable with the level of immigration and feel they are out of place in twenty-first century Britain. Without acknowledging that you can't really understand the political divides in modern Britain. Neo-liberalism and the tech boom have deepened inequality and the free-market ideology that has pushed globalization and the global village is facing a backlash across the Western world. Austerity and the third wave of neo-liberalism dealt a damaging blow to a country already suffering from inequality and globalization. The financial crash and subsequent implementation of austerity decimated communities and public services in Britain. Unrestricted freedom of movement has not been without major flaws, populations in cities remain segregated, people remain resentful of immigration levels whilst acknowledging that immigration has bestowed many benefits upon us. Without control of immigration policy from Europe, we are breaking down the idea of borders for better or worse. A question I found myself wondering whilst writing this book was, what makes a nation if you cannot define its borders? We increasingly surrender ultimate sovereignty to higher powers for ease of trade and make our borders increasingly more permeable. So is a nation-state a valid idea anymore? Do we have a national culture to protect? Is there any point in worrying about these concerns at all? It's almost inevitable that the world will become increasingly more connected so it's worth considering whether you feel that Britain has its own culture and whether it is worth preserving. If you're leaning towards a yes on these questions then you may be more sympathetic to what I believe was one of the major forces that gave us Brexit. The feeling that our nation and our culture is being eroded. You cannot put a price on that. The Anywheres still fail to understand that the economic warnings will not reverse the people's decision. Management writer Paul Leadbeater outlined this beautifully:

'The Remain campaign was all about money and how much people would lose...The Leave campaign was all about restoring a semblance of meaning to people's lives.'

I urge everyone who feels that Brexit should be reversed to consider the Somewheres who say they want control back in their lives, however tangible a concept that may actually be. Until we acknowledge that we cannot begin to move forward as a country.

Part 2

The Campaign

5. The Weaponized Propaganda Machine

Power is in tearing human minds to pieces and putting them together again in new shapes of your own choosing.
George Orwell, 1984

As we've already seen, data gathered by companies like Facebook, Google, and Twitter allows them to target adverts based on our every click. They can build detailed profiles about our personality, complex webs of information that allow them insight into what sort of adverts we are more likely to click on, what time of day, or day of the week it is, how many times we have visited a specific page, how long we spend on each page. They can predict whether or not we will react to certain types of adverts and wrap in a nice bow to sell off to the highest bidder. We understand how our data, social media, our deeply divided society, and our loss of trust in traditional media left us open for exploitation. Now it is time to understand just who was behind the campaign of digital misinformation and political psychological warfare that tore British politics to pieces.

SCL Group

Two years ago, almost no one on the planet had ever heard of the SCL Group. Their existence was known only to political insiders and a smattering of journalists. Yet since Brexit and Trump, they have found their work, both past and present, has come under immense scrutiny after they became intertwined in two of the greatest political upsets of our generation. SCL, or Strategic Communications Laboratories, claims to have worked on more than 100 election campaigns around the world. They have been employed by NATO, the Ministry of Defence, and the US State Department. Their purported area of expertise is in 'psychological operations', changing people's minds through 'informational dominance' rather than simple persuasion and campaign tactics. Their mission statement reads: 'Our vision is to be the premier provider of data analytics and strategy for behaviour change. Our mission is to create behaviour change through research, data, analytics, and strategy for both domestic and international government clients.'

In other words, they use personal data to map populations and figure out how to target political messaging. Dr Emma Briant wrote about SCL in her book Propaganda and Counter-terrorism: Strategies for Global Change. She claims that the company have been:

> making money out of the propaganda side of the war on terrorism over a long period of time. There are different arms of SCL but it's all about reach and the ability to shape the discourse. They are trying to amplify particular political narratives. And they are selective in who they go for: they are not doing this for the left.

The company pledges strict confidentiality, assuring clients that 'absolutely no information concerning any of our past projects will be made available under any circumstances'.[23] SCL was founded in 1993 by Nigel Oakes, but his experience in the obscure and shady world of secretive political consulting and campaigning goes back much further. Oakes founded Behavioural Dynamics in the 1980s and quickly acquired a reputation for highly effective political messaging. In 1992, Oakes spoke to a trade journal about his work: 'We use the same techniques as Aristotle and Hitler...We appeal to people on an emotional level to get them to agree on a functional level.'

He studied at Eton and claimed on the SCL website to have attended UCL before retracting the statement. At one time he worked for the Saatchi & Saatchi advertising agency and was

148

involved with work on Margaret Thatcher's image. In 2000, Oakes had a little trouble whilst allegedly conducting 'psychological warfare' operations for the Jakarta government. He complained to the Sunday Times that 'he was caught up in a dangerous web of intrigue and disinformation following criticism of his media-monitoring centre' – but we will get to that a little later. By 2005, SCL was expanding its operation. Roger Gabb, Rollo Gabb, and Alexander Nix joined Oakes to form the SCL Group, branching out into military and political consultation and data analytics. Their new mission would be to provide 'data, analytics and strategy to governments and military organisations worldwide'.

Roger Gabb, the 79-year-old founder of Western Wines Limited (the UK's largest branded supplier of South African wine), is a member of the board of directors at SCL. He owns a 25 per cent stake in the company through his own holdings and the Glendower Settlement Trust, a fund linked to him and his wife. Rollo Gabb, Roger Gabb's son, was also a founding member of SCL and remains on the board to this day. Since 2004 the senior Gabb has given over £700,000 to the Conservative Party, both nationally and to his local Ludlow party branch. This included a donation of half a million in 2006, which made him one of the largest political donors in British political history. Unsurprisingly, Gabb was pro-Brexit. During the campaign he was fined £1000 by the Electoral Commission for failing to include his name and address in pro-Brexit adverts he placed as a director of Bibendum Wine.

The main shareholders include Alexander Nix, the Gabbs, as well as Nix's mother and sister. Baron Jonathan Marland, David Cameron's pro-Brexit former trade envoy, was also previously a shareholder through a family trust. Marland was the Conservative Party treasurer from 2003-2007 and in 2015 he was awarded the Order of Merit of Malta. Property tycoon Vincent Tchenguiz was a 24 per cent shareholder (worth 4 million at the time) via his company Consensus Business Group.

Between 2005 and 2013 Tchenguiz donated £21,500 to the Conservatives. Other noteworthy members of the SCL Group include a handful of former military personnel on the company's board of advisers. Rear Admiral John Tolhurst and Colonel Ian Tunnicliffe, a former strategic communications expert at the Ministry of Defence, were both key advisers to SCL. Chris Naler, an ex-commanding officer of the US Marine Corps operations centre, who recently started work at Iota Global, is a partner of the SCL group. IOTA Global worked with SCL and NATO to train almost 100 students from Ukraine, Moldova, and Georgia in Behavioural Dynamics Institute Target Audience Analysis Methodology and in basic Strategic Communication principles. They were described as acting 'as a real counter to the insidious Russian propaganda'. Sir Geoffrey Pattie, a former Conservative defence and industry minister, also took a central role in the company for its first 3 years but resigned as a director in 2008. The SCL director and chairman is Julian Wheatland, a chairman of the Oxford Conservative Association.

SCL has become intertwined with both the British and American military establishments. Governments around the world have long been interested in the psychological operations so it is no surprise to see numerous high-ranking military personnel involved in the company. The Brexit campaign attempted to use the psychological warfare techniques that SCL had pioneered on the British electorate. Whether you think it is possible that this had a marked effect on the referendum is a question we will address in the coming chapters, but the reality is that this group was tied up in the biggest electoral earthquake in modern British politics.

Early Days of SCL

Behavioural Dynamics was founded by Nigel Oakes in the late 1980s and exists as a part of the SCL web. He took the experience he had running Behavioural Dynamics and put it to work with the newly-formed SCL. It seems that in the late 1990s and early 2000s they engaged in routine political consulting and PR work. Reports from the WSJ and The Independent explored work that they were carrying out in Thailand and Indonesia. They have always worked in secrecy, favouring ethically questionable campaign techniques. In Jakarta, Indonesia, in 1999, Oakes worked as an image consultant to President Abdurrahman Wahid, who was facing financial misconduct allegations. The company was described in The Independent[24] at the time as 'one of the hidden wonders of Jakarta', though after some trouble with the government it 'evaporated as suddenly as it had appeared'.

Their headquarters in Jakarta included a grandiose room brimming with high-tech computers. The Observer described the room as looking like the villain's computer-filled complex from the 1995 James Bond film Goldeneye (not by accident either as SCL hired the company that built the Goldeneye film set to put together another operations centre). From there they produced a series of TV messages/adverts from the 'Foundation of Independent Journalists' and monitored stories about the client, Mr Wahid.

According to the Asian Wall Street Journal: 'This included the screening of television commercials stressing religious and ethnic harmony that gave implicit backing to the beleaguered president. The centre also held a seminar on journalistic ethics and independence, but shielded from participants the fact that it was being funded by the presidential palace.'[25]

The Independent, who reported on the story, seemed to believe that it was mainly cosmetic: 'It was just like a movie set to impress the clients, to calm down the family,' said one Indonesian who visited it, 'They are really desperate.' There were also reports that SCL tried to add a story to an Indonesian paper based on a fake government document and that they operated through a web of shell companies that obscured the source of its funding. They were eventually paid between $300,000 and $2 million for their work. A local Indonesian employee in Oakes' operations room, dubbed the Jakarta International Media Research Centre, told The Independent: 'We didn't know the purpose of it all, we just did what he asked. We called him Mr Bond because he is English, and because he is such a mystery.'[26] After the article was released, Oakes flew quickly to Singapore and shut down all operations and contracts in Indonesia.[27] In the late 1990s, they also held a $2.1 million contract in Kuala Lumpur, during which they were accused of being involved in voter manipulation that was aimed at keeping young people at home.

Post 9/11, they began to market themselves as experts in anti-terrorism and anti-jihadist messaging. They found governments around the world were willing to invest heavily in anything labelled 'psych-ops' and that is exactly what SCL were promising to anyone who might open their cheque books. They were 'a communications company for a dangerous world' and boasted that BDI (Behavioural Dynamics Institute), their own in-house research group, kept an office at the Royal Institution; known as one of Britain's top scientific bodies. According to SCL marketing materials, BDI gave them an edge in 'psychological warfare' and 'influence operations'.

A 2005 Slate article described pitches they were making at the time to governments of the world, espousing their belief that their strategic communications were 'the most powerful weapon in the world'. That same year, at Defence Systems & Equipment International, the United Kingdom's largest military trade fair, they pitched their 'ops centre' as a central tenant through which they could 'override all national radio and TV broadcasts in a time of crisis'. This ops centre sounds much like an evolution of their set-up in Indonesia, focusing on the spectacle and theatricality of politics and crisis.

They gave a few examples of how this could work:

Example Scenario #1

There is a smallpox outbreak in London. Rather than mention smallpox, they would use the ops centre to spread the word of an accident at a chemical plant. The news and media are given updates about the path of a chemical gas cloud and people stay indoors awaiting confirmation that it is safe to go outside. The smallpox outbreak can be contained more easily as the population believes almost any trip outside could be fatal.

SCL estimated that by following their advice the death toll would be in the thousands, as opposed to predictions of up to 10 million had other measures been taken.

Example Scenario #2

There is a country that has recently transitioned to a democratic state in South Asia. Struggling with corrupt politicians and rising civil unrest that threatens to bubble over into revolution, the monarchy steps in to temporarily seize power, aided and abetted by SCL steering the media narrative from their ops centre.

These are legitimate examples given by SCL. They have a long history of willingly subverting and distorting the truth to further their clients' goals. Misinformation and deceit are their bread and butter. Mark Boughton, the SCL spokesperson, said at the time: 'If your definition of propaganda is framing communications to do something that is going to save lives, that's fine.' These aren't exactly modern tactics; Operation Fortitude saw the allies use this sort of misinformation to hide the true location of the D-Day landings.

The year 2005 was a marked turning point for SCL, they were simultaneously launching themselves on the defence market and the homeland security market. Expanding from being a data analytics firm working to promote political campaigns and products, to one that also worked with a military focus. Whistle-blower and former employee Christopher Wylie provided documents to parliament in which SCL bragged of their use of religious leaders to help suppress the vote in the 2007 Nigerian elections. The brochure he gave to parliament also shows that they considered 'bribing' citizens to vote for the incumbent regime. They ultimately decided against this because they feared voters would simply take the money and vote for whom they wanted, not because it is morally or ethically questionable. Instead, they concluded that 'a more effective strategy might be to persuade opposition voters not to vote at all'. To this end, they organized 'anti-poll rallies' in areas with high support for opposition parties replete with spiritual and religious leaders 'to maximize their appeal especially among the spiritual, rural communities'. Local commentators described the election as the most corrupt, unruly, and violent election in the country's history, with reports of ballot stuffing, stolen and tampered election materials, and underage voting.

Another SCL brochure discovered by the BBC claimed that during the 2010 elections on Trinidad and Tobago, they painted graffiti across the island to help their candidates message that he was 'listening to a "united youth"'. The Great Hack, a Netflix documentary on Cambridge Analytica and the Facebook data scandal, explains how they promoted apathy in an attempt to drive down the Afro-Carribean youth vote. The campaign was called 'Do So' which means don't vote. The turnout for 18-35-year-olds was 40 per cent lower than expected (in an election where a 6 per cent swing was all that was required) according to claims made by Alexander Nix.

In 2010 Prime Minister Gonsalves of St Vincent and the Grenadines accused SCL Group of funnelling foreign money into his opponent's campaign and running a smear campaign against him. The leader of the opposition party denied receiving foreign funds from SCL Group, but said that it did receive other forms of assistance from the company. The Times has since uncovered documents from 2011 in which SCL admitted to working against Gonsalves with a 'targeted digital attack'. They manipulated the Google search algorithm so that, 'within three weeks every single reference to him on the first two pages of Google…referred to the candidate's horrific track record of corruption, coercion, rape allegations and victimisation'.

In 2010, they worked on the re-election campaign of Denzil Douglas, the prime minister of St Kitts and Nevis. According to The Times, they were behind a sting operation in which the opposition leader, Lindsay Grant, was caught on camera agreeing to sell land to a British buyer below market rate in exchange for a $1.7 million donation. A video of the conversation was posted on YouTube by an account that has not been used since and was reportedly run by SCL, called 'investigativerep1965'. In 2013 they carried out some more work for the Trinidad government, under contracts with the country's National Security Council. Under the guise of security work, they proposed a scheme to capture citizens' browsing history, recording phone conversations for a police database and analysing it to produce scores for each citizen on how likely they were to commit a crime. In the same year, they were involved in the Kenyan presidential election, working on the campaign of Uhuru Kenyatta, who was under indictment for crimes against humanity at the International Criminal Court. The charges were later dropped and Kenyatta won the election with 50.1 per cent of the vote. Cambridge Analytica was also involved in the Kenyan presidential election in 2017. The result was challenged in court but their candidate won the second-round election regardless. Brexit Party MEP and former head of media for UKIP Alexandra Philips was first asked by Channel 4 if she worked for them in July 2019 responding: 'I didn't work for them at all. That's libellous…I'm being very serious now. You're actually propagating a load of misinformation that's been put online…based on nothing…If you want to talk about the Cambridge Analytica campaign, speak to them, not me. I don't know them. I really don't know the people.'

The next week she admitted to Channel 4 that she had worked for Cambridge Analytica, who ran the media operation for the Kenyan president, after Channel 4 released a recording where she discusses being under contract with the firm. Philips later said when questioned by Labour MEP Julie Ward in a European Parliament session discussing foreign electoral interference and disinformation she had worked freelance for a consultancy that worked for another firm which folded into Cambridge Analytica and accused Ward of 'taking her information from conspiracy theorists on Twitter, FBPE hashtag people who want to stir up misinformation'. It's a familiar response, threats of legal action and claims of crazy conspiracy theories prior to admissions of truth. These people are supposed to be experts in crafting messages and obscuring the truth, so muddying the waters about their own work is second nature to them. In 2015, they were tangled up in the Nigerian elections once again in conjunction with an alleged SCL subsidiary, AggregateIQ. They were part of a team that produced and disseminated 'incredibly anti-Islamic and threatening' videos on social media designed to discredit and attack the main rival to the incumbent, Muhammadu Buhari. The videos depicted scenes of people being dismembered, decapitated, and their throats being cut, leaving them to bleed out in a ditch.

AggregateIQ worked on this project alongside Black Cube, an Israeli private intelligence firm who were hired by Harvey Weinstein to disrupt reports accusing him of sexual assault and misconduct. Christopher Wylie alleged that Black Cube was tasked 'to hack the now-president Buhari to get access to his medical records and private emails'. Their work was then handed to Cambridge Analytica by AggregateIQ. This is the perfect illustration of how the SCL group use webs of sub-contractors to obscure who is doing the real work. Cambridge Analytica contracted AggregateIQ, who in turn passed along information supplied by Black Cube, who describe themselves as a 'private intelligence agency', were accused of being part of a dirty ops campaign against former Obama administration officials, and were founded by the former SCL shareholder Vincent Tchenguiz. They deny having ever been involved with SCL or working in Nigeria and boasted on camera about having performed covert operations to attempt to sway an election in Malaysia during the Channel 4 undercover investigation into their work. A leaked briefing accused them of igniting old divisions and using old voter suppression techniques on a digital scale:

'Many of the techniques of social influence and control being used today have their roots in the COUNTER-INSURGENCY doctrines used to suppress the movement for Malaysian independence more than half a century ago. They have since been supercharged with the help of new technologies, big data analysis and social media.'

All Malaysian government officials deny ever working with SCL, but leaked emails show ongoing communication and strategic discussion, as well as joint pitches involving government officials for election messaging and campaigning. They pitched to the supposedly independent but state-owned Oil and Gas firm Petronas to campaign in support of the right-wing Barisan Nasional. As part of the proposal, they pitched political psychographic community profiles, a turnout model, and an emotional model of the electorate. Part of the work focused on 'inoculating' opposition ideas by creating a list of simplified policies and dismissing them as ridiculous, to prime opposition voters to reject them out of hand. It's difficult not to compare it with the way that the press primes the British population to reject ideas that might challenge the status quo. SCL also helped Rodrigo Duerte win the 2016 Philippines presidential race, emphasizing his qualities as a strong leader and rebranding him as a tough crime fighter.

Routine denial of any involvement is a recurring theme of

anywhere SCL are uncovered. Secrecy is their game and the ease with which they can traverse the globe, operate through webs of shell companies and sub-contractors, without much, if any, oversight should scare you. SCL is just one of the thousands of private military contractors working around the globe on behalf of governments. Untoward campaign tactics have been their bread and butter around the world, but it is only recently that they have turned their attention to elections in western developed nations. Until the last few years, SCL had found it difficult to break into the campaigns of western nations as they already have a pool of election talent that they will recruit from. Lynton Crosby dominates the Conservative electioneering in the modern age, whilst the Labour Party tends to focus more on local campaigning and grassroots campaigns rather than top-down organization. America was already overflowing with over-priced election consultants, data scientists, and campaign managers. The New York Times claimed that Cambridge Analytica experimented abroad, including in the Caribbean and Africa, so that their modus operandi of secrecy could be maintained. They are far less likely to come under the same level of scrutiny, where 'privacy rules are lax or nonexistent'. Perhaps they were simply perfecting their craft? Regardless, if SCL were to move beyond work in Africa and the Caribbean, they needed to find a way into the inner circles of Anglo-US political campaigning.

Cambridge Analytica is Born

The more you can make your organisation invisible the more influence it will have.
The Family

You may be wondering why we are focusing on the SCL group. After all, it was Cambridge Analytica who were plastered over the internet following the data scandal that is set to cost Facebook some $5 billion. Cambridge Analytica is simply one part of the massive web of companies who fall under the SCL umbrella. SCL Group is the parent company of Cambridge Analytica. A parent company is essentially a group, company, or conglomerate that owns a collection of smaller firms under one name. For example, Disney is a parent company to Pixar and Lucasfilm. The very nature of SCL's business means that being secretive is a huge asset. SCL operates as a large web of companies and vehicles, where work can be contracted and subcontracted out, obscuring exactly who is doing what and where the work is being done. By 2013, whispers of SCL had reached Steve Bannon's ears. At the time he was running Breitbart News out of Washington and was engaged in what he saw as a full-frontal culture war against the left wing in the US.

Christopher Wylie told The Guardian, 'Bannon believes that politics is downstream from culture. They were seeking out companies to build an arsenal of weapons to fight a culture war.'

The political strategist first came to public attention as the head of Breitbart News, the far-right digital news outlet. A former officer in the US Navy and vice president of Goldman Sachs, he co-founded Breitbart News in 2007 with Andrew Breitbart to be 'the Huffington Post of the right'. He served briefly as campaign manager for Donald Trump's presidential campaign, was appointed as Trump's Chief Strategist in the White House (before leaving in August 2017), and sat on the National Security Council until April 2017. Emails seen by The Guardian revealed that Bannon found SCL through Mark Block, a Republican strategist. He reportedly sat beside a cyberwarfare expert for the US air force on a plane, who suggested he speak to SCL because they did 'cyberwarfare for elections'. Back in 1997, Block was banned from Wisconsin politics for 3 years and fined $15,000 after violating election laws.

Rumours that Bannon and Boris Johnson had been in touch were also discussed but dismissed by Boris in 2018 when he described the theory as a 'lefty delusion whose spores continue to breed in the Twittersphere'. However, in June 2019, a video was released from mid-2018, prior to a Johnson speech that would blame Theresa May for the Brexit divisions and problems saying she was 'dithering' and leaving the UK in a 'miserable limbo' amid a 'needless fog of self-doubt'. In the video, Bannon remarks: 'Today we are going to see if Boris Johnson tries to overthrow the British government. He's going to give a speech in the Commons, I've been talking to him all weekend about this speech. We went back and forth over the text.'

Boris got to know Bannon after the Trump victory in 2016: 'Right after we won, Boris flew over. Because their victory was as unexpected as ours. I got to know him quite well in the transition period,' he said in clips for the documentary The Brink, which follows Bannon during the 2018 mid-terms after being kicked out of the White House by Trump.

Wylie 'n' Nix

Christopher Wylie grew up in British Columbia, Canada. He left school at 16 with nothing but a diagnosis of ADHD and dyslexia. At 17 he landed a job in the offices of the Canadian opposition leader and by 18 he was learning about data from Obama's national director of targeting. He taught himself to code at 19 and at 20 began studying law at the London School of Economics. Whilst studying for a PhD in fashion trend forecasting, he stumbled across a paper that proposed that personality traits, rather than say class or place of birth, could inform a person's political leaning. With this inspiration, he devised a plan to harvest Facebook profiles and use the data to build psychological profiles that would allow people to be targeted with political ads tailored to their personality. That's all it remained for a while though, simply a wild idea. That is until he got a call from Alexander Nix.

Alexander Nix was educated at Eton College and Manchester University. He began his career as a financial analyst with

Baring Securities in Mexico and thereafter in the UK with Robert Fraser & Partners LLP, a boutique corporate finance and tax advisory firm. In 2003 he left the financial sector to join the SCL Group as a director. Once there he was tasked with growing SCL internationally, together with opening new markets for SCL's many behavioural products and services. In 2007 he began to focus on developing the elections division, opening new offices in Washington DC and Delhi and growing the global staff to over 300 employees. Over the past 9 years, he has worked on more than 40 political campaigns in the US, Caribbean, South America, Europe, Africa, and Asia. Nix loves to boast, once claiming a 100 per cent success rate in 100 elections operations across Africa, Asia, and Western Europe.

In 2012, Wylie found himself doing some work for the Liberal Democrats but was lured away to work for SCL as a research director across the entire SCL group when they told him: 'We'll give you total freedom. Experiment. Come and test out all your crazy ideas.' He told Carole Cadwalladr at the Observer: 'It's like dirty MI6 because you're not constrained. There's no having to go to a judge to apply for permission.'

Wylie's predecessor had met an untimely end, after some work with Kenyan politicians in 2015 he was found dead in a hotel room. Once inside the company, Wylie worked on everything from British and US military contracts to election work in the Caribbean and US congressional races. Later he became a source for the Guardian/Observer investigation into Cambridge Analytica and testified in front of the parliamentary DCMS committee.

He left SCL in 2014. In the Netflix documentary 'The Great Hack', Julian Wheatland (then acting CEO of Cambridge Analytica) accused him of trying to 'kill the company'. Wylie founded his own company, Eunoia Technologies. Eunoia is ancient Greek for beautiful thinking and the company offered 'psychographic microtargeting' and 'multi-agent system voter behaviours simulation'; he said that he wanted to build the 'NSAs wet dream'.

Eunoia, who had two ex-Cambridge Analytica employees alongside Wylie, Mark Gettleson, and Tadas Jucikas, pitched unsuccessfully for the Trump campaign in 2015. Eunoia pitched Vote Leave their microtargeting services but Cummings turned them down, opting for AggregateIQ instead. After accusations from SCL that they were stealing clients, Eunoia shut down in October 2017. Resignation emails were uncovered from July 2014, his contract was reportedly for 19 hours per week and he was not a founder as he has claimed. When leaving Wylie took several hundred pages of company documents and a complete copy of the Facebook dataset. Alexander Kogan gave Wylie full access to his Facebook Dataset.

Bannon and Nix met in 2013, around the same time that Wylie came on board at SCL. Bannon and Wylie quickly hit it off after chatting about elections, culture, and how ideas can live and evolve online. As soon as Wylie began discussing his ideas for mapping personality traits to target voters, Bannon was hooked.

> [Bannon] got it immediately. He believes in the whole Andrew Breitbart doctrine that politics is downstream from culture, so to change politics you need to change culture. And fashion trends are a useful proxy for that. Trump is like a pair of Uggs, or Crocs, basically. So how do you get from people thinking "Ugh. Totally ugly" to the moment when everyone is wearing them? That was the inflexion point he was looking for.

With Bannon convinced that SCL could be a tool in his culture war, he decided to introduce Mix and Wylie to one of the richest political donors in America. Robert Mercer.

The Mercers

Robert Mercer, born 11 July 1946, is a US billionaire who made his fortune pioneering in AI (Artificial Intelligence) and machine learning. He is known as a brilliant computer scientist and the co-owner of one of the most successful hedge funds on the planet. Renaissance Technologies was the first to use bots and AI as part of their overall trading strategy, replacing hedge fund managers with computer programs. His daughter Rebekah, who has a maths degree from Stanford, runs the family foundation, through which they fund numerous right-wing candidates and super PACs. They also fund Breitbart and trust Steve Bannon as a close adviser.

Rebekah was fond of Wylie from the moment they met in her New York apartment. He had flown out with Nix to meet Robert and Rebekah. 'She loved me,' he told The Guardian, 'she was like, "Oh we need more of your type on our side!"' Both she and Bannon saw 'the gays' (Christopher Wylie's words not mine) as early adopters, they set fashion trends. 'He figured, if you can get the gays on board, everyone else will follow. It's why he was so into the whole Milo [Yiannopoulos] thing.'

Robert Mercer saw the potential in the technology they were claiming to be pioneering. He felt that it could make him, as the New York Times described it, 'a kingmaker in Republican politics'. He may have been bankrolling this new venture, but Mercer understood just what it could be capable of if it was deployed correctly. Wylie said after their first meeting that he was intrigued but needed more than simply theories and research papers.

'In politics, the money man is usually the dumbest person in the room. Whereas it's the opposite way around with Mercer. He said very little, but he really listened. He wanted to understand the science. And he wanted proof that it worked.'

Professor David Miller has been critical of those who have suggested that Mercer may simply have thrown money at this firm without any proof they were worth their salt: 'Robert Mercer did not invest in this firm until it ran a bunch of pilots –

controlled trials. This is one of the smartest computer scientists in the world. He is not going to splash $15m on bullshit.'

To begin with, he agreed to help fund a $1.5 million pilot programme in the November 2013 Virginia gubernatorial race to test their psychographic messaging software. They backed Republican attorney general Ken Cuccinelli but he lost the race. The Mercers were still impressed enough with their work to continue to invest in the firm. Cambridge Analytica managed to win the bid to work on the Ted Cruz presidential campaign. They agreed to provide $15 million to help SCL expand into the US on a more permanent basis. They set up a new company, incorporated in Delaware, as a part of the SCL web named Cambridge Analytica. The new company would have a licence to the psychographics platform developed by Christopher Wylie's team. Mercer and Bannon wanted to fuse big data analytics, social media, military-grade 'psych-ops', and 'information operations' and turn them on the US electorate.

Bannon is reportedly the one who suggested the name, he held a stake in the company and served as a vice president. It was Mercer, however, who held the principal stake. Alexander Nix was to serve as CEO. At the time, the New York Times reported that the company was merely a shell and that all the contract work was to be carried out by the SCL group. They spoke to former employees who claimed that any contracts that Cambridge Analytica was awarded would be taken on by SCL in London and overseen by Alexander Nix. They were warned in 2014 that this could violate US election laws limiting the involvement of foreign nationals in US elections.

Initially, Cambridge Analytica worked with a few 2014 midterm candidates. They also did hundreds of thousands of dollars of business with the former National Security Advisor and renowned war hawk, John Bolton's Super PAC (for whom Robert Mercer is a funder), supporting conservative candidates campaigning on national security-centric issues. They also worked on the Ted Cruz presidential campaign, but, evidently, they were unsuccessful. The Cruz campaign said their data was worthless and disputed their payments, which is believed to be at least $750,000 in 2015 alone. The new company's early work was focused around Bannon's culture war and his anti-establishment, economic nationalist message. A year before Trump announced his candidacy for president, Cambridge Analytica were testing and probing a large group of disenfranchised, white Americans, with messaging on a border wall, 'race realism', and 'draining the swamp' of Washington's political elite.

Christopher Wylie revealed that back in 2014 Steve Bannon had even ordered Cambridge Analytica staff to test messaging on Vladimir Putin and Russian aggression and expansion in Eastern Europe. According to Wylie, this was the only foreign leader that was specifically researched, not Kim Jong Un, not Angela Merkl, not Erdogan, just Putin. They were discussing Putin with focus groups and 'testing images of Vladimir Putin and asking questions about Russian expansion in Eastern Europe'.

With Ted Cruz comprehensively beaten by candidate Trump, Cambridge Analytica and Robert Mercer hopped on the Trump train along with (almost) the entire Republican Party. Only a handful of half-hearted 'never-Trump' Republicans remained and their disloyalty was quickly forgotten and brushed under the carpet as Trump defied conventional political wisdom to rise higher and higher in the polls. Some raised their heads in opposition following the release of the Access Hollywood 'Pussygate' tapes, but these were soon forgotten as Trump suffered little to no discernible consequences in the polls.

When Cambridge Analytica began work on the Trump campaign, they found the digital side of the campaign was a mess. According to Nix, they essentially took charge of the entire digital operation and the online propagandizing. However, both Trump aides and Cambridge Analytica staff are adamant that they did not use psychographics in their campaign. They claim that they didn't have the time to create one of their 'super samples' that we discussed earlier and used Republican Party voter data instead. Nix told the BBC that they used what he described as 'legacy psychographics' that were originally built for the Cruz campaign.

Despite Trump's constant defiance of odds and expectations, Clinton's loss seemed to come out of the blue. In the aftermath, Cambridge Analytica was keen to take credit for Trump's upset, but there are disputes over just how influential they were. In December 2016, The Spectator's Paul Wood asked: 'Are Cambridge Analytica brilliant scientists or snake-oil salesmen?' It is a fair question. Were this group simply lucky to attach themselves to the anti-establishment sentiment of Trump and Brexit, or were they the ones who galvanized and enhanced the brewing cultural clashes that took place?

The Weaponized Propaganda Machine

By leveraging automated emotional manipulation alongside swarms of bots, Facebook dark posts, A/B testing, and fake news networks, a company called Cambridge Analytica have activated an invisible machine that preys on the personalities of individual voters to create large shifts in public opinion.

Scout.AI

By now you must be wondering exactly what this magical piece of software is that intrigued Steve Bannon enough to bring it to Robert Mercer. Who in turn was willing to fork out $15 million to see it brought to life. Cambridge Analytica's website boasts of their ability to help clients gain the advantage over political opponents in this exact way, utilizing thousands of data points to build a 'psychographic profile' of targeted voters. The firm claims it can predict voting patterns by combining personality surveys and digital personal data on every American adult. They told the Washington Post that for the Trump campaign they offered suggestions on where to hold rallies and where volunteers should knock on doors. Jonathan Albright, a professor of communications at Elon University, North Carolina, described Cambridge Analytica as a central point in the right's 'propaganda machine'. Christopher Wylie even gave written testimony to the Senate judiciary committee that both Cambridge Analytica and its parent company SCL were able to perform 'black ops' that included breaking into computer systems to gather intelligence.

In America, their primary objective was voter disengagement and to persuade Democratic voters to stay at home using tactics that they had honed in elections across Africa and the Caribbean. They wanted to cast doubt in the minds of swing voters as to who was the most dangerous candidate – painting Clinton as a criminal who ought to be locked up. Remember hearing 'Lock Her Up' or 'Hillary For Prison'? Nix did an interview with TechCrunch in November 2017, discussing how advertising in the commercial world can be applied to the political realm: 'There's no question that the marketing and advertising world is ahead of the political marketing, the political communications world...there are some things which is "best practice digital advertising", best practice communications which we're taking from the commercial world and are bringing into politics.'

The application of branding and marketing techniques from the advertising world to politics is not a new idea. Simple, direct messages and branding in politics have almost always been a part of successful mass movements and political campaigns. Lord Timothy Bell, once the driver behind Thatcher's media campaigns, argued that the simplification of political messaging would 'help ordinary people understand it'. He hoped to transform the way people thought, shifting the national conversation towards neo-liberal ideas: 'Advertising is about having an idea which captures the public's imagination and makes them change their attitudes or their behaviour, and politics should be the same thing.'[28] The Conservatives used their 'coalition of chaos' and 'strong and stable' rhetoric to both good and bad effect in the 2015 and 2017 general elections; the Republican Party in America (prior to 2016) had long campaigned on the idea of 'family values', and Labour movements around the world frequently use variations on 'standing up for the working class'; 'For the many, not the few' may ring a bell. Obama, for all his eloquence and skills as an orator, focused around a single word during his 2008 campaign: 'Change'. Cambridge Analytica hoped to use simple messaging and target voters based on personality. They categorize people by their interests, their life choices, their careers and hobbies, rather than their age and identity. In a way, they are attempting to leverage the complete opposite of identity politics in order to build a coalition of voters. Identity politics, at its very root, is based upon facets of your life that you have no control over as a child. Where you are born, your ancestors, your family, your sexuality, not the things you choose for yourself like your hobbies, interests, or your career path. Obviously, these choices are influenced by the place you are born and grow up, you're unlikely to find many American football fans in Finland, Arctic Monkeys fans in rural Kansas, or Iron Brew fans in Dorset.

You will probably have all heard the phrase, actions speak louder than words. Cambridge Analytica believes that actions speak louder than identity. That to truly understand a person you need to look at how they choose to spend their life and free time, rather than the more traditional age, race, location demographics that have typically dominated political polling, canvassing, and campaigning. The difference between campaigns of the past and Cambridge Analytica, or for that matter almost any sophisticated modern campaign, was the sheer amount of data available to access. We've already seen just how easy it is for big corporations to gather massive amounts of your personal data. Now we will examine how that was and can be exploited by bad actors and political campaigns.

In 2013, two psychologists at Cambridge University's

Psychometrics Centre, Michael Kosinski and David Stillwell, ran a research project where they legally harvested Facebook data. They published a peer-reviewed paper that claimed they could determine everything from personality traits and political partisanship, to sexuality and more simply by correlating and examining Facebook likes and the results of a personality quiz. They used a quiz called myPersonality to score users on the 'big five' personality traits – Openness, Conscientiousness, Extroversion, Agreeableness, and Neuroticism and correlated them with the Facebook likes of each individual. Nix explained to Bloomberg's Sasha Issenburg,

'Your behaviour is driven by your personality and actually the more you can understand about people's personality as psychological drivers, the more you can actually start to really tap into why and how they make their decisions, we call this behavioural microtargeting and this is really our secret sauce if you like.'

Some of these patterns are quite strange; for example, people who liked 'I hate Israel' on Facebook also tended to like Nike shoes and KitKats. One internal email seen by The Guardian showed that they were particularly interested in Facebook users who 'liked' Mitt Romney, Walt Disney World, the US Marine Corps, and Coca-Cola. Brian Resnick of Vox.com argued that whilst these personality traits may have an effect over our decision making on political issues, we are also influenced by 'our ideologies, and our personal history'. Though he does concede that these are all intertwined. Our personalities are informed by our genetics and crafted by our personal history, just as our personalities, in turn, construct our ideologies. That seems fairly straightforward in theory. How difficult can it be for data scientists and psychologists to take what they know about advertising to particular personality types and apply it to political messaging? Isn't that what politicians have been doing for years? Conservatives in America have spent decades honing the Fox News brand to represent exactly what they know appeals to the Republican base, whilst at the same time steering them in the direction they want. The British press has arguably been even more successful in cultivating an anti-EU audience based on fears of immigration and a loss of sovereignty.

Nigel Oakes' expertise from BDI was truly brought to life with the ability to micro-target adverts based on personalities and hobbies. He had long attempted to influence electorates by targeting social groups (especially self-selecting ones) with a strong sense of identity. In a typical SCL project, they would speak to tens of thousands of people through numerous polls, surveys, and different sub-contractors. Rather than ask what they felt about certain issues or political figures, they would ask 'how do you feel about life?' This gave them insight into local and individual concerns; whether those reflect reality or are a legitimate grievance is irrelevant. If you ask about a feeling, you get much more of an insight into the community mood and the feeling on the ground in any particular area.

Dr Spectre

Dr Michal Kosinski was a PhD candidate at Cambridge University's Psychometrics Center whilst studying the correlation between Facebook likes and personality traits. Zurich's Das Magazine profiled Kosinski in 2016, reporting:

> with a mere ten 'likes' as input his model could appraise a person's character better than an average coworker. With seventy, it could 'know' a subject better than a friend; with 150 likes, better than their parents. With 300 likes, Kosinski's machine could predict a subject's behaviour better than their partner. With even more likes it could exceed what a person thinks they know about themselves.

Kosinski published another paper in November 2017 entitled

'Psychological targeting as an effective approach to digital mass persuasion'. The study that ran on some 3.5 million users found that:

Persuasive appeals that were matched to people's extraversion or openness-to-experience level resulted in up to 40 per cent more clicks and up to 50 per cent more purchases than their mismatching or unpersonalized counterparts. Our findings suggest that the application of psychological targeting makes it possible to influence the behaviour of large groups of people by tailoring persuasive appeals to the psychological needs of the target audiences.

Kosinski concluded that by using data gathered solely from Facebook combined with an OCEAN personality test, he could predict political leanings and use this data to target and persuade voters. SCL/Cambridge Analytica soon hired another scientist from the university, Dr Aleksandr Kogan, to do the same for them. Kogan approached Kosinski on behalf of SCL Elections, to inquire about licensing his model to them. But Kosinski declined, fearing the consequences of this technology being used by a firm with a shady past in elections.

Just a few months into 2014, Kogan and SCL teamed up to build a model similar to Kosinski. Since it was simply a research paper, out in the world for everyone to see, there was nothing he could do to stop them from replicating his methods. They used Mechanical Turk (MTurk), a crowdsourcing marketplace run by Amazon, to recruit people to take the personality quiz. Kogan paid Amazon MTurk workers $1 each to take the OCEAN quiz, in exchange for all of the data linked to both their own Facebook profiles and those of their friends. Imagine the vast amount of information you can garner access to through just one person. How many friends do you have on Facebook? 400, 500, 800, 1000? They were able to harvest the data of hundreds for the price of one. Kogan told Facebook that the data would only be used for academic purposes, not for commercial ones. Numerous users eventually flagged the task as violating the MTurk terms of service: 'They want you to log into Facebook and then download a bunch of your information,' complained one user at the time.

Kogan's app, called 'thisismydigitallife', pulled data from an average of 160 other people's profiles. Emails from Christopher Wylie revealed that nobody from Cambridge Analytica had checked whether this data harvesting was legal. Facebook was seemingly incredibly hands-off about the practice. Wylie told The Observer: 'Their security protocols were triggered because Kogan's apps were pulling this enormous amount of data, but apparently Kogan told them it was for academic use. So they were like, "Fine".'

This breach of data was initially reported by The Guardian at the end of 2015 when Harry Davies published the first report on how Cambridge Analytica was harvesting and using Facebook data on the Ted Cruz campaign. Upon seeing this report, employees at Facebook quickly identified the source of the information leak and moved post-haste to secure the data and ensure it had been deleted. In August 2016, a mere 9 months later, lawyers for Facebook wrote to Christopher Wylie, 'This data was obtained and used without permission...It cannot be used legitimately in the future and must be deleted immediately.' Just a few months out from the presidential election, this was a little late to be intervening. Despite their rapid action and investigation into the matter, Wylie had by this time not been at SCL or CA for the best part of 2 years. 'Literally all I had to do was tick a box and sign it and send it back, and that was it,' says Wylie. 'Facebook made zero effort to get the data back.'

Facebook was eventually fined $5 billion for privacy violations in the US and £500,000 in Britain. In the amazing corporate world that we live in, their stock price ticked up as investors had been told Facebook had already anticipated and set aside money for such an eventuality. A $5 billion fine for leaking the private information of 87 million people to a private political consultancy with military-grade psychographic software who were involved in the two biggest political upsets in the modern world is considered business as usual, nothing to worry about. Facebook's deputy general counsel said in a statement that Dr Kogan, 'SCL Group and Cambridge Analytica certified to us that they destroyed the data in question'.

In Wylie's first call with Carole Cadwalladr from The Observer, he told her he had receipts, invoices, emails, and legal letters from inside Cambridge Analytica. These detailed the story of how, between June and August 2014, the profiles of more than 50 million Facebook users had been harvested. Most damning of all, he had a letter from Facebook's own lawyers stating that Cambridge Analytica had acquired the data illegally.

In the summer of 2014, Kogan's business partner boasted on LinkedIn that their private company Global Science Research (GSR) 'owns a massive data pool of 40+ million individuals across the United States – for each of whom we have generated detailed characteristic and trait profiles'. SCL held a contract at the time with GSR. They had agreed to pay data collection costs for GSR in order to improve 'match rates' in the datasets that SCL already held or to improve GSR's algorithm's 'national capacity to profile capacity of American citizens'. SCL was paying Kogan to better pair Facebook data with other datasets they had accrued of the US population. Kogan has claimed that GSR stores Facebook data anonymously and that although they did sometimes use MTurk for data collection, they 'never collected more than a couple thousand responses on MTurk for any one project, or even across all projects for a single client – the vast majority of our MTurk data collection as a company is in the form of surveys only'.

He began harvesting the data in June 2014, costing Cambridge Analytica a cool $800,000, a little over 10 per cent of the $7 million they spent on data acquisition leading up to the 2016 presidential election. He was even allowed to keep a copy of the harvested data for his own research. This bought Cambridge Analytica 50 million raw profiles, of which 30 million could be matched to other data the company had acquired via addresses or other personal information. They were able to get all this from 270,000 users who agreed to the data harvesting. A total of 30 million from 270,000. Not a bad rate of return. This was the data that helped Wylie to build the models that they had promised to the Mercers. In April 2018, Facebook confirmed that Cambridge Analytica illegally gained access to up to 87 million profiles, most of whom are from the US. Brittany Kaiser, a former Cambridge Analytica executive, believes it could be more. She told the DCMS committee: 'I believe it is almost certain that the number of Facebook users whose data was compromised through routes similar to that used by Kogan is much greater than 87 million.'

Early on in the course of the parliamentary investigation, Facebook was far less forthcoming with information, denying that Cambridge Analytica could have used data from the social network. Facebook's UK director of policy, Simon Milner, was questioned by the parliamentary DCMS (Digital, Cultural, Media, and Sport) committee investigation into the Brexit campaign and use of personal data:

> **Christian Matheson (MP for Chester):** 'Have you ever passed any user information over to Cambridge Analytica or any of its associated companies?'
>
> **Simon Milner:** 'No.'
>
> **Matheson:** 'But they do hold a large chunk of Facebook's user data, don't they?'
>
> **Milner:** 'No. They may have lots of data, but it will not be Facebook user data. It may be data about people who are on Facebook that they have gathered themselves, but it is not data that we have provided.'

In another hearing by the same committee, Rebecca Pow, MP for Taunton Deane, asked Cambridge Analytica's CEO, Alexander Nix: 'Does any of the data come from Facebook?' Nix replied: 'We do not work with Facebook data and we do not have Facebook data.'

Despite this denial from both Facebook and Cambridge Analytica, Christopher Wylie has a copy of the executed contract, from 4 June 2014, between SCL and GSR. It details Facebook data harvesting and processing in order to match it to personality traits and voter rolls. Some wilder theories suggest that Facebook was complicit, not simply incompetent. Given the storm of fake news, bots, trolls, and newsfeed manipulation that Facebook was dealing with at the time, it seems much more likely that ensuring data wasn't used correctly or legally was simply not a priority for them. Data protection laws were flimsy and the company was making more money than ever off advertising revenue. They were running to catch up with the beast they had unleashed when they created an addictive platform open to large-scale manipulation that hosted a profile for the majority of people on the planet.

Bizarrely, at one point Kogan even changed his name to Dr Spectre (though he has subsequently changed it back to Dr Kogan). This is either unknowingly ironic or incredibly sinister, given that in the original Bond films Spectre was attempting mass manipulation of entire populations. In a video responding to the allegations surrounding Cambridge Analytica, they released a video that said explicitly 'Cambridge Analytica is no Bond villain,' so perhaps they were aware of the connotations. Despite the major controversy surrounding his work for Cambridge Analytica, he is still a faculty member at Cambridge University.

To help them build their system, Cambridge Analytica also purchased numerous consumer datasets for absolutely everything they could get their hands on. They amassed magazine subscriptions, airline travel, shopping habits, land ownership, and more and fed them into their voter-profiling machine by matching common data such as the address, phone number, or email address. David Miller, a professor of sociology at Bath University, explained that the ultimate goal was 'to capture every single aspect of every voter's information environment'.

The purchase of consumer datasets is perfectly legal, but the way in which they used them to construct voter profiles was unprecedented. They bought from data brokers and third-party organizations selling information about swathes of the population. Nix likes to boast that this allowed them to construct a personality profile for each of the 230 million adults in the US with up to a staggering 5000 data points. Now, this is unlikely to be the case for everybody; but the fact we have to ponder over how true this could be is a little terrifying. Nix told TechCrunch in an interview in November 2017: 'This is publicly available data, this is client data, this is an aggregated third-party data. All sorts of data. In fact, we're always acquiring more. Every day we have teams looking for new data sets.'

Using legal methods, a private company funded primarily by one billionaire, that has popped up using unscrupulous campaign tactics in elections time and again, has a database encompassing almost every citizen in (arguably) the world's most powerful country. Jonathan Albright believes that new data pulled from Facebook and Twitter is being continually meshed into this system, which would explain what Nix means when he says the data is being constantly updated and refined. He is terrified of the power of social networks being used to influence populations: 'This is a propaganda machine. It's targeting people individually to recruit them to an idea. It's a level of social engineering that I've never seen before. They're capturing people and then keeping them on an emotional leash and never letting them go.'

Scout.AI, a web-based AI project, went even further than this. After in-depth research work with Professor Albright, Samuel

Woolley, head of research at Oxford University's Computational Propaganda Project, and Martin Moore, Director of the Centre for the Study of Media, Communication and Power at Kings College, concluded that: 'This phenomenon was about much more than just a few fake news stories. It was a piece of a much bigger and darker puzzle – a Weaponized AI Propaganda Machine being used to manipulate our opinions and behaviour to advance specific political agendas.'

They accused Cambridge Analytica and SCL of building a propaganda machine that preys on the most vulnerable individuals, homing in on their biggest fears and worries and using them to manipulate public opinion on an unprecedented scale.

'Many of these technologies have been used individually to some effect before, but together they make up a nearly impenetrable voter manipulation machine that is quickly becoming the new deciding factor in elections around the world.'

Perhaps this technology is something we ought to be a tad concerned about?

Channel 4 Undercover

As a part of a 4-month investigation, Channel 4 went undercover posing as representatives of a wealthy client interested in their services for an upcoming election in Sri Lanka. After exchanging a few emails, a meeting was arranged between the 'client', Cambridge Analytica's Chief Data Officer Alex Taylor, and managing director Mark Turnbull. When intelligence gathering was mentioned during one of the meetings, Turnbull told the fake client: 'We have relationships and partnerships with specialist organisations that do that kind of work...You know who the opposition is, you know their secrets, you know their tactics.'

When these sorts of tactics have been alleged by whistle-blowers or journalists, SCL has always denied all accusations of underhand tactics. These are no longer whispers and rumours of shady campaign tactics based on conspiracy theories and wild accusations. It's coming straight from the horse's mouth. The Channel 4 investigation gave us an absolutely crucial insight into how CA operate, how they sell themselves to clients and the power that they claim to have to sway voters via any means necessary. During the meeting Turnbull went on to explain:

> The two fundamental human drivers when it comes to taking information onboard effectively are hopes and fears and many of those are unspoken or even unconscious...our job is to drop the bucket further down the well than anybody else, to understand what are those really deep-seated underlying fears and concerns. It's no use fighting an election on the facts, it's all about emotion.

They appeal to the most primal base emotions that people can feel, the primary drivers of people's actions. In the futuristic TV show 'West World', where AI robots are designed as characters in a game, these base emotions are described as 'cornerstones'. This is the foundation upon which their entire character is built and it is our own individual cornerstones that Cambridge Analytica hoped to understand and then exploit. The tactics they suggested are very reminiscent of some of the work they allegedly did in the recent Kenyan and Nigerian elections, where fake news and provocative viral videos played on people's fears about disease, infrastructure, poverty, Islamic extremism, and corruption. They publicly deny almost all involvement in these elections, but in private Turnbull told Channel 4 that they had been a part of the Kenyatta elections in 2013 and 2017. They took credit for almost every facet of the campaign.

During a third meeting between the Channel 4 'client' and CA executives, questions were raised about the nature of intelligence gathering on opponents. Turnbull nonchalantly mentioned that they know of a number of private organizations filled with ex

MI5 and MI6 employees who can find 'all the skeletons in his closet'. They explained how such information must be released discreetly and at the exact moment: 'It has to happen without anyone thinking, that's propaganda.' They believe that anything they release has to feel organic and not choreographed in any way. If people can easily identify propaganda, then the next logical question is, 'who put that out?' The most important part of disseminating 'junk news' or information that has been acquired through less than legal means is to ensure it feels like real journalism. Turnbull explained that: 'We just put information into the bloodstream of the internet and then watch it grow. Give it a little push every now again.'

In the series of meetings Cambridge Analytica also spoke openly about their ability to operate through a web of shell companies to maintain secrecy. At the third meeting, Alexander Nix was also present and told Channel 4: 'We're used to operating through different vehicles, in the shadows...I look forward to building a very long-term and secretive relationship with you.'

At one of the initial meetings, Turnbull said that they aren't in the business of fake news or entrapment, as it crosses a line. However, in the meeting attended by Nix, these sorts of tactics seemed to be very much on the table. When questioned on deep digging for dirt or compromising information he told the client that whilst they are excellent at intelligence gathering, they employ others to gather dirt on opponents or manufacture it themselves. Nix interjected: 'Equally effective can be to just go and speak to the incumbents and offer them a deal that is too good to be true and make sure that video is recorded. These sorts of tactics are very important.'

Nix listed several example scenarios, such as sending someone posing as a wealthy developer to offer a large amount of money to finance a candidate in exchange for some land or contractual promises or using women to seduce, distract, or butter up politicians: 'I'm just giving you examples of what can be done and what has been done,' he said, 'These are things that don't necessarily need to be true, as long as they are believed.'

To keep their role under wraps they will often come into foreign countries under different company names, or aliases altogether. They set themselves up with fake IDs and pose as tourists, or students on research projects, 'I've had a lot of experience with this,' Nix told the undercover reporter. Turnbull even spoke about how they have had recent success subcontracting their work for a project in what they describe as an Eastern European country. They claimed their employees simply floated in and floated out without anyone noticing. Perhaps the most shocking titbit uncovered by this investigation was their claim that in reality, because the candidate doesn't understand what is going on with Cambridge Analytica – evident from their lines of questioning – that they are the puppet. That this shady, unaccountable, foreign-funded web of consultancies, campaign groups, and big data scientists have become self-anointed leaders of world politics, shaping elections as they see fit.

David Miller has expressed serious concerns about the involvement of Robert Mercer in the company and subsequently its involvement in elections around the world. He described it as 'an extraordinary scandal that this should be anywhere near a democracy. It should be clear to voters where information is coming from, and if it's not transparent or open where it's coming from, it raises the question of whether we are actually living in a democracy or not.'

They speak of offering to bribe foreign officials, disseminating information without a brand to avoid it being traced, and using Proton mail with a self-destruct timer in order to avoid emails being leaked. All this was admitted and openly discussed with just a handful of meetings. Do you still trust this company when they say they weren't involved in the Brexit campaign?

It is worth noting that Nix is known to exaggerate and embellish to get a client on board. Former CA executive Brittany

Kaiser described Nix as a man willing to say almost anything to win clients, 'Alexander is known to oversell everything to close the deal.' Regardless, Nix was suspended from Cambridge Analytica as CEO after this investigation was revealed and broadcast on Channel 4 News. The company said in a statement:

> The board of Cambridge Analytica has announced today that it has suspended CEO Alexander Nix with immediate effect pending a full, independent investigation.
>
> In the view of the board, Mr Nix's recent comments secretly recorded by Channel 4 and other allegations do not represent the values or operations of the firm and his suspension reflects the seriousness with which we view this violation.

Nix told reporters 'appearances can be deceptive' when asked about the Channel 4 film. Do you think he was suspended because of what he said? Or because he was caught saying it? The best way to look at the information gathered during this Channel 4 investigation is to line it up with allegations that have been made against Cambridge Analytica and SCL in the past. Do these statements seem consistent with the rumours of underhand electioneering tactics, misinformation, and targeting of people's most primal fears and desires to achieve their clients' electoral goals?

AggregateIQ

I've spent quite a few pages covering the SCL group and their creation of Cambridge Analytica. But Cambridge Analytica is just one of the many companies in the wider SCL web. They use numerous different shell companies and different vehicles to outsource work and payments in order to obscure the real recipient of funds and exactly who is performing what work and where. These shadowy operations allow SCL and similar firms to operate in relative obscurity and remain unknown to the majority of voters. AggregateIQ is one of such sub-contractors.

Run by Zach Massingham, a former university administrator, AggregateIQ (AIQ) used to be a low-profile political consultancy that, among other things, develops highly-targeted Facebook advertising. It was set up in 2013 by Massingham out of Victoria, British Columbia and is reported to have around just 20 staff. This tiny Canadian marketing company is credited by some insiders as being the reason for the success of the Brexit campaign. Vote Leave communications director Paul Stephenson called AggregateIQ 'instrumental in helping the Leave campaign win...they transformed Vote Leave's digital offering and helped us to contact voters over one billion times online', whilst Dominic Cummings commented that Vote Leave owed 'a great deal of its success to the work of AggregateIQ...We couldn't have done it without them.' Data released by the Electoral Commission showed that roughly 40 per cent of money spent by leave groups during the campaign was on services provided by AggregateIQ (AIQ). Their website states that: 'AggregateIQ delivers proven technologies and data-driven strategies that help you make timely decisions, reach new audiences and ultimately achieve your goals.'

They claim to be specialists in fields such as:

- Audience Persuasion
- Message Testing
- Public Opinion Polling
- Online Engagement and Intervention
- Audience Analysis

Aside from that, their website gives little indication as to who they are, or how they achieve their goals. Run a quick Google search and very few stories come up pre-referendum, perhaps a little odd for a firm credited with causing one of the most seismic referendum results in British history. They believe in the value of repetition and simplicity: 'You always want to try and reduce everything down to the simplest form of the argument and then repeat those simple lines again and again and again and that becomes your brand...Knowing when to spend what money, and where, and what the impact is going to be, is actually very important.'

Christopher Wylie told Channel 4 that AggregateIQ was set up originally as SCL Canada, for some staff who were unable to be as mobile as other people or groups within the SCL umbrella. An anonymous Cambridge Analytica employee who spoke to The Observer explained that Christopher Wylie was the real figure behind AggregateIQ: 'He's the one who brought data and micro-targeting [individualized political messages] to Cambridge Analytica. And he's from west Canada. It's only because of him that AggregateIQ exists. They're his friends. He's the one who brought them in.'

Wylie also claimed that the Intellectual Property was owned by Cambridge Analytica and SCL, even though they were technically a separate company. When the Electoral Commission wrote to AggregateIQ to ask about their links to Cambridge Analytica, they responded saying that it had signed a non-disclosure agreement that was outside British jurisdiction – or as Vote Leave described it, 'a clean bill of health'. The same source for The Observer, however, also confirmed that the two companies were one and the same:

'The Canadians were our back office. They built our software for us. They held our database. If AggregateIQ is involved then Cambridge Analytica is involved. And if Cambridge Analytica is involved, then Robert Mercer and Steve Bannon are involved.'

SCL removed a listing for SCL Canada from its site in March 2017. The listed phone number was that of Zach Massingham, the director of AggregateIQ. When questioned about it, a spokesman for SCL said it was an outdated listing of a former contractor who had done no work for Vote Leave.

Almost all of AIQ's contracts came from either Cambridge Analytica or Robert Mercer – they wouldn't have been able to exist without their contracts. CEO Jeff Silvester said roughly 80 per cent of AIQ's revenue came from SCL between 2013 and mid-2015. They paid AIQ $575,000 to build a system to manage modern political campaigns; a platform to co-ordinate canvassing, automated emails, and target adverts. An intellectual property licence revealed a binding 'exclusive' 'worldwide' agreement 'in perpetuity' for all of AggregateIQ's intellectual property to be used by SCL Elections.

In a 4-hour appearance before the DCMS committee, Christopher Wylie described how AIQ was effectively the Canadian arm of Cambridge Analytica/SCL, receiving business as a sub-contractor. At the time of the referendum, it was operating almost as 'an internal department of Cambridge Analytica. It didn't have a website and no contact number. The only public contact number was SCL's website.' In contrast, COO Jeff Silvester told the Times Colonist, that: 'AggregateIQ has never been, and is not a part of, Cambridge Analytica or [its parent firm] SCL. AggregateIQ has never entered into a contract with Cambridge Analytica.'

Wylie said he was surprised that Dominic Cummings, Vote Leave's campaign director, had discovered AIQ, which did not have its own website. AggregateIQ say they have had a website since their launch in 2013. Wylie had one meeting with Cummings in late 2015, when he made an unsuccessful pitch for work. At the time of the referendum, AggregateIQ and Cambridge Analytica were working together, being paid by Mercer-funded organizations to work on Ted Cruz's presidential campaign in America. In one article Carole Cadwalladr alleged that several anonymous sources told her that the two companies shared the same database. The DCMS committee concluded that, where

AIQ and SCL worked together, both staffs had full access to some of the same databases. Nix brushed this off as consultancy work, training them on putting their software into action.

Intriguingly, AggregateIQ had a non-compete clause with Cambridge Analytica, which does suggest a higher level of co-ordination between the two wings of SCL. A non-compete clause is where a subsidiary company agrees not to enter the same profession or marketplace in an attempt to undercut the larger firm. Leave.EU announced in November 2015 that it was going to be working with Cambridge Analytica so AggregateIQ would have needed explicit permission to work with Vote Leave so as to avoid any lawsuits if they are a subsidiary.

Emails and files obtained by the tech website Gizmodo found that software being used by CA during the 2016 US election was designed by AggregateIQ. The files were discovered by Chris Vickery, the research director at UpGuard, a Californian cyber-risk firm. They contained thousands of pages of code and internal notes, emails, and discussions between AIQ staff. The files revealed that AIQ were the developers for the campaign apps used by Ted Cruz, Texan Governor Greg Abbott, and for Ukrainian steel magnate Serhiy Taruta, head of the country's newly-formed, pro-Russian, Osnova party. Vickery also found a config file that suggested collaboration between CA, AIQ, and Breitbart and references an app they pitched to Breitbart News.

In an internal forum, AIQ developers discussed a project known as 'The Database of Truth', a system that 'integrates, obtains, and normalizes data from disparate sources, including starting with the RNC Data Trust...The primary data source will be combined with state voter files, consumer data, third party data providers, historical WPA survey and projects and customer data.'

The RNC Data Trust is the Republican Party's primary voter profile provider. AIQ was collating and organizing huge quantities of voter data, using the RNC voter database as the starting point and building a huge network of information about the US electorate. It seems that AIQ was working on collating a super sample of the US electorate for Cambridge Analytica, bringing together numerous sources of data, including the main RNC voter database – just as Alexander Nix told MPs.

The DCMS committee report on AIQ and Cambridge Analytica/SCL detailed their doubts that the two were separate companies: 'There is clear evidence that there was a close working relationship between Cambridge Analytica, SCL and AIQ. There was certainly a contractual relationship, but we believe that the information revealed from the repository would imply something closer, with data exchanged between both AIQ and SCL, as well as between AIQ and Cambridge Analytica.'

Similarly, the ICO expressed doubts, describing the relationship between the two companies possessing '"a permeability" between the companies above and beyond what would normally be expected to be seen'.

In the end, this little company with just 20 staff made a touch under £3.7 million on the Brexit vote. A total of £2.9 million from Vote Leave, £625,000 from BeLeave, £100,000 from Veterans for Britain, and £32,000 from the DUP. Whether you believe they were two separate companies or not, AggregateIQ has Cambridge Analytica's fingerprints all over them. They shared staff, gave them almost all their initial contracts, and AggregateIQ developed their campaign platform, all whilst SCL held all the intellectual property rights.

SCL has a long history of using shell companies and sub-contractors to cloud their activities in a web of mysteries. They have repeatedly been accused of covert means of electioneering, using digital propaganda and graphic videos. They have used psychographic voter targeting, worked alongside the Ministry of Defence and NATO, and are in possession of technology that has been declared a weapon by the British government and was export-controlled until 2015. Every controversy they become embroiled in, they leave in a hurry, denying any involvement. They played a role in both Trump and Brexit and have attempted to distance themselves from both campaigns. These two (or maybe one) companies were on the right side of two of the most seismic events in world politics in decades. In two populations deeply divided and still hurting after the 2008 crash and withering from the slow rot of globalization on former industrial towns and cities, they found the places to hit us hardest. Communities and families were turned on one another, hatred was encouraged, outrage was celebrated for its viral potential. The intrusion they masterminded into the personal data of 87 million Americans cost Facebook $5 billion and they didn't even break a sweat. They just made some promises to be more accountable and Mark Zuckerberg did some podcasts to show how serious he was about it all. They helped turn the referendum debate into a firestorm that is still burning bright. Worst of all we are all stuck arguing about how to deal with the new fires, whilst the old ones still burn.

Military Ties

Psy-ops is short for psychological operations. It essentially describes any form of warfare that engages in psychological manipulation or mind games. Genghis Kahn, leader of the thirteenth-century Mongolian Empire, is considered by many to be the greatest conqueror in history. He often used psychological tactics as a complement to his vast hoards to devastating effect. He believed that it was much easier and more efficient to conquer new lands if the enemy had already surrendered before the battle began. Kahn's generals would threaten the utter destruction of villages if they didn't surrender, settlements that resisted were burned to the ground and the survivors were massacred. Word quickly spread of these horrors and the next villages would think twice about resisting the will of Genghis Kahn. Each soldier would light three torches at night to give the impression that his army was much larger than it was. Sometimes brushes and rakes were tied to the tails of horses as they rode across dusty valleys to create massive dust clouds as if many thousands of soldiers were marching across the plains. During WW2, the allies used misinformation to confuse the German high command as to the exact date and locations of the Normandy D-Day landings. In more modern warfare, the CIA has been known to use rogue TV broadcasts to influence populations in Panama and Cuba. In the 1991 Gulf War, American forces would drop leaflets telling Iraqis they would be bombed the next day if they didn't surrender. If that didn't encourage them to raise the white flag, they would be carpet-bombed and the following day more leaflets would be dropped again urging survivors to surrender.

There has been a psychological element to warfare for as long as war has existed and as warfare has developed and technology has evolved, ever-more innovative and subtle ways of conducting warfare are becoming routine. Wars are seldom fought on the battlefield anymore; instead, they are fought through cyber-attacks and online propaganda. Marshall McLuhan wrote in 1969: 'World War III is a guerrilla information war with no division between military and civilian operation.'

In a study done by the Computational Propaganda Project at Oxford University, Samantha Bradshaw and Philip N. Howard found that the activity of 'cyber troops' has become the norm on social media. In Troops, Trolls and Troublemakers: A Global Inventory of Organized Social Media Manipulation, they define cyber troops as 'government, military or political party teams committed to manipulating public opinion over social media'. The global phenomenon has become ever-more pervasive online and can be a significant force in shaping online discourse and discussion. The report looked at 28 countries including Britain, America, France, and Germany. They found that every authoritarian regime that they studied was using social media propaganda on their own public, whereas the 'democratic' nations were almost guaranteed to be using similar techniques on foreign populations. You might consider Boris Johnson's £100 million campaign to promote a no-deal Brexit or his use of bots to interact with his Facebook and Twitter posts as examples of this in a democratic nation.

In January 2015, the British Army announced that their 77th Brigade would 'focus on non-lethal psychological operations using social networks like Facebook and Twitter to fight enemies by gaining control of the narrative in the information age'. Their primary objective of this would be to shape public behaviour through the use of 'dynamic narratives' as a counter to political propaganda distributed by terrorist groups. The Army spokesman told the press that:

> 77 Brigade is being created to draw together a host of existing and developing capabilities essential to meet the challenges of modern conflict and warfare...It recognises that the actions of others in a modern battlefield can be affected in ways that are not necessarily violent and it draws heavily on important lessons from our commitments to operations in Afghanistan amongst others.

It is not news to the British military establishment that warfare is changing, war is not fought on the battlefield anymore, it is fought online and through digital propaganda. One of the scariest parts of the growth of private psy-ops contractors is that this sort of behaviour has evolved from simply being deployed by national militaries to being outsourced to firms like SCL and Palantir, owned by the Facebook investor and PayPal founder Peter Thiel, and being used in political campaigns.

We've already mentioned in passing the military links between Cambridge Analytica, their founders, funders, and the psychological warfare techniques they have levelled on sovereign populations around the world. Yet so far we have only scratched the surface to the vast web of military links and contracts that SCL is a part of. It makes sense that the first people to see the potential of Dr Kosinski's original research were the defence and military establishment. Militaries around the world have long been researching and using more basic or blunt psychological operations techniques, but the availability of massive datasets on entire populations via social media and commercial operations gave them a power they could only have dreamt of in the past. Boeing, a major US defence contractor, funded Kosinski's PhD and DARPA, the US government's secret Defense Advanced Research Projects Agency, is cited in at least two academic papers supporting Kosinski's work. Information operations are just one strand of the 'five-dimensional battle space' that the US military operate in. SCL, for example, was paid for conducting counter-extremism operations in the Middle East, and the US Department of Defense has contracted it to work in Afghanistan. According to testimony given to the DCMS committee from Brittany Kaiser, Cambridge Analytica's business development director, she has seen documents where Nigel Oakes (co-founder of the SCL Group and the head of its defence division) discussed how the company's audience-targeting methods were 'export-controlled' by the British government up until 2015.

'That would mean that the methodology was considered a weapon. Weapons-grade communications tactics – which means we had to tell the British government if that was going to be deployed in another country outside the United Kingdom.'

Brittany Kaiser told Commonwealthy.com in 2016 that the underpinnings of Cambridge Analytica's political methods are the same social scientific research and data science techniques that were used by the military: 'This was most often actually used in defence. We work for the Department of Defence and intelligence agencies in counter-terrorism operations with this exact same similar methodology. And now we decided to start building up a database to work in politics.'

Documents passed to the DCMS committee by Christopher Wylie confirmed that SCL had 'routine access to secret information' and carried out a training programme that included a 'classified case study from current operations in Helmand' in Afghanistan. They were individually commended by the UK Ministry of Defence for training they gave to a psychological operations warfare group and received an endorsement from the UK Psychological Operations Group in 2012 who declared that they would 'have no hesitation in inviting SCL to tender for further contracts of this nature'. SCL worked with the British military in Afghanistan and Libya and across 15 different psychological operations projects worth an estimated £350,000. They worked with the Foreign Office on counter-terrorism strategies in Pakistan involving 'strategic planning to counter violent jihadism'. The MoD also worked with SCL Insight (one of their subsidiaries) on a £42,000 data analytics contract as recently as February 2018. Wylie is particularly concerned about the power of this private psychological operations firm working with governments around the world whilst simultaneously working on political campaigns.

'The company has created psychological profiles of 230 million Americans. And now they want to work with the Pentagon? It's like Nixon on steroids.'

SCL and their subsidiaries have worked inside governments across the world, on political campaigns and military psychological operations. Their military work is focused on waging psychological and digital warfare to aid military intervention and national security in conflicts in the far corners of the globe. Now they have turned their digital weaponry upon the British people, shouldn't we be at least a little worried? Set aside the referendum for a moment, forget the issue itself and try to picture how you might feel if they were involved in any vote or campaign in the future. How much power do you think they would have to influence an election? If you think they have any chance of impacting the outcome of a democratic vote, then should we allow them to operate? Is psychographic voter targeting a step too far? A step beyond traditional marketing tactics into something more morally grey?

These are questions that you may have already been asking yourself. You might be getting nervous, anxious, or even angry. How have we allowed this to become the new normal? Should we just lie down and accept it? Political campaigning has always been based on creating coalitions and appealing to a majority of the population, but should this level of manipulation (or at least attempted manipulation) be accepted? Should we accept that military-grade psychological warfare techniques have been turned on the British electorate in an attempt to change the future standing of the entire country, economically, politically, and on the world stage? Cambridge Analytica is just one of many private security and intelligence firms making a fortune off the digitization of politics.[29] Most of the divides in our society have been bred by the actions of the powerful, by those who comprise the modern establishment, but the vulnerabilities of our modern electoral system to the tech industry were brought by our own negligence. We failed to understand early on, what the internet meant for elections and the influence they were capable of exerting upon a nation's politics. Carole Cadwalladr cautioned in her TedTalk on Facebook interference in elections that unless we change the law now, we may never have free and fair elections again. The technology is only going to get better and better at understanding how and why we make political choices and we're going to be more and more exposed unless we make a concerted effort to protect our electoral process.

Russian Connections

I could pretend that to avoid sounding like a deranged conspiracy theorist, Russian individuals were not meaningfully connected with Cambridge Analytica, Vote Leave, and Leave.EU. Sadly, there are connections of note. I feel it would be a disservice to my goal to help you understand why the Brexit vote happened and who stands to benefit, to not examine the plethora of links to Russian business and intelligence. I'm not going to start drawing wild conclusions or connecting dots that don't exist, just lay out what we know and let you make of it what you will.

Alexander Nix told the DCMS committee:

'We have never worked with a Russian organisation in Russia or any other company. We do not have any relationship with Russia or Russian individuals.'

So that must be that. If Alexander Nix tells us in a parliamentary hearing that SCL or Cambridge Analytica has never worked with Russia or any Russian individuals, then I guess we have to believe him. Nix has repeatedly proved himself to be a straight-talking, honest, and transparent businessman. What reason could we have to doubt him? Perhaps the pitch they made to Lukoil, the Russian oil and gas giant, simply slipped his mind. Nix emailed Christopher Wylie on 17 July 2014 discussing a memo they had been asked to write for the firm to explain how their services would apply to the petroleum industry. 'They understand behavioural microtargeting in the context of elections,' but were, 'failing to make the connection between voters and their consumers.' He said the work was to be shared with the CEO, former Soviet oil minister and associate of Putin Vagit Alekperov. Alekperov and Lukoil answer to Putin and have been used as a vehicle to exert Russian influence beyond their borders. For example, in 2016 it was revealed that a pro-Russian adviser to the then Czech President had been paid by the firm.

The presentation that they eventually put together was barely to do with their customer base at all. Instead, the documents bragged about a 'rumour campaign' designed to spread fear during the 2007 Nigerian elections and pushed the fact that they were psychographic messaging experts. Senator Adam Schiff told the media in a statement: 'Mr Wylie testified that Cambridge Analytica's CEO [Alexander] Nix marketed Dr Kogan's research on the American electorate in his original outreach to Lukoil.' Bill Browder, who is leading the campaign to enforce international sanctions against Russia, told Carole Cadwalladr at the Observer:

'Everyone in Russia is subordinate to Putin. One should be highly suspicious of any Russian company pitching anything outside its normal business activities.'

What could a Russian oil giant, who answers to Putin, need with psychographic messaging? Is it plausible that they are acting as intermediaries? Providing either services or expertise to the Russian government via Lukoil. Wylie said: 'What I witnessed at Cambridge Analytica should alarm everyone. Cambridge Analytica is the canary in the coalmine of a new Cold War emerging online.'

The connections don't end there. Dr Kogan is still a faculty member at Cambridge University but is also an associate professor at St Petersburg University. He has received grants from the Russian government to conduct research on 'Stress, health and psychological wellbeing in social networks'. During the congressional hearing on Russian interference in the US election, on Wednesday 16 May 2018, Wylie revealed that Aleksandr Kogan, who created the application to harvest Facebook user profile data, was working on Russian funded 'behavioural research' projects at the same time.

'This means that in addition to Facebook data being accessed in Russia, there are reasonable grounds to suspect that CA may have been an intelligence target of Russian security services... (and) that Russian security services may have been notified of the existence of CA's Facebook data.'

Wylie also claimed that Cambridge Analytica had used Russian researchers as part of its data-harvesting operation and 'openly shared information on "rumour campaigns" and "attitudinal inoculation"' with companies and executives linked to the Russian intelligence agency FSB. On top of the use of troll farms, bots, and fake news, Russia was also targeting voting machines in the US in 21 states. According to Jeanette Manfra, head of cybersecurity at the Department of Homeland Security, 'We saw a targeting of 21 states and an exceptionally small number of them were actually successfully penetrated.' 'Without doubt,' she added, 'we were able to determine that the scanning and probing of voter registration databases was coming from the Russian government.'

Michael Flynn, the former Trump administration official, was sacked and is under investigation for failing to disclose meetings he held with Russian officials. Flynn actually worked as a consultant for Cambridge Analytica. The Wall Street Journal reported that US investigators have looked into reports that depicted Russian hackers exploring how they could hack Hillary Clinton's email server and pass the files to Flynn. The leak of the Paradise Papers left further question marks over Russian influence in social media when it was revealed that Russian business person Yuri Milner, who also owns a stake in a company co-owned by Jared Kushner, Donald Trump's son-in-law and senior White House adviser, coordinated Russian state investment in both Facebook and Twitter. Milner claimed that Facebook and Twitter were unaware of the source of the investments, which came from VTB (a Russian state-controlled bank) who invested $191 million in Twitter in 2011, and a financial arm of the state oil and gas firm Gazprom who financed an offshore company which held some $1 billion in Facebook shares.

The motivations here are unclear, whether they simply saw a financial gain to be made from a growing industry, or they wanted a greater insight, influence, or understanding of how social media works and did work – in order to manipulate it. This would require incredible foresight on the part of the Russian state, though interestingly Karen Vartapetov, the director of sovereign ratings at Standard & Poor's, said the Russian government had 'a strong influence on VTB's strategic and business plans' even when these were not expected to be lucrative. 'VTB plays a very important role for government policies, including implementation of some less profitable and socially important tasks,' said Vartapetov.

Tom Watson, then deputy to Jeremy Corbyn, spoke at a fringe event at the Labour Party Conference condemning Russian interference in Western elections. He accused the Kremlin of having 'reinvented blitzkrieg for the digital age' in their campaign of misinformation, malicious technology, and dark money.

All of us need to wake up to the true scale of what's been going on. Now is the time when the government must drop the three wise monkeys act: see no evil, hear no evil, speak no evil – about the biggest threat to the integrity of our democracy. The Russian attack. It's time we woke up to the reality that Russia has reinvented the blitzkrieg for the digital age. A new strategy to attack far behind our old defences, to attack us from within.

Watson called for a full-scale public inquiry, on a par with the Mueller investigation currently ongoing in the US into this 'dark story about the frontiers of the new Cold War'. In the report on Russian interference in the US election, Robert Mueller was unambiguous about the level of Russian activity; he confirmed that 'The Russian government interfered in the 2016 presidential election in sweeping and systematic fashion.' If you have to ask yourself why Russia would be even remotely interested in the UK leaving the EU, consider what Russia would gain if the UK were to leave the EU. It divides Europe and the West, distracts them from what Russia is doing because of internal conflicts, and economically weakens the UK and the EU (at the very least in the short term). It is also worth noting that the objective need be no more than simply stirring up unrest in the UK. Christopher Wylie spoke at a Labour fringe event alongside Tom Watson, explaining that Russia may want to cause internal struggles and divisions within Britain and America, with no goal other than chaos: 'If you are Russia, your goal is not to advance a particular political ideology. Your goal is to divide what you see as your geopolitical foes...Chaos is your objective, and that happens on all sides. It's not just UKIP.'

The company intertwined with the Brexit vote works alongside militaries and world governments on waging psychological warfare and the behaviour change of entire populations. They use huge amounts of personal data to map and target electorates and are not afraid of using dirty or underhand tactics to achieve their goals. They illegally harvested Facebook data and have ties to a nation that has been actively involved in a large-scale, co-ordinated series of cyber-attacks and online misinformation campaigns attempting to disrupt elections in a number of western democracies. If that doesn't suggest that we need to be wary of attempted Russian influence on our politics and that our electoral laws need reform, I'm not sure what does.

6. Vote Leave, Take Back Control

For both Leave and Remain there was to be one officially designated campaign. For Leave, Vote Leave were the eventual winners of the designation ahead of Leave.EU and Grassroots Out (GO). The lead campaign on each side was afforded a £7 million spending cap, compared to £700,000 given to the other campaign groups who wished to form. Vote Leave initially rejected the immigration heavy campaigning of Nigel Farage and Leave EU, opting to highlight issues such as the UK contribution to the EU budget, the ECJ, and British Parliamentary Sovereignty. They focused on three words that will forever be printed in the memory of those of us who lived through the 2016 campaign: Take Back Control. Vote Leave was comprised mostly of Conservative MPs, including big names such as Michael Gove, Boris Johnson, Steve Baker, Andrea Leadsom, Dominic Rabb, Liam Fox, and Chris Grayling. However, they also boasted a cross-party coalition that included Labour MPs Frank Field, Gisela Stewart, and Ian Davidson, as well as then UKIP MP for Clacton, Douglas Carswell. Vote Leave employed two renowned Conservative political strategists to co-ordinate the campaign; Dominic Cummings as the campaign director and Matthew Elliott as the chief executive.

Vote Leave was first brought together in the kitchen of Tory MP and arch-Eurosceptic Bernard Jenkin. There that night were Steve Baker, Dominic Cummings, Matthew Elliott, and Owen Paterson. In May 2015 they all agreed that Cameron was not going to achieve enough reform from the EU and thus wanted to be a part of the campaign to leave the EU.[30] In a press statement at the beginning of their campaign, Rob Oxley outlined the Vote Leave message:

Technological and economic forces are changing the world

fast. EU institutions cannot cope. We have lost control of vital policies. This is damaging. We need a new relationship. What happens if we vote 'leave'?

We should negotiate a new UK-EU deal based on free trade and friendly cooperation. We end the supremacy of EU law. We regain control. We stop sending £350 million every week to Brussels and instead spend it on our priorities, like the NHS and science research.

We regain our seats on international institutions like the World Trade Organisation so we are a more influential force for free trade and international cooperation.

A vote to 'leave' and a better, friendlier relationship with the EU is much safer than giving Brussels more power and money every year.

(For the record each individual member of the EU has a seat on the WTO as does the EU as a whole so technically we are over-represented).

Eventually, the name 'Vote Leave, Get Change' was settled upon, which later became 'Vote Leave, Take Back Control'. Three-word political phrases rarely encapsulate so many feelings and invoke so many disparate grievances. It encouraged people to take back control from immigrants, the EU, the modern world, the establishment, the PC brigade. Any villain you wanted could be projected on the canvass of ' Take Back Control'.

Dominic Cummings
Anybody can start a fire, he's not the messiah.
Craig Oliver (in Channel 4's Uncivil War)

A lot has already been written on the subject of Dominic Cummings. The almost messianic reverence that some Tories hold for him is fascinating. By leading the campaign against unelected bureaucrats, he has inadvertently become the most powerful unelected bureaucrat in Britain. Cummings is married to the former commissioning editor at The Spectator and daughter of Sir Humphrey Wakefield, Mary Wakefield. He graduated from Oxford in 1994 aged 22 and moved to Russia to set up an airline in the new Russian Federation. He toiled away for 3 years and managed to charter just one flight in the time but the company never took off.

Upon his return to the UK, he began work in politics and served as campaign director of business for Sterling from 1999 to 2002. He later worked as director of strategy for Conservative Party leader Iain Duncan Smith tasked with modernizing and detoxifying the modern Conservative party. He lasted a grand total of 8 months.[31] He also worked on the campaign opposing a Northern Regional Assembly which won 78 per cent of the vote. He is perhaps most famous (pre-referendum at least) for his 7 years spent as right-hand man to Michael Gove, including as his Chief of Staff after the 2010 General Election. Whilst working as a special adviser at the Department of Education, he was described as 'the paramilitary wing of Michael Gove' – probably due to his highly aggressive use of the @toryeducation Twitter handle to attack anyone who criticized Gove or his work. Farage described Cummings as an 'interesting bloke but clearly a bit domineering – or attempts to be domineering – of every situation that he is in'.[32] He was sanctioned by the ICO (Information Commissioner's Office) for failure to respond to FoI requests and it was eventually leaked that he had deliberately used Gmail in order to avoid such requests. The London Evening Standard described him during the referendum as 'Intense, iconoclastic, verbose' and made allusions to a reputation as 'the Tory Che Guevara'. When it was alleged by The Guardian that there were links between Robert Mercer, Cambridge Analytica, and Leave. EU, Dominic Cummings wrote angrily on Twitter declaring that the piece was 'full of errors & itself spreads disinformation' and that 'CA had ~0 per cent role in Brexit referendum'.

His campaign strategy was described as: 'Don't talk about immigration'; 'Do talk about business'; 'Don't make the referendum final'; 'Do keep mentioning the Charter of Fundamental Rights and the over-reach of the European Union's Court of Justice.' Owen Bennett outlines their strategy in The Brexit Club as 'Saving money. Science. The NHS. These were the areas that Vote Leave felt would win over the undecideds.' He is the one credited with coining the slogan 'Take Back Control', which became a central part of the campaign messaging effort. Don't get the wrong impression from his desire to avoid immigration as a topic, he is not in any way, shape, or form, a placid or unconfrontational figure. He seemed to upset a number of people within the campaign, the board attempted to sack him before the campaign began, and he openly feuded with Leave EU (the campaign group fronted by Nigel Farage). He has maintained his reputation as a foul-mouthed contemptuous figure since his arrival at Number 10. Tim Shipman wrote in All Out War about how Steve Baker dubbed Cummings, 'political special forces. If you don't care about what collateral damage you sustain, he's the weapon of choice. He operates with the minimum of civilized restraint. He is a barbarian.'

He was also found to be in contempt of parliament after refusing to appear before the DCMS committee a second time. He accused them of grandstanding and spreading lies. Most importantly, he was crucial to the success of the Leave campaign. Both Tim Shipman and Craig Oliver confirm in their books that most of the major players involved with Vote Leave credit the victory to Dominic Cummings.

Matthew Elliott

Matthew Elliott was the chief executive of Vote Leave. The Leeds-born LSE graduate had worked successfully as campaign director on the No to AV campaign during Cameron's first term as prime minister and was now charged with directing the effort to see Britain be the first nation to exit the European Union. The BBC described him as 'one of the most effective lobbyists at Westminster'. Elliott founded the TaxPayers' Alliance (TPA), a think tank/lobbying group who mirror the Tea Party in America and are pro-Brexit advocates of global free trade. He also founded Business for Britain (BfB), who became a forerunner to Vote Leave, and the think tank Politics and Economics Research Trust (PERT), in 2004. In 2012 Elliott was sought out by a man the Home Office now believes was a Russian spy. Sergey Nabolin was the first secretary in the Russian Embassy's political sector in London. When Elliott got engaged in 2014, Nabolin was the first to congratulate him. He eventually left the UK in 2015 after his visa expired following the Alexander Litvinenko murder. Perhaps most interestingly, Elliott was a founding member of Conservative Friends of Russia and in 2012 he embarked upon a 10-day trip to Moscow.

Dominic Cummings and Matthew Elliott (Vote Leave Chief Executive) worked alongside each other on the 2011 No to Alternative Vote campaign. This campaign laid the groundwork for how the Leave campaign would approach digital campaigning. The Financial Times commented in an interview with Cummings:

'That campaign made exaggerated emotive claims [and] also recognised that the Advertising Standards Authority had no power to regulate political ads, however misleading.'

When they came together in October 2015 to found Vote Leave, they knew how powerless the current regulators were to oversee modern campaigning. The capability of social media to target adverts had grown exponentially in the years since the No to AV referendum and Cummings was keen to put that power to good use. Elliott and Cummings had focused on the cost of the new AV system and its complexity. One of their posters showed a soldier and read: 'He needs bulletproof vests NOT an alternative voting system'.[33] It laid the groundwork for the Vote

Leave campaign.

Physicists and Secrets

Dominic Cummings holds some colourful views on modern politics and politicians more broadly. He may be angry, belligerent, arrogant, and somewhat highly strung, but his take on the way the British public felt on Europe was somewhat prophetic. In an article in The Times in June 2014, Dominic Cummings wrote:

'The combination of immigration, benefits, and human rights dominates all discussion of politics and Europe. People think that immigration is "out of control" and puts public services under intolerable strain.'

He also noted that 'people now spontaneously connect the issue of immigration and the EU'. In an interview for The Economist, he reasoned that simplicity was the key: 'The Eurosceptic world has thousands of books and zillions of pamphlets and has been talking about this for many decades. The challenge is not to say more things. The challenge is to focus, to simplify things.'

In June 2015, Cummings wrote: 'The official out campaign does not need to focus on immigration. The main thing you need to say on immigration is "if you are happy with the status quo on immigration, then vote to stay IN".'

The campaign exercised constructive ambiguity combined with data-informed focus. Dominic Cummings was adamant throughout the campaign that Vote Leave should never commit to a single trade model, because the public didn't understand the various institutions that comprise our EU membership and trading relationship, nor were the opinions of any two Eurosceptics the same. Each wanted something completely different, so better to leave it undefined. Ambiguity was a deliberate strategy, much like Trump's, to allow voters to project onto him whatever outcome they envisioned. Cummings told Vote Leave staff: 'No one knows what the Single Market is!

No one knows! No one will know what it is by the end of this campaign. Period.'[34]

Cummings makes a point that we touched on in Chapters 3 and 4. The EU is complex and most people have little understanding of how it works. The potential future relationship with Europe has such a wide range of potential options, here are just a few examples:

1. Leave the EU and stay in the single market and the customs union
2. Leave the single market but stay in the customs union
3. Stay in the single market but leave the customs union
4. Leave all three
5. Leave with a trade deal
6. Leave without a trade deal
7. Join the European Free Trade Association and stay in the single market
8. Join the European Free Trade Association and leave the single market
9. Leave everything but maintain all existing policing and security arrangements as well as European co-ordination on disease control

The list goes on...

Cummings was happy to take advantage of misconceptions and a lack of understanding. He was happy to play fast and loose with the truth. But, as we explored in the previous chapter, politicians have lied pretty consistently throughout history. Populists love to offer vague solutions and simple answers to big complicated questions. These aren't new tactics. What separated this campaign from those before it was the previously unparalleled use of data. Prior to the 2016 referendum, there was no web-based canvassing software for the UK that allowed live use and live monitoring. Vote Leave was forced to build their own software, something that had been tried unsuccessfully by other British political parties. Cummings wrote on his blog in November 2016:

One of our central ideas was that the campaign had to do things in the field of data that have never been done before. This included a) integrating data from social media, online advertising, websites, apps, canvassing, direct mail, polls, online fundraising, activist feedback, and some new things we tried such as a new way to do polling...and b) having experts in physics and machine learning do proper data science in the way only they can – i.e. far beyond the normal skills applied in political campaigns.

Conservative MEP Daniel Hannan described the scientists as 'a group of west coast American academics' who had been recruited 'in great secrecy' and specialized in astrophysics or similar fields. He claims that they 'found this way of scraping data off people's Google searches and feeding it into a program to tell you, by postcode, where your voters were.'

They designed a system which allowed them to feed in the UK electoral roll. This allowed them to target, on a street by street level, where they thought leave voters were more likely to reside and where they should focus canvassing efforts. It contained star ratings for local teams to rate how likely each street was to be fruitful for them. Feedback was crucial to hone and improve their models because of limited time and resources (both in financial terms and sheer man-power). They spent almost their entire budget on digital communication and online campaigning. With this money, they hired physicists and quantum information specialists. This may seem like an odd move, but Cummings explained their choice:

If you want to make big improvements in communication,

my advice is – hire physicists, not communications people from normal companies and never believe what advertising companies tell you about 'data' unless you can independently verify it. Physics, mathematics, and computer science are domains in which there are real experts, unlike macro-economic forecasting which satisfies neither of the necessary conditions – 1) enough structure in the information to enable good predictions, 2) conditions for good fast feedback and learning.

Cummings preferred that the physicists and data scientists were kept a secret from other politicians involved in the campaign because they were only interested in 'having boozy lunches with Farage gossiping about what would happen after we lost'. They were untrustworthy and notorious for leaking to the press so he decided to keep the physicists and data scientists safe from prying eyes and unwanted attention. He was obsessed with testing, data, and feedback and discussed it frequently on his blog. 'Data was really important for Dom,' Wylie noted during his parliamentary testimony. He frequently laments the ineptitude of politicians to understand data and make use of it correctly, lambasting them for being focused on Facebook 'likes' when discussing the digital presence and over-estimating the impact of more traditional forms of media (such as TV debates). He despises politicians who don't understand the modern media landscape and was convinced he could run an incredibly successful campaign focused on big data and digital advertising. Cummings described their process in much the same way that Nix talks about his work with Cambridge Analytica. They tracked response data and constantly refined and renewed ads based on what was working, continuously feeding back data, absorbing more and more information. It's political A/B testing, in the exact same way as Google and Facebook carry it out. Obama was the first major politician to use these techniques in a political campaign, but the referendum was the first time it was used in Britain.

When this data was combined with reports from canvassing street teams and national polling data, they claimed that they were able to build a clear picture of the state of their campaign. Reading Cummings' blog you get the impression that the campaign wouldn't have been possible without such ease of access to data:

'Data flowed in on the ground and was then analysed by the data science team and integrated with all the other data streaming in. This was the point of our £50m prize for predicting the results of the European football championships, which gathered data from people who usually ignore politics.'

One advert that provoked media attention was 'Predict the European Championships and win £50 million – the amount we send to the EU every single day'. The odds of winning the contest - which Vote Leave funded through an insurance policy - were calculated at one in 5,000,000,000,000,000,000,000,000. It was a competition set up by Vote Leave to encourage the sort of disaffected Somewheres that would not be reached by traditional political advertising. A total of 120,000 signed up to the competition, and every entrant received a text in the final 24 hours reminding them to vote – the texts were sent to half a million people.[35] It wasn't just Leave targeting football fans, Stronger In worked out which teams might be worst hit by immigration restrictions and targeted pro-Remain ads at fans of clubs like Arsenal[36]. For a political campaign to be successful, just like in any good business, they need to understand the people they are trying to target. Before social media, the sort of data found in the '50 Million Remains' dataset would have been all but impossible to access, but now technology has opened the door to people who could have easily ignored the political realm entirely. In the end, they inspired more votes than any single cause in British history.

Data on less engaged citizens is like gold dust to campaigns attempting to target disaffected voters. Martin Moore, Director of the Centre for the Study of Media, Communication and Power at King's College, London, explained the importance of this kind of data:

> What's clear from the ad is that they had identified a particular group of people who are really hard to reach. Working-class young men who actively ignore and reject politics. It's hard to get their contact details and hard to get them to turn out to vote but this was central to Project Waterloo – increasing turnout among particular demographics, especially young working-class males, by sending them messages that Leave knew would provoke a response.

Vote Leave spent the majority of the 10-week campaign message and model testing, then spent almost their entire advertising budget in the final days in a last stand blow-out. They wanted to get their robustly tested messages out in front of people as close to D-Day as possible, they wanted to be the freshest thing in their mind when they approached the polling booth. In his blog, Dominic Cummings proposed that Brexit ultimately came down to 'about 600,000 people – just over 1 per cent of registered voters'. This is unerringly similar to the results of the presidential election in America, which ultimately came down to some 80,000 voters scattered across three swing states. In 2015, the Conservatives targeted just 200,000 swing voters in marginal constituencies[37] and won a surprise majority. Really it becomes a question of whether you believe enough adverts could sway 600,000 people in Britain to vote to leave the European Union.

Dark Ads

It used to be that how you voted depended very much on your class or where you were born or grew up. But in recent years, people have been, as Alexander Nix puts it, 'buoyed by the availability of information and a plethora of options available on the internet' to look outside of values espoused by their family or their neighbours in order to find their own identities and beliefs. Nix claimed to have incredibly precise insights into what voters wanted, down to the level where he claimed in an Op-Ed for Campaign Live that they discovered 'a small pocket of voters in Iowa who felt strongly that citizens should be required by law to show photo ID at polling stations'. He claims that by targeting voters on a more individual level, they were able to swing the Iowa Caucus for Ted Cruz – though ultimately this wasn't enough to win him the nomination.

According to Martin Moore, Project Alamo, the digital wing of the Trump campaign, was using 40-50,000 variations of adverts. These were continuously tracked to determine their salience and effectiveness and adapted based on the results. They designed Facebook ads and scripts for phone canvassing and door-to-door use to communicate their message in the most amenable way possible for different categories of voters. For example, for those who were designated part of the 'Temperamental' personality group, it was decided that campaigners should take the line that showing your ID to vote is 'as easy as buying a case of beer'. Or for those categorized as being in the 'Stoic Traditionalist' group the best message was that showing your ID in order to vote 'is simply part of the privilege of living in a democracy'. Just as with the titles of advertising groups that Facebook places you into, these titles are just attempting to give a literary description to the shared data points and patterns in each category.

Based on users' responses to these posts, Cambridge Analytica was able to identify which of Trump's messages were resonating and where. That information was also used to shape Trump's campaign travel schedule. For example, if targeted voters in Kent County, Michigan, clicked on an article about bringing back jobs, then it was time to schedule a Trump rally in Grand Rapids that focuses on economic recovery. As is the case with most of these techniques, talking to voters about region-specific issues is hardly something CA pioneered. It doesn't take a complex algorithm to work out that it would be pointless to discuss the improvement of transport in London when addressing a crowd in Liverpool. The difference here is that these techniques have been refined and enhanced significantly by big data analytics.

From their monstrous vault of user data, the Trump digital team identified 13.5 million persuadable voters and modelled which combinations of these voters they needed in order to get themselves over the line. The US uses a strange weighted system to count their votes known as the Electoral College. Each state is allocated a certain number of electors and the winner of the state-wide election is granted all the electors from that state (except in the case of Maine, which allocates its electors proportionally) as the candidates race to 270 electoral college votes.[38] Just like Vote Leave, they relentlessly tested and refined their messages. They were focused on finding voters who would not traditionally vote Trump or Republican.[39]

At one point, in response to the data, Brad Parscale said he 'took every nickel and dime I had out of everywhere else, and I moved it to Michigan and Wisconsin'.[40] Jared Kushner suggested he started campaigning in Pennsylvania after seeing the data as well. Pundits called it crazy, questioning why Trump would be trying to penetrate Clinton's 'blue wall'. In the end, Trump won all three states. Cambridge Analytica built a system capable of assessing target voters' responses to say, an article about Clinton's negligence over her email server and serve up more ads based on those responses. Continually refining both itself and its knowledge of voters allowed them to shape their digital campaign, and identify areas where their message was particularly resonant. Ultimately it was victories in Michigan, Pennsylvania, and Wisconsin by tiny margins that won Trump the election. Vote Leave developed their voter targeting software with AggregateIQ, who helped build 'The Database of Truth' for Trump during his campaign, whose intellectual property is owned by Cambridge Analytica and SCL. The adverts used on Facebook have become known as 'dark posts' or 'dark ads'. They can only be seen by those who are posting the advert, and those being targeted by it. There is no regulation, no fact checks, no oversight, and no accountability. When Gerry Gunster appeared on Panorama in 2017 he explained very clearly how these adverts could have been used during the Brexit referendum:

> You can say to Facebook, 'I would like to make sure that I can micro-target that fisherman, in certain parts of the UK,' so that they are specifically hearing that if you vote to leave you will be able to change the way that the regulations are set for the fishing industry...Now I can do the exact same thing for people who live in the Midlands who are struggling because the factory has shut down. So I may send a specific message through Facebook to them that nobody else sees.

The targeted nature of these posts makes it so difficult to conduct oversight. Anyone can place political adverts on Facebook, with no requirement to prove their source or validity. As a part of the parliamentary inquiry into fake news, Damian Collins, chairman of the Culture, Media and Sport Committee, has pointed the finger at Facebook, claiming that they need to be more accountable for its role in these elections and in political campaigning in general:

> Historically, there have been quite strict rules about the way information is presented and broadcasters work to a very strict code in terms of partiality and there are restrictions on the use of advertising. But with something like Facebook you have a media which is increasingly seen as the most valuable media in an election period but which is totally unregulated.

A politician heaping blame on someone else isn't exactly front-page news, but it does raise an intriguing question: who is accountable here? During the EU referendum, the Vote Leave campaign paid for 1 billion ad impressions (how many times an advert will be seen). Just to put that in perspective – for every single person that voted in the referendum (some 33.6 million people) Vote Leave paid for 29 impressions on social media; 29 times for every single person. Imagine the cost involved if you needed that level of advertising in print, radio, billboards, or television. It would be astronomical. The ads would be publicly available for everyone to see and there would be far more scrutiny over their content. Facebook allowed campaigners to bypass all of these obstacles and plug directly into the beating heart of digital life. These adverts made up a huge bulk of the digital spend with AggregateIQ. Zach Massingham explained: 'Though we are listed as one of the largest expenditures, the reality is the vast majority of that money was for online advertising to those groups of people the campaign wanted to reach.'

Emily Las, a New York digital marketer, found a smattering of what appear to be Vote Leave 'dark ads' online. They included a video that claimed: 'Turkey is joining the EU. Our schools and hospitals already can't cope.' It told viewers that 76 million people were preparing to land on British soil and swarm the NHS and education system - it was viewed by some 515,000 people. Facebook was asked by the UK parliament's DCMS committee to disclose the Brexit ads as part of its enquiry. Eventually, Facebook released a few adverts run by AIQ for the official Vote Leave campaign, BeLeave/Brexit Central, and the DUP.

One reads: 'The EU is expanding. Turkey is one of Five new countries joining the EU. The EU will cost us more and more' and goes on to list the populations of Turkey (76 million), Albania (2.8 million), Macedonia (2.1 million), Montenegro (0.6 million), and Serbia (7.2 million). An alarm bell symbol on another is accompanied by, 'Turkey, Albania, Serbia, Macedonia, &

Montenegro are joining the EU,' and asks 'Will this hurt the UK?' Another reads simply: 'Turkey (population 76 million) is joining the EU. Vote Leave, take back control' with a picture of an open door made from a British passport. Each advert was tailored to our individual personality (or at least what we let Facebook see). For the environmentalists, one ad reads: 'The EU blocks our ability to speak out and protect polar bears!', for tea addicts 'The European Union wants to kill our cuppa', or one for the mild Eurosceptics featured a more sensible line on immigration with Boris Johnson pictured announcing: 'I'm pro immigration, but above all I'm pro controlled immigration.' Older voters were hit with ads about the cost of the EU and young voters with adverts quoting old Jeremy Corbyn speeches: 'The EU takes away from national parliaments the power to set economic policy and hands it over to an unelected set of bankers.'

We've been able to see just a handful of the ads that were blanketed across social media during and after the referendum campaign. Vote Leave had found their niche and they were hitting voters hard with the same lines over and over, digitally and on TV and radio. Cummings had realized there was no oversight on these adverts and was not going to let truth stop him from causing the biggest upset in British politics. One advert seen between 2 and 4.9 million times was targeted almost exclusively (99 per cent) at English Facebook users — and included the claim that: 'EU protectionism has prevented our generation from benefiting from key global trade deals. It is time we unite to give our country the freedom to be a prosperous and competitive nation!' BeLeave were slightly more subtle with their approach, urging target recipients to back a 'fair immigration system' or an 'Australian-style points-based system' but without making any direct references to any specific non-EU countries. BeLeave also created a handful of ads which focused on EU regulation of modern technology as a reason to back Brexit. They criticized EU regulation of digital streaming services and ride-sharing apps like Uber, 'We can't let EU regulators keep us in the past. Learn More'. Or 'The EU should not be forcing quotas on streaming. Learn More'.

The most problematic part of these dark ads is the lack of oversight, there is no factual test, regulatory barriers, no ombudsman to complain to if adverts are misleading, disingenuous, or just straight-up lies. That is, unfortunately, a huge part of the internet. We have to use our own judgement to determine the validity of claims we see – 'Will this supplement in my Facebook feed really make me burn twice as many calories?' 'Does this Nigerian Prince really need my help?' 'Do HMRC really owe me £13,000?' Twitter has now banned all political advertising, but it remains to be seen as to whether Facebook will follow suit.

All of these seem easy to decipher, they are obviously extreme examples. But do remember that if no one clicked on these adverts, they would not still exist. Because we are permanently plugged into the news cycle through social media, we have to be on constant alert. It's exhausting, never-ending scepticism, but it is what is required from all of us in twenty-first century society to remain informed and aware of what exactly is going on in the country. For far too long it has been easy not to care, to watch from afar and assume everything was running smoothly enough. We have out-lived that luxury and to ensure the survival of our very democracy we will be forced to tune in and educate ourselves.

Facebook has since issued a statement declaring that all ads running on its platform display an associated Page — in the top left corner, where users can click through to find out more. Although the relative sizes of the ads when they appear in the news feed means it is possible people could have clicked on an imprint-less ad without noticing it was being run by a Brexit campaign.

Initially, Vote Leave tried to stay clear of an immigration

driven campaign because they bought into the idea that Farage's perceived racism turned off more voters than it brought in. They had to make their campaign more subtle. Initially about taking back control of laws and borders and the cost of immigration, then slowly moving towards a more immigration-focused campaign strategy. You may be tempted to say that this was data-driven, that testing had revealed immigration-based arguments played best. Dominic Cummings and Paul Stephenson discussed the transition to immigration as far back as 2015, they believed that to go hard on immigration too soon would turn off voters at the beginning: 'It's there, it's a massive issue, we can go hard on it at the end – and we probably will go hard on it at the end – but we lose a whole bunch of people if we do it straight away.'[41] Farage told journalist Tim Shipman that he felt the moment the campaign changed was when Vote Leave began discussing the Australian points-based immigration system that he had long advocated for, 'within 48 hours I thought "we're going to win this"'.[42]

These dark ads were all able to fall on the fertile ground due to the cultural and political climate we inhabit. The loss of trust in mainstream media led people to look elsewhere for news whilst the algorithms on Facebook, Twitter, Google, and YouTube helped us construct echo chambers and epistemic bubbles that reinforced, radicalized, and fed our own belief systems. The ability for political campaigns to harvest data and target adverts with no oversight allowed social media to be flooded with hidden propaganda. It took advantage of the poor quality of online debate, our inability to objectively assess sources, and, if you were deemed by algorithms from Cambridge Analytica or Facebook to be a potential swing voter, you were bombarded with the same messaging over and over. You might hear ideas repeated in the bar, on your timeline, or discussed on the evening news.

As ideas slid seamlessly from memes, 'junk news', or dark

ads, to comment sections, through blogs and into the mouths of politicians, they became part of the national political conversation. The source of the original point or comment becomes irrelevant once the discussion has begun. Take the debate over Turkey as an example; the idea was propagated by dark ads on Facebook, repeated by members of the Vote Leave and Leave.EU campaigns and discussed in comment sections, Facebook groups, and links posted all across social media. It was plastered across the front pages and came up time and again in debates on TV and on YouTube. Turkey has been applying to the EU since 1987, the UK has a veto. This is all prefaced on Turkey overcoming human rights concerns, corruption within government and the courts. By 2015, of the 33 chapters of membership, Turkey had only negotiated one successfully – science and research, in 2006.[43] Yet, none of this seemed to matter (or even be mentioned). Turkey continued to rattle around as part of the debate. Perhaps most ironically, Brexiteers Boris Johnson and Daniel Hannan were founders of Conservative Friends of Turkey and Johnson declared a few months after the referendum that he would campaign to help Turkey join the EU.

When I first began writing and researching for this book, I had mystical ideas about the power of big data analytics. The data alchemists could descend from their Mount Olympus bestowing superhuman predictive powers upon those with a big enough cheque book. As I read further into the capabilities, I felt slightly underwhelmed at the predictive powers that they possessed. Whilst they can successfully identify your political beliefs, sexual orientation, and hobbies, as well as likes or dislikes, their ability to predict personality OCEAN traits was barely above random, hovering around 60 per cent. For a brief moment, my illusions had been shattered. Perhaps all the claims about the power of big data to influence politics were lies. Perhaps Cambridge Analytica was selling snake-oil.

In Outnumbered, David Sumpter expresses serious doubts

over the actual impact of microtargeting on social media. He reasons that this is no more powerful than human judgement[44]. Cambridge Analytica achieved two upsets in 1 year, there is something more than just luck going on here. Its true power lies in its sheer scale and the unaccountability that it provides to political campaigns. They can throw as much money at these adverts as they please with little to no oversight of the content or the source. They can happily flood social media with misinformation on misleading claims. Winning an election or referendum, especially one as partisan and binary as the Brexit vote (or the 2016 presidential election), is achieved by altering the minds of millions of people. The majority of people were already sold on one side or the other, long before the votes were cast. In the case of the Brexit vote, some Eurosceptics had been waiting decades to stick it to the bureaucrats in Brussels. Vote Leave only needed the support of enough of the swing voters, the independents, the undecided. If you invade social media with broadly targeted messaging, inducing fear and resentment amongst those who you believe to be receptive to your ideas, success need not be measured by turning millions of voters with a 100 per cent success rate, it simply needs a few thousand here and there. Bombard the population with your message over and over and you're likely to win over some converts, even if it is only temporarily, i.e. until the vote takes place. Anti-EU sentiment in the UK peaked during the week of the referendum vote when Vote Leave was spending most of their money. With the ability to reach into the Facebook feed of almost every eligible voter in Britain, it is not accuracy but scale that becomes important. Something around 1 billion impressions might be enough.

It would be lovely to be able to breathe a sigh of relief and tell yourself that the dark Brexit ads were confined to during the referendum. Sadly not. In the year to October 2018, a website known as mainstreamnetwork.co.uk spent an estimated £250,000 on anti-Chequers (the rough agreement put together by Tories during a marathon cabinet retreat in 2018) pro-Brexit adverts. One unknown website essentially footed half the bill that Facebook was sanctioned with by the ICO for data breaches and misuse during the Brexit referendum. It was insignificant for Facebook, they earn billions a year selling you and your data, so why on earth would they stop now? There are no legal requirements to make their advertising process more transparent and seemingly none on the way with the British government all but paralyzed dealing with Brexit itself. This is still happening and will continue to happen until we legislate against it.

BeLeave in Britain

BeLeave was founded by Darren Grimes, a then 23-year-old fashion student from County Durham. Grimes was a paid-up Liberal Democrat party member with a talent for graphic design and social media marketing. The BeLeave logo (not dissimilar to the Vote Leave logo) can be found on Vote Leave's own website, where BeLeave is listed as an 'outreach group'. They pursued a different type of digital campaign to the other pro-Brexit groups. They wanted to target younger or more progressive voters who would be expected to vote Remain, by focusing on the failure of the EU to be forward-thinking or progressive enough. The group's treasurer turned whistle-blower, Shahmir Sanni, told The Observer that:

> Vote Leave understood that they couldn't win the referendum if they specifically targeted angry Ukippers. They knew that they needed to target young liberals…They needed to target Green party members that didn't like the EU's environmental laws or liberal Eurosceptics like me that did hold fiscally conservative values but were socially liberal and understood the EU didn't support everyone, that it only benefitted Europeans.

Some of their online campaigns focused on:

- Why holders of EU passports could come freely to the UK whilst Commonwealth citizens could not.
- Attacking the EU for policies it claimed 'have driven African farmers into poverty'.
- How EU policies made it impossible for Britain to abolish the 'tampon tax'.
- EU penalties that could make Netflix streaming more expensive.

They were initially much more successful with their digital campaign than much of the fear-mongering rhetoric online spread by other pro-Brexit groups. Their Facebook posts were engaging more people than most paid advertisements by the larger campaign groups. One of the BeLeave videos reached 41,000 people in 1 day without any paid promotion. 'With funding, we could triple this amount,' they wrote in a pitch for extra funding from Vote Leave. When, in the final weeks, Vote Leave neared their spending limit of £7 million, senior directors suggested to BeLeave that, if they set up as a separate campaign, they would receive a donation for their own personal use. After initially expecting a donation in the tens of thousands, they were told to set up a bank account to prepare for a donation of £625,000.

BeLeave worked out of Vote Leave's headquarters and Carole Cadwalladr claimed that their website was co-ordinated and paid for by Vote Leave's head of outreach Cleo Watson. A Vote Leave campaigner that spoke to Buzzfeed said Grimes was often seen at the Vote Leave office and that he sat adjacent to high-ranking staff members. Shahmir Sanni told The Guardian that Grimes was well known at Vote Leave's campaign HQ. 'Everyone knew who Darren was...Everybody congratulated us and knew what role we'd played. He knew exactly how important we'd been.

He's a close friend of Dom Cummings.'

AggregateIQ boss Zach Massingham and Grimes ignored the suspension of campaigning out of respect for Jo Cox, the Labour MP who was tragically murdered during the campaign. Messages exchanged between some AggregateIQ and BeLeave employees released by the DCMS committee showed that they began running dark ads on Facebook just one day after her murder. The head of AggregateIQ, Zach Massingham, wrote to Darren Grimes, the co-founder of BeLeave, 'Once we turn everything back on we'll start to see results based on the new segments.' Grimes replied, 'Oh, fantastic.' Campaigning was not meant to resume for another 2 days, but the nature of the dark ads meant that the only oversight possible was hindsight. Shahmir Sanni told The Guardian:

'Zach was working in the Westminster office. He knew exactly what was going on with Jo Cox and he was communicating with Dom Cummings day and night.'

Vote Leave raised £9.2 million from members of the public in the entire 5-month regulated campaign period. In a blog after the campaign, Cummings wrote that Vote Leave had begun to raise far more money than it could legally spend in the last few weeks of the campaign. They donated 5 per cent of their funds to other campaign groups after this was 'suddenly allowed in the last few weeks of the campaign by the Electoral Commission'. He initially claimed that the organization got a letter from the Electoral Commission, signing off on these donations. But Carole Cadwalladr revealed in The Observer that the EC (finally) told her, 'we can't find any record of any exchange with us on the subject of donations between them from that period'.

Vote Leave drew up the legal documents for BeLeave to create a bank account so that it could accept donations of its own. Vote Leave's legal director said in an email to Grimes in May: 'Following our discussion I attach a typed-up first draft of the constitution.' But the donation never arrived in the bank account, it was sent directly to AggregateIQ in their name without ever touching the new BeLeave bank account. It was made clear to Sanni by Grimes that they wouldn't have control over how the money was spent. Grimes claims their spending, 'was done in isolation of Vote Leave...we didn't discuss with Vote Leave how we would spend the money apart from telling them that it was for our digital campaign and that is why we asked for the money to be paid directly to the company were working with, AggregateIQ'. Once the Electoral Commission began looking into the donation, Grimes said that he was impressed by the AggregateIQ website, but cached data shows that AIQ did not have a website at the time. AIQ, as we know, claims to have had a website since 2013.

In almost any referendum, there are likely to be numerous different groups campaigning on each side for a plethora of reasons. During the Brexit referendum campaign, this was no different, and the limit on spending per campaign group was set at £700,000 with the designated campaign allowed £7 million. Backing a vote to leave the EU were:

- Vote Leave
- BeLeave
- Veterans For Britain
- DUP
- Leave.EU
- GO

You may be asking what there is to stop powerful or wealthy groups from simply setting up numerous campaign groups in order to dodge spending limits? British electoral law expressly forbids any sort of collusion or co-ordination between groups. The Electoral Commission states that:

In our view, you will be very likely to be working together if:

- you have joint advertising campaigns, leaflets or events
- you co-ordinate your activity with another campaigner – for example, if you agree that you should each cover particular areas, arguments or voters
- another campaigner can approve or has significant influence over your leaflets, websites, telephone scripts or other campaign materials

According to Commission guidelines:

'When you work together in a joint campaign with a designated lead campaigner all the spending counts towards the lead campaign group's spending limit.'

It is, however, specified that 'Making donations to another campaigner is not working together.' If they are 'spending money as part of a coordinated plan or arrangement', then it's 'working together'.

'If campaigners work together as part of an agreed plan or arrangement, the combined referendum spending will count towards the limits for each campaigner involved. This may mean that campaigners involved will need to register even if they spend less than £10,000 individually.'

If groups work together they must declare the spending together towards the spending limit of each campaign involved in the co-ordinated plan. It is also illegal to set up numerous different campaign groups under separate banners, all of whom will co-ordinate together secretly whilst acting independently to the public and the Electoral Commission. Grimes also received £50,000 from an individual Vote Leave donor in the final 10 days of the referendum. The donor was Anthony Clarke and approached Grimes directly to offer the money (the following day he donated £40,000 to Vote Leave). Grimes told Buzzfeed:

'[He was a] donor that got in contact with us, that we checked against the electoral roll to ensure was permissible – he was... We received donations in a standard legal way and have reported them according to the rules.'

The timing of the donations meant they did not have to be declared until after the result was known, thus they could not be scrutinized before the vote. The total of £675,315.18 given to Grimes via four donations spread over 8 days took him close to the £700,000 limit any registered individual was legally allowed to spend in the campaign. Sanni told Channel 4 that everything that he and Grimes did was run past Stephen Parkinson, that they were essentially reporting to him. Then after the campaign, Sanni alleged that Grimes was being coached by Vote Leave staff members, being told what to say and what not to say. They were specific about exactly what to say if quizzed about AggregateIQ – that it was a donation in kind for services used by BeLeave.

Parkinson claimed in a blog post that he and Sanni had an 18-month personal relationship, ending in September 2017. That he only offered advice to Sanni in a personal capacity and that he apologized if the lines had become blurred. Sanni is gay but hadn't yet come out to his family, some of whom, including his sister, still live in Pakistan, where homosexuality can mean death. The post was taken down quickly upon request, but a journalist from the New York Times had received Parkinson's statement as an official comment from Theresa May. Parkinson later said Sanni should not have expected to go public with his story and keep their relationship a secret: 'I cannot see how our relationship, which was ongoing at the time of the referendum and which is a material fact in the allegations being made, could have remained private once Shahmir decided to publicise his false claims in this way.'

There's also evidence that BeLeave shared a dataset with Vote Leave. The House of Commons DCMS committee released a letter Facebook sent to the Electoral Commission noting that Vote Leave and BeLeave both used three sets of data to target audiences which covered the same audiences. Both groups strongly denied any co-ordination. Gareth Lambe of Facebook admitted that these were 'the exact same audiences'. The dataset that Facebook refers to in the letter is entitled '50million_ remains'.

The Guardian suspected that this was likely to be drawn from the competition that Vote Leave ran which offered fans the chance to win £50 million if they correctly predicted the outcome of every game in the European Championships that year. Dominic Cummings admitted that the competition to win £50m was a data-harvesting exercise on his blog.

Veterans for Britain

Veterans for Britain was registered by David Banks. He lived in the United Arab Emirates for 4 years, working in media relations across the Middle East. Banks was later to become the group's director of communications. They were set up 'to put forward the Defence and Security arguments for the UK to vote to leave the European Union' and have an interesting web of connections that has been explored by OpenDemocracy in incredible depth.

Lee Rotherham, former director of special projects for Vote Leave, became Executive Director of Veterans for Britain in October 2016. At Vote Leave, Rotherham's role included: 'coordinating with specialist researchers working in parallel for allied think tanks and groups...and maintaining formal and informal outreach across the wider Eurosceptic movement'. Rotherham has ties to Matthew Elliot's think tank, the TPA, and the Freedom Association, and now owns his own think tank, The Red Cell.

Veterans for Britain was led by their chairman, Major General Julian Thompson, a British army veteran who fought as far back as the mid-60s. He argued that it was NATO which had kept peace in Europe, not the EU. Richard Kemp, a former commander of British forces in Afghanistan with close ties to the Saudi Arabian regime, was on the advisory board. Gwythian Prins, another name on the advisory board, was on the academic advisory council of the climate change sceptic campaign group the Global Warming Policy Foundation. During the referendum, whilst he was an active board member at the Charity Commission, he was accused of failing to act impartially after he published an essay in support of Brexit. Charles Ronald Llewelyn Guthrie (or Field Marshal Lord Guthrie), a shareholder in Peter Thiel's Palantir Technologies, sits on the advisory board. Guthrie is a senior adviser to the chairman of Arcanum Global, a private intelligence agency that caters to governments and private companies to provide 'a host of bespoke strategic intelligence services'. Guthrie was also a non-executive director of Gulf Keystone Petroleum from 2000 to 2015 according to his House of Lords record. It's registered in Bermuda but operates mostly in Iraqi Kurdistan. He was the director of Petropavlovsk, a mining company from the far east of Russia, from 2008-2015, and was called 'Tony's General' due to his close relationship with Tony Blair.

Veterans for Britain only declared two donations to the Electoral Commission (EC). A sum of £100,000 from Vote Leave paid directly to AggregateIQ and £50,000 from Arron Banks' firm Better for the Country Ltd (who were also investigated by the EC). When The Observer asked Veterans for Britain where they heard about AggregateIQ, David Banks, Veterans for Britain head of communications, said: 'I didn't find AggregateIQ. They found us. They rang us up and pitched us.'

Rotherham spoke to openDemocracy about his time working at Vote Leave during their investigation into the Dark Money of Brexit. He said, he 'was in touch with a range of Eurosceptic campaigners, of which VfB [Veterans for Britain] was one group' – this in itself is not illegal and he denies all allegations of co-ordinating campaign activities and expenditure, denies referring AggregateIQ to the group, and denies being behind the £100,000 donation.

Investigations Galore

The Electoral Commission ruled that BeLeave spent their £675,000 with AggregateIQ by illegally co-ordinating with Vote Leave. The money should have been declared as spending by Vote Leave and meant Vote Leave spent almost £500,000 over the £7 million limit. Bob Posner, EC Director of Political Finance and Regulation & Legal Counsel, didn't mince his words. The investigation 'found substantial evidence that the two groups worked to a common plan, did not declare their joint working and did not adhere to the legal spending limits. These are serious breaches of the laws put in place by parliament to ensure fairness and transparency at elections and referendums.'

Darren Grimes was fined £20,000 after spending £675,000 on behalf of BeLeave (a non-registered campaigner) and wrongly reporting that spending as his own. The decision was later overturned on appeal on the basis that the Electoral Commission forms were too complex and that Grimes had filled them in to the best of his ability. The judge ruled that the EC had set too high a bar for determining whether BeLeave was a legitimate campaign organisation and the fine that had been levied was disproportionately high.

Vote Leave was fined £61,000 by the Electoral Commission and was referred to the police for further investigation after refusing to cooperate with the EC investigation and refusing to attend interviews. They were repeatedly obstructive and when documents were eventually made available they were found to be incorrect or incomplete. Bob Posner said the commission uncovered 'serious breaches of the laws put in place by parliament to ensure fairness and transparency at elections and referendums'. Matthew Elliott described the report as 'riddled with errors' and having got its 'conclusions completely wrong'. Vote Leave also handed the Electoral Commission an incomplete and inaccurate spending report, with invoices missing for £12,849.99 worth of spending.

The Electoral Commission noted that there appeared to be a pattern of coordination and raised the possibility that they could have been illegally working with other campaign groups. Christopher Wylie put forward a compelling case to the DCMS committee in May 2018.

> So, the first question that I have is: why? Why is it that all of a sudden this company, that has never worked on anything but Cambridge Analytica projects, that had no public presence, somehow became the primary service provider to all of these supposedly independent and different campaign groups... When you look at the accumulation of evidence, I think it would be completely unreasonable to come to any other conclusion: this must be coordination, this must be a common purpose plan.

Vote Leave were also fined £40,000 by the Information Commissioners Office for sending 196,154 unsolicited emails. What's more, they were willing to smear the whistle-blower who brought many of these issues to light. They denied, deflected, refused to cooperate with investigators and put up quite a hefty legal battle. Before coming forward with his story, Sanni went on to work for the TPA with Matthew Elliott. He was then fired when he went public with his story about BeLeave and took the TPA to an employment tribunal on grounds of unfair dismissal. Before he took his story to the press, he confronted Chief Executive John O'Connell who advised him against it. The TPA fought the case but dropped it after Sanni alleged that there was a co-ordinated effort to discredit him being made by a coalition of nine groups centred around 55 Tufton Street (we'll have more on them later), including the TPA, the office of Peter Whittle, former leader of the UK Independence Party, Civitas, The Adam Smith Institute, Leave Means Leave, The Global Warming Policy Foundation, Brexit Central, The Centre for

Policy Studies, and The Institute for Economic Affairs. Sanni's legal filing said he believed that the whistleblowing had been discussed at their monthly Tuesday meeting. Sanni threatened to demand disclosure of communication between the groups if they fought the case. The TPA dropped their challenge on 'pragmatic grounds'.

The Liberal Democrats were also fined £18,000 and Stronger In £1250 for failure to return a complete spending review. VfB also inaccurately reported a donation it received from Vote Leave. The Electoral Commission made it very clear in their report that they considered the fines they dished out to be 'inadequate for serious offences of electoral or referendum law' and the law needed a serious overhaul.

'Looking forward, we have recommended that government and parliament in the UK should change the law to enable us to impose substantially higher fines in line with other comparable regulators.'

OpenDemocracy has also raised further concerns over possible co-ordination, after reporting that Vote Leave, Leave. EU, GO, UKIP, and the DUP all used a tiny branding agency called Soopa Doopa, based in a house in Ely, Cambridgeshire. Vote Leave spent £637,000 with this agency, whilst the DUP spent nearly £100,000.

Vote Leave broke the law and have refused to cooperate with the Electoral Commission. If you don't care that they broke the law you're either incredibly cynical or just a partisan hack. Maybe you just don't care enough about politics at all to even be cynical. This does not in any way mean we should ignore the root causes of the vote, my gripe with this goes far beyond Brexit itself. It's a dangerous precedent to allow lawbreaking to go unchallenged, especially when the body charged with enforcing the law is crying out that the law is not fit for purpose in the modern world. The rule of law is a foundation of modern western democracy; if that is eroded then the state and the justice system hold less legitimacy. Technology is making it easier and easier to circumvent ageing electoral laws not designed for this kind of campaigning and our institutions lack the power to enforce what meagre laws we have.

In the final days of the referendum, Vote Leave spent almost their entire advertising budget. They bought themselves 1 billion views of dark ads aimed at exploiting the deep divides of Britain. They spent months testing which adverts were most receptive and collating data on voter groups, then bombarded swing voters with misinformation over the last week of the campaign alongside the firm who built the 'Database of Truth' for Cambridge Analytica. From what we have seen, these ads were propagating serious misinformation on issues like Turkey and other countries joining the EU. Misinformation and digital campaigning can be incredibly effective at polarizing an already divided society, attacking people's worst fears is an efficient way to get them riled up and emotional about a topic. It is imperative that dark ads be regulated or banned outright in future, for the integrity of our election process, though it seems unlikely that Facebook would cooperate willingly with these laws. Do you believe 1 billion targeted adverts could sway the right 600,000 people to change their vote?

7. Leave.EU

They may not have won the official designation, but Nigel Farage and Aaron Banks were determined to pump all their money, resources, and political capital into ensuring that Britain was freed from its European shackles.

In 2015 Nigel Farage was considering his position as UKIP party leader. He had just been defeated a seventh time as a parliamentary candidate. But his party had swept the European elections, pushing the Conservatives to third position, and now they had won 4 million votes in a general election. Cameron won a majority and had committed to a referendum on Europe before the end of 2017. The former City of London metals trader had led UKIP on and off since 2006 and he had pledged to resign if he didn't win the seat in Thanet.[45] UKIP members and donors alike begged their 'man of the people' to stay and the pint-swilling former commodities broker quickly gave in. After all, there was a referendum to win. He was determined not to let 'the posh boys' take over the campaign and lose. This was something he had been fighting for his entire life and the very reason he had founded UKIP. He was concerned that the 'Paleosceptics', the ageing Tory backbenchers who had argued against Europe since its conception, would run a campaign for Westminster, by Westminster, and from Westminster and would fail to generate enough grassroots support to win the referendum.[46]

Leave.EU was funded almost entirely by Aaron Banks. Banks first announced himself on the political scene with a £1 million donation to UKIP in October 2014. It was initially going to be a £100,000 donation until William Hague said he had 'never heard of him', at which point he increased it to £1 million.[47] It later became just over £400,000 in cash instalments over the next 6 months. Banks is so fond of Farage that after his success with Brexit he rented a £4.4 million house for him in Chelsea, complete with brand-new furniture, bills all included of course. He found a little spare change lying around to lease a 50k car complete with a driver, a private office, and a PA. Banks even chipped in a few hundred thousand to promote 'Farage' the brand in America. Goddard Gunster reportedly billed Banks' Southern Rock for a £108,684 Brexit party for Nigel Farage in Washington in July 2016. I'll say nothing about the irony of celebrating Britain's 'Independence Day' in a former colony. The bill included an £11,305,41 interview with Fox News anchor Tucker Carlson. They later billed Southern Rock £64,064 for a 'Nigel Farage Brexit Policy Luncheon' as well.

The insurance mogul ended up as the biggest pro-Brexit donor having given a £6 million loan to Leave.EU and £2.1 million to GO, a separate group, through his Better For The Country Ltd campaigning firm. He was one of UKIP's biggest individual donors and, in total, has spent £10 million on political contributions.

Following the election, Eurosceptics in the Conservative Party were waiting for the results of Cameron's renegotiation with Europe. They couldn't credibly say that they had waited to see what the prime minister had brought back from Brussels if they rejected it out of hand. After a while Banks became impatient and decided to set up his own Out campaign called 'In the Know'. The referendum was initially going to be offering the question 'Should Britain remain a member of the European Union? Yes/ No?', so this was to be a hilarious play on words.[48] In the Know were so keen to start the referendum campaign, they already had merchandise produced and branded before the question was changed upon recommendations from the Electoral Commission and were forced to scrap it all.[49] When the question was changed, voteleave.com was quickly purchased and someone set the page up to redirect to a YouTube clip of Rick Astley singing his 1987 classic, 'Never Gonna Give You Up'. (This is a long-running joke on the internet known as 'Rickrolling'.)

Elliott and Cummings were determined not to have Farage involved in the main campaign and the two campaigns openly fought with each other.[50] Farage was considered toxic by huge portions of the Conservative Party; they felt that 'if he couldn't win Thanet then UKIP couldn't win the referendum'.[51] Banks played psychological games with his rival campaign group, offering Cummings £250,000 to quit and work for him and calling Elliott to brag about their number of donations.[52]

To his credit, Farage did initially try to get the two campaigns to merge, but Elliott told Banks at the meeting that, 'I'll take your money but I have total control.'[53] Leave.EU also offered Lynton Crosby and his firm Crosby Textor £2 million to run the campaign but they turned him down.[54] Although Farage is a rumoured technophobe, he wanted to be able to use social media in a way they never had in an election campaign. He was keen to harness things like YouTube, which had helped him gather a cult following with all his speeches in the European Parliament being shared amongst Eurosceptics online.[55]

There were some delightful figures involved in Leave.EU, the DC to Vote Leave's Marvel. Alongside Aaron Banks and Nigel Farage stood George Cottrell, co-director of Brexit fundraising for UKIP. He worked in banking, specializing in 'offshore investment'. William Cash, a former UKIP candidate (not to be confused with Conservative MP Bill Cash), said that Cottrell's understanding of 'the murky and complicated world of shadow banking, secret offshore accounts and sophisticated financial structures' got him the job. In his book, Aaron Banks describes Cottrell as 'posh to the point of caricature and wilfully abrasive, but extremely generous when it comes to picking up the bar tab'. In December 2016 Cottrell was convicted of fraud as part of a money-laundering scheme. He served 8 months in prison on a plea deal.

Communications director Andy Wigmore played a significant

role in the campaign. Wigmore is Bank's right-hand man, half Belizean and half British, he actually represented Belize at the 2014 Commonwealth Games for shooting. The former Conservative Party operative and Banks are 'virtually inseparable' and refer to each other as Banksy and Wiggy. Wigmore had spent most of his life in communications but was appointed to the board of Southern Rock in 2014 and joined Eldon Insurance in December 2015, with no history of working in the industry.

Jim Mellon, a friend and business partner of Banks, gave £100,000 to the Leave.EU campaign, despite being a citizen of the Isle of Man and unable to vote in the referendum. Mellon was the one who first introduced Banks to Nigel Farage. Mellon made his estimated £920 million fortune in the wake of the breakup of the USSR. As the Russian state began to sell off its former state industries to private investors, Russian citizens were given certificates worth a small share of the post-Soviet state. Many Russian citizens vastly under-estimated their worth, considering them to be worth about the same as a bottle of vodka. Mellon bought up huge numbers of these certificates for next to nothing and within weeks he was a millionaire many times over. Mellon also co-founded the Regent Pacific Group in Hong Kong, who earned the nickname the 'Vulture Fund' for their unscrupulous business tactics. A vulture fund is a term for a company or fund that buys up poorly performing companies at below-market values in an attempt to turn them around and make short-term profits. An arrest warrant was issued by South Korean authorities in 2000 and renewed several times before expiring in 2010 over accusations that he was involved in the manipulation of share prices of the Regent Pacific Group subsidiary, Regent Securities. Mellon denied the allegations and was never formally arrested.

Richard Tice was the co-founder of Leave.EU who later became co-chair of Leave Means Leave. The millionaire property developer is also CEO of the £500 million asset management group Quidnet Capital who boast of their expertise in 'distressed debt'. A hedge fund will buy up the debt of struggling firms at a discount, either taking control or selling the assets as part of liquidation for more than they paid for the debt. It's disaster capitalism on a smaller scale. As co-chair of Leave Means Leave he has repeatedly rubbished the idea of a transition period, calling it 'completely unnecessary', and co-wrote a letter to Theresa May in December 2017 urging that 'it should be non-negotiable that the UK is free to diverge from EU rules and regulations when it leaves the EU on March 29th 2019'.

Raheem Kassam was a UKIP activist and former chief adviser to Nigel Farage. In 2014 he was appointed London editor of Breitbart News. Kassam also worked at the TPA at one time, the free-market lobby group founded by Matthew Elliot. He published a book in 2017 under the title 'No Go Zones: How Sharia Law Is Coming to a Neighborhood Near You' and told conspiracy king Alex Jones in an interview on Info Wars that 'there are vast swathes of Europe, and indeed here in the United States now, that are turning into enclaves for migrants...establishing their Koranic law, their Islamic rules'. He also ran to succeed Farage as party leader under the slogan 'Make UKIP Great Again'.

Farage gave his full endorsement to the campaign at the UKIP Conference in Doncaster, though he did later say he backed both campaigns because they were targeting different audiences. Leave.EU was going to be run differently to the idiots at Vote Leave. They didn't understand the ground game, the grassroots of UKIP, or the ordinary bloke on the street. In order to win the nomination and the referendum, they needed a way to compete with a campaign run by the political establishment and thankfully 2015 was providing them with the perfect case study.

Politics Killed the Reality Star

Presidential campaigns in America are incredibly long. They start 18 months to 2 years in advance and require more energy, resilience, and money than most of us will ever possess. Trump was already lighting up the Republican primary race when the Brexit campaigns were being set up. The first time Farage joined Trump on stage he said: 'Folks, the message is clear, the parallels are there...Remember, anything is possible if enough decent people are prepared to stand up against the establishment.'

Andy Wigmore, Leave.EU's communications director, described the Leave campaign as a 'petri dish' for the Trump campaign. He said: 'We shared a lot of information because what they were trying to do and what we were trying to do had massive parallels.' This is an example of Leave.EU using what I call Trumped-up politics. I felt I needed to use the term Trumped Up for two reasons:

1. Trumped-Up politics is about mimicking the tactics of Donald Trump, whereas the Americanization of politics is a slightly broader term.
2. Trumped Up sounds much better than Trumpisation.

The Brexit and Trump campaigns have been compared so much now it almost feels like a cliché, but there are several strands to Trumped-Up politics that I want to identify for you. They're often used by authoritarians but Trump has his own little flair with which he dominated the 2016 election. The three strands I want to highlight here are:

- Lies, insults, and vague solutions. All designed to outrage and draw the attention of the media. Break all norms and never apologize.
- Attack the press. Everything you don't like is fake news.
- Be the outsider. Harness the anti-establishment message. Make everything into a war, harness the anti-PC (Politically Correct) and liberal backlash.

I'm not sure how many of you watched the 2016 presidential

race unfold as closely as I did. I was living in Canada at the time writing for a local magazine and it was all over the news every day. Trump was the logical conclusion of America, the reality TV star, the real-life President McBane, 'elected to lead, not to read'. There were moments that will stick with me, that made me think, 'well, that has to sink him now, no one could survive this scandal'. The most vivid for me was the release of the 'Pussygate' recording. In case you need reminding, here is exactly what he said:

You know, she was down on Palm Beach. I moved on her, and I failed. I'll admit it. I did try and fuck her. She was married...I moved on her like a bitch. But I couldn't get there. And she was married. Then all of a sudden I see her, she's now got the big phoney tits and everything. She's totally changed her look...

Yeah, that's her. With the gold. I better use some Tic Tacs just in case I start kissing her. You know, I'm automatically attracted to beautiful — I just start kissing them. It's like a magnet. Just kiss. I don't even wait. And when you're a star, they let you do it. You can do anything. Grab 'em by the pussy. You can do anything.

Numerous Republicans denounced him and condemned him for it, including then-Speaker of the House Paul Ryan. Farage saw it differently: 'He's not running to be Pope,' he told Fox News. I used to believe that there was something capable of derailing Trump, that a revelation or an insult or a lie would be so great that it would derail him. I have since realized that there is no getting that crazy train off the tracks. He is made of some material that is not yet known to man. He lied, insulted, and bragged his way to victory. Banks believed that Leave.EU could use these tactics to build the Brexit movement. He and Wigmore flew to the US in August 2015 to get a first-hand taste of a Trump rally.

They openly ran what they called a 'Trump-style campaign' to generate publicity, 'do something controversial and not apologise for it. That was the usual method.' Tim Shipman wrote in All Out War that, '[Banks] decided as a deliberate strategy to be louder, more aggressive and more controversial than anyone else'.[56] In The Bad Boys of Brexit the Leave.EU funder described them as, 'blunt, edgy, and controversial, Donald Trump-style... If BBC Producers aren't spluttering organic muesli over their breakfast tables every morning, we won't be doing our job.'

Anti-fascist organization Hope Not Hate have credited Raheem Kassam with urging Farage to pursue a 'shock and awful' TV debate strategy. The pint-swilling Brexiteer has never been a vanilla figure. When he arrived late for a meeting in Wales in 2014, he blamed 'open-door immigration' for the traffic. By the time the 2015 General Election came around, he had become no stranger to using shock and outrage to his advantage. In the 2015 General Election leaders' debates, Farage complained of migrants using the NHS to get HIV treatment. By the time the Brexit campaign rolled around, Farage had become utterly shameless. Polling done before the referendum had told him that immigration was the biggest fear that people held about Europe and he was determined to exploit that:

If you think another 75 million poor people should have access to come to Britain, to use the Health Service, to use our primary schools, to take jobs in whatever sector it may be – if you think it's a good idea for our borders now to reach Iraq and Syria, then please vote to stay inside the European Union, because that is what is coming down the tracks at you.[57]

Leave.EU considered using faked photos of an alleged attack involving a migrant and released an apparently fake video that showed 'how easy it was to cross the channel'. Brexit campaigner and regular guest on Sky News's The Pledge, Phil Campion was accused of faking a film where he crossed the channel with imitation migrants. Leave.EU used the video to prove how easy it was for migrants or refugees to get into Britain illegally from Europe. Once the DCMS committee began looking into Banks and Leave.EU he sent committee member and Tory MP Damian Collins's constituents a letter calling him a 'disgrace' and a 'snake in the grass'. Alastair Campbell, Tony Blair's spin doctor, a man not unfamiliar with bending the truth, was taken aback by the way honesty was abandoned in 2016: 'I can't remember campaigns where you mount the campaign based on a lie, and then when it's exposed, you just keep going, as Johnson and co did.'[58]

After the 2015 attacks in Paris and Brussels and an NYE assault of a woman by migrants in Cologne, Leave.EU tweeted: 'The free movement of Kalashnikovs in Europe helps terrorists. Vote for greater security on June 23. Vote #Leave.' Farage echoed the statement. Wigmore was ecstatic, 'We knew it would be outrageous – it was. The vitriol that we got from the press worked...You spent absolutely no money whatsoever getting Nigel headlines.'[59]

Presidential runs can be incredibly costly endeavours; in 2016 Hillary Clinton spent a mind-blowing $1.2 billion, though Trump only spent $650 million. His early spend was a fraction of what is usually spent in a crowded primary, less than $20 million. Trump used outrage for free publicity and Leave.EU was determined to do the same. They blasted out deliberately provocative adverts and statements to dominate the news cycle and attract people who would not frequently vote. Wigmore told The Guardian: 'If people are outraged, you can do one of two things. You can ignore it and then it dies, or you can react and take it down, not apologise, but then see what the reaction is.' Banks claimed that they were able to generate millions of pounds of unpaid press coverage by being provocative. He told the New Yorker: 'We played the media like a Stradivarius, if we spent eight million in the referendum, we got thirty-five, forty million in free publicity.'

YouTuber Nerdwriter1 called Trump the 'Magician in Chief' in homage to his mystical ability to avoid consequences for his ever-growing list of scandals. He references the earliest known book of magic in English, 'Hocus Pocus'; one of the four traits required for magic is 'gestures of Body as may lead away the Spectators Eyes from a strict and diligent beholding his manner of conveyance'. It's a slightly more elegant version of David Cameron's description of Boris Johnson as a greased pig. Not only does controversy draw attention to you and allow you to control the narrative, it also acts as the perfect distraction from a previous scandal; 24 hours is a long time in today's news cycle. Trump and the Leave campaigns hopped from controversy to controversy, between the frying pan and the fire. The Argentine author Cesar Aira wrote in 2001: 'Any change is a change in the topic.'[60]

On 27 November 2016, the New York Times published a comprehensive look at the Trump business empire around the world and how his business interests might conflict with his ability to act impartially as president. Around 12.30 that afternoon Trump tweeted: 'In addition to winning the Electoral College in a landslide, I won the popular vote if you deduct the millions of people who voted illegally.' By the time that was out of the news cycle, Trump was already tweeting about how flag burners should be jailed or lose their citizenship. It's effective because it demands attention. It provided hours of free news coverage, increases your exposure to the wider public, and gives you control of the news cycle – you have framed the day's news coverage and forced your opponents to spend the day responding to your comments rather than promoting their own agenda[61]. Banks and Wigmore are a provocative pair not afraid to bend the truth, in front of the House of Commons DCMS committee

Banks said: 'We certainly weren't afraid of leading journalists up the country path, the same with politicians...Journalists are the cleverest, stupidest people on earth. They are clever, but they want to believe some of this stuff.'

The attention goes where Trump wants it to go. I'm not in the camp of people who believe Trump is a genius who craftily manipulated the media and political world. I think he is a thin-skinned narcissistic con man, he lashes out because he can't handle criticism, he can't be controlled and has no self-control or attention span to understand anything new in any depth. He does understand how to sell a brand, though: the Trump brand. When I wrote this book the number of lies Trump had told since he became president sat at a little over 12,000 (according to the Washington Post tracker). The truth means nothing to him. The entire world is a sales pitch and they've got to buy Trump. Trump socks, Trump steak, Trump Wine, and now the Trump Whitehouse.

The Leave.EU Facebook page was similarly blusterous. One post read, 'IMMIGRATION WITHOUT ASSIMILATION EQUALS INVASION', whilst another warning of the danger of freedom of movement was posted with a picture of a ticking bomb. The 'Breaking Point' poster was a low point in provocative campaigning. The highly controversial and shameless dog-whistle to racism was unveiled on the morning of Jo Cox's murder. Its reaction provoked Banks to pump money into controversial Facebook videos during the 2-day campaign hiatus. In a leaked email chain, Leave.EU's CEO, Liz Bilney, agreed, and noted that whilst campaigning was paused the video 'could get a lot of take up'. Banks replied, 'Exactly – press it harder.' Gawain Towler, former director of communications for UKIP, spoke about Banks' less than friendly behaviour:

'Of course they are going to make enemies. They make enemies because they don't play by the rules, because they've been written by other people.' All rules should only be permissible to the author of the rules apparently. So everyone should just make up their own rules? Seems like a fair society to me.

In No Is Not Enough, Naomi Klein warned that: 'Every election becomes an arms race, and the problem with arms races is that they are very difficult to slow down.' Needing to amp up the rhetoric to remain controversial and noticeable will become harder and harder. To set themselves out from the crowd politicians are likely to pitch themselves as ever-more extreme, lest they seem to be compromising with the enemy. Brexiteers have successfully pushed their rhetoric to the point where anything that is not the hardest Brexit possible is a betrayal. The Liberal Democrats have shifted from a democratic platform of a second vote to a desire to cancel the entire endeavour with an act of parliament. Theresa May went from the second Iron Lady to a Remainer saboteur; we went from the point where leaving would be a carefully managed procedure to potentially leaving with no deal because any Brexit that leaves ties to Europe is now a betrayal. Farage and Boris have both been accused of being Remainers (Farage by a caller live on his LBC show). No Brexiteer may ever be pure enough to truly deliver Brexit. The betrayal talk is effective because it is easy to parrot and, more importantly, it is provocative.

Trump's tweets are emotionally charged. Trump wants the reader to know exactly how they are supposed to feel. His habit of ending tweets with a single word or phrase like 'sad', 'big problem', 'witch hunt', or 'so true', has been widely mocked, but it can be a powerful framing device and form of communication. Trump, more than any other politician, speaks through Twitter. You can hear him reading the tweets (tell me I'm not the only one who reads his tweets in his voice?). It's been suggested that this makes him connect with people more through Twitter than most politicians. Deliberate or not, it allows him to emotionally frame his tweet and better connect with his supporters.

We lived through an age filled with bland politicians and

governed by an ideology that simply offers two versions of the status quo. Demands for change that would have bubbled up in trade unions, through demonstrations, and the usual political channels, has found its release valve in the digital world. All the hatred, the passion, the emotion that used to be found in the real world, in political movements, has been pushed online. Goodhart suggests that this resistance 'has reappeared in the chaotic and often shrill digital world'. The current dynasty of politics has been labelled as the 'banter era', where only the most ridiculous things are likely to occur. The modern media's pursuit of clicks above all else has enabled the fringes to dominate politics. In the Road to Somewhere, David Goodhart lays the blame at the feet of the press: 'A mass media that rewards the shocking and belligerent can act as a de-civilising influence; it is hard to imagine the triumph of Donald Trump in a pre-social media age.' Personalities have always dominated politics, that's nothing new. Figures like Trump and Farage (and now Boris) are the logical conclusion of a media that rewards outrage and rejects complexity. Most of the coverage surrounding the passage of the various pieces of Brexit legislation has focused on whether the bill will pass, not how it would affect the country. It's political theatre and not in any way helpful to the wider public. Comments that Trump and Brexit have killed comedy because reality is funnier than parody were widespread in 2016 and 2017. A reality TV host is leading the most powerful country in the world and politics in Britain is becoming more and more like the US, driven by entertainment value. Politics has killed the reality star.

Banks' use of the Leave.EU Twitter account was certainly a homage to Trump, he frequently abused Remain voters and posted wild unsubstantiated claims about Germany processing over 400,000 migrants every 40 days and about Turkish immigrants preparing to flood UK soil. They went as far as to ask: 'What does BSE mean to you? Britain Stronger in Europe or…Mad Cow Disease?' It's childish and provocative. It pushes buttons and demands it be addressed or recognized. It's pure 'Toddler in Chief'. Tell me these quotes from Banks don't sound like vintage Trump:

'Leave.eu is the biggest viral political campaign in the UK, with 3.7 million engagements last week on Facebook alone. Dwarfing political parties and other groups.'

'Channel 4 is packed with ex-Guardian journalists and left-wing activists, who create Fake news for a living!'

'The campaign must be doing something right to annoy all the right people consistently.'

The second Trump trademark I want to discuss here is attacking the press. It's an attempt to undermine the very institutions of the state and democracy. Make it personal if you can. The press are the enemy. They are there to prop up the liberal elite and line their own pockets. They are 'fake news'.

The idea that the press is 'fake news' is not entirely untrue. That's the most dangerous part and why it was so effective. On both sides of the Atlantic, they are obviously partisan and the majority support the ruling establishment because they are owned by the ruling establishment. One thing almost every mainstream outlet loves is war. They cheered on the war in Iraq, in Syria, in Afghanistan, and will cheer on the next war in Iran, Ukraine, or wherever it happens to be. The type of war that the press doesn't enjoy is one being waged against them. They flounder, they don't know what to do when someone doesn't respect their institution. CNN is 'fake news', they employ no real journalists, do no investigation, rarely break a story themselves, unless the story is something outrageous that was said on their channel. They do nothing but provide an empty political theatre in the form of their TV studio, somewhere to scream and shout at the enemy whilst they oversee it all, just waiting for the next clip to be cut and packaged for virality.

Trump was willing to play with the press, more than

any candidate in modern political history. Clinton actually encouraged the press to cover Trump early on in what was called the 'pied piper' strategy, believing that he would be the best person for her to take on in the main contest. Trump kept CNN waiting for hours at times, constantly streaming an empty stage as they waited with bated breath for the next outrageous scandal. The media lapped up Trump's madness, he was their golden cash cow, always three words away from dominating the next 24 hours of news coverage. In a way, the press in the US were caught in an abusive relationship, one they cultivated. They loved Trump, he drove up ratings with his unfiltered stream of consciousness. At the same time, they were receiving more and more abuse as the battle against CNN and MSNBC escalated. At rallies, the press core and camera crews often became the focal point of anger and hatred. The mainstream media were the enemy and Trump was prepared to go to war for the coverage. Leave.EU had a similarly paradoxical relationship with the press. Farage frequently appears on BBC programming, only to spend the time complaining of bias and how the media are dead-set against him. During the campaign the heads of Leave.EU were prepared to publish the personal numbers of the BBC's head of Westminster Robbie Gibb, Matthew Elliott, Dominic Cummings, Robert Oxley from Vote Leave, and UKIP's Douglas Carswell to lobby them to let Farage be a part of the Wembley debate.[62] Andy Wigmore described the Trump mantra: 'His way of doing things was to create as much noise by being as outrageous as he possibly could. We took that strategy and employed it...We had to play the press like Trump has, like the string of a lute.'

Trump's attacks on the press often get personal. In one of his famed early-morning Twitter rants, he called Mika Brzezinski, the co-host of MSNBC's 'Morning Joe', 'low I.Q. Crazy Mika' and claimed in a series of Twitter posts that she had been 'bleeding badly from a face-lift' when she attended the Mara Lago New Year's Eve party. Trump has known Brzezinski for a number of years and the pair are friends privately. This was either the calculated attack of a sociopath controlling the press narrative with skill and expertise or it was the uncontrollable lashing out of a spoilt narcissist who cannot handle criticism. Either way, it is tremendously effective. The best press strategy in the world folks, believe me. Banks had no issues matching Trump like-for-like with his attacks on the press. One journalist in particular has been a lightning rod for hatred and abuse, from Banks himself and the wider public: the 'Crazy Cat Lady'. Carole Cadwalladr described the campaign of abuse in a piece for The Guardian:

'Who has called me hysterical, insane, a lunatic, a mad woman, a conspirator, a loony, a mad cat lady, a nasty piece of work, a criminal, a bully, a mad cat lady, a loony, a tinfoil hat nutter, a hacker, a mad cat lady, a loony, a bitter Remoaner, a lone conspiracy theorist, an enemy of the people.'

The first time Cadwalladr wrote about Cambridge Analytica was December 2016. Since then she has been the recipient of a personal campaign of abuse or 'trolling' by Leave.EU and Arron Banks. They reported her to the police, Banks allegedly has an information file on her, and has engaged in quite a strong campaign against her on Twitter as well. She was depicted in a scene from the classic movie Airplane; her face was pasted onto a hysterical woman who people are lining up to slap to calm down. The last in the line is holding a gun. The caption reads stop being so hysterical and the whole video is set to the Russian national anthem. That was posted as an official video from the Leave.EU social media account. Cadwalladr accused them of spending the entirety of summer 2017 launching daily jabs at her on social media. Dominic Cummings has also accused her of spreading a 'loony conspiracy theory'. Carole has been showered with prizes for her journalism including British Journalism Awards' Technology Journalism Award, Specialist Journalist of the Year 2017 at the National Society of Editors Press Awards,

Orwell Prize for Political Journalism, and Reporters Without Borders 'L'esprit de RSF' Award (amongst others).

Banks has already chosen to take legal action against Carole following the TED talk she gave on how social media corrupts democracy. Not against TED the organization, not against The Guardian or The Observer, whom she writes and works for, but her personally. Carole has outright stated that Banks is 'trying to use litigation as a weapon against me to harass me and stop me doing journalism'. It's an attempt to silence journalists through intimidation and fear and can lead down a very dark road.

Before The Great Hack, the Netflix documentary about Cambridge Analytica and the Facebook data scandal, was even released, Banks was threatening to sue them. Legal action always seems to be the first line of defence. In 2019 press freedom campaign groups and charities authored a joint letter to the government warning that: 'The legal claim against Ms Cadwalladr, issued on 12 July by lawyers acting for Arron Banks, is another example of a wealthy individual appearing to abuse the law in an attempt to silence a journalist and distract from these issues being discussed by politicians, the media and the public at a critical time in the life of our democracy.'

You have to make the media scared to print the most damaging sources, that's how to avoid scrutiny. It's how dictators behave. Banks has said that, 'Carole Cadwalladr will have to stand up her wild claims in court and face the consequences or apologise.' The case had not yet been to court at the time of writing – maybe it never will.

Since Boris Johnson arrived in Number 10 there has been a clear and concerted effort by individuals inside Downing Street to spread misinformation via unsuspecting journalists. Journalists are often keen to get little snippets of insider news from a 'source inside No. 10'; anonymous leaks are often incredibly helpful in understanding what is going on inside an administration, but they can also be abused by journalists and politicians alike.

In September 2019 the Mail ran with the headline – 'Number 10 probes Remain MPs' "foreign collusion"'. The story was repeated the following day in the Daily Express, The Sun, The Times and on Breitbart. As has become the norm, 'a senior No 10 source' was quoted commenting: 'The government is working on extensive investigations into Dominic Grieve, Oliver Letwin and Hilary Benn [who tabled the Bill] and their involvement with foreign powers and the funding of their activities. Governments have proper rules for drafting legislation, but nobody knows what organisations are pulling these strings.'

Then, on The Today Programme, BBC presenter Nick Robinson asked Johnson about the investigation. He responded that there were 'legitimate questions' to be asked of the MPs. When Downing Street was asked by Peter Oborne and OpenDemocracy they confirmed that no investigation was taking place. The string of 'fake news' stretched from The Mail to the BBC without anyone asking whether the investigation was actually taking place. Robert Peston, the ITV News political editor, regularly falls foul of repeating government lines. On 25 September 2019, he cited a 'senior government source' who claimed it was possible for the PM to get around the Benn Act (the piece of legislation that attempted to stop Boris Johnson pushing the UK into a no-deal Brexit). Legal experts said this was rubbish, but the idea continued to bounce around the political sphere unimpeded. A former communications director at the Treasury commented that: 'That may be how Number 10 wants to operate: to allow the prime minister to look statesmanlike while the dodgier tactics emerge from an unnamed source.'

When Amber Rudd resigned from the Johnson government, she said she had frequently requested to see its legal advice on the prorogation of parliament and was refused by the Attorney General Geoffrey Cox. She even suggested that Cummings had intervened to stop her from being shown the legal text. Two weeks after her resignation, Tim Shipman, the Sunday Times political editor, tweeted that 'a govt source' had told him that Rudd was given 'every opportunity' to see the legal advice but chose not to. By publishing the quote anonymously Shipman was allowing Rudd to be called a liar by someone inside the government with no repercussions or need for proof. In his piece for OpenDemocracy, Oborne pulled no punches:

> Dodgy stories and commentary linked to Downing Street or government sources started to appear in the press and media after Johnson installed his own media team...With the prime minister's evident encouragement these Downing Street or government sources have been spreading lies, misrepresentations, smears and falsehoods around Fleet Street and across the major TV channels. Political editors lap it all up.

When the Yellowhammer document (the government assessment of the impact of a no-deal Brexit – not the worst-case scenario as was often claimed) was leaked at the beginning of Boris Johnson's term, the blame game began. The media, egged on by anonymous government sources, turned the leak into a Cluedo-esque search for the culprit; rather than examining the actual content of the document. The Times ran with the headline 'Boris Johnson accuses ex-ministers over Brexit chaos leaks', whilst The Daily Telegraph went with 'No-deal leak blamed on Hammond's Remainers.

This is a deliberate tactic to use a compliant press to spread the government line without the need to commit to scrutiny. By remaining anonymous it allows sources (and more specifically Dominic Cummings) to make unaccountable statements that are paraded around as the truth from inside government. The unwillingness to scrutinize these claims and the willingness of political editors to publish these statements is a symptom of the Mediacracy we discussed in Chapter 3. Trump, Leave.EU, and now the Johnson administration all pulled the levers of the press, manipulating them to their own gain and to date, the mainstream press has no comeback.

This brings us to the final tenet of Trumped-Up politics; be the outsider. As the public has become increasingly more hostile to political insiders, the new political vogue has become the outsider. Bernie Sanders almost won the democratic nomination out of nowhere, Jeremy Corbyn emerged from obscurity to lead the Labour Party, and Trump won the Republican nomination by virtue of having never worked in politics before. Being an outsider is now seen as an advantage to the point where even Jeb Bush (the brother and son of two former presidents) tried to claim during the 2015 primary campaign that he was a political outsider. It's a principle shared by Trump's former chief strategist, Steve Bannon. If you want to drain the swamp you can't be a part of the swamp. Farage has been a Bannon fan since 2012 when he invited Farage to spend a few days with him in New York and Washington, where Farage met the Breitbart team. Bannon has held a close relationship with Nigel Farage since and founded the UK wing of Breitbart in order to support UKIP. He declared this move as the latest front 'in our current cultural and political war'. Of Bannon, Farage once said, 'I have got a very, very high regard for that man's brain.'

After his success in the Brexit campaign, Farage was cheered as a hero at the Republican National Convention. There he met political maverick Roger Stone and Alex Jones, though he was more interested in securing a meeting with the former Apprentice star (Trump reportedly thought he could continue producing from inside the White House prior to his victory). At the convention, Farage also ran into the delegation of the Mississippi Governor Phil Bryant and they were invited to a Trump fundraiser. Bryant was a Farage fan, having seen his European Parliament speeches on YouTube. Trump and Farage first met on stage at a cocktail reception for around 60 donors in Mississippi. Trump was on stage when he asked, 'Where's Nigel? Where's the Brexit guy?' Farage made his way on stage where Trump greeted him with a hug and declared, 'This guy is smart. This guy is smart. We've got to do what he does.' Trump even suggested at one point that Farage should be made Britain's US ambassador.

Before Farage appeared on stage with Trump for the first time, he was a little taken aback by the atmosphere. A bubbling Trump rally, sound-tracked by a chorus of 'lock her up' and 'build the wall', was surely an intimidating spectacle to behold. But once he arrived on stage he loved every second of it. Farage now describes Trump as 'absolutely' his friend and has defended Trump on numerous occasions. He brushed aside Trump's dog-whistle to white nationalism after the death of an anti-racism protestor in Charlottesville when he said there were very fine people on both sides of the neo-Nazi march. In 2017, Farage appeared at rallies in support of accused rapist and paedophile Roy Moore who Trump had backed (if you remember we looked at this election campaign in Chapter 2).

Accompanied by Banks and Wigmore, on 12 November 2016, Farage became the first foreign politician to meet President-elect Trump. He told the New Yorker: 'The funniest bit was going out on the balcony for a smoke and being told by the Secret Service we could be targets for snipers.' After arriving unannounced they were welcomed in by Steve Bannon and spent around an hour with Trump, who was busy taking congratulatory calls from world leaders.

Bannon's Breitbart was accused by whistle-blowers within UKIP in 2017 of carrying out a, '"deliberate strategy" by Breitbart to wield influence over the Party in ways that emphasised views against migrants and other far-right positions'. They also said that Breitbart employees were working as unpaid UKIP volunteers and if true would constitute an indirect political donation by a foreign donor since Breitbart is owned by Robert

Mercer. The anti-fascist organization Hope Not Hate have described Breitbart's wider political agenda:

> Its political aims are to undermine and destroy the liberal democratic progressive consensus – understood as left-wing cultural hegemony – and the societal norms which are derived from it. Key here is a rejection of multiculturalism, manifest as opposition to immigration and liberal refugee policies. More generally its content stands in opposition to supposedly left-wing concepts such as feminism, LGBT+ rights and minority rights more generally.

Farage has been heavily critical of European leaders like Jean Claude Junker and Angela Merkl. Yet despite his disdain for democratically elected leaders, like Trump, he has confessed of admiration for Vladimir Putin. The Brexit Party leader told The Guardian in 2013 that he was the world leader he admired most. He, like Trump, admires the strongman. He described Trump in the second presidential debate as performing like 'a silverback gorilla...He is the leader of the pack, he is the leader of the tribe.'

Whether influenced directly by it or not, the UK political arena and the Brexit debate mimicked the Steve Bannon 'culture war' ideology that Trump embodied so well. Bannon's philosophy dictates that in order to bring about change in a political system or culture, you have to go to war – with elites, elitism, the establishment, with everything and everybody that stands in your way. That might include the press, the political norms, conventional wisdom, or facts themselves. Brexit and Trump both harnessed the anti-PC backlash against the Millennial 'snowflakes'.

Dr Emma Briant believes that, for Bannon, Britain was a key entry point through which he could aid the rise of right-wing populism across Europe and use it to help spread his vision of economic nationalism across the Atlantic to European shores.

He hoped to target and boost the National Front and Marine LePen in France, AfD in Germany, and FPO in Austria – amongst other groups. The UK was a crucial political battleground in upending the global political structure. A former employee of Bannon's who wished to remain anonymous told The Guardian: 'He believes that to change politics, you have to first change the culture. And Britain was key to that. He thought that where Britain led, America would follow. The idea of Brexit was hugely symbolically important to him.'

Everything has to be viewed through the lens of a cultural war where breaking the political system (perhaps beyond repair) is an acceptable casualty of the culture war. Brexiteers like Farage, Johnson, and Davis embraced this attitude and rejected conventional realpolitik, whether consciously or unconsciously. Brexit became a war on the political establishment, on the 'Westminster Bubble' that had for too long ignored the real people of Britain – the Somewheres. This was a battle for the soul of Britain, to rescue the sovereignty and independence of the United Kingdom from the clutches of European bureaucrats. This was not simply a fightback against the establishment, it quickly became much more than that.

Much like Trump was able to harness the xenophobic nature of middle America, the Brexit campaign opened wounds that many thought had begun to heal and disappear from British society. Brexit was fought on a war footing. The middle ground of discussion and complexity was swept aside as battle lines were drawn across the British Isles; Leave vs Remain, the elite vs 'the people', the powerful vs the disaffected, Anywheres vs Somewheres. The resentment of immigration, the dilution of 'British culture', and the rejection of the Anywhere worldview came bubbling up from the depths, wielded by a willing and eager Leave campaign. Legitimate discussions about immigration were shelved to be replaced by a war on the harbingers of multiculturalism. Banks and Farage fit the PC backlash like a glove. In 2013, Banks criticized former pupils of the school he attended who gave evidence against a teacher accused of sexual abuse – who later served 10 years for his crimes. He even came to his defence, acting as a character witness, and claimed those speaking out against the teacher were simply a part of today's 'victim culture' and were 'crying over spilt milk'. In the same interview Banks added that 'I abhor homosexuality and abuse of any kind.' He has also described fellow Eurosceptic Douglas Carswell as 'borderline autistic with mental illness wrapped in'.

Trump's ironic ascension to champion of the traditional working man was quite unbelievable for a man who lived his entire life in the aristocracy of New York. Craving the approval of its elite, whilst he looked on from his gold-plated Penthouse in Trump Tower. Farage, the public schooled former city trader turned career Brexit campaigner, was a similarly odd choice as 'man of the people'. For all their screaming about fighting the elite, they were both intertwined with wealth and power. Farage, much like Trump, was held up as the everyman, the champion of the working class, a straight-talking warrior who was just like you and me, sent to fight for the soul of Britain against the tyranny of Brussels and the EUSSR.

You can see and hear the Bannon culture war rhetoric in the language of the Brexiteers, the politicians, and the pro-Brexit tabloids. If you aren't with them, you are against them, a traitor to British ideals and to the very idea of Britain itself. To question their motives, their arguments, or their logic makes you an enemy, not a sceptic. You must be a remoaner and an official paid-up shilling member of the latte-drinking liberal elite. It allowed the Leave campaign to dismiss any and all questions and criticism throughout the entire campaign. To question the idea of Brexit, the unshackling of Britain from the chains of Europe to set sail into the wide world must mean you hate Britain. Do you hate Britain? Farage told Sam Knight at the New Yorker: 'There are no norms. They have gone. I love it.'

Data Dolphins

The official launch of Leave.EU took place on 18 November 2015. American political strategist Gerry Gunster explained what their strategy would entail. 'The one thing that I know is data,' he said. 'Numbers do not lie. I'm going to follow the data.' Banks had hired Gunster for his record. He had won 30 out of the 32 referendums he had taken part in in the US. With Banks and his cheque book backing them up, they were able to poll up to 100,000 people to get a clear view of the state of opinion across Britain.[63]

Leave.EU understood exactly who they had to target in order to win the referendum. This is common practice in politics, you identify the groups with whom you believe your message will have maximum penetration. Early on Leave.EU identified several categories of voters that they deemed as persuadable; this wasn't just about appealing to UKIP or Conservative voters, they needed Labour voters onside as well. These groups included those who left school early, currently work in lower-paid industries, and are struggling to get by, living pay cheque to pay cheque. According to Leave.EU's analysis: 'They are resentful of New Labour for allowing large-scale immigration and for failing to respond to their anxieties and concerns. For these groups the Labour party is dominated by professional politicians or socially liberal London-centric elites who treat them with disdain or condescension.'

It describes them as 'socially conservative in many respects' and 'not trusting of external sources of information such as politicians and the media if it does not conform to their world view. They are also slightly neurotic, which leads them to emphasise the unfairness in issues such as welfare or immigration.'

They had, in a way, identified the Somewheres that David Goodhart describes in The Road to Somewhere. UKIP brought a significant advantage to the Leave side, they already had spent years mapping and understanding the heavily anti-EU vote, where the hardcore support was and who to target digitally. Remain had no such body or party to draw upon, they were starting from scratch. Leave.EU, Cambridge Analytica, the RMT Union and Trade Unions Against EU, and pro-Brexit Labour MP Katie Hoey got access to Labour's 2015 election data prior to the official beginning of the Brexit campaign. The dataset contained 107,406 postcodes labelled 'blue-collar' and 131,691 identified as 'deprived and disaffected'. The datasets are believed to have been compiled by Ian Warren, who was headhunted by Labour for Ed Miliband's campaign after the success he had with UKIP in 2010. Warren, however, was not amongst the 'Man of the People's' cult following:

'Should Mr Farage be used, it should be done sparingly and only to "keep the pot boiling" for such voters. Mr Farage could be used effectively at times of a specific crisis in migration, for example, to underline the negative effects of immigration on working households.'

He met with Cambridge Analytica to discuss the use of this data at the end of 2016. A February 2016 email from Warren to Aaron Banks, Kate Hoey, Julian Wheatland of Cambridge Analytica, Brittany Kaiser, Liz Bilney, and Andy Wigmore, discussed his datasets and encouraged them to come to him for advice if they required any. When Warren was asked by a journalist on a call whether he had the right to retain and use the data compiled during his time at the Labour Party, he abruptly ended the call. Andy Wigmore confirmed that it was Labour data that informed where they deployed Nigel Farage.

The Great Hack follows the stories of Brittany Kaiser and David Carroll as a part of the Facebook and Cambridge Analytica data scandal. Whilst Kaiser was a student, she had worked for Amnesty International and on the 2008 Obama campaign as part of the media team. She began to become disillusioned by their apparent lack of impact upon the world. That's when she met Alexander Nix. He told her, 'let me get you drunk and steal your secrets', and in December 2014 she was offered a job at Cambridge Analytica. In The Great Hack, she describes how joining the company changed her, the people she socialized with, and her outlook on life – she became more conservative, even joining the NRA to help her better understand the right wing of US politics. Kaiser worked as a senior executive at the firm until January 2018 and at one point even had a key to Steve Bannon's townhouse in Washington. When asked to testify in front of the DCMS committee, Kaiser told parliament that she had seen with her 'own eyes' how Leave.EU had targeted customers of Eldon Insurance – owned by Banks – using their private data to promote anti-Europe messaging and that employees of Eldon Insurance staffing a call centre were working for Leave.EU. She told MPs:

'They all had a computer, and a headset, making calls that I assume were normally sales calls, or calls for customer assistance and advice, and instead they were calling people to undertake a survey – they were talking to those people about their interests in leaving the European Union and issues around Brexit.'

Kaiser also told the committee that Banks asked Cambridge Analytica to combine data from different sources to build their voter targeting software: 'He asked us to design a strategy where we could work with Leave.EU, UKIP and Eldon Insurance data together.' During a visit to Eldon Insurance HQ around November 2015, she found that Eldon employees were actively working on the Leave.EU campaign. She saw them taking survey data and discussing views on Brexit and alongside another Cambridge Analytica colleague, she gave advice to them on how to improve the survey methodologies. She told the DCMS committee,

'I was under the impression, by what they told me, that every single individual that they were pulling up to call was actually a lead or a current customer of Eldon Insurance or Go Skippy... They had probably already been doing that around a month or two.'

An OpenDemocracy investigation found that Eldon employees had been working for Leave.EU undeclared and that Eldon had been operating as an extension of Leave.EU. Numerous staff moved over from Eldon temporarily, despite Banks' frequent public assertations to the contrary. One anonymous employee told OpenDemocracy: 'You were told to stop what you were doing and do something for Leave.EU or Grassroots Out or the GO movement.'

On Tuesday 12 June, Aaron Banks and Andy Wigmore were set to appear before the DCMS committee, but on the preceding Friday the insurance duo put out a letter about how they were refusing to attend and accusing the committee of colluding with pro-Remain groups. In the letter released on Twitter, Banks wrote:

'It is perfectly clear that the committee, which comprises only of Remain supporting MPs, is conducting a coordinated "Witch Hunt" of Leave groups involving the Electoral Commission & the ICO. You have called no witnesses from the Remain campaign or associated groups.'

He accused the committee of colluding with the Fair Vote Project, who have taken legal action in the US alleging that Leave.EU data was illegally sent abroad to be processed at the University of Mississippi.

Brittany Kaiser told parliament that Banks had set up Big Data Dolphins to work with a team of scientists at the University of Mississippi after he stopped negotiations with Cambridge Analytica. Banks denies the allegation and complained that the MPs had released evidence from a witness in that case early 'in order to aid this group'. The case has since been dismissed by a US Chancery Court.

Cambridge Analytica
We've talked a lot about Cambridge Analytica, they denied having ever done any work for Leave.EU, but questions

remain unanswered. Arron Banks said that they did speak to Cambridge Analytica about working with them, 'if we won the official designation – but we didn't'. In The Bad Boys of Brexit, for the entry dated 22 October 2015, Banks wrote: 'We've hired Cambridge Analytica, an American company that uses "big data and advanced psychographics" to influence people.' Banks has since walked back his claim, disputing that they ever hired them or paid for any work. He claims that their fee was too high and that they were attempting to illegally subvert campaign finance laws. He tweeted, 'CA wanted a fee of £1m to start work & then said they would raise £6m in the states. We declined the offer because it was illegal.' When questioned on this by the parliamentary committee on fake news, Nix responded: 'That is totally untrue.' A leaked email from 2015 showed that Banks asked Cambridge Analytica about fundraising in America for Leave.EU, 'We would like CA to come up with a strategy for fundraising in the states and engaging companies and special interest groups that might be affected by TTIP' — the controversial Transatlantic Trade and Investment Partnership that would allow corporations to sue governments over lost profits. Cambridge Analytica even responded saying they were on board with the idea and would develop a proposal which would include 'US-based fundraising strategies'.

Wigmore said that Robert Mercer had been 'happy to help' and Cambridge Analytica had given its services to the campaign for free. It was the general secretary of UKIP, a British lawyer called Matthew Richardson, who arranged Leave.EU's introduction to Cambridge Analytica. Wigmore told the press: 'We had a guy called Matthew Richardson who'd known Nigel for a long time and he's always looked after the Mercers. The Mercers had said that here's this company that we think might be useful.'

Brittany Kaiser sat on the panel at the Leave.EU launch event and was described on the Leave.EU Facebook page as their director of program development. She discussed the 'large-scale research' that would identify what people were really interested in and how this would 'help inform our policy and our campaigns'. When speaking to Bloomberg about their work, Kaiser commented that the first stage of her work with Leave.EU involved interviewing 'close to half a million Britons'. Typical polling samples conducted by firms such as YouGov are of about 1200 people. This sort of research would cost hundreds of thousands of pounds, but nothing has been declared or accounted for by any campaign. A now-deleted post on Leave. EU's website, entitled The Science Behind Our Strategy, reads, 'While Cambridge Analytica will be helping with the data, Goddard Gunster...will be helping us turn that data into a comprehensive strategy'.

In November 2015, Andy Wigmore tweeted a link to a PR Week article discussing how they were working with Cambridge Analytica. Then, on 2 February 2016, Banks tweeted: 'Our campaign is being run by Gerry Gunster (won 24 referendums in the USA) and Cambridge Analytica experts in SM.' (This post has since been deleted, though screenshots exist). In an interview in February 2016, Alexander Nix told Campaign magazine: 'Recently, Cambridge Analytica has teamed up with Leave.EU... We have already helped supercharge Leave.EU's social media campaign by ensuring the right messages are getting to the right voters online.' Then in March 2016, Brittany Kaiser gave yet more details: 'Well, actually right now we are working on the Brexit campaign so we are working with all three of the main parties...It's a very exciting campaign because it has forced the British government to run their third ever national referendum.'

Long after the referendum, Banks was still saying that they had worked with Cambridge Analytica. In January 2017, Banks responded to a tweet about the company with: 'Interesting, since we deployed this technology in leave.eu we got unprecedented levels of engagement. 1 video 13m views. AI won it for leave.' Andy Wigmore told The Observer that Cambridge Analytica harvested personal data and targeted voters on Facebook with anti-EU messaging. He described Facebook as a crucial and powerful tool for Leave.EU's armoury and remarked that the accuracy of the technology was 'really creepy'. A leaked 10-page document produced by Cambridge Analytica for Leave.EU titled 'Big Data Solutions for the EU Referendum', claims that their tech was capable of singling out Brexiteers among voters, donors, politicians, and even journalists. By February 2017, Nix was starting to play down the work done with Leave.EU. He told Bloomberg Businessweek: 'We did undertake some work with Leave.eu, but it's been significantly overreported.'

When questioned on these links by The Observer, a Cambridge Analytica spokesman said: 'Cambridge Analytica did no paid or unpaid work for Leave.EU.' Lawyers for Cambridge Analytica and SCL Elections accused The Observer of taking part in a libellous campaign of vilification, designed to besmirch the reputation of their clients. They claimed the stories contained significant inaccuracies and that their clients had done nothing wrong, broken no laws, infringed upon no one's rights and had not been part of a 'shadowy' or unlawful campaign to subvert British democracy. Just days after Cambridge Analytica denied any involvement in the Brexit referendum, Richard Tice, the Leave EU co-founder, spoke to Bloomberg on the phone and stood by his earlier statements that CA had worked for Leave EU and that their denial was 'down to politics'.

When Alexander Nix was quizzed by parliament on the issue he told them unequivocally that they only did some initial scoping work for them, pitching to them, during one meeting that he attended, and that both he and Cambridge Analytica were the victims of a runaway press who jumped onto a dangerous conspiracy theory.

We've been, again, crystal clear to all media including The Guardian, who really propagated this story from day one, based on nothing. Carole Cadwalladr has made it her personal mission to come after us again, living in denial about the outcome of the election. She cannot accept that the British people wanted to leave Europe and she's made it her mission to vilify us. We did not work on Brexit. We didn't do a little bit of work. We didn't do a lot of work. We did no work on Brexit. We were not involved in the campaign for either Leave.eu or Vote Leave, at all.

On 21 April 2017, the Electoral Commission began their first investigation into Leave.EU. They wanted to look specifically at whether all Leave.EU's donations had been permissible and if their spending return was accurate. At 3.37am the following morning, Alexander Nix sent an email to Kaiser and other CA executives stating that the company had 'nothing to worry about' from the Electoral Commission. Nix was keen to get out in front of the story and ensure that the 'narrative' was that 'we did not end up working together'. He was concerned that it would be argued that they had contributed to the campaign in the form of 'goodwill' and was keen to avoid this becoming the dominant part of the story.

He wrote: 'Whilst there is no law against "lying", I think that we need to establish the narrative that precipitated these two admissions, such that we can mitigate loss of credibility...both the press release and Brittany's comments indicate that CA had already completed work for the campaign.'

Kaiser told parliament that the CA work that had been done included analysis of data provided by UKIP. This work took a number of weeks and required 'at least six or seven meetings' with senior officials from Leave.EU. Kaiser said that she felt she had lied by repeating Cambridge Analytica's official line that it had done 'no paid or unpaid work' for Leave.EU. She confirmed that Leave.EU did not pay for the work: 'In my opinion, I was lying...In my opinion, I felt like we should say, "this is exactly what we did".'

Kaiser said that initial work began in autumn 2015 when she visited the UKIP and Leave.EU offices. Both organizations were happy to share proprietary data with CA's lead scientist, David Wilkinson. He asked for access to Facebook pages, subscriber, donation and local group data, email engagement, and call centre records. However, it is unclear as to how much of the data he was actually given access to. What we do know is that CA did some work based on UKIP data. UKIP had done some survey work on why people wanted to leave the EU (or why they didn't) and also had a bank of membership data that helped CA build some personality profiles on British voters. Kaiser said, 'that was work that would normally be paid for'. Despite this initial work, it seems a full report was never delivered after Leave.EU pulled out of the deal and no payments were made. In a letter to Damian Collins in July 2019, Kaiser stated that she believed that the datasets processed by Cambridge Analytica were later used by Leave.EU. She also alleges that: 'Despite having no signed contract, the invoice was still paid, not to Cambridge Analytica but instead paid by Arron Banks to UKIP directly. This payment was then not passed on to Cambridge Analytica for the work completed, as an internal decision in UKIP, as their party was not the beneficiary of the work, but Leave.EU was.' An email from Julian Wheatland reads, 'I had a call with Andy Wigmore today (Arron's right-hand man) and he confirmed that, even though we haven't got the contract with Leave written up, it's all under control and will happen just as soon as Matthew Richardson has finished.'

Banks and UKIP have both denied that any money was transferred and say that neither received any data from Cambridge Analytica. Ian Lucas from the DCMS committee has called for the Electoral Commission to reopen their investigation, but no action has been taken so far.

When Nix was questioned by parliament on the Campaign

Live piece that discussed how Cambridge Analytica had teamed up with Leave.EU, he brushed it off as the work of an 'overzealous PR consultant' based on work they were hoping to do for Leave.EU. When asked about Brittany Kaiser appearing at the Leave.EU launch and her speech on work they were about to undertake with Leave.EU, he told MPs:

'It is not unusual, when you are exploring a working relationship with a client, to speak in public together about the work that you hope to undertake.'

OpenDemocracy also revealed that Cambridge Analytica discussed working with Banks' firm, Eldon Insurance, despite previous claims that Leave.EU had never involved Eldon or Cambridge Analytica. Invoices received by the Electoral Commission also revealed that Leave.EU was making payments to a firm named Advanced Skills Institute. The company is otherwise known as ASI Data Science. They have done work alongside Cambridge Analytica and share a host of current and former employees with them. Both have publicly denied having any formal relationship. ASI Data Science also worked with the Home Office on a £600,000 contract developing a tool that can reportedly detect '94 per cent of Daesh [IS] propaganda with 99.995 per cent accuracy' on online platforms.

Leave.EU were the subject of two separate investigations; one by the Information Commissioner's Office about possible illegal use of data and another by the Electoral Commission. They were concerned about CA's 'use of personal data' and announced that they were initiating a wider investigation into 'the data protection risks arising from the use of data analytics, including for political purposes'. British law forbids donations from foreign donors, in order to maintain the integrity of the British Electoral system. The Electoral Commission defines a donation under the Political Parties, Elections and Referendums Act 2000 (PPERA) as 'money, goods or services given to a party without charge or on non-commercial terms, with a value of over £500'.

A permissible donor includes any one individual on a UK electoral register, most UK-registered companies, UK trade unions, LLPs, building societies, and unincorporated associations that carry out business or other activities in the UK. It is illegal for a company to be used as a front or middle man for a foreign actor to channel money to a UK party. If you receive a donation, you have 30 days to decide whether or not to accept it and you are required to ask where the donation is from and consider whether the donation is from a permissible donor. If you are unsure, you must return the donation within 30 days.

Cambridge Analytica is a US company, owned by US citizen Robert Mercer. Thus it would be illegal to offer their services, consulting or technological, to a British company in kind as it would constitute a gift/donation. They cannot legally provide services in the form of donations to a UK campaign or political party, yet they don't appear on the Leave.EU campaign spending records. In front of parliament, Nix maintained that 'No company that falls under any of the group vehicles in Cambridge Analytica or SCL or any other company that we are involved with has worked on the EU referendum.' The idea that any foreign entity, company, or individual should be trying to influence the UK electoral process or political landscape should be cause for concern for anyone who cares about the direction of politics in this country. There is nothing patriotic about allowing a foreign billionaire to aid political movements that have severely disrupted Britain's political landscape.

Money, Money, Money

Better for the Country Ltd provided £12.4 million in 'administrative services' to Leave.EU up until May 2016. A business associate of Aaron Banks has claimed that because these donations and services were given before the referendum spending cap took effect in April 2016, they are perfectly legal. This £12m includes the £9m figure Banks was already known to have donated/

loaned to Leave.EU. He also gave £2 million to GO via Better for the Country Ltd in the form of 'merchandise, leaflets, billboards, pens, badges and other paraphernalia'. Questions have been raised over how he could afford to invest so much in political campaigning.

In September 2013, Banks was forced to resign from Eldon and Southern Rock by Gibraltarian regulators after Southern Rock was found to be trading whilst technically insolvent. He had to provide £60 million in extra funding to keep the company together, on top of £40 million he already claimed to have pumped in to save the company. Yet, just a year later, he had the funds to bankroll UKIP, buy some diamond mines, invest in chemical companies, wealth management firms, and even set up a few money-draining political consultancies. Banks' 2014 spending alone came to an estimated £5 million – odd considering the financial strain he was under ensuring Southern Rock stayed afloat. This is estimated to be just under a quarter of his total gross earnings of £22m – from his various businesses – since 2001. OpenDemocracy were keen to hold a spotlight to Banks' financial dealings and questioned how it was possible for him to have spent so much money on politics, without a hidden source of income.

Our review of the publicly available records for Banks' business empire, and his own public statements has revealed a patchwork of legal disputes, regulator interventions, and poor corporate governance. Two of Banks' claimed previous employers have denied he ever worked for them. The value of his businesses is materially lower than Banks' own inflated boasts and, while still a wealthy man, was he wealthy enough to give so much to the Brexit campaign, without some other undisclosed source of income?

Wigmore claims that Banks was able to fund Brexit through the sale of the New Law Group. In 2014, NewLaw Legal was sold in a deal that valued it at £35 million. However, according to the Financial Times, Banks had sold his share of the company 18 months prior to the sale, for an estimated £1.75 million. Banks himself states that much of his fortune was made from the sale of Brightside, an insurance company he co-founded.

Private equity firm Anacap bought out his company Brightside in 2014 for a reported £127 million, but Banks claimed to have made £145 million from the sale (a 144 per cent share). Company documents reviewed by openDemocracy show Banks made £22 million from share sales, £1.2 million in salary from serving as the group's CEO and Chief Insurance Officer, and just £270,000 in dividends. The firm has also since alleged in court that they discovered 'serious and widespread failings' throughout the company, many of which dated from Banks' time as CEO and Chief Insurance Officer. They also claimed in court that:

- All the purchases of Banks' companies were found to be worth less than Brightside had paid for them.
- The E-systems software he acquired barely functioned.
- The Brightside website was hacked and remained inoperable for more than a month.
- The company was 'in breach of its banking covenants and insolvent on a net asset basis'.
- There was no system in place for handling client funds.

Whilst he was at Brightside, Banks had been able to prop up and re-finance Southern Rock through the purchases of E-Cars, E-Systems, E-Development, and E-Bike. An investigation by Gibraltar Financial Services Commission and the Financial Conduct Authority in London concluded that Southern Rock had been trading without sufficient reserves. This is when Banks was forced to resign and was effectively barred from holding a position within an insurance company.

Southern Rock was eventually able to turn a £42 million profit in 2015 by selling rights to future income to ICS Risk Solutions for £77 million. They sold the rights to the 'ancillary income' on its motor insurance policies for £17.5 million, and the rights to the 'finance arrangement fees' for £60.2 million – all for only 197,000 motor insurance policies. The sale coincidentally came just a few days after Louise Kentish (Banks' wife) was appointed to the ICS board. Banks claims to own 90 per cent of ICS, but a Source Material investigation found that he only owns 50-75 per cent. The relationship between the companies is under observation by Gibraltar's Financial Services Commission. These cash injections meant that Southern Rock met new EU solvency laws which were described by Banks as 'a good example of something no-one really wants' being imposed by Brussels.

Banks is not alone in his troubles. The co-founder of Southern Rock, Alan Kentish, has had a wild ride over the past few years. In October 2017 the CEO of the STM group was arrested over failure to notify the authorities of potential money laundering. Staff filed reports of suspicious activity 19 times in 18 months, yet none of these incidents were passed to financial regulators. Eventually, they were acquitted, but they were told that they had to clean up their act and their money-laundering compliance officer was banned from holding a regulated position in Jersey. Banks invested in STM Group in 2004 and was the largest shareholder until 2015 when he sold up. STM is mainly involved in setting up offshore trusts that make it difficult to discern the owner of certain companies or assets, what they call 'wealth preservation solutions'. In 2014, Banks bought over £600,000 worth of shares to add to £900,000 he already owned.

In 2002 STM were sued by UK tax authorities for setting up a trust for someone suspected of fraud via a £100-million VAT scam. Early in 2017 regulators told them that they were 'fundamentally concerned' about its compliance with anti-money laundering laws. They were also concerned with STM investing pension savings into Trafalgar Multi-Asset Fund which collapsed in 2016 and is now under investigation by the serious fraud office.

In 2015 they became the first company in the history of Jersey to be prosecuted for money-laundering compliance failures whilst managing operations for Henley & Partners. STM has been fined twice in the past 2 years and Kentish has been banned temporarily in Malta after he failed to tell regulators in Jersey that Gibraltar regulators forced him to resign Southern Rock directorship.

In April 2014, Banks bought £2 million of shares in an AIM-listed chemicals company called Iofina – a sector he had shown no prior interest in. It had never turned a profit and drained large amounts of capital as chemical prices shrank due to reduced demand. In June 2014, he set up Chartwell Political, a PR company that eventually worked on the Leave campaign along with Jim Pryor, a former Tory party spokesman who had also worked on FW deClerk's campaign against Nelson Mandela in South Africa. The company racked up losses of over £300,000 by June 2015. He continues to control Southern Rock and Eldon Insurance, owner of the GoSkippy brand, through his Isle of Man-based holding company ICS Risk Solutions.

The real question here is, if he does (or had) a hidden income source that paid for his Brexit donations, then who is behind it? Tom Keatinge, the former banker at JP Morgan now working as an anti-money laundering expert at the Royal United Services Institute, has commented that even when looking only at publicly available information about Banks' businesses, 'red flags do pop out all over the place'. To him the refinancing of Southern Rock 'appears, from an outside perspective, to be an attempt, at several points, to conjure value from thin air'.

Russia Connections

Just as I stated when mentioning Russian connections in Chapter 5, I would be doing myself a disservice to ignore the plethora of connections between the Leave.EU campaign and representatives of the Russian state. Back in November 2017 Banks issued a statement rubbishing the idea of any connection between himself, Russian money, and the Brexit campaign. He wrote in a lengthy statement that: 'The Guardian allegations of Brexit being funded by the Russians and propagated by Ben Bradshaw' were 'complete bollocks…My sole involvement with the "Russians" was a boozy six-hour lunch with the ambassador where we drank the place dry (they have some cracking vodka and brandy).'

In September 2015, Andy Wigmore met the suspected intelligence officer and Russian diplomat Alexander Udod at the UKIP conference. Not long after he arranged a meeting with the Russian Ambassador, Alexander Yakovenko. Udod was thrown out of the country after the Sergei Skripal poisoning. During November 2015, Aaron Banks and Andy Wigmore attended several events at the invitation of the Russian ambassador, who has been a subject of interest to the Mueller investigation

They visited the Russian embassy the day after the Leave.EU launch event, where they first discussed a business deal involving six Russian gold mines in Siberia with Russian businessman Siman Povarenkin (a rumour flew around that they even drank vodka distilled for Joseph Stalin). In a June 2018 interview, Wigmore told The Washington Post his goal for the meeting was to discuss finding a buyer for a banana plantation in Belize. It's unclear whether the deal went ahead, the only evidence we have to the contrary is a Banks tweet from 17 July 2016: 'I am buying gold at the moment & big mining stocks.'

In February 2016, Banks flew to Moscow to discuss the mining deal further, the gold mines were reportedly owned by the Russian state-owned Sberbank. The Guardian reported that the deal could have reaped profits in the billions of pounds. Banks told the DCMS committee that the deal was simply a proposal that never went through. Also reported to have taken part in the deal was Field Marshal Lord Guthrie of VfB and Peter Hambro. Hambro, also known as 'Goldfinger', co-founded Petropavlovsk (for who Guthrie was a director for 7 years) based out of London with massive operations in the desolate far east of Russia. The Leave.EU duo audaciously invited Yakovenko and another senior Russian diplomat to a pub in Millbank to watch the referendum results come in (sadly Yakovenko had commitments in Moscow). Yakovenko asked them for a number for someone from the Trump transition team, which they were happy to supply. These meetings continued post-referendum as well. On 19 August (the day Steve Bannon was named as Trump's new campaign manager) Yakovenko met Banks and Wigmore before they travelled to Mississippi with Nigel Farage where Trump introduced him as 'Mr Brexit'.

A July 2018 report by the DCMS committee spoke of how keen Banks and Farage are to play down any Russian contacts or links, often attempting to shut down conversation as long as the Russians are mentioned. This isn't the first journalist he has refused to talk to on these sorts of issues; when he was questioned by an Independent reporter on a meeting with a Russian official in 2013 he quickly stopped the interview. Farage has also been named as a person of interest by Robert Mueller in his investigation of the Trump campaign and attempted Russian interference in the US 2016 Presidential Election.

Farage says he has never visited Russia, but in March 2017 two senior members of his party, Nigel Sussman and Richard Wood, were among a crew of mainly far-right politicians to visit Crimea, illegally annexed by Russia from Ukraine in 2014. The trip was described by the Moscow Times as a disinformation exercise by the Russian government designed to 'help Putin score points at home'. A senior member of Farage's parliamentary group staff in Brussels, Kevin Ellul Bonic, has been accused of orchestrating a smear campaign against a critic of the Kremlin.

In September 2014, Banks also bought a Bristol-based family

jewellery shop that was running at a loss and lent the firm some £200,000. By February of 2015, he owned four diamond mines in South Africa, in the midst of a struggling diamond market. One of the mines Banks picked up had collapsed in value from a reported £12 million valuation in 2005, to as little as £200,000 by the time Banks bought it. Banks' wife, Katya, is Russian. Her first husband recalled that not long after their wedding Katya told him: 'I do not love you. I am not married to you in Russia. And, if you ever disobey me, you will feel the full force of my father's connections.' He told the New Yorker that her father had reportedly boasted 'about his connections with the Russian Mafia'.

The chair of the US House Intelligence Committee, Democrat Adam Schiff, said there were 'parallels and interconnections in abundance' between Russian efforts to influence the US election and their apparent part in the Brexit vote. In January 2018, a US Senate minority report suggested possible ways Russia may have influenced the Brexit campaign. It stated:

> The Russian government has sought to influence democracy in the United Kingdom through disinformation, cyber hacking, and corruption. While a complete picture of the scope and nature of Kremlin interference in the UK's June 2016 referendum is still emerging, Prime Minister Theresa May and the UK government have condemned the Kremlin's active measures, and various UK government entities, including the Electoral Commission and parliamentarians, have launched investigations into different aspects of possible Russian government meddling.

The Mueller Report, released in 2019, dealt with sweeping Russian efforts to disrupt the 2016 presidential election with the social media warfare strategy. The IRA ran a large-scale misinformation campaign, spread and publicized WikiLeaks email dumps and also used trolls, bots and memes to spread both conflict and outrage. It was not that the Russians had to set the fire to themselves, they simply had to fan the flames and watch an already divided society tear itself to pieces. Banks owns a host of businesses in southern Africa, including a handful of diamond mines. He was subject to two investigations by South African authorities, one over reports he was laundering diamonds from other parts of Africa.

Andrew Weiss, an expert on Russia at the Carnegie Endowment, believes that Russian officials are fearful of the Western 'regime-change agenda' and believe it may be turned on Putin's Russia. He told the New Yorker: 'Russia felt they needed to push back hard...They wanted to promote cleavages in the West, and that's where their promotion of populist and nationalist groups and—I think—their support of Brexit fits in.'

Don't Get DUPed

The Democratic Unionist Party was founded by the Reverend Ian Paisley in 1971 at the start of the Troubles, a conflict that grew out of a campaign for equal treatment of Catholics and Protestants. It is a grassroots working-class party, with a heavy religious focus, who oppose gay marriage, the concept of man-made climate change, and a woman's right to an abortion.

They had links with loyalist paramilitaries during the Troubles and at one time attempted to found their own 'loyalist defence militia', called 'The Third Force', that would work alongside the Police and British soldiers – by 1981 Paisley claimed they had 15-20,000 members. During the Troubles, they opposed The Sunningdale Agreement, The Anglo-Irish Agreement, and the Good Friday Agreement, all of which were attempts to restore power-sharing to Northern Ireland. However, in 2006, they worked together with Sinn Fein and put together the St Andrews Agreement, which restored power-sharing to Northern Ireland until 2016, when the RHI (Renewable Heating Incentive) scandal and the ensuing election left Stormont out of action. The DUP and Sinn Fein, as the largest Unionist and Nationalist parties, are both required to rule together in coalition or there can be no government. It's been over 1000 days since Northern Ireland had a functioning government and there seems to be no rush to fix that any time soon. We almost seem to have accepted it.

Over the past 20 years, the DUP have slowly eclipsed the Ulster Unionist Party as the largest Unionist party in Northern Ireland, and are currently the largest party in the Northern Irish assembly. Up until the last election, they had used this position of power to oppose gay marriage and abortion legislation, amongst other things, by exploiting the 'Petition of Concern'. A 'Petition of Concern' is a measure designed to stop sectarian discrimination in the legislative process by preventing legislation from passing if it is signed by 30 or more MLAs from a Nationalist or Unionist party. The measure was designed when no one party had enough votes to use the motion, but from 2003 until the end of the last assembly, the DUP have been able to manipulate it to their advantage.

It would be easy to mistake people from Northern Ireland as backward, intolerant, bigoted, or religiously obsessed, all because around one-third of people will vote for the DUP. That is a common misconception; people look across at us from mainland Britain and wonder how we can seriously elect politicians like Sammy Wilson, who believes the world is 6000 years old and that climate change is a myth. The answer is not that Northern Ireland is filled with religious extremists, rather our entire political system and every single political conversation is framed by one question – are we British or Irish?

Northern Ireland voted to remain in the EU by a majority of 56 per cent to 44 per cent (turnout in NI in the Brexit referendum was the lowest in the UK, with just 62 per cent of eligible voters casting a ballot). Yet a study released at the end of May 2018 by the UK in a Changing Europe group found that 69 per cent would favour Remain if there was another vote. Perhaps this is because those in Northern Ireland are more familiar with the border issue, they are aware of the significant amount of cross-border travel and trade that is facilitated by an open border and of the consequences (both socially and economically) of the re-emergence of a hard border.

Border posts, however light-touch and frictionless, are almost guaranteed to become targets for dissidents resentful of the new border. It has been repeatedly pointed out that cameras, once targeted by terrorists, protestors, or paramilitaries, can become guarded cameras or patrolled areas, which will eventually become fixed border checkpoints. Border communities would be devastated by any new border checks, Northern Ireland could be thrown into turmoil by the economic consequences and the potentially violent political fallout. It is impossible to predict accurately how dissidents on both sides of the sectarian divide would react to a new border. Given the significance of the fragile peace that has grown out of the Good Friday Agreement (and subsequently the St Andrews Agreement), Northern Irish folks are more than aware of the potential for Brexit to derail that peace. The constitutional question of a united Ireland is at the forefront of many minds as a result of Brexit and the tension between the largest Unionist and Nationalist parties is so highly strung that they have been unable to agree to terms on which to form a government for 3 years. We're already living through a fraught political time.

These fears are not unfounded. Research by Professor John Garry and Professor Brendan O'Leary has given a glimpse at what may lie beyond the decision to implement any sort of border in Ireland. They found that one in five Catholics would find camera-based technology at the border 'almost impossible to accept'. Over half of Catholics and 70 per cent of Catholics who support Sinn Fein would find customs checks 'almost impossible to accept'. If customs agents were protected by British soldiers almost three-quarters of Catholics, and 82 per cent of Catholics who support Sinn Fein, would find the arrangement almost impossible to accept. More than a quarter (28 per cent) of Catholics would vote for a united Ireland if the UK remained in the EU, whilst 53 per cent would back a united Ireland if there was a hard exit in which the UK left the customs union and single market. The research also found that there were strong expectations that protests against checks at the Irish border or between Northern Ireland and the rest of the UK would quickly become violent. Even when the possibility of a second vote is taken off the table, 61 per cent of the population still favour the UK as a whole remaining in the customs union and single market – a position being pushed by both Sinn Fein and Alliance. Even an Irish Sea border would cause upset within the North with 29 per cent of Catholics and 28 per cent of Protestants stating that they would find East-West customs checks 'almost impossible to accept'.

During the last parliament, the DUP and their ten MPs in Westminster held an extremely disproportionate amount of power. Having been bought by a cool £1 billion in funding for Northern Ireland, they pledged their support for a flailing Conservative government scratching around parliament for the votes to give them a majority. The DUP pushed relentlessly for a hard Brexit whilst maintaining that there can be no regulatory diversion from the rest of the UK and no border in Ireland or the Irish Sea. They have always been Eurosceptic, but their pursuit of a hard Brexit, absent of widespread public support, seems odd in a way. Their devotion to ensuring Northern Ireland remains on par with the rest of the UK is somewhat contradictory to their desire for divergence on issues like abortion, gay marriage, and transparency of political donations. So is this more than simple political ambiguity and opportunism? They withdrew support for Boris Johnson's deal after opposition from grassroots unionists and meetings with representatives from the UDA and the UVF.

DUP representative Jim Wells claimed that the decision to support the Leave campaign in the referendum took 'all of five minutes'. The DUP have traditionally been Eurosceptic. For Wells, asking if the DUP was pro-Brexit was 'like asking if we were royalist — it's just the way we are'. There was more disagreement within the party than Wells would have you believe, younger party members were reportedly more pro-Europe than the older generation leading the party. MLAs Alistair Ross, Simon Hamilton, and David McIlveen were described by two young party members as 'reformers rather than ardent leavers'. Aaron Banks claimed in his book that the DUP demanded 'cold, hard cash in exchange for their support'. The DUP extorted the Conservative Party for £1 billion for Northern Ireland as a part of their confidence and supply deal and we now know they received £435,000 for their support of the Brexit campaign.

The source of the donations wasn't originally clear due to laws designed to keep donors protected during the height of the violence in Northern Ireland, but the group behind the donation has since been named as the Constitutional Research Council (CRC). The mysterious CRC was confirmed in February 2017 to have donated £435,000 to the DUP, of which they routed £425,000 into pro-Brexit ads in mainland Britain, not Northern Ireland. This spending included a £282,000 advert reading 'Take Back Control - Vote To Leave' in the Metro and almost £100,000 worth of campaign merchandise. The CRC was simply a front group for the true source of the donation. The true source of the donor was set to be retroactively revealed, but following a rule change by the Conservative administration, they will now remain anonymous. The new transparency laws were set to come into effect from 1 January 2014 when the law was first passed. However, the then secretary of state for Northern Ireland, James Brokenshire, pushed the date back to 1 July

2017 following the Conservative-DUP coalition deal (though any connection between the two has since been denied). The Northern Ireland Office told Channel 4 that James Brokenshire 'does not believe that it is right or fair to impose retrospective regulations on people who donated in accordance with the rules set out in law at the time'. Every other major party in Northern Ireland supports backdating donor transparency to January 2014, just as the legislation sets out. This isn't the first time the Tories have been caught out obscuring donors and donations. A 2014 Observer investigation found that the United and Cecil Club was pouring £285,000 into the Tory party with no obvious information on donors or the origin of the money.

The CRC's chair and former Scottish Conservative parliamentary candidate Richard Cook is the only name or contact that we have for the organization. The CRC has been named by OpenDemocracy as a potential front organization used to funnel money anonymously in British politics. It has no formal or legal status and refuses to name its members. The DUP chose not to ask where the money was coming from and just got on with spending it. Steve Baker, a former junior minister in the Department for Exiting the European Union, also received £6500 from the CRC when he was chairman of the European Research Group (ERG), a pro-Brexit caucus. When Christopher Howarth, the senior researcher for the ERG, was quizzed on the donation, he told The Observer that, 'It's a registered donation from a permissible donor. That's all the information you would need.' Cook spoke to the Sunday Herald about the donation, insisting that it was from a legal, UK-based donor:

'The CRC is regulated by the Electoral Commission. We operate solely in the UK. We accept donations only from eligible UK donors. We donate solely to permissible UK entities. Any suggestion that we have done anything else is basically defamatory.'

Even if the donor is legitimate, we have a right to know

who is funding politics in the UK. Questions still remain over why the anonymous donor chose to bequeath to a Northern Irish party more money than they had ever spent on an election, who then proceeded to spend the vast majority on campaigning outside of Northern Ireland. Cook admitted that he had only visited Northern Ireland twice in the past 6 years, so there seem to be very few reasons to donate to the DUP aside from the transparency laws. Full disclosure of who is funding our politicians is crucial to a healthy and functioning democracy. In an ideal world, we would have publicly-funded elections, money has no place in politics. We need to understand where this money came from and why the Conservative government chose to keep the identity of the donor hidden from the public.

The CRC was purportedly set up during the Scottish independence referendum in 2014 after disagreements within the 'Better Together' campaign group. Cook, who now lives in Glasgow, ran for parliament in 2010 against the Labour incumbent, Jim Murphey, who was briefly Scottish Labour leader in 2015. Cook once owned DDR Recycling, who eventually went out of business, owing taxpayers some £150,000 and dumped illegal waste on an international scale. BBC Spotlight followed a case where a shipment of 'rubber material' was sent from Felixstowe to India. It was, in fact, tyre waste that has been illegal to dispose of in landfill sites since 2006. When the Indian authorities questioned the labelling of the product, DDR Recycling sent them a fake test of the material sent from Grapevine UK Ltd, a recruitment agency owned by a fellow director of his. Cook claimed to have left the company in 2009, but company documents show he remained the director until 2014.

Whilst in business DDR won an £80 million contract in Kiev, shipping 20,000 tonnes of used railway per year over the course of a number of years. When BBC Spotlight investigated they found that the company was registered in a residential area, was virtually unknown within Ukraine, and gave off every whiff of being a front company. The company appears to have never even been in the business of recycling or selling railways. When they visited the building the company was registered to, they found it was an old soviet tower block and the BBC crew were harassed as they attempted to film outside the state bank where one of the invoices they had obtained had led them. After some time they were able to uncover that the person listed on the company account was a Hans Ernst Bastian, a convicted grain fraudster. The CRC has contracts worth over £1 billion scattered across the globe in countries including Russia, Syria, Australia, South Korea, and Malaysia. FBI Agent Gregory Coleman told Spotlight he felt that many of these contracts may be fake. Coleman is the agent who famously toppled the Wolf of Wall Street, Jordan Belfort.

In 2012, the BBC reported that Cook was involved in a £640-million deal with the Port Qasim Authority in Pakistan. But the company never filed any documents with Companies House and Cook Consulting (UK) Ltd was dissolved by June 2015. Cook has a habit of using front companies to hide the true source of money or contracts. Time and again he has registered companies, failed to produce accounting documents, and subsequently dissolved the company, leaving little to no trace, and he has been caught actively committing fraud against the Indian government. We cannot trust this man to be acting in the best interests of the British people, nor can we allow information crucial to the transparency of our electoral process to be swept under the rug. Cook also has strong links to Saudi Arabia, in 2013, he founded Five Star Investment Management Ltd with the former head of SA intelligence, Prince Nawwaf bin Abdul Aziz, whose son is Saudi Ambassador. The firm never filed any accounts with Companies House and was dissolved in December 2014.

DUP MP Gregory Campbell told Source Material that he felt that the onus was not on the DUP to investigate as to whether the source of the CRC donation was a permissible donor. Rather he declared that it was up to the Electoral Commission. Electoral law states that any incorporated company that donates more than £25,000 must be registered with the Electoral Commission, an OpenDemocracy investigation found that the CRC was linked to a £6000 fine imposed by the Electoral Commission, though they have refused on numerous occasions to provide any further information about the fine. All we know is that it was a sanction connected to a political donation in Northern Ireland. They gave no name, offence, or summary of the decision.

Think about how crazy that is for a second. Laws that were designed for secrecy during a time of violent conflict in Northern Ireland, that were meant to be repealed, are now protecting the identity of a donor who funnelled £435,000 into the Brexit referendum. The largest donation in Northern Irish political history came from a group fronted by a fraudulent businessman, who seems to be part of a web of contracts designed to hide the movement of money around the world. The ruling party, whose majority in parliament was being propped up by the party that received the donation, reversed their decision to reveal the source of the donation. The Electoral Commission refuses to release any details and the DUP will not reveal the source of their donation except to say that either they didn't check whether it was a permissible donor, or that they checked and that they have covered all legal obligations required of them. Even following the BBC Spotlight investigation, the Electoral Commission thought that it was not in the 'public interest' to investigate, even if crimes had been committed.

It's a question of understanding who wanted the UK to leave the EU, poured hundreds of thousands of pounds anonymously into campaigns, and how they might stand to benefit from the vote. Either the Conservative government are so determined to leave the EU that they are willfully ignoring or actively shutting down any questions that arise that may question the legitimacy of the campaign or they don't wish to reveal uncomfortable truths about who is pulling the strings in the innermost circles of British politics. There is no good reason for a donor who has gone to such lengths to remain anonymous, to be forgotten or ignored when we are discussing the most seismic political event of most of our lifetimes.

Aaron Banks has been referred to the National Crime Agency after the Electoral Commission said it had 'reasonable grounds to suspect' that Banks was not the source of the £8 million he donated to pro-Brexit campaigns. They believe the money may have come from Rock Holdings, which would be impermissible as they are incorporated in the Isle of Man.

Leave.EU and Eldon Insurance were fined £120,000 by the ICO for data law breaches. Leave.EU appealed and had the fine reduced overall from £135,000. Eldon were fined £60,000 after over a million emails sent to Leave.EU subscribers contained marketing for the Eldon Insurance firm's GoSkippy services. Leave.EU was fined £45,000 for this breach and a further £15,000 for 'using Eldon Insurance customers' details unlawfully to send almost 300,000 political marketing messages'. Banks brushed it off on Twitter saying that they may have accidentally sent a newsletter to customers. The ICO disagreed and said it had uncovered a 'disturbing disregard for voters' personal privacy'. Better For The Country Ltd was fined £50,000 for sending people text messages without having first gained their permission to do so.

An investigation by the NCA into the source of Banks' funding was controversially dropped due to 'insufficient evidence':

'The NCA has found no evidence that any criminal offences have been committed under PPERA or company law by any of the individuals or organisations referred to it by the Electoral Commission.'

The inquiry found that Banks took a loan from Rock Holdings Ltd, which he owned, and that was the source of the funding.

'There have also been media reports alleging that Mr Banks has been involved in other criminality related to business dealings overseas. The NCA neither confirms nor denies that it is investigating these reports.'

Leave.EU was also fined £70,000 by the Electoral Commission for spending violations during the referendum campaign. An investigation by the Electoral Commission found that they overspent by at least £77,380 – 10 per cent over the limit for non-party registered groups – but that the actual figure may have been 'considerably higher' due to the 'incomplete and inaccurate' information about spending that the group provided. Bob Posner, the commission's director of political finance and regulation and legal counsel, described the breaches as 'serious offences' and suggested that the fine would have been bigger but for a cap on the amount that the commission can levy: 'The rules we enforce were put in place by parliament to ensure transparency and public confidence in our democratic processes.' The investigation found no evidence that Cambridge Analytica had made donations or provided any services aside from some 'initial scoping work'.

Aaron Banks dismissed the findings altogether: 'We view the Electoral Commission announcement as a politically motivated attack on Brexit and the 17.4m people who defied the establishment to vote for an independent Britain...The EC went big game fishing and found a few 'aged' dead sardines on the beach. So much for the big conspiracy!'

Why does it matter if Cambridge Analytica and subsidiaries worked with the Leave campaign? There are two key reasons: first, they broke electoral law. Second, Vote Leave and Leave. EU refused to cooperate with investigations by the Electoral Commission and the Information Commissioners Office. When police raided Cambridge Analytica HQ in London, they were already shutting down operations and quietly setting themselves up again as Emerdata. Just as SCL has disappeared from countless countries and denied any involvement in shady electioneering tactics, they disappeared from Britain in a puff of smoke. How AggregateIQ were found by Vote Leave, BeLeave, the DUP, and VfB remains unclear. Until 2015, all their work seems to have come from Robert Mercer. The Brexit campaign appears to have been their first major election not funded by the hedge fund billionaire.

SCL have used propaganda, divisive misinformation, admitted bribery and operating through a web of shadow companies. They have repeatedly popped up around the world, embroiled in election and corruption scandals, and now their fingerprints are all over the Brexit campaign. Cambridge Analytica, the company at the centre of the data scandal that has cost Facebook $5 billion, did initial work for Leave.EU, and AggregateIQ, which appears to be a subsidiary, and have worked alongside them on several campaigns, including the Trump campaign. AggregateIQ built software for Trump and Vote Leave; all of their intellectual property is owned by SCL. If we allow this to be forgotten, we are just opening ourselves up to the same kind of interference in every future election, with better and better technology being deployed. You can't deny the vote happened. Nor can you declare the referendum void, though it was technically only advisory. But I'll leave that argument unopened.

In the Channel 4/HBO dramatization of Brexit, The Uncivil War, Dominic Cummings repeatedly talks of hearing the country groaning, as if the very bedrock of the country was preparing for a seismic shift. The vote to leave the EU was a cry for help from a country under strain. Growing inequality, a barbell economy, 20 years of privatization and deregulation gave us the 2008 crash. It was followed up by the hammer blow of austerity, hitting the poorest parts of Britain already on the ropes after years of globalization had outsourced manufacturing.

The economic divide that has been growing since the 1980s has been joined recently by the new cultural divide, those feeling left behind by the modern world and those thriving in it: the Anywheres against the Somewheres. These economic hardships fused with a backlash against modern liberalism and PC culture, the dissatisfaction with the state of the neo-liberal low wage economy blended with the loss of identity and cultural erosion. The loss of a sense of community that bound us all together was accompanied by the rise of the internet, where we have divided ourselves up into digital clusters, each part of our own little network. It has been said too many times to count but, in a connected world, we really are more divided than ever. Opportunistic campaigns used this connectivity and the vast availability of personal data to understand us and target with adverts meticulously tested and designed to trigger us, to gaslight us, to turn us against one another. None of the discussion here is about how these voters could be enthused by Brexit due to the positive impacts on their lives. Nor is there any talk of any economic benefits to Brexit for them – it is about exploiting fears and using mass datasets to target these fears more efficiently than ever before. But the underlying problems still remain, we are a divided nation. More worryingly we are a distracted nation. This debate is taking years out of our political system and there is a backlog of problems that need to be addressed more and more urgently. I fear that once this whole debate is reconciled and we achieve some sort of progress, leaving or remaining, we will be faced with a bottleneck of legislation and important issues will be sacrificed for the hot topic of the day. Education spending, climate change, cybersecurity, electoral law reform, Northern Irish devolution, Scottish Independence, student loan debt, NHS funding, and many more issues will all be on the table, that's going to take years and a lot of co-operation to sort through. Being distracted means we haven't seen what is also on the horizon: the fourth wave of neo-liberalism and the disaster capitalists eyeing a hard Brexit.

Part 3

The Blue Print

8. Disaster Capitalism

Three successive waves of neo-liberalism have assaulted Britain since the rise of Thatcher. The journey we've been on in this book thus far was necessary to understand how Brexit became a melting pot of long-term problems and how politicians and campaign groups exploited this . Now it is time to understand the next step. The post-Brexit chaos will be used to enact the fourth wave of neo-liberal consolidation. That means more privatization, more public spending cuts, and more globalization.

James Meek, the author of Disaster Capitalism, blamed the legacy of Thatcher for the rise of free-market neo-liberalism. He argued that Thatcher and her successors have 'done all they can to sell off the nation's bricks and mortar...Only to be forced to rent it back at inflated prices from the people they sold it to'[64]. Privatization is the mantra and running government like a business the only accepted logic. In the words of British song-writer Beans on Toast, 'Everything's for-profit, everything's for-profit.' Brexit will be used as a jumping-off point to force unrestrained neo-liberalism upon the British population.

From Friedman to Osborne

Milton Friedman is the father of free-market economics. His ideas gave birth to Thatcherism in the UK and Reaganomics in the US. Friedman and the Chicago school of economics argued that impositions of the state like minimum wages, public education, price controls, and taxation upset the equilibrium of the market. Their mission was to purify the market of all hinderance and let it be free. The recipe is simple, cut taxes on the wealthy, cut back regulations, and cut back and sell off the state to pay for it. The modern embodiment of these ideas was born in April 1947 in the Swiss village of Mont Pelerin at a gathering of 40 academics, economists, and journalists. Later called the Mont

Pelerin Society. It had been put together by Austrian-born British economist Friedrich Hayek, who claimed that 'we have progressively abandoned that freedom in economic affairs without which personal and political freedom has never existed in the past'. The Mont Pelerin Society believed that the crisis of the Western world that had led to two world wars was the result of ' a decline of belief in private property and the competitive market'. The only way forward was to restore the 'laissez-faire' economic model of the nineteenth century, emphasizing the reduction of state involvement in day-to-day life, which had given way to a more interventionist style of governance.

The free-market idea, now almost universally accepted amongst the ruling class in Britain and America, was thought to be far too radical in the 1960s and was wholly untested in the modern world. Thus it was necessary to impart a shock to the system to help ease the transition to pure freedom of capitalism. This is the process articulated by Naomi Klein in The Shock Doctrine: 'First came an intense crisis – then came the Blitzkrieg of pro-corporate policies.' This could be anything, a military coup, a financial crisis, or a natural disaster, but anything, sufficiently hyped by politicians, could be used as a window of chaos to exploit.[65]

The 'Shock Doctrine' is so titled because of the likeness to the process of torture on interrogation victims. The desire to return torture victims to a blank slate upon which a new person can be built. Similarly, Friedman and his disciples sought to put their ideas to work on a blank slate created by inducing the country into a state of shock. Psychologists in the CIA believed in regressing victims to a 'pristine state' in which they could be moulded and Friedman imagined the possibilities of returning markets to pure unhindered capitalism. No regulations, trade barriers, or government interference. Friedman believed that the only way to cleanse an economy of its bad habits and market distortions was to deliver 'bitter medicine', the shock. As part of the declassified MK Ultra experiments, the CIA tried to use electroshock therapy to clear distortions and bad patterns in the human brain.

When the CIA assisted Pinochet's military takeover of Chile in 1973 it was seen as the ideal opportunity to implement Friedman's ideas. As Pinochet's economic adviser Friedman helped him enact what he called a 'shock treatment' on the country to push through radical reforms. Klein describes how 'Friedman predicted that the speed, suddenness, and scope of the economic shifts would provoke psychological reactions in the public that facilitate the adjustment'.[66] Before Pinochet's coup, he had lost the election to socialist Salvador Allende. With the help of the CIA, he overthrew Allende and dished out the shock treatment. He privatized the public-school system, healthcare, nurseries, cemeteries, and more. All of this in a country that had chosen left-wing policies before the coup.[67] When the economic shock failed to jolt the Chilean economy into health, Friedman personally visited Pinochet, who was immediately converted to a disciple of the Chicago school. Friedman told Pinochet that the reason the economy was struggling was because some remnants of the old economy still remained. He dutifully continued to cut spending, taxes, and regulation to shock the economy back into life. Friedman literally prescribed 'shock therapy' for Chile, branding it the only solution. By 1982 the economy was in crisis, national debt exploded, unemployment hit 30 per cent, and hyper-inflation loomed. 'The Piranhas', a group of wealthy businessmen in Chile, had bought up state assets on borrowed money and run up debts worth $14 billion. Pinochet was forced to nationalize many of these businesses (just as his former opponent Allende had done) and was able to keep the economy afloat because of the state-owned copper company that at one point made up 85 per cent of exports. The Chilean project is held up as a miracle of free-market economics, but in reality, it was a disaster. The 'miracle' growth in Chile occurred a decade after the Chicago Boys/CIA shock treatment, after re-nationalizing many industries that had been sold off. By that time, 45 per cent of the population had fallen below the poverty line (in the late 1970s, Chileans could spend three-quarters of their income buying bread).

It may be comforting to believe that this policy could never be pursued in the developed world. That a government would never wilfully take advantage of a crisis to take more power for themselves (maybe I'm underestimating your cynicism). This ideology has been applied throughout the Western world as globalization took hold and multinationals worked hand in hand with governments and private military to spread the good word of Friedman.

The free-market idea is an example of the closed-loop systems discussed in Black Box Thinking. If something is going wrong in an economy, Friedman's logic suggests that the problem must be that the market is not free enough. The response to every crisis, whether engineered deliberately or via negligence, is to further advance the neo-liberal agenda and roll back the state. When Boris Yeltsin sent tanks to set fire to the Russian parliament and arrested the opposition leaders, it cleared the way for the Russian state assets fire sale, the NATO attack on Belgrade in 1999 preceded rapid privatization in Yugoslavia, and the 9/11 attacks allowed the free market to be bestowed upon Iraq. Artificial debt crises were engineered in Canada, Asia, and Britain that allowed unpopular waves of public spending cuts to be pushed through as necessary to deal with the debt.

The Homeland Security and private surveillance industry blew up after the September 11 attacks. Bush announced a never-ending war on terror in which everything could be outsourced. The Bush administration exploited the post-9/11 chaos and 'war on terror' to privatize everything from soldiers and interrogation to gathering and mining data on the public itself. In 2003 the US government handed out 3512 contracts for security functions, from 2004-2006 they gave out more than 115,000. The global homeland security industry was valued at $200 billion in 2007, $431 billion in 2018, and is expected to grow to $606 billion by 2024.[68]

Paul Bremmer, director of Henry Kissinger's consulting firm, was named by George W. Bush as the chief envoy in Iraq. From inside the Green Zone (known by some soldiers as the 'emerald city'), Bremmer sought to remake Iraq as the model free-market economy. The tax rate was to be set at a flat 15 per cent, all state assets were to be sold off, and the government was to be substantially downsized to make way for private industry. They even brought in Russian experts on 'economic shock therapy' to share their experience of the collapse of the USSR and the asset fire sale that created the class of Oligarchs that still exist today. Yegor Gaidar, otherwise known as Russia's 'Doctor Shock', explained the importance of rapid change, so that the Iraqis didn't have time to fight back against the measures. 'Iraq's missing billions' disappeared into the privatization pit, never to be seen again.

War and military violence is just one type of shock that can be exploited. Anything that provides sufficient confusion, chaos, and distraction can be used as the priming electroshock to wipe the slate clean and install the privatization agenda. Just 14 days after the destruction of Hurricane Katrina, the Republican Study Committee led by now Vice President Mike Pence produced 'Pro-Free Market Ideas for Responding to Hurricane Katrina and High Gas Prices'. The list predictably prescribed dropping labour standards and cutting huge portions of the public sphere.[69] Within days of the disaster in New Orleans, Joseph Canizaro (one of the city's wealthiest property developers) was describing the destruction as 'a clean sheet' from which they could profit.[70] Within 19 months, whilst many of the poorest residents of the city were still unable to return to their homes, privately-run Charter schools had taken over most of the public-school system

– there were just four state-run schools left – and teachers unions had been dismantled.[71]

Private Security Contractors from Iraq like Blackwater and Haliburton have seen the potential for their involvement in the domestic market dealing with natural disasters (a domestic market worth $3.4 billion in no-bid contracts thus far).[72] The mantra of Paul Pindar is, 'Never miss a good opportunity to make money from a disaster'. Pindar is the boss at Capita, a firm who specialized in business process outsourcing and have made a tidy profit on the outsourcing of the British state, taking on payroll and administration duties for the health and education services. Pindar famously told the public accounts committee in 2013 that the reason army recruitment was falling was the 'disadvantage that we actually have no wars on'.[73] Capita was at the centre of a scandal where the Department for Work and Pensions was forced to send civil servants to help with work that had been outsourced to the firm. They were processing PIP payments so slowly that in some cases recipients had died before receiving anything.

The idea of a pure and free market became intertwined with the idea of personal freedom. Friedman himself said, 'Underlying most arguments against the free market is a lack of belief in freedom itself.' In reality, the free-market ideology surrenders the power of the individual to the invisible hand of the market, or rather the invisible hand of capital. Shaping the economy to give the monied interests the greatest freedom at the expense of the wider populace who see wages, rights, and opportunity stripped away in the name of profit. In each country where the Chicago Boys have had their way, inequality has soared, be that Argentina, Indonesia, or Chile (which remains one of the most unequal countries in the world 40 years on). We are experiencing the visceral impacts of this ideology on Britain, we now live in one of the most unequal societies in the developed world. Alex Niven writes,

'As Thatcher and her political successors have progressively remodelled Britain so that it is a country in which ancient interests share power with the profiteers of liberal aspirationalism, we have seen a return to the pre-twentieth century arrangement.'

Whilst Thatcher is credited with the first wave of neo-liberalism, it was the second wave under Tony Blair and New Labour which marked the takeover of Friedman's ideology of both major parties in the UK. Instead of the wholesale privatization that occurred under Thatcher, the changes made under Blair were less drastic, but important steps in the neo-liberal transformation of Britain.

Private Finance Initiatives (PFIs), though first implemented by John Major's government, were expanded under Tony Blair. A PFI is a contract with a private company to provide public services that governments had previously run themselves. Instead of borrowing the money themselves, governments outsource this to firms who borrow the money from the City to fund the project and typically pay them back over the course of 25 years. It allows governments to hide the scale of their borrowing and spending by keeping it off the books. The theory is that the private sector, in its pursuit of profit, will be more efficient than the public sector and provide services cheaper and more effectively than the government would be capable of. In reality, the corporate world extracts every last ounce of profit, leaving unaccountable bare-bones structures in place of our public services. The Strathclyde Police Training and Recruitment Centre was financed through a PFI. The money paid by the government goes to Strathclyde Limited Partnership, it then flows through ten companies or partnerships and arrives at the Guernsey-based International Public Partnerships Limited. From there it winds its way through a host of different shell companies and financial vehicles, with accountants and lawyers taking their respective fees, to individuals and other firms in London, the United States, Jersey, Germany, and beyond. The police centre which cost £18 million to build will cost the government £112 million between 2001 and 2026 with most of that money being siphoned off to shareholders and tax havens. In 2017 the 700 PFI contracts were valued at just under £60 billion, yet the taxpayer will be billed for over £300 billion by the time these contracts run their course. New Labour promised to only hand out these contracts if they were cheaper than the public sector equivalent. Philip Hammond did state in 2018 that PFI contracts would no longer be used, though we know how much that means in modern British politics and he has since had the party whip withdrawn by Boris Johnson over his stance on a no-deal Brexit.

Though Blair sought to offer a third way between socialism and free markets, allowing the market to flourish whilst protecting the individual, economic interests had far more sway than public opinion. Professor Anthony King, author of Who Governs Britain, described Blair's government as the 'first ever Labour government to be openly, even ostentatiously pro-business'. Blair laid the foundation for the mass privatization of the NHS and other public services by welcoming private corporations into the running of public services under the premise of 'public service reforms'. It's no coincidence that senior Tories refer to Blair as 'The Master'. By the time Cameron, who described himself as 'the heir to Blair', and Osborne arrived in government the British economy had been primed for the next wave of neo-liberalism by the biggest financial crash since 1929.

The Big Short

In June 1815, Nathan Rothschild's courier came barrelling into London. Britain had won the Battle of Waterloo, defeating Napoleon in a heroic stand-off later immortalized by ABBA. Upon receiving this information he did not celebrate, cheer, or rush to tell his friends. There was work to do. He had received word of the victory a full day in advance of anyone else and immediately started offloading British bonds. Other investors feared that Rothschild had heard that Napoleon had won and began frantically selling government bonds that would be worthless when official word broke that Wellington had lost to the French. As prices plummeted Rothschild began buying up British bonds and when he sold them at the market peak 2 years later he made a fortune. He was the true father of disaster capitalism, famously stating that 'the best time to invest is when there is blood in the streets'.

Disaster capitalism functions by delivering a massive shock to an economic system and then exploiting the resulting chaos to expand market share or profit by betting against the market. In the words of Petyr Bailysh from George RR Martin's Game of Thrones, 'Chaos isn't a pit, chaos is a ladder.' By plunging the economic, political, and social system into disarray, you are best poised to exploit it. There are winners in every disaster. This idea is hardly strange or unknown to the public, it is on full display in pop culture – the remake of James Bond's Casino Royale had disaster capitalism as a major plot point. The villain, Le Chiffre, was providing illicit banking services to the world's criminals and using that money to take out massive bets against the stock of an airline set to launch a brand-new airliner. At the same time, he was arranging for a terror attack to sabotage the unveiling of the new plane. In theory, the stock value of the airline would plummet after the successful attack and he would make millions of dollars betting against the stock. Thankfully, Bond was on hand to put a stop to the bomber, but it illustrates exactly how this would work in the real world.

Prior to the financial collapse in 2007, banks had begun to trade more and more in Asset Based Securities (ABS). An ABS pools thousands of loans together, which are chopped up to be sold and traded on the markets with no real connection to the initial value of the loans. Within these packets of loans, the risk rating of the loans varies, and the good loans are packaged up with higher risk loans (those rated more likely to default) to help offset the risk to investors. On top of the packaging of these financial bundles, banks also placed huge bets on the performance of these securities, with hedge funds and investors getting in on the action, placing bets on the outcome of those bets. Any loans not deemed fit for an ASB were pooled into huge financial instruments called CDOs (Collateralized Debt Obligations). As soon as the CDO was large enough, these badly rated loans were stamped with a triple-A rating and sold as if they were a AAA mortgage. The financial system became totally disconnected from the reality of the world they were living in or the value of the assets they were trading.

Banks were handing out loans to anyone who could sign a contract, offering introductory mortgage rates to make the loan seem affordable. When these introductory rates expired and default rates skyrocketed, investors suddenly realized they were sitting on top of billions in toxic debt and assets. It began a shockwave that was felt universally, the largest global financial crash since 1929. Lehman Brothers, a financial institution that had stood through a civil war and two world wars, shut its doors. The National Audit Office revealed that bank bailouts cost the British taxpayer £1.162 trillion. The 2008 crash was the perfect shock. It was devastating, chaotic, and softened up the public to accept the implementation of a brutal regime of austerity that punished the poorest and not those who caused the crisis.

During the US mortgage crisis, Michael Burry (played by Christian Bale in the Hollywood adaptation of the story The Big Short) and Scion capital produced an investment return of 489 per cent. They quadrupled their money taking out short bets against the US housing market before closing down for Burry to concentrate on personal investment. Taking a short position means that you are essentially betting that specific stocks or financial instruments will go down in value. Burry spotted that the US housing market was based on a whole stack of mortgages being packaged up and sold off as AAA-rated loans, almost guaranteed to pay off, when they were filled with the lowest-rated mortgages that exist – those who had no deposit, no income, no means of paying off the money as soon as the variable rates kicked in. The mortgages were sold with low introductory rates that would sky-rocket in 2007, so when defaults started pouring in the banks holding and betting on the housing market were left holding AAA-rated bonds and securities that were worth nothing. The entire system began to collapse on itself and the world was left to clean up the mess that greed and gambling had created.

When Boris Johnson was announced as prime minister on 23 July 2019, it was hoped he would provide a 'Boris Bounce' at the polls. A little bump as this charismatic Eton old boy took to the wheel. What very few people mentioned were the donations he received as he took part in the leadership contest, where he raked in £655,500 in campaign contributions, two-thirds of which (£432,500) came from a mix of hedge funds and City traders. Many of these donors had worked with Johnson during his time with Vote Leave; according to investigations from Byline Times (a freelance crowd-funded journalism site),

'Crispin Odey, Paul Marshall, Peter Cruddas, Jon Moynihan, Jon Wood, Robin Birley, David Lilley, Philip Harris, JCB and The Bristol Port Company all donated (directly or indirectly through companies they and their co-directors are involved with) to Johnson's leadership campaign and also contributed more than £2 million to the Vote Leave campaign.'

Over £4.5 billion in short positions have been taken by hedge funds that financially backed Boris for the leader of the Conservative Party, either directly or indirectly, and another £3.7 billion had been taken out by firms who contributed to Vote Leave. That is £8.27 billion betting on the British currency to drop in value. It's an absurd amount of money, most of us couldn't even imagine what we could do with £8.2 million, let alone a thousand times more. These hedge funds, having backed a decision that could cause decades-long damage to the UK, are proceeding to take up billions of pounds in bets that our currency will lose its value and make a fortune from it.

The UK spends around £250 billion a year on outsourcing and contracting, or around 13 per cent of annual GDP. That's just under one-third of annual public spending. Mitic CEO Ruby McGregor Smith told Management Today, 'outsourcing has always been positive during recession', it's seen as a way of kickstarting the economy allowing private capital to take advantage of the sale of government assets. In reality, it further concentrates wealth and power in the hands of those at the very top, allowing them to turn valuable public services into profit. Ron Van Steden of Vrije University Amsterdam (and Dutch government adviser) explained to the Financial Times how companies like G4S 'follow a salami technique: slicing off a small part of public services to see how far they can go'. The Cameron regime succeeded in privatizing libraries, schools, forests, child protection services, green energy, foreign aid, public transport, and elderly care. These services are seen as potential profit, something that could be commercially exploited if it weren't for the pesky government getting involved. There is no room in this ideology to consider the quality of service or the value of public assets; Royal Mail was undervalued by £180,000,000 by Vince Cable when it was auctioned off. Outsourcing continues regardless of the result.

In January 2018, the facilities management and construction firm Carillion went into liquidation. They left behind a pension liability of around £2.6 billion owed to 27,000 people (who will now be partially reimbursed by the Pension Protection Fund), debts worth £2 billion to their suppliers, sub-contractors, and creditors, and £7 billion in total liabilities. This was less than 12 months after paying record dividends of £79 million to shareholders in March 2017. Carillion was given contracts for hospital maintenance, schools meals, defence accommodation and was put under pressure by government ministers to take contracts at a lower cost than it was possible to provide the service. The report from parliament was damning:

> Carillion's rise and spectacular fall was a story of recklessness, hubris and greed. Its business model was a relentless dash for cash, driven by acquisitions, rising debt, expansion into new markets and exploitation of suppliers. It presented accounts that misrepresented the reality of the business, and increased its dividend every year, come what may. Long-term obligations, such as adequately funding its pension schemes, were treated with contempt. Even as the company very publicly began to unravel, the board was concerned with increasing and protecting generous executive bonuses. Carillion was unsustainable. The mystery is not that it collapsed, but that it lasted so long.

Despite the firm issuing profit warnings, Theresa May continued to award contracts to them, perhaps in a futile attempt to keep the company afloat. We throw money at the bottomless pit of privatization and continue to expect better results. The police and army stepped in in 2012 after, despite being the recipient of a £284 million contract, G4S were unable to provide enough private security personnel for the Olympics. G4S continues to benefit from millions of pounds of government outsourcing contracts, everything from security to prisons and immigration facilities. We continue to lower taxes for the wealthy and expect wealth to trickle down. In the Financial Times in December 2011, they ran the headline, 'Even donors admit that Tory MPs' desire to cut the 50p top rate of income tax is because these rich City donors are so close to the party'.[74] An ICM poll found even 65 per cent of Conservative voters opposed the move at the time and yet the policy was pushed through within a year of the Tories arriving in government.[75] In the 1983 novel Sudden Death by

Rita Mae Brown, antagonist Susan Reilly recalls what fictional sports writer Jane Fulton told her: 'Insanity is doing the same thing over and over again, but expecting different results.' (It's a quote that is often misattributed to both Einstein and an ancient Chinese proverb.) We as a population are doing the same by enabling the disciples of neo-liberalism to continue to enact their holy trinity of tax cuts, public spending cuts, and privatization. The very essence of modern capitalism is, as Owen Jones put it, 'a publicly subsidized racket, where the real scroungers are to be found not at the bottom of society but at the top'. In 2017, billionaires around the world made more money than they had in the history of the planet. Their wealth increased by a full fifth to an astonishing £6.9 trillion. Now clearly some of that can be attributed to inflation, but I challenge you to find any country in which the GDP is growing at 20 per cent. The gap between the rich and poor of the world is only getting larger and larger and as they amass more money, power, and influence, they acquire even more power to entrench the system that gave them their wealth and new ways to expand and grow their bank accounts and their influence. It is a vicious circle fed by human greed.

Let me draw your attention to one particular act of privatization that illustrates the problem. In April 2017 the UK Government agreed on a deal to sell off the Green Investment Bank (GIB) for £2.3 billion to a consortium led by an Australian bank, Macquarie. The Macquarie Group are frequently referred to as 'The Millionaires Factory' because of the massive paycheques and bonuses paid out to their executives. Chief Executive Nicholas Moore and his management team took three of the top five places on 2014's list of highest-paid executives in Australia, despite the series of scandals that embroiled the firm at the time. Australian Shareholders' Association chairman Ian Curry commented that, 'No one seems to have lost their position, or seem to have lost their entitlements.' The Government retained a 'special share' in the GIB to protect its 'green purposes', which is to be managed by a newly-formed Green Purposes Company Ltd. The consortium that purchased the GIB consists of the Macquarie European Infrastructure Fund 5 (MEIF5) and the Universities Superannuation Scheme (USS), which is the UK's largest private pension scheme, which holds around £50 billion in assets. USS assumed £600 million in liabilities to help fund the investment, stacking more on the already £17.8 billion deficit that it is currently running. Nick Mabey, chief executive of E3G (the think tank who developed the concept for the GIB), described the move as 'completely reckless' and said that it threatened to 'destroy investor confidence, which in turn will damage both energy security and the UK economy'.

The GIB was launched in November 2012 backed by £3 billion of public money. The bank posted a pre-tax profit of £100,000 for the financial year 2014/2015. Following a period of investment, development, and construction during which the fund lost £5.7 million in the financial year 2013/2014, the GIB was beginning to profit from the investments that it had made. The GIB chief executive, Shaun Kingsbury, even predicted that the 2014/15 returns suggested that the bank's shrewd investments 'should deliver a return for the taxpayer of eight per cent a year'. The government developed and incubated this fund and the second it turned profitable it was sold to the private sector at a bargain price. This is pure corporatism. Where the state is there to support and care for corporations over the people, providing corporate welfare in the form of tax breaks, subsidies, and bailouts at the expense of the taxpayer.

The idea of the Green Investment Bank was for the government to front research and development costs and encourage the sector to grow in Britain. In this it was wholly successful, for every £1 invested by the bank, £3 of third-party investment has been stimulated. This was to help David Cameron sell himself as being the 'greenest government ever' - a pledge he quickly abandoned. The Green Investment Bank was a key part of the British government's involvement in actively combating climate change and adhering to its current zero-net carbon by 2050 commitment. Yet when the opportunity came, this was abandoned in favour of the Friedman ideology and was sold off to the 'Millionaire Factory'. It was just another asset for Macquarie to strip. Macquarie have been plagued with scandals and allegations across numerous different divisions of their operations over the past decade. In 2010, the group was accused of a practice known as 'telephony bundling', which puts telecommunications services together with electronic goods or other equipment. Customers would sign up with a telecommunications firm on the understanding they would receive televisions, laptops, phones, or other electronic goods for free, but then would be hit with bills for tens of thousands of dollars under multi-year rental contracts for the equipment from a separate finance company.

In August 2014, 160,000 Macquarie Bank clients were invited to seek compensation after clients suffered heavy losses from poor advice dating back to 2004 – when the bank first obtained a financial services licence. The Australian Securities and Investments Commission (ASIC) uncovered misconduct and flawed financial advice given by its planners to clients. They faced accusations that they handed out answers to compulsory professional development exams so Macquarie advisers could cheat. On top of this, they were deliberately labelling clients as sophisticated wholesale investors so their money could be invested in risky products without the protection given to retail investors. In June 2017, it was reported that Macquarie Group were facing a major class action over allegations that some of its investment advisers artificially inflated the price of a small mining company before a sudden collapse wiped out many of its investors. The bank's brokers were accused of deliberately ramping up prices by brokering a deal to buy a Brazilian iron-ore mine project with a potential value of $34 billion that turned out to be a worthless patch of jungle.

A former divisional director at Macquarie, who has since left the bank, pushed the stock aggressively among his network of wealthy investors. It was described as the classic 'pump and dump', where stock is purchased at a low price before releasing positive, and often misleading company announcements, often promulgated on social media, on online forums, or by word-of-mouth, to temporarily raise the stock price. The Sydney Morning Herald reported that during a trip to deal with part of the acquisition of the mining company, two Macquarie executives 'repeatedly drugged a colleague with valium and laxatives'. They proceeded to send photos of the unconscious man to Macquarie staff in Australia in an attempt to ruin his reputation at the firm – those responsible were not reprimanded at the time, despite executive knowledge of their misconduct. According to Australian Securities and Investments Commission (ASIC), between 2008 and 2013 traders disclosed confidential details of client orders to third parties and revealed material information about Macquarie's trading activity in relation to large Australian-dollar trades. Traders were also discovered to be 'deliberately "triggering" prices in order to meet client orders' and attempting to manipulate the market. Macquarie was accused of running a 'farcical' compensation programme, in which a minute proportion of customers were compensated. The firm was accused of 'using its widespread failure to document advice to clients, to now deny people compensation, arguing that its brokers and financial planners gave no personal advice'.

In November 2016, the Macquarie Group admitted trying to act as a cartel to influence the benchmark rate for the Malaysian ringgit on eight separate occasions in 2011. They agreed to settle with a fine of $6 million and alleged that the conduct involved a single, junior trader who was fired in 2012 and that no senior management or any other Macquarie employees were involved in or aware of the conduct. Macquarie have also acquired a rather toxic reputation in the US for their purchases and subsequent mismanagement of public services. Since acquiring the controlling share of the 14.3-mile Dulles Greenway expressway for $615 million they steadily increased toll fees (it is now one of the most expensive in the world) and pushed traffic into residential areas, which caused chaos and outrage. They also own the Chicago Skyway, a 7.8-mile toll road which cost them a one-time upfront payment of $1.8 billion. An increase to $4 per driver on 1 January 2013 made the Skyway the most expensive toll per mile of any interstate toll system in the United States, costing motorists who use it daily approximately $2000 per year. After acquiring Aquarion, the private water utility company, for $860 million, they increased rates in Connecticut by 31 per cent. Prices had not risen in the 9 years before Macquarie took over. These rate hikes all occurred whilst investors were enjoying a 9.59 per cent annual rate of return. A Macquarie-led consortium purchased Puget Sound Energy, the largest energy company in Washington, which provides electricity and natural gas to Seattle and the surrounding area for $7.4 billion. This was financed in large part by borrowing $4.2 billion and they were accused of willingly planning to 'saddle Puget Energy with debt, sapping its financial standing and creating pressure in the future to raise rates'.

The GIB was sold at a £700,000 loss on the original investment of public money to a clearly corrupt firm with a history of asset-stripping just as it began to turn a profit for the state. The goal here isn't to help it grow in the private sector, despite what then Business Secretary Sajid Javid may say. The goal is the shrinking of the state, at whatever cost. It is not relevant whether it may be better for certain industries to be state-owned, for oversight, accountability, or performance. These are a hindrance to the market.

Corporatism as an ideology, the intertwining of the state and private industry, has triumphed alongside neo-liberalism.

In a way, they are one and the same. Privatization and no-bid contracts are a form of corporate welfare, subsidizing the corporate world by pouring taxpayers' money into a bottomless pit of shell companies and tax havens. It's a direct transfer of wealth from the public purse to corporate Britain. Britain has been stripped and sold off to the world. The nation that once ruled the globe is now owned by the rest of the world. Our nuclear power stations are owned by the French company EDF and the brand-new nuclear power station at Hinckley C is a joint French/Chinese project set to cost billions more than originally estimated. Our biggest chemical company, ICI, has been sold off to Holland, and Cadburys, the chocolate soul of Britain, to the American firm Kraft, who have outsourced production despite promises it would keep up local employment. ARM Holdings, who conduct tech research and development on computer chips and tech infrastructure, was sold in 2017 to Japanese Softbank for £24 billion along with all their mobile technology, used by Apple, Sony, Samsung, HTC, and Nokia.

A total of 70 per cent of UK rail routes are now wholly or partly owned by foreign states. Unlike our own government, the Dutch, French, Italian, and German governments are all shareholders in British rail firms. The only UK-owned franchises are FirstGroup, Stagecoach, and Virgin Trains. The UK government was actually forced to take over from Virgin Trains East Coast in June 2018 as the route was found not to be as profitable as originally projected. One of the most common tactics of foreign owners is to load the company with debt, asset strip the company and then walk away as the company folds. To squeeze every last penny out of the company they may cut pay, pension contributions, delay paying suppliers, or even buy up competitors to force up prices in an artificial monopoly. As cashflows temporarily spike they pay shareholders massive dividends and then if the company goes bust they are liable for normally just 2 per cent of the value of the company because of the magic of 'limited liability'. Social care provider Southern Cross was bought by the US firm Blackstone, saddled with debt, and left to slide into insolvency. Boots was sold in 2007, asset-stripped, and its HQ moved to Switzerland to avoid tax. It's now owned by Walgreens, the US pharmaceutical company.

By 2016-17 the jaws of privatization had begun to swallow huge portions of the NHS, especially in England. Almost 70 per cent (267 out of 386) of contracts worth £3.1 billion were awarded to private care providers. By 2018-19 that number had risen to £9.2 billion paid out to private companies, up 14 per cent from the previous year. An astonishing 44 per cent of spending on mental health services for children and teenagers went to private firms and 30 per cent of mental health budgets overall. Companies like Virgin Care have been only too happy to take up these opportunities, raking in £1 billion in NHS contracts, all whilst paying no tax in the UK (as their parent company is based in the British Virgin Islands). They were simultaneously suing six NHS commissioning care groups after they failed to win an £82 million care contract. The Conservatives scrapped the Nation Audit Office in 2015 whose job it was to hold the government to account on their spending. In a brazen act of outsourcing, it now relies on 'armchair auditors', that's the general public, to scrutinize the accounts by releasing the data online.

The financial sector, since Thatcher's 'Big Bang', has become a more and more integral part of the British economy. The City of London is the financial centre of the world (though that power could slip away post-Brexit) and because of its vast wealth and power, it seems only natural that the neo-liberals would look after capital in twenty-first century Britain. At the end of 2011, Cameron vetoed an EU treaty that would have introduced a continent-wide transaction tax and restrictions on short-selling to try to cut back on reckless speculation. Osborne went to court to stop the EU placing a cap on bankers' bonuses. The neo-liberal double act were truly protecting the most vulnerable in society.

In 2012 around 2700 bankers were paid more than $1 million.

In the decade prior to the 2008 crash, the UK financial sector grew at twice the pace of the rest of the economy. By 2011 the financial sector was worth 9.4 per cent of the entire country's economic output. The City has come to dominate the British economy, even more so than in America. In the book The Finance Curse: How Global Finance Is Making Us All Poorer, Nicholas Shaxson argues that an over-powerful financial sector is comparable to the economic consequences suffered by countries with the resource curse. The resource curse (or paradox of plenty) is when a country with an abundance of minerals or fossil fuels fails to translate resources into economic growth. This happens because foreign multinationals or governments often exploit the resources of the country (often through war, just look at Iraq) or the country focuses too much investment on their abundant resource and neglects other areas of the economy. Shaxson uses the example of Angola, where the influx of oil money pushed up local prices of goods, housing, and basic amenities. The high prices meant it was impossible for local businesses to compete with imported goods, decimating agriculture and the local economy. The rising cost of property in Britain has similarly made it more and more difficult for British companies to compete with foreign competitors. The dominant financial sector draws talent and resources away from government, civil service, and smaller private industries. A paper from The Sheffield Political Economy Research Institute indicated that the oversized financial sector in London had cost the UK £4.5 trillion from 1995-2015 in lost talent and investment whilst blowing up the price of property and other assets. Shaxson argues that the oversized financial sector in Britain has caused the same misery in Britain as the abundance of oil has caused in numerous third world countries, with the consequences disproportionately hitting the most vulnerable:

'Finance is a great geographical sorting machine, dividing us into offshore winners and onshore losers. But it is also a sorting machine for race, gender, disability and vulnerability – taking value from those suffering reduced public services or wage cuts, and from groups made up disproportionately of women, non-white people, the elderly and the vulnerable – and delivering it to the City.'

It's clear austerity exacerbated existing divisions in British society. It severely widened the gap between the richest and the poorest. The hollowing-out of the economy over the past 20 years means Britain resembles more and more a feudal society, with the ruling establishment all but separate from the working classes. The neo-liberal ideology, membership of the EU, and the narrowing of the Overton window have meant issues like immigration control, nationalization of industries, and the prioritizing of national citizens over EU citizens have been ignored by the Anywheres who run the country. Those left behind by globalization, the destruction of industry, the transition from a skills-based to a knowledge-based economy, and the mass expansion of higher education were left without recourse, representation, or remedy to their problems. Worst of all, austerity was a political decision, driven by the neo-liberal ideological campaign to privatize and corporatize. The 2010 Conservative government chose the aftermath of the financial crash and the ensuing recession to cut back state spending, privatize and sell off public assets. It was an ideological political decision to implement these sweeping cuts, one that contributed to the anti-establishment backlash that was the Brexit vote. Don't believe me that austerity was a political choice? Did you think the government was broke, that the vaults were empty and the Conservatives inherited the UK coffers in 2010 with nought to be found in them except an IOU from Gordon Brown?

From 2009 to 2012 the Bank of England (BoE) created £375 billion out of thin air, equivalent to £6000 for every man, woman, and child in the UK, before adding another £70 billion to the bill in 2016. Maybe you didn't even know that the Bank of England could do this, or that they ever had. Sounds suspiciously like a magic money tree doesn't it? They did this using a financial mechanism known as Quantitative Easing. This is not solely a BoE practice, between 2008 and 2015, the US Federal Reserve created more than $3.7 trillion to pump into the economy, whilst the EU has created around $600 billion across the Eurozone. But why do this?

When a national economy is struggling, as was the case around the world in the wake of the 2008 crash, governments often look for ways in which they can pump in money in order to keep the economy from stagnating. Cutting interest rates is often how national governments will attempt to encourage growth in times of recession or economic stagnation, but when interest rates hit zero, or close to zero, governments need another way to encourage growth and borrowing. They do this by electronically creating money – this is as simple as adding numbers to the Central Bank's computer – and using it to buy bonds or debts from banks or pension funds. The theory goes that this will increase the amount of money in the system and encourage businesses to spend. When this money was added to the economy artificially, it pushed up stock prices by 20 per cent. The richest 10 per cent of Britons saw a £322,000 bump in the price of their assets. Out of every £1 created, only 8p ever made its way to the real economy as most stock owners reinvested the money in financial markets, where it is unlikely to ever be seen by those who truly need it. The money ends up in the hands of those at the very top and rarely trickles down to the people who are struggling at the very bottom end of the income scale.

The campaign group Positive Money have argued that this money should have been injected at the very roots of the economy, not at the very top. They argue that this technique could be used to create money for infrastructure projects, to build hospitals, schools, affordable housing, solar or wind farms, whatever society needed. Positive Money estimate that if this was carried out with even a small portion of the amount created by the Bank of England from 2009-2012, that every £1 invested could grow the economy by £2.80. This is an ideological crusade based on the work of Milton Friedman. Corporate welfare has been normalized as common sense, public spending has been vilified, and government spending is becoming a de facto wealth transfer from the taxpayer into the pockets of offshore finance. It is not luck that this ideology has come to dominate the politics of the British elite, the goals of the corporate world and the free-market ideology go hand in hand – diminish all obstacles to profit. But to do that you need influence in the way governments craft legislation.

The Right-Wing Noise Machine

Lewis F. Powell was a lawyer and corporate lobbyist who was later appointed to the Supreme Court. In 1971, he wrote a secret memo for the US Chamber of Commerce called Attack on American Free Enterprise Systems. It called for corporate America to be more aggressive in moulding and influencing how people thought about politics, government, and business in the US. He implored the corporate lobby to expand the pro-business media, expand their reach in academia, reduce the power of unions, and take over the government. Documentary maker Jen Senko describes this as the pursuit of one-party rule. Noam Chompsky has also made the case that the US has become a one-party state: the Business party. He also believes the UK is not far behind America on the road to corporate governance. Whilst on the Supreme Court, Powell pushed his pro-corporate ideology. His opinion in First National Bank of Boston v. Bellotti declared that private donations to political campaigns should be protected in the same way as individual speech. It paved the way for the Citizens United ruling that made unlimited contributions to Political Action Committees (Super PACs) completely legal.

Super PACs are private campaign groups who may not co-ordinate with candidates directly.

The Lewis Powell memo (as it became known) was a call to arms against the marginalization of the free-market and pro-corporate ideology. It certainly galvanized corporate America. In 1971 there were 175 business headquarters in Washington DC. A decade later that number had grown to 2400. Powell believed devoutly in the fusion of business and government, 'If you don't know your senators on a first name basis, you are not doing an adequate job for your stockholders.' The right wing of US politics created an all-encompassing media eco-system, from Fox News through to Breitbart, the Daily Caller (another right-wing news site) and Talk Radio. After the poor performance of Richard Nixon against JFK in the televised debates and defeat in the election, the Republican Party realized that they needed a plan to take advantage of the new medium of TV. They wrote a plan to 'put the GOP on TV'. This was the foundation for Fox News, the basic theory was 'people are lazy' so they created a network where 'the thinking was done for you'. They pioneered the art of the soundbite with Richard Nixon when he was finally elected president in 1968. This media eco-system was named the Republican Noise Machine, a loud, ceaseless barrage on every medium available. Brock was once a part of the Republican noise machine. He was famous for his attacks on Bill Clinton and Anita Hill in the American Spectator, a conservative magazine funded by billionaire Richard Mellon Scaife whose fortunes come from oil, banking, and aluminium. In 2002 he released Blinded by The Right, a memoir on how he had been a part of a co-ordinated campaign funded by right-wing groups to smear the left and confuse the public. His later book The Republican Noise Machine: Right-Wing Media and How It Corrupts Democracy detailed the way in which the Conservative right, funded by billionaires and corporate America, coordinates to push free-market ideology and smear anything that challenges it. The right has come to dominate in America despite a majority of the US public backing most of Bernie Sanders' policies: universal healthcare, free college tuition, and an end to corporate money in politics. He is considered far left by their standard. Bradford Plumer summarized how the noise machine works perfectly in a Mother Jones interview with Brock from 2004:

> Fringe conspiracies and stories will be kept alive by outlets like Rush Limbaugh, the Washington Times, and the Drudge Report until they finally break into the mainstream media. Well-funded think tanks like the Heritage Foundation overwhelm news reporters with distorted statistics and conservative spin. Mainstream cable news channels employ staunchly right-wing pundits — like Pat Buchanan and Sean Hannity — to twist facts and echo Republican talking points, all under the rubric of 'balance.' Meanwhile, media groups like Brent Bozell's Media Research Center have spent 30 years convincing the public that the media is, in fact, liberal.

They created a web of think tanks to produce pro-free market white papers, reports, legislative plans, etc. They set up organizations demanding huge cuts in spending such as Americans for Prosperity, the National Tax Payers Union, Citizens Against Government Waste, and FreedomWorks, who posed as neutral bodies but pumped out free-market propaganda. They had to win students over at a university level and build an academic case for free markets to legitimize their arguments. In the 1960s there were less than 50 right-wing think tanks in the US, by 2000 that number had grown to 350.

One of the things I really struggled with when writing this book was balancing brevity with detail. I was determined to pack it with information and try and make it easy to understand and read. I know I've dished out a lot of information about a lot of different MPs, campaign groups, lobbyists, and the like. I'm trying to give you a picture of just how interconnected this world is. How, rather than one individual or corporation exerting huge influence over public policy or government decisions, it is a mesh of donors and lobbyists using soft power to push ideas in support of or directly funded by their clients. They rub shoulders with politicians at research events, charity dinners, by inviting them to speak at conferences or taking meetings with them in their official capacity as lobbyists. Money still wins elections, so money is still used to buy influence. Want to influence government policy in Britain? Here is a simple guide:

1. Pick your area of public policy. Let's say you want to turn Essex into a car park.
2. Amass some wealth through hard work or inheritance.
3. Found a think tank to produce reports in favour of your ideas. Let's call ours the Centre for Radical Innovation (CRI). They could author a report on the social and economic benefits to be gained from levelling the whole county for concrete – population reduction, job creation, decreased demand for housing in the area.
4. Register yourself as an educational charity to avoid taxation on donations.
5. Hire some lobbyists to work on your behalf and cite the reports produced by the CRI as evidence to back your proposal.
6. Throw a charity dinner and invite the relevant MPs or government minister to speak at the event (all expenses paid or in exchange for some campaign contributions). Better yet, hire them on an extravagant salary as a consultant or adviser for a few hours a month.
7. Wait and see how many of your ideas make it into legislation (or how many you oppose die in committee). You might even have some lobbyists or perhaps CRI produce draft legislation which MPs (or Member

of Congress in America) can use as a template for government legislation.

I am not suggesting that any of these individuals or groups can have a major impact on public policy or legislation, it is difficult to influence government decisions, just ask any backbench or opposition MP. What spinning a web of aligned groups and interests does is hijack the prevailing wisdom, shift the Overton window, and push governments towards adopting pro-corporate ideas. It allows pro-corporate, neo-liberal ideas to become the accepted wisdom, regardless of facts or public opinion. The revolving door between the corporate world and the political world is made easier by the web of think tanks that have sprung up in the UK. Over the past 30 years, the Establishment has built a network of think tanks and charities designed to make the case for free markets and neo-liberalism. In 'The Establishment', Conservative Robert Halfon tells Owen Jones that think tanks fuelled Thatcher's transformation of Britain, 'If you look at the Thatcher revolution, that was all powered by think tanks.' Guardian writer Aditya Chakrabortty describes this as 'one legacy of neo-liberalism: fencing off the means of knowledge production, claiming it as theirs'.

In the 1970s, free-market groups including the Institute for Economic Affairs (IEA), Centre for Policy Studies (CPS), and the Adam Smith Institute together founded the St James Society to mimic the Philadelphia Society in the US. The annual Philadelphia Society conference was a who's who of free-market Conservatives. Madsen Pirie, the founder of the Adam Smith Institute, stated that: 'Our aim was almost to try and build another consensus – or not quite consensus, but to create the impression that a tide was surging in that direction.'[76] They were determined to upset the post-war status quo that was generally more socialist and less supportive of privatization and lowering trade barriers. To do that they had to begin by creating an academic backing for their argument, or at least a perceived one. Thus they pumped money and resources into creating think tanks to produce free trade papers and proposals.

Let's take an example. The Legatum Institute is a right-wing free-market think tank funded by the New Zealand born Chandler brothers, who made billions during the 1990s in Russia. After making their fortune investing in Honk Kong real estate, they formed the investment firm Sovereign Global in Monaco to focus on transitioning industries in Russia, Latin America, and Eastern Europe. Legatum is just a single wing of a large Dubai-based hedge fund that gives millions to the Legatum Foundation, which in turn provides the money to run the Legatum Institute. In 2017 their ties to the Brexit department and the background of Christopher Chandler came under scrutiny from the Charity Commission. Conservative MP Bob Seely said that he and four other MPs had seen documents from Monaco's security department that related to 'national security and money laundering' and included information supplied by the DST intelligence agency, France's equivalent of MI5. The files indicate that Chandler had been 'an object of interest' to the DST since 2002 because of suspicion that he was working for Russian intelligence services.

The Mail on Sunday published a detailed story on Chandler's alleged ties to Moscow. It claimed that Legatum's economics director, Shanker Singham, had met Boris Johnson and Michael Gove, and had co-ordinated a letter written by them to Theresa May demanding a hard Brexit. In the letter, they cited an IEA plan to slash top-rate taxes and begin a red-tape fire to make the UK attractive for businesses post-Brexit. Singham held discussions with leading cabinet Brexiteers on multiple occasions and saw representatives of David Davis's department six times in the year up to August 2017. Legatum's CEO, Baroness Stroud, co-founded the Centre for Social Justice think tank alongside Iain Duncan Smith and was previously his special adviser. Matthew

Elliot, head of Vote Leave, is a senior fellow, Toby Baxendale, who helped run Andrea Leadsom's Tory leadership campaign, is a trustee of the charity, and Theresa May, then home secretary, was a guest speaker at the 2015 Legatum summer party. The foreign funders of the hard-Brexit think tank stand to benefit substantially from heavy deregulation of environmental restrictions, tax evasion laws, and workers' rights. Guy Shrubsole, a campaigner at Friends of the Earth, commented that,

'Legatum's demands for deregulation after Brexit, and its full-throttled support for letting the market loose, raise questions about who is trying to profit from the Brexit process. People who voted 'leave' were urged to do so to 'take back control' - not cede control to a shadowy network of think-tanks and backroom lobbyists.'

The Charity Commission launched a probe into whether Legatum's push for a hard Brexit goes beyond its educational remit as a charity emphasizing to 'advance the education of the public in national and international political, social and economic policy'. Legatum was only able to gain charitable status in 2010 after overcoming questions from the UK Charity Commission over whether it would be able to advance 'education in the charitable sense rather than simply promoting a particular point of view'. There are countless links between the Institute and senior government ministers. A former Legatum adviser, Crawford Falconer, is Britain's chief trade negotiations adviser, second in command in the Department for International Trade. The Brexit Department has failed to respond to various freedom of information requests about its relationship with Legatum. The Mail on Sunday photographed Shanker Singham, director of economic policy at Legatum, and Michael Gove at a behind-closed-doors Commons seminar on Brexit, also attended by Number 10 and US embassy officials. The Mail claimed that this was the most recent of at least seven meetings with ministers over the past 14 months, prompting further questions over the access Legatum now has to the government. The investigation by the Charity Commission found that Legatum had 'crossed a clear line' in its political work. They were instructed to take down a pro-Brexit report on their website, and their work is to be monitored closely. Singham left the charity in March 2018, followed by Matthew Elliott in May, in the light of the controversy and ongoing investigation. Legatum has abandoned its work on Brexit for the foreseeable future.

This is, unfortunately, as in the case of the Green Investment Bank, just the tip of the Iceberg. In Britain, we also have a network of right-wing think tanks with shady funding streams pushing the neo-liberal case. In the UK many of these groups operate out of 55 Tufton Street, including Matthew Elliot's TPA. Number 55 Tufton Street is owned by Richard Smith, a former trustee of Matthew Elliot's pro-Brexit Politics and Economics Research Trust, and houses:

- Global Warming Policy Foundation (GWPF)
- TPA
- Business for Britain (Until October 2015)
- Vote Leave (which became Leave Means Leave)
- The European Foundation
- UK2020
- Civitas
- New Culture Forum
- Global Vision
- Brexit Central (a pro-Brexit news site founded by Matthew Elliott)
- Migration Watch UK

The Global Warming Policy Foundation (GWPF) was established in 2009 by former Conservative chancellor Lord Lawson with the explicit goal to challenge the 'extremely damaging and harmful policies' that are being proposed as part of our fight against man-made climate change. Because it is registered as a charity it is not required to supply its sources of funding, but director Benny Peiser has assured the public that GWPF does not receive funding 'from people with links to energy companies or from the companies themselves'. Known to have donated to GWPF are the 'godfather of Tory donors', Michael Hintze (who also donated £225,000 to Vote Leave) and Neil Record, who donated £450,000 to the Conservatives between 2010 and 2017. Matt Ridley is a former chief of Northern Rock, an ardent climate change denier, and a Murdoch journalist for The Times and The Sun. Ridley is on the Academic Advisory Council of the Global Warming Policy Foundation and is a policy adviser for UK2020. He appeared on stages with BfB and was involved with the Vote Leave campaign. He receives revenue from two open-cast coal mines on his estate in Northumbria worth roughly £336 million and has previously used his House of Lords seat to oppose renewable energy measures. He breached the Lords code of conduct in a 2014 debate on fracking after failing to mention his personal investment in the Weir group who make fracking equipment. Ridley has complained that 'red tape' is stifling science in the EU, citing the EU ban on neonicotinoid pesticides known to be harmful to bees. In 2014 they were ruled to have breached their charitable status by blurring fact and fiction and breaching impartiality rules in their educational services on climate change. The Charity Commission commented in their report: 'The website could not be regarded as a comprehensive and structured educational resource sufficient to demonstrate public benefit. In areas of controversy, education requires balance and neutrality with sufficient weight given to competing arguments. The promotion of a particular view or position would not equate to education.'

Former Tory MP Peter Lilley (now Lord Lilley) sits on the GWPF advisory board. He was one of only five MPs to vote against the UK's Climate Change Act in 2008 that, although critiqued by groups like Friends of the Earth and WWF for not going far enough, received almost universal cross-party support to map out the government's long-term plan for climate change targets. Lilley is on the board at Tethys Petroleum, a Cayman Island-based oil and gas company. In January 2018, he spoke to a Chinese businesswoman claiming to represent 'high net worth individuals' in Hong Kong and China. He elaborated on how he expected to receive a peerage in the next round of honours and that he had close links to Brexit minister Steve Baker and special access to International Trade Secretary Liam Fox's department. The woman, who was an undercover Channel 4 reporter, told Lilley that he would be an ideal candidate to sit on the advisory board of Tianfen Consulting, a strategic communications firm. He also boasted of his regular meetings with the ERG, a faction of Eurosceptic Tory MPs pushing for a hard Brexit who have been headed by Jacob Rees-Mogg since January 2018. He appeared to offer up his influence in post-Brexit Britain. Lilley reported Channel 4 to Ofcom over the broadcast.

The TPA was founded by Matthew Elliott in 2004. They sell themselves as a 'non-partisan grassroots campaign for lower taxes and better public spending'. Their website declares that 'the TPA is committed to forcing politicians to listen to ordinary taxpayers'. They make themselves media-friendly and release short research notes for press releases – saving journalists from reading long and complex research papers. Employees of the TPA regularly appear on BBC programming posing as impartial representatives of regular citizens. Elliott hoped that they could operate less like a think tank and more like a lobby group. They took inspiration from Americans for Prosperity and Americans for Tax Reform, the lobby groups funded by the oil billionaires, the Koch brothers. Elliott's wife Sarah once worked at the Americans for Tax Reform and credits its boss, Grover Norquist, for inspiring the way the TPA operates.

After the Thatcher years, the low taxes, small state rhetoric wasn't making the impact they wanted. Though Blair was happy to push on with some privatization and had bought into globalization as the future, he still believed in a role for the state. The Conservatives were almost trying to match Labour's spending pledges until the 2008 crash. When Labour made the argument that we needed to continue to spend our way out of recession, the Tories backed a period of austerity, to tighten our belts and rein in reckless spending. By reckless spending, we mean public services, the welfare state, and social care. Not fossil fuel subsidies and costly, unaccountable outsourcing. The goal of the TPA is, according to Owen Jones, 'to demonize public spending, portraying hard-earned taxpayers' money as gratuitously wasted on gimmicks and perks'.[77] The TPA is part of the World Taxpayers Associations, an international coalition of anti-tax, free-market campaign groups that includes the Australian Taxpayers' Alliance, Americans for Tax Reform, the Austrian Economics Center, and the Canadian Taxpayers' Federation. At the 2016 Conservative Party Conference, they hosted a free trade event alongside the Competitive Enterprise Institute (CEI) and the Heritage Foundation, two other US-based free-market climate science deniers funded by the fossil fuel lobby. The TPA is intertwined not only with powerful international corporate interests, but with the most powerful people in Britain and the right wing of British politics. The confidential guest list for their post-2010 roundtable discussion included Douglas Carswell, the first UKIP defector from the Conservative Party, Eurosceptic MEP Daniel Hannan, Aemon Butler of the Adam Smith Institute, Mark Littlewood from the IEA, Richard Ritchie, UK Director of Government Affairs at BP, and blogger Paul Staines.[78]

In the US, the Tea Party is a libertarian faction of the Republican Party that pushes for free trade, low taxes, and low regulation on behalf of corporate America under the guise of a grassroots movement demanding freedom and liberty. Owen Paterson has set up his very own British franchise in the form of UK2020, who want to release Britain from climate change regulations and targets that hinder the free market. Matt Ridley and Tim Montgomerie, founder of the website ConservativeHome and a former senior fellow at the Legatum Institute, are advisers for the group. Paterson gave a speech to the GWPF in which he declared that climate change predictions have been 'consistently and wildly exaggerated'. In an article for ConservativeHome in 2016, he branded the NHS not 'fit for purpose' and advocated for insurance-based models like Japan, Singapore, and Canada. He used the think tank to pay for £39,000 worth of overseas trips, including one to the US to promote post-Brexit trade, and refuses to disclose the donor. Paterson is also on the political advisory board of Leave Means Leave, who are calling for a 'WTO Brexit'.

Civitas, another 'neo-liberal' think tank in 55 Tufton Street, began life as the IEA Health and Welfare Unit and was spun off as its own institution in 2000. They have produced work arguing for the privatization of NHS services and have been criticized by Transparify for their opaque funding arrangements. The trustees of Civitas are Sir Alan Rudge, who is an adviser at the GWPF, and Lord Nigel Vinson, a former GWFP donor.

The New Culture Forum (NCF) is a more culturally focused think tank, who believe that cultural debates have become dominated by 'the left'. The first line on their website reads, 'Culture, it is said, is upstream from politics', echoing the Steve Bannon philosophy word-for-word. The NCF supported Brexit and have published a book by founder Peter Whittle titled 'Being British: What's Wrong with It?' as part of their war on the 'triumph of cultural relativism and political correctness in the opinion-forming fields of the media, academia, education and culture'. Michael Gove, Richard Smith (the owner of 55 Tufton Street), Tim Montgomerie, former UKIP deputy leader Peter Whittle, Lord Nigel Vinson, and Matthew Elliott all sit on the advisory board. The NCF is funded by PERT, a tax-focused research charity founded in 2004 by Matthew Elliot.

As well as the NCF, they fund the TPA (to whom they have given around £2 million), the pro-Brexit group BfB, and the CPS, another free-market think tank. Richard Smith is a trustee and former director and the Vote Leave donor Richard Barbour was formerly a director. Barbour was also a director at Civitas until 2010 and donates to the Bruges Group, another neo-liberal think tank. In its first 2 years, PERT gave £505,000, more than 90 per cent of its total funding, to the TPA. Emma Reynolds, the Labour MP and former shadow minister for Europe, wrote to the Charity Commission about concerns over the charitable status of both PERT and the TPA: 'PERT may be in breach of charities' legally binding commitments to preserve their independence, specifically regarding political activity and the delivery of charitable objectives.'

This stream of funding continues to this day. The Charity Commission investigation found that there was no oversight or procedure in place to ensure that research funded by the charity was furthering the impartial goals of the charity and asked them to put in place more formal arrangements to ensure more impartiality in the future. However, impartiality feels difficult when 97 per cent of their funding goes to overtly pro-Brexit causes.

Elliott is also on the advisory board at the Eurosceptic think tank, The European Foundation (chaired by Conservative MP Bill Cash), alongside Richard Smith, David Davis, Sir Graham Brady (former chairman of the 1922 committee), former Tory leader Iain Duncan Smith, Owen Paterson, and a handful of other Conservative MPs. The European Foundation was formed in October 1992 to oppose the Maastricht Treaty. It was initially funded by Sir James Goldsmith, leader of the British Referendum Party at the time, and later by Margaret Thatcher, who later became Patron of the Foundation. In 2009 they published a report arguing that humans are in no way responsible for climate change titled, '100 reasons why global warming is natural'. The author of the report, Jim McConalogue, warned that the Copenhagen climate summit could lead to 'nonsensical targets' to reduce emissions and a 'burdensome regulatory agenda'.

Policy Exchange was founded in 2002 by a group of Tory MPs (including future front-bencher Michael Gove and junior minister from the Cameron government Nick Boles[79]) and two former Asda executives, Francis Maude and Archie Norman. Several former Policy Exchange figures went on to be special advisers in the Cameron government, such as Alex Morton who was appointed to the Social Security Advisory Committee after authoring a report that advised the sell-off of council property. Policy Exchange has been described as the most influential think tank on the right of British politics, advocating for free-market solutions to public policy problems. Transparify rated their funding structure as '"highly opaque," one of 'a handful of think tanks that refuse to reveal even the identities of their donors'. They have advocated for a 'WTO Brexit' claiming that Britain would thrive by leaving the EU without a trade deal.

These groups are part of a wider network of right-wing free-market think tanks that are being used to expand and maintain the neo-liberal status quo. An investigation by DeSmog UK found that many of these groups were being funded by climate change deniers and US billionaires waiting to pounce on the post-Brexit UK. The free-market believers in the UK drew inspiration from the US conservatives. In Britain, the post-war consensus was one in support of state intervention and ownership of industries. Through the 1970s, they promoted their ideas through the media and by founding a number of think tanks and campaign groups to give academic credence to their arguments. They present themselves as neutral, grassroots movements put together by concerned citizens who want the best outcome for the nation, but are instead a way for the wealthy to lobby and influence government policy.

Just down the road from 55 Tufton Street is the Adam Smith

Institute, one of three think tanks at the centre of the Thatcher revolution. It was founded in 1977 by Madsen Pirie and Eamon Butler, one year after the two-hundredth anniversary of the publication of The Wealth of Nations, a kind of bible for free-marketeers around the world. Pirie believed that the market was the greatest force for good and that public services would perform much better upon privatization. They outlined visions for the outsourcing of local government services, the privatization of public transport, the slashing of the top rate of tax (from 83 per cent to 40 per cent), and the liberalization of alcohol licensing laws that were later put in place by Thatcher.

Alongside the ASI, Thatcher relied on the IEA and the CPS to provide her with legislative inspiration. The IEA is a free-market think tank and 'educational charity' whose trustees include Nigel Vinson, Neil Record, and Michael Hintze — all of whom donate to the GWPF. The IEA has been at the centre of a push to allow US corporations access to deregulated post-British markets. A 6-month investigation run by Greenpeace in collaboration with The Guardian found that Michael Carnuccio, CEO of the US-based E Foundation for Oklahoma, had promised donors the ability to influence Brexit policy via the IEA. This would include the ability to shape agricultural, environmental, and food standards. Discussions were had over how to sell chlorinated chicken to the British public through a co-ordinated media campaign with the IEA's director-general Mark Littlewood:

'Mark starts talking about how to get a free trade agreement done, what I need in the United States is I need some partners and I need a big media push on the May government and others...in the UK.'

Carnuccio told an undercover reporter that they were pitching Shanker Singham's access and influence within Westminster, including connections with Liam Fox, Michael Gove, and Boris Johnson:

'If they don't know them, then we just explain they're the

free-market organisation that is the private sector trade advisor right now through working in that capacity with Shanker, so they have the access, they have the influence.'

The investigation also found director Mark Littlewood claiming that Shanker Singham, who was working with the IEA at the time, was drafting a post-Brexit US and UK trade deal that he would attempt to get both governments to sign. He arranged for meetings between potential investors, Steve Baker (then a Brexit minister), and officials at the Foreign Office and the Department for International Trade. Singham was also a policy expert at the US-based Heartland Institute who has been bankrolled to the tune of at least £676,500 by ExxonMobil since 1998, though their funding sources are currently kept under wraps. The Union of Concerned Scientists found that 'nearly 40 per cent of the total funds that the Heartland Institute has received from ExxonMobil since 1998 were specifically designated for climate change projects'. Legatum's Alden Abbot has also produced a report for the Heartland Institute and was a deputy director at The Heritage Foundation.

During what Littlewood described as a 'lucrative' 13 stop US tour, he told potential donors that Brexit provided an opportunity to 'shed' restricting EU regulations. The idea was to sell a vision of deregulated Britain to US interests. For example, Singham was an advocate of dropping the EU precautionary principle. It states that if there is a possibility that a specific policy could cause harm to the public or the environment, and if there is no scientific consensus as to whether it is healthy, that these policies shall not be pursued. He proposed a deal that would lower British safety standards for food and would allow a hormone fed beef and chlorine-washed chicken to be sold on the UK market.

Unearthed, the investigative outlet run by Greenpeace, also revealed that the Bison Club – a group of donors from US agriculture and energy – was planning to raise $250-400,000 to lobby on post-Brexit trade. The IEA has claimed that this group simply does not exist. I had the opportunity to interview Mark Littlewood for my podcast about their proposals for a post-Brexit Britain, where they played down fears of how disastrous a 'no-deal' Brexit would be for the UK economy. When I quizzed him on the accusations made by Greenpeace and The Guardian, he argued that it was preposterous that the IEA, a small think tank, could have the ability to influence government policy.

The IEA have close ties to Conservative MP Owen Paterson, who, during his time as the secretary of state for environment, food and rural affairs, cut funding for climate change adaptation by around 40 per cent. He also stated on BBC Radio 4's Any Questions? in June 2013 that 'the temperature has not changed in the last 17 years', a commonly repeated climate denier talking point. It carefully picked a period between a peak and trough in global temperatures, but when taken in the context of the past 100 years looks much more foolish. Look closely, the period in question is from 1997-2013. Paterson took advantage of an all-expenses-paid trip to the States to speak at the Heritage Foundation (a Koch Brothers funded think tank) in March 2015 and has since spoken at a few other anti-regulation think tanks including the CEI. The CEI has been outspoken against what they call, 'global warming alarmism' and in 2009 their director of energy and global warming policy told The Washington Post, 'The only thing that's been demonstrated to reduce emissions is economic collapse.'

Hintze has also historically been a backer of Boris Johnson, and the two worked together alongside Michael Gove at Liam Fox's now dismantled think tank, The Atlantic Bridge, which lobbied to increase trade links between the UK and US. The Atlantic Bridge is known for its 2007 partnership with the American Legislative Exchange Council (ALEC), a Koch Brothers enterprise who produce template pieces of legislation that would reduce environmental protections and /or other 'red tape'. The charity was shut down in 2011 following a Charity Commission investigation that found it had partaken in heavily politicized work. Hintze was also on the advisory board of BfB. Mark Littlewood contributed as a part of the editorial board to their 1000-page Brexit 'bible', which provided intellectually digestible weight behind the Brexit campaign.

The IEA, TPA, CPS, ASI, and Civitas are members of the Atlas Network. A Washington-based non-profit encompassing 450 free-market groups around the world. The Atlas Network is funded by climate deniers and fossil fuel magnates, including the Koch Brothers who own the largest private fossil fuel company in America. The Kochs have previously collaborated with ExxonMobil to fund the Committee for a Constructive Tomorrow (CFACT), who are one of the most effective climate denial groups in the US.

The CPS was co-founded by Margaret Thatcher in 1974 to combat the Keynesian consensus of British politics. They were committed to the free-market ideals of Hayek and Friedman, encouraging and successfully arguing for the privatization of British Telecom and the introduction of private industry to the telecommunication sector. More recently they issued reports that successfully lobbied for the lower rate of corporation tax and against the proposed 'mansion tax'. When they had their thirty-fifth anniversary in 2009, David Cameron credited their role through the 1970s with 'a great rebirth of intellectual ideas, of intellectual vigour, and of intellectual leadership'.

Consumer Watchdog Tobacco Tactics conducted some research into the Adam Smith Institute, CPS, and the IEA. They have each received secretive funding from the tobacco industry and produced research and reports that were used to lobby in opposition to stronger anti-smoking regulations:

'We found that the Adam Smith Institute has created a structure so opaque that it concealed not only who gave money, but also who took it, leaving us unable to determine where close to one million pounds given by American donors had ended up.'

The IEA, CPS, and the Adam Smith Institute were all given an abysmal E rating (the scale runs from A-E) by the watchdog Who Funds You, as were the TPA and Policy Exchange, for their opaque and secretive funding structures.

I don't want to make it seem like I am suggesting that these groups are all actively working together on some grand, meticulous, decades-long conspiracy. I don't believe they are quite that competent. Rather it is an entire community of partially aligned and partially competing entities and individuals who benefit from broadly the same policies and would suffer from measures that they collectively oppose - fracking bans, environmental regulation, and the EU-wide crackdown on tax evasion, amongst other things. The think tanks have become so intertwined with government that their goals seem to almost merge as one. Jen Senko, who produced The Brainwashing of My Dad, a documentary that examines the power of Fox News to manipulate and change viewers, calls the takeover of the free-market right-wing ideology in America 'the slow boiling coup'. I spoke to Senko for my very first podcast episode, she told me: 'The right's idea was to divide and conquer and separate us and they've successfully done that. So now we can't talk to each other.' I believe we are witnessing the culmination of a very similar situation in the UK. For decades in the US, the right-wing noise machine has created a pastiche of media, academia, and lobbying all in pursuit of reducing the size of the state. In the 1970s Thatcher welcomed in the age of neo-liberalism, signalling the takeover of the upper echelons of British politics by the free-market ideology. To achieve this goal, Nicholas Shaxson alleges in The Finance Curse: How Global Finance Is Making Us All Poorer that the British establishment 'shapes laws, rules, thinktanks and even our culture so that they support it. The outcomes include lower economic growth, steeper inequality, distorted markets, spreading crime, deeper corruption, the hollowing-out of alternative economic sectors and more.' This ideology now permeates every powerful institution in Britain, from the press and think tanks, to politicians and the civil service.

Are they succeeding? Between 2010 and 2015, the massive gulf in wealth inequality in the UK widened even further. The GDP of the richest regions in Britain went from more than eight times the national average to 11.5 times the national average whilst the poorest regions saw their GDP dip. The disciples of Friedman and Thatcher have succeeded in concentrating the wealth of Britain in the hands of very few, selling off the state, and rolling back regulations. But the EU stood in the way of truly free markets and maximum deregulation.

Shock and Chaos
Politicians struggled to separate their ambitions for Britain from their own ambitions and their families' ascent into the six figure income class.
James Meek, Private Island

In the book No Is Not Enough, Naomi Klein condemns Friedman's ideology as an assault on the public interest:

The goal is all out war on the public sphere and the public interest, whether in the form of antipollution regulations or programs for the hungry. In their place will be unfettered power and freedom for corporations. It's a program so defiantly unjust and so manifestly corrupt that it can only be pulled off with the assistance of divide-and-conquer racial and sexual politics, as well as a nonstop spectacle of media distractions.[80]

The ultimate goal was to create a blank slate upon which the free-market could be introduced. In Chile, Argentina, Uruguay, and Indonesia, right-wing coups paired free market economists pushing economic 'shock therapy' with terror dished out by militaries and police forces. Many of the economists were students of Friedman himself. The Ford Foundation and Rockefeller Foundation sponsored Chilean students to attend the Chicago School of Economics as a way of growing the academic influence of their ideas in Chile. The graduates who returned home built their own little Chicago School in the Pontifical Catholic University of Chile. The Heritage Foundation has credited them with transforming Chile into one of the world's most business-friendly nations and Latin America's best-performing economy.

Klein repeatedly compares the shocks experienced by these economies to the trauma experienced by victims of torture in countries like Chile and Iraq, 'The shock doctrine mimics this process precisely, attempting to achieve on a mass scale what torture does one on one in an interrogation cell.' The goal of the brutal electroshock techniques was to produce a blank slate upon which a new person could be built. The shocks were designed to soften up the victim, to 'depattern' them. There is a breaking point at which a victim of torture or electroshock therapy is much more susceptible to suggestion and willing to do or say things they would not normally. The economic remedies prescribed by the 'shock doctors' are so unpalatable to the general public that they cannot be implemented without shock and chaos, manufactured or natural.

At the end of the Korean War, 21 US prisoners of war declared that they would not return home, but instead they wished to remain in China. The fear of Communist states brainwashing prisoners or citizens was rife in America and the US military and CIA began their own programmes to help understand how the human mind could be reprogrammed. One of the scientists they turned to was Donald Ewen Cameron, a Scottish psychiatrist who experimented with an assault of psychiatric drugs, sensory deprivation, and electroconvulsive therapy. Between 1957 and 1964 he performed the MK Ultra experiments in Montreal on innocent US and Canadian civilians, many of whom suffered only mild conditions like anxiety disorders or post-natal depression. In Chile, Argentina, America, and now Britain, shock treatment was dished out to a mostly healthy body. His goal was to reach the tipping point where patients could be remoulded with little resistance. This is why shock was used to implement highly unpopular free-market policies. You have to reach that point of chaos to ensure a less resistant population. Cameron reportedly kept patients in states of coma for weeks at a time, whilst playing tape loops on repeat and used electroshock therapy doses 30 to 40 times higher than normal – not that electroshock can ever really be considered a normal course of treatment.

Peter Hargreaves donated just a smidge over £3 million (£3.2 million if we're counting) to the cause to free Britain from the EU stranglehold. The 69-year-old founder of stockbroker Hargreaves Lansdown told Reuters that Brexit would give the British economy a shot in the arm, 'It would be the biggest stimulus to get our butts in gear that we have ever had.' He talked of defeating the evils of mainland Europe with wartime spirit, 'It will be like Dunkirk again...We will get out there and we will become incredibly successful because we will be insecure again. And insecurity is fantastic.' Insecurity is fantastic with those of us with the money to take advantage of it. Create chaos and leverage the madness, it's pure shock doctrine. He believes that the EU creates an unnecessary extra burden on UK businesses with red tape: 'Some of the regulation that we have to obey is bizarre and by people who have never been to Britain and wouldn't know how to spell financial services.'

He offered up Singapore as a template for how Britain could operate outside the EU as a low-regulation tax haven. He argued that 'no deal' would only cause a little market turbulence, after which the UK would quickly become prosperous again, just like Singapore, 'That little insecurity that they were no longer part of Malaysia, it was an inspiration. I honestly think that would be good for us too.' Hargreaves has also been keen to cut public spending despite the massive cuts to public services to date. He's a free-market purist and has also advocated for a 'no-deal' Brexit, telling Bloomberg, 'The best option is no deal...No deal would give us free trade with Europe because the three biggest economies in Europe, outside Britain, are huge exporters to the UK.' Despite this, he has claimed he would stake his entire £3.6 billion fortune on getting a free trade deal with Europe, or namely France, Germany, and Italy, though that would have to be via a EU free trade deal. Shares in Hargreaves Lansdown hit an all-time high in May 2019.

Multinationals will let nothing stand in the way of profits and they are more than prepared to engage governments and militaries in their plans to grow their revenue. From the moment Allende was elected in Chile, he was at war with corporate America. Nixon instructed the CIA to 'make the economy scream' whilst an 'Ad Hoc Committee on Chile' was formed to deal with the crisis. The committee included US companies with major mining operations in Chile, Pfizer Chemical, Bank of America, and the committee leader, the International Telephone and Telegraph Company (ITT), who stood to lose out if Allende nationalized the Chilean phone company. They would not let Allende succeed. Not because he posed a danger to his citizens or the world; US Senate reports from the time show that Allende posed no threat to democracy in Chile. His populist left-wing politics could not be seen to succeed in transforming the country positively at the expense of the wealthy. Together with the CIA and Chicago School economists, they plotted Pinochet's coup. Taking inspiration from military coups in Brazil and Indonesia, they put together an economic plan known as 'the brick', that would slash regulation, rapidly sell off state assets, and cut taxes for the wealthiest. The goal was a total economic transformation that could only be achieved when married with violence, torture, shock, and chaos.

In 1964 Brazilian General Humberto plotted to overthrow the democratically elected left-wing government. He wanted to strip back welfare programmes and open Brazil up to multinationals and privatization. Though the coup began more peacefully than in Indonesia the following year, it was later revealed that some 'subversives' were captured and tortured. This was nowhere near the scale of terror that Pinochet would embark upon a decade later, killing over 3000 people and interning 80,0000. The 1965 coup by General Suharto in Indonesia was accompanied by the massacre of between 500,000 and 1 million people. It was a brutal regime of terror designed to create the conditions for the economic shock therapy that was to follow. Just as the Chicago Boys had provided the economic blueprint for Pinochet, a group of Indonesian academics known as the Berkley Mafia (who had been educated in the free-market doctrine at the University of California) issued Suharto with academic backing. Though not as extreme as the Chicago Boys, the Berkley Mafia, many of whom were appointed as economic advisers to the dictator, ensured that within 2 years the country's natural resources were being divvied up amongst the largest mining and fossil fuel companies in the world whilst they enjoyed tax breaks and the low wage economy.

In 1981, after an inspiring trip to Chile in 1981, Friedrich Hayek wrote to Thatcher encouraging her to pioneer free-market ideas in Britain using the Chilean transformation as a model. Yet when Thatcher wrote back she dashed his hopes, telling him, 'I am sure you will agree that, in Britain with our democratic institutions and the need for a high degree of consent, some of the measures adopted in Chile are quite unacceptable. Our reform must be in line with our traditions and our Constitution. At times the process may seem painfully slow.' Thatcher didn't believe that shock therapy was viable in the UK. It was too severe to impose on a democratic nation, so whilst she was supportive of Pinochet, she believed it was not possible to so rapidly remodel the British economy.

Nixon too, despite his facilitation of the Pinochet revolution, was unwilling to put the free market to work in the US. The US economy was in a tough spot, rising unemployment and inflation meant Friedman expected Nixon, whom he declared came 'closer to expressing a philosophy compatible with my own', to implement Chicago School economics in their homeland. Despite naming a Friedman disciple in Donald Rumsfeld (who would go on to oversee the George W. Bush military privatization post 9/11) as an economic adviser, Nixon put price and rent controls in place – a move that Friedman described as 'a cancer that can destroy an economic system's capacity to function'. Nixon was victorious in the next election before the Watergate scandal forced his resignation.

In Britain, Thatcher pioneered the ownership society. She wagered that by helping low-income residents to buy council houses at reduced rates, they would buy into her unrestrained capitalism that drove up house prices and benefitted those who owned property and assets. It was a far cry from an overnight success story. By 1982 unemployment had doubled under Thatcher and opinion polling on her government had dropped to 18 per cent. Her personal approval rating hovered around 25 per cent. On 2 April 1982 Argentina invaded the Falkland Islands, an outpost that Thatcher had previously shown disdain for, cutting defence and financial aid through her first 3 years in government. There were suggestions that her foreign policy was begging Argentina to invade. General Galtieri was struggling to keep the country under control as it underwent its 'shock therapy' and wagered that the only thing stronger than anti-elite sentiment in Argentina was anti-imperial hatred. Thatcher jumped at the chance to become the true 'Iron Lady'; in just 11 weeks, at the cost of 255 British soldiers and 655 Argentinians, Thatcher's government soared to 59 per cent approval, riding to victory on a wave of nationalist pride and she declared that

Britain must now turn its attention to 'the enemy within'.

In Chile, Argentina, Bolivia, and Uruguay, it was necessary to break the unions with physical force. They were likely to provide the highest level of resistance to the neo-liberal economics that governments were trying to impose upon their respective nations. Thatcher waged an ideological war on the miners, more concerned with breaking them than finding a solution to the strike. She carried out a military level counter-surveillance operation to infiltrate, destabilize, and sabotage the unions. Thatcher was ready to show that unions could not stand against the power of the state. Reagan was similarly harsh to union action, sacking 11,400 air-traffic controllers in a single day for striking. In Britain, 3000 extra police a day were brought in to defeat the miners' strike by any means necessary. Author of The Enemy Within Seamas Milne documented the war on the miners that involved 'militarised police occupation of the coalfields; the 11,000 arrests, deaths, police assaults, mass jailings and sackings; the roadblocks, setups and false prosecutions'. By 1985 she had succeeded. Thatcher had broken the most powerful union in Britain. Ironically, the Falklands War, codenamed Operation Corporate, allowed Thatcher to promote her own Operation Corporate in Britain, beginning a near 40-year reign of corporate dominance. Her use of the Falklands was proof that you didn't need extreme violence or unrest inside a country to implement Friedmanite economics.

Around the same time, there was another neo-liberal success story emerging in South America. In 1984 Bolivia was undergoing a democratic revolution after almost 2 decades of intermittent authoritarian rule. The previous year, Reagan had imposed economic sanctions on Bolivian coca farmers (the leaf that can be refined into cocaine) that transformed half the country into a military zone. Export revenue was cut in half and inflation peaked at 14,000 per cent prior to the 1985 elections. The choice was between former dictator Hugo Banzer and the former elected president Vctor Paz Estenssoro. The race was incredibly tight and the final ruling on the election was left to the Bolivian Congress. Paz was declared the winner, reportedly with the help of Senator Gonzalo Snchez de Lozada (in Bolivia, he's known as Goni). Goni, one of Bolivia's wealthiest men and a Chicago School graduate, was then appointed to a secret economic team alongside Harvard economist Jeffrey Sachs. Paz brought in Sachs to stabilize the economy after he claimed he could end the inflation crisis in a single day.

He prescribed a 300 per cent hike of oil prices, massive cuts to social spending, unrestricted imports, and the downsizing of state companies to prepare for privatization. Paz, who had overseen the nationalization of many industries during his previous tenure, was about to impart neo-liberal shock therapy on an unsuspecting country. One of the main authors of the plan compared the rollout of their economic vision to the pilot who dropped the first atomic bomb on Hiroshima, 'When he saw the smoke he said: "Oops, sorry!" And that's exactly what we have to do, launch the measure and then: Oops, sorry!' To avoid resistance it was all packaged into one executive decree, the Bolivian equivalent of 'the Brick'. Sachs succeeded, in 2 years inflation was down to a manageable 10 per cent and he was praised as an economic hero the world over. The New York Times hailed him as the 'evangelist for democratic capitalism'.

Inside those 2 years unemployment rose from 20 per cent to 30 per cent, real wages dropped 40 per cent, whilst a wealthy group of businessmen saw their fortunes grow bountifully. Hundreds of thousands of secure full-time jobs with pensions were replaced with ones with no protections or benefits. When policy makers became uneasy over the human cost of the policies, Sachs told them: 'When it really gets out of control you've got to stop it, like a medicine. You've got to take some radical steps; otherwise your patient is going to die.' In an ironic twist, a story that began with Reagan's economic war on coca farmers ended

2 years later with 350,000 people working as part of the drugs trade; poverty-stricken Bolivians were pushed to grow coca out of economic desperation induced by free-market shock therapy. Bolivia was proving, however poorly, that it was possible to impart these policies to an unwilling public inside a democracy, with no violent coup or war involved. Paz ran on a nationalistic platform, only to open the country up to a flood of foreign imports and sell off state assets. Economist John Williamson described it as 'voodoo politics'. Except, there was resistance, unions organized protests and strikes only to be greeted with armed police. As he passed his economic atomic bomb, Paz declared a 3-month state siege, gassed and arrested protestors, and used the military to round up union leaders and fly them to a remote jail in the Amazon. As ransom, he demanded that the union protests came to an end; which they soon did. A year later he declared a second state of siege as resistance to his programme grew once again into protests. Paz rounded up union leaders and two former Labour ministers and held them in internment camps for two-and-a-half weeks until the strikes were called off again. Those who continued to strike found themselves out of work and living in the burgeoning shanty towns and slums around La Paz. The rise of homelessness and poverty follows in the wake of every neo-liberal takeover as wages are pushed down and the middle class decimated. When the Chicago Boys were unleashed upon Uruguay real wages dropped 28 per cent and roaming groups of scavengers and homeless people became the norm on the streets of Montevideo. Britain has seen a 165 per cent increase in rough sleepers since the Tories took power in 2010. It's estimated that more than 14 million people now live in poverty, all whilst CEO pay has doubled and the top 10 per cent of households now take home about a third of all income and own two-thirds of all wealth.

Thatcher and Paz showed these policies could be married to state violence and still applauded as democratic, a major milestone for the global free-market revolution. Klein wrote in The Shock Doctrine, 'Bolivia provided a blueprint for a new, more palatable kind of authoritarianism...one carried out by politicians and economists in business suits rather than soldiers in military uniform.' In each case, it seems that the economic shock therapy must be accompanied by a cultural, social, or psychological shock. War at home or abroad is an excellent trigger, but the authoritarian treatment of societal resistance is another disturbing trait. As the patient convulses in the electro-treatment, the dosage is turned up to ensure compliance and effectiveness. It's estimated that between 100,000 and 150,000 people were captured and tortured in South America during this period, but that pales in comparison to the victims of economic torture. Rodolfo Walsh, Argentina's top investigative reporter at the time, wrote in anguish, 'It is in the economic policy of this government where one discovers not only the explanation for the crimes but a greater atrocity which punishes millions of human beings through planned misery.' Chilean political prisoner Orlando Letelier looked on in exile at the destruction of his country's economy for the benefit of a few wealthy interests at the expense of the population at large. In 1976 he wrote, 'during the last three years several billion dollars were taken from the pockets of wage earners and placed in those of capitalists and landowners...the concentration of wealth is no accident, but a rule'.

Letelier was an economist who fled Chile when Pinochet took over. He was heavily critical of the world press and governments who failed to make a connection between the brutal regimes of terror and neo-liberalism that were ravaging the country. To the outside world, there was no connection; Pinochet was a dictator, a brutal one at that, but the economic changes he was making were celebrated by the Chicago School and free-market believers round the world. There was in the words of Letelier, 'an inner harmony' between the free market and unlimited terror. This style of economics cannot be imposed peacefully. Friedman didn't quite see it that way, commenting: 'I do not regard it as evil for an economist to render technical economic advice to the Chilean Government.' He went as far as to claim the Chilean saga had been a triumph of democracy, 'The really important thing about the Chilean business is that free markets did their way in bringing about a free society.' Friedman's colleague Arnold Harberger was immensely proud of the work his Latino students did in Chile. He once commented, 'I feel prouder about my students than of anything I have written.' It's chilling that they take so much pride in holding up the brutal dictatorships of South America as shining examples to model ourselves on. Worst of all, we did adopt their policies, not accompanied by physical violence on the same scale, but through other forms of shock therapy.

The third wave of neo-liberalism may not have had the same open brutality that Thatcher engaged in when brutalizing the unions, but it was brutal nonetheless. Cuts to the welfare state have been equated to an assault on the most vulnerable in society. The 'hostile environment' policy was designed to invoke fear in immigrants and the Windrush scandal was a shocking example of a government abandoning its citizens. The brutal 'fit for work' assessments, that have naturally been outsourced to the much-maligned Atos, have been condemned as a war on the most vulnerable. Peter Beresford, professor of social policy at Brunel University London, denounced the highly controversial welfare assessments:

'It is becoming increasingly difficult not to associate such catastrophic policies with something deeper, something more visceral...The current direction of travel of social care and welfare reform doesn't merely represent harsh policy or even reactionary ideology. Instead it is a deliberately prejudiced, vicious attack on a significant minority of the population.'

Between December 2011 and February 2014, 2380 people

died after their Employment and Support Allowance (ESA) was cut because they had been declared fit for work; though ministers insisted that these deaths could not be linked to the welfare reforms. The Grenfell fire disaster killed 72 people and injured 70 more, despite numerous safety warnings, and amounts to manslaughter by gross negligence. The extra cost of the fire-resistant cladding was less than £300,000. The council was running a budget surplus, had issued a top-rate tax rebate a few years ago, and had access to around £300 million in reserve funds.

The Red Tape Fire

Every single post-Brexit economic model released by the Treasury found that the UK would be worse off under any Brexit scenario. These scenarios were far worse in the case of a hard Brexit, and catastrophic under a no-deal scenario. This is the shock. Then comes the wave of privatization and tax cuts. In the case of economic fallout from Brexit, or the recession that seems to be looming, the only way that the British economy could survive will be to cut regulations, taxes, and roll back the state to make Britain attractive to investors. That will be the remedy prescribed by the disaster capitalists. Are European nations causing you too much bother with their environmental protections, their harmonized tax structure, or their workers' rights? No problem, Britain doesn't worry about any of this. Come and abuse your workers, stash your money offshore, and dump harmful industrial waste wherever you want.

The phrase 'clean break' or 'clean Brexit' has been frequently used to describe the act of leaving the EU with no withdrawal deal. The language is eerily reminiscent of the blank slate that CIA torture experts and the Chicago Boys both sought to rebuild a person or economy on top of. Clean does not mean painless, easy, or prosperous, it means chaos. Shock and chaos. This is the only way in which the British population will accept the fourth wave of neo-liberalism. Within moments of the BBC declaration that Leave had won the vote, the free-market think tank the CPS was outlining the 'opportunities' that Brexit would create to remove environmental and financial regulations:

'The weakness of the Labour party and the resolution of the EU question have created a unique political opportunity to drive through a wide-ranging...revolution on a scale similar to that of the 1980s...This must include removing unnecessary regulatory burdens on businesses, such as those related to climate directives and investment fund[s].'

The free-marketeers were wasting no time in getting to work. This is the opportunity for the next dose of privatization and tax cuts. The TPA have already suggested a 'no-deal peace package' that proposes cuts to corporation tax, business rates, income tax, stamp duty, and air passenger duty. Shanker Singham of the IEA and Legatum has proposed a global zero-tariff trade arrangement for a post-Brexit Britain. Unsurprisingly, the CPS have also backed these plans, putting forward a post-Brexit economic plan that encouraged cutting corporation tax, lowering all tariff barriers, and dismantling the harmful red tape that is holding back business.

In the months after the referendum, George Osborne proposed a further cut to corporation tax from 20 per cent to 15 per cent in order to stem the loss of profit that would come from any potential loss of business. There was no such tax cut promised for the struggling families who will be hit harder by the economic fallout of whatever form Brexit might take. In January 2018, Liam Fox proposed that the UK could join the TPP, a free trade deal encompassing a host of different nations with different cultures, economic needs, languages, and currencies (remind you of anything). It has been heavily criticized for its favouring of corporations' rights over citizens. Nick Dearden spelt out the disastrous consequences:

TPP would limit dozens of powers which governments use to protect citizens and their environment, and push the balance further in favour of big business. It would extend the monopoly rights of big pharmaceutical corporations, cutting off the citizens of poorer countries from affordable life-saving drugs, while also making it harder for the NHS to negotiate cheaper prices for medicines. It would gut the ability of local government to use taxes to stimulate local farming and the local economy. The 5,000-page deal doesn't even mention the words 'climate change' but would make it harder for governments to introduce environmentally friendly policies.

Fox, who became a prominent Brexiteer during the campaign, has been a vocal proponent of proposals and legislation to cut regulations, taxes, and public spending. He is part of the ERG and has close ties with a number of the think tanks in 55 Tufton Street. A leaked document from Liz Truss's Department for International Trade showed that she was preparing to put pressure on Environment Secretary Theresa Villiers to lower food and environmental standards post-Brexit. The briefing noted that the UK would be under significant pressure to 'accommodate' American requests to lower the UK's regulatory measures in order to achieve a trade deal with America. When speaking at an IEA event, Truss was asked if post-Brexit trade deals could lead to a race to the bottom on environmental standards, Truss didn't deny the possibility and simply stated that she wanted to take 'a free-market approach'.

Crispin Odey manages about £6.5 billion (he's estimated to be worth around £1.1 billion himself) for his clients at Odey Asset Management and gave £870,000 to Vote Leave. Jacob Rees-Mogg's Somerset Capital Management was initially a wing of Odey Asset Management and Odey later donated to the Mogg's 2015 election campaign. On the morning after the Brexit vote,

Rupert Murdoch's former son-in-law pocketed earnings of £220 million in the space of just a few hours. He took out short bets against the pound and raked in profits as the UK markets dropped sharply in the wake of the referendum result. Odey, who had donated £873,000 to the Brexit campaign, told the press: 'I think I may be the winner.' His fund sadly lost 49.5 per cent of its value in 2016 as he continued to bet against the pound. He made a fortune during the financial crisis betting against the market and it seems he hoped to do the same with the post-Brexit economy. He took out £500 million in short bets against UK government bonds and large firms like Debenhams, ITV, and TalkTalk, making a fortune as the market crashed and burned. He has complained about the tightening of EU regulations on hedge funds and claimed that new EU banking laws would create a 'terrifying' environment for investors. His luck didn't last too long, he continued to place pessimistic bets on the UK economy which has kept growing, albeit at the slowest rate in Europe.

Jacob Rees-Mogg is a leading member of the ERG. His asset management fund has opened two Irish funds to insulate themselves from the impact of Brexit. Somerset Capital Management, the investment house he co-founded, has established two billion-pound funds in Dublin since 2016. Somerset Capital Management, who initially operated as a wing of Odey Capital Management, isn't even managed from the UK; instead, it is managed via subsidiaries in the tax havens of the Cayman Islands and Singapore. Rees-Mogg, the eloquent and patriotic Brexiteer, has defended the structure in the past, stating, 'I do not believe people have any obligation to pay more tax than the law requires.' He was also revealed in the Paradise Papers leak to have owned some 50,000 shares in Lloyd George Management, an investment firm based in the British Virgin Islands and made a tidy £520,000 when it was bought by Canada's Bank of Montreal in 2011. Rees-Mogg has no real say in the firm to influence decisions, but it illustrates a point. The richest in our society will be just fine, they have the capital, connections, and the opportunities to protect themselves from the harshest economic consequences of Brexit. The vast majority of us don't. Not only that but if the Brexit deal restricts freedom of movement, the entire country will have fewer opportunities to live and travel in other parts of the world. Rees-Mogg earned an average monthly payment of £14,983 during 2017/18, visiting the asset managers three times a week for just an hour at a time. He is an ardent believer in the free market and has frequently espoused the desire to use Brexit as a reason to slash regulation. He told the Treasury Select Committee:

'We could, if we wanted, accept emissions standards from India, America, and Europe. There'd be no contradiction with that...We could say, if it's good enough in India, it's good enough for here. There's nothing to stop that.'

Boris Johnson's cabinet was put together for a single purpose, to fulfil the dreams of the Thatcherite free-market revolution. Four newly minted members of Johnson's cabinet co-authored the book Britannia Unchained: Foreign Secretary Dominic Rabb, Home Secretary Priti Patel, Secretary for International Trade Liz Truss, and Business Secretary Kwasi Kwarteng. It's a savage attack on the UK's 'bloated state, high taxes and excessive regulation' and labelled British workers as 'among the worst idlers in the world'. Patel argued when she was employment minister that, 'If we could just halve the burdens of the EU social and employment legislation we could deliver a £4.3bn boost to our economy and 60,000 new jobs.' Chancellor of the Exchequer Sajid Javid's original intellectual hero is said to be Ayn Rand, the patron saint of US Republicans and a staunch advocate of 'greed is good' economics. Javid, though sadly not part of the clique that authored Britannia Unchained, is a keen believer in its principles. He has proposed cutting corporation tax in Britain from 17 per cent (already the lowest in the G20) to

12.5 per cent and abolishing the 45 per cent top rate of income tax. The purist believers in the free-market ideology now occupy the great offices of state, including Prime Minister. At the first leadership hustings for the Conservative Party in 2019, Boris bragged openly about his support for the banks that plunged us into recession in 2008:

'Can you think of anybody who stuck up for the bankers as much as I did? I defended them day in, day out, from those who frankly wanted to hang them from the nearest lamppost.'

One of the harmful regulations that the Brexiteers have singled out for review is the Working Time Directive. It limits the working week to 48 hours and ensures rest-time of 11 hours between shifts and paid lunch breaks, though workers can choose to wave the 48-hour limit if they so choose. Brexiteers argue that scrapping this law will allow businesses flexibility and workers to earn extra 'vital overtime cash'. The renewable energy directive has also been predictably pinpointed as a harmful source of EU regulation. It requires the UK to generate 15 per cent of its energy from renewable sources by 2020. Much to the horror of many human rights campaigners, Theresa May even mused on removing Britain from the European Convention on Human Rights post-Brexit.

Mark Sedwill, cabinet secretary and head of the civil service, is currently compiling a Brexit 'brick'. An economic plan dubbed 'Project After' to put in place post-Brexit that will deliver the neo-liberal trifecta of deregulation, lower taxes, and the sale of public assets. This vision for a post-Brexit Britain has been described as the 'Singapore-on-Thames' model and 'Thatcher's Fourth Term'. The US is pushing us to accept lower data protection laws for the giants of Silicon Valley, allow pharmaceutical companies to push up drug prices, and, a-la TTIP and TTP, they want to give US multinationals the right to sue the British government in 'corporate courts' if they pass laws that hinder business such as a sugar tax or anti-fracking laws. It's no wonder that the free-marketeers are touting Singapore as a model for the post-Brexit economy. They ranked second in the World Bank index of 190 countries for 'ease of doing business'. The Development Finance International and Oxfam Report in 2018 ranked Singapore number 149 out of 157 countries for commitment to reducing inequalities and last in terms of redistributive progressivity of tax policies.

The UK's wealthiest resident, Sir Jim Ratcliffe, was an ardent Brexiteer. He is the founder and CEO of the petrochemicals company INEOS and is worth an estimated £21 billion. Despite his support for the Brexit cause (during the campaign, Ratcliffe claimed that the UK would be 'perfectly successful' outside the EU) and having just been knighted for services to business and investment, he is leaving Britain for the sunny Mediterranean tax haven of Monaco. Ratcliffe may be unaware, but in Monaco, residents don't pay any income tax. Two of INEOS's top executives are expected to join him in Monaco. He was previously critical of Britain's tax regime and INEOS even relocated to Switzerland for 4 years to save on corporation tax. Friends of the Earth revealed that INEOS has lobbied the government to find ways around carbon taxes and levies if the UK leaves the EU.

Sean O'Grady, deputy editor of The Independent, wrote a piece that called on Britain to 'create an ultra-low tax economy to attract inward investment of every kind. We can't expect the world to believe in Britain because we have clean air and pretty countryside. There needs to be a hard financial incentive. The message needs to go out that Britain is somewhere you can make – and keep – your money.' Former Tory leader Ian Duncan Smith has argued that by leaving the EU, 'we can reduce the cost on business and on individuals by reducing regulations which will improve our competitiveness, our productivity and therefore ultimately our economy.' He called for a 'root and branch review' of the costly regulatory burden the EU imposes on the UK. Owen Paterson has called Brexit a 'once in a lifetime opportunity' to escape the EU regulatory burden. Thatcher's chancellor Lord Lawson believes that Brexit presents the chance to finish Thatcher's quest of freeing the market, 'Once out of the EU, we have the opportunity to do this on an even larger scale with the massive corpus of EU regulation. We must lose no time in seizing that opportunity.' As any other patriotic Brexiteer would do, Lawson has since applied for French residency.

John Bolton, Trump's short-lived national security adviser and notorious warhawk, was in frequent communication with Liam Fox and Chris Grayling whilst they were in Theresa May's Cabinet. He is a senior fellow at the Koch Brother's funded American Enterprise Institute and has publicly called for a 'clean Brexit' to allow the UK to sign a free trade deal with the US. Bolton has also endorsed South America's latest free-market authoritarian, Jair Bolsonaro. The Brazilian president appointed a foreign minister who believes climate change is a 'Marxist plot' to stifle western economies and wants to open up the Amazon to miners, farmers, and construction companies. A US government consultation with agri-businesses revealed demands for the UK to accept lowering food standards, dropping the safety threshold for pesticides, abandoning biotech regulations, getting rid of traceability and colour warning labelling, and removing safety restrictions on beef, pork, and poultry.

Of all the red tape that the Brexiteers are fighting against, one area seems to provoke more objections than any other – taxation and finance. Theresa May committed the UK to become the low tax haven of Europe (hoping to steal the mantle from Ireland), promising 'one of the most business-friendly economies in the world' and 'the lowest rate of corporation tax in the G20'. It seems unlikely that Boris Johnson or any future Conservative will renege on that commitment. Adam Posen, President of the Peterson Institute for International Economics, and a well-known economist, raised fears that the UK would double down on its commitment to the financial sector:

'My concern, in part based on comments by the leadership of the pro-Brexit vote, is that they essentially double down on being a financial centre. That they say "We want to be the offshore financial centre for Europe. Oh look, the Chinese are going to start trading renminbi in London, it's going to be great."'

Tax havens share three common characteristics:

1. Financial secrecy, allowing companies to hide their income and assets from government taxation
2. Loose tax rules and low tax rates
3. Lax financial regulations, which enable secrecy and money laundering

British territories and dependencies include four out of the ten places on earth that have done the most to 'proliferate corporate tax avoidance' according to the corporate tax haven index. The UK itself ranked thirteenth on the list. The report that accompanied the research commented that, 'The UK, with its corporate tax haven network, is by far the world's greatest enabler of corporate tax avoidance and has single-handedly done the most to break down the global corporate tax system, accounting for over a third of the world's corporate tax avoidance risks.'

When the network of British Crown Dependencies and Overseas Territories is considered a single entity, it ranks number one on the Tax Justice Network's financial secrecy index as the biggest threat to global financial transparency. Britain is the world's largest enabler of tax evasion. Crown dependencies and overseas territories only have to give information on the true owners of offshore companies if it is requested by law enforcement officials.

HM Revenue and Customs estimate that it lost about £2.7 billion through tax avoidance and £4.4 billion through tax evasion in 2013/14. That's about £7.1 billion altogether. Overall, it estimates about £34 billion in taxes goes uncollected each year.

But not all of it is because of tax evasion and tax avoidance. HMRC are chronically under-staffed and under-resourced. Despite every £1 spent on new staff for its large business compliance service bringing in an extra £97 extra in tax. The National Audit Office revealed in 2014 that one in five large businesses in Britain paid zero tax and research by the Trade Unions Congress estimates that Britain's elite dodge £25 billion in taxes every year. Perhaps, and understandably so, the EU fears Britain becoming another offshore tax haven for European multinationals and some MPs fear the UK could end up on that blacklist post-Brexit. Ironically, Panasonic is moving its European HQ from London to Amsterdam because it fears that Britain will become a tax haven. They would face back-taxes in their home market if the UK further lowers corporate tax rates.

The big four tax accountants in Britain offer tax minimization services. They gain their expertise through literally helping the government to formulate policy. Firms like Ernst & Young are contracted in to help write the tax code, then go off and sell their services to clients advising on how to get around the law. They advocate the use of complex corporate structures to avoid tax and locate headquarters and tax bases in tax havens or low tax areas like Luxembourg. They use 'transfer pricing' to help shift profits offshore by using two subsidiaries of the same parent company to exchange goods and capital across borders, charging what they claim to be competitive prices on a competitive market. Small and medium businesses cannot compete, they don't have the resources to set up and manage these complex tax arrangements.

Starbucks has outsourced its tax burden via offshore subsidiaries by purchasing coffee through these offshore companies. Starbucks' European business paid an effective UK tax rate of just 2.8 per cent in 2017 – $5.9 million of tax on profits of $213 million, Amazon paid just £4.5 million on £8.7 billion in revenue, and Apple UK paid just £10 million in tax on British sales of £1.2 billion. Not only are these companies offshoring profits, but they are also receiving tax breaks from the government; in 2016 Amazon received £1.3 million in tax credits. Facebook's offshore structure means that they paid £15.8 million in tax on £1.3 billion in sales in Britain. Facebook was able to reduce its £15.8m tax bill further by claiming £8.4 million in tax credits from granting its employees shares in the company. That means the net tax it paid was £7.4 million.

The Tax Justice Network estimated that if Google registered UK advertising sales in the UK (rather than in Ireland), that they would have been liable for £1.5 billion in taxes, compared to the £67 million that they paid in 2018. They calculated that Google revenue in the UK could be almost £10 billion, compared to the £1.4 billion that they were taxed on. That could pay a year's salary for 60,000 nurses, 50,000 police constables, or 50,000 secondary school teachers.

Tax avoidance is for the wealthy, a privilege of having an army of accountants to find every loophole possible. It's an expense that small businesses can't afford, they can't compete with corporate giants. Britain's tax havens have for years been a way for those with the resources to do so to hide money out of the reach of HMRC. A 2013 report from Oxfam estimated that £4.7 trillion of the £12 trillion sitting in tax havens around the world was being held in accounts in British overseas territories and crown dependencies. The Panama and Paradise Papers leaks gave us just a glimpse of the complex web of offshore structures that help the wealthy to avoid tax, scrutiny, and the reach of government interference. In the book Moneyland by Oliver Bullough, he discusses the financial arrangements of the now-convicted money launderer and former Trump campaign manager Paul Manfort. He maligns the meticulous skill required to unpick offshore financial arrangements:

'Trying to draw the complexity of the financial arrangements between all these entities is a job for a whole team of law enforcement professionals; it's all but impossible for a layman.'

That is a major part of the appeal. At a time when the EU and other world governments are trying to clamp down on tax havens, Britain is doing all it can to keep this offshore world, or 'Moneyland', in the shadows. By creating a web of offshore vehicles and holding companies you can obscure the flow of capital and hide practices like tax evasion and money laundering. Using offshore companies is not illegal, but it makes it more difficult to scrutinize illegal practices. It's a global issue. The EU loses an estimated £506 billion to tax avoidance each year. A Global Financial Integrity report found that since 2011, developing countries have lost $1 trillion annually because of corrupt or illegal deals, many of which involved anonymous offshore companies. Global Witness, an NGO who campaign against corruption and human and environmental abuse, pronounced the offshore world 'a gateway for corporate abuse and corruption'. Tax havens have enabled the flow of £68 billion out of Russia via the British overseas territories between 2007 and 2016. The National Crime Agency report found that there are 'hundreds of billions of pounds' being laundered through Britain annually. Previous estimates were only £36-90 billion. It's been estimated by Gabriel Zucman of the University of California that an astonishing 40 per cent of overseas profits made by US multinationals are sent to tax havens. A total of 60 of the top 500 largest companies in the US paid zero tax in 2018, including General Motors, Amazon, and Netflix. Numerous Trump former and current advisers and cabinet members hold funds offshore, including former secretary of state Rex Tillerson, Treasury Secretary Steve Mnuchin, and Trump's ambassador to Russia, Jon Huntsman. Commerce Secretary Wilbur Ross was revealed to have business investments with a Russian shipping company with ties to a Russian oligarch subject to US sanctions and Vladimir Putin's son-in-law. Stephen Bronfman, a key part of Justin Trudeau's successful bid for the leadership of the

Canadian Liberal Party in 2013 and general election victory 2 years later, was accused of using a complex web of entities in the US, Israel, and the Cayman Islands to avoid paying millions in taxes in the US, Canada, and Israel.

The European Commission has already declared that Ireland failed to collect up to €13 billion in taxes from Apple, in a case set to be heard in the European Court of Justice (ECJ). This is not an isolated case either, Luxembourg has also been accused of granting Amazon illegal tax benefits worth €250 million, the European Union has ordered Amazon to pay back the taxes as it amounts to illegal state aid under EU law. European Competition Commissioner Margrethe Vestager said in a statement:

> Luxembourg gave illegal tax benefits to Amazon. As a result, almost three-quarters of Amazon's profits were not taxed...In other words, Amazon was allowed to pay four times less tax than other local companies subject to the same national tax rules. This is illegal under EU state aid rules. Member states cannot give selective tax benefits to multinational groups that are not available to others.

After initially opposing calls to clamp down on tax havens, the government backed legislation that requires 14 overseas territories, including the British Virgin Islands and the Cayman Islands, to bring in public ownership registers before the end of 2020. The UK, however, does not have the power to impose these laws on Jersey and Guernsey or the Isle of Man. In 2017, the EU published their first tax haven blacklist which put Jersey, Guernsey, the Isle of Man, Bermuda, and the Cayman Islands, on a 'greylist' of tax havens who have said they will reform their tax structures and review their 0 per cent corporate tax rates. The UK tried unsuccessfully to allow these jurisdictions to avoid screening by the EU's tax experts but was overruled. The UK also signed up to the Extractive Industries Transparency Initiative which requires companies incorporated in the UK to disclose payments made to government agencies including overseas and will soon force companies with a contract for oil, gas, or mining to reveal their beneficial owners.

Whilst Britain isn't whole-heartedly rejecting any regulation of tax havens, the British government hasn't exactly been the poster-child for transparency and accountability of tax havens. Britain and Europe have a fractious relationship when it comes to tax evasion and avoidance regulation, many British MPs and MEPs have frequently been at odds with the majority of European states when it comes to cracking down on tax dodging multinationals. The EU has often complained about British attempts to slow crackdowns on tax evasion. In 2013 George Osborne introduced a law concerning CFCs (Controlled Foreign Companies) that allowed UK parent companies to avoid paying tax on interest paid on loans to their offshore subsidiaries. Without these measures, the interest income would be taxed in the UK because the HMRC would disregard the offshore shell and allocate the interest income to the UK parent company. These set-ups aren't illegal but can be challenged by HMRC. For example, Ithaca Energy, an oil firm with headquarters in Aberdeen, was revealed in the Paradise Papers to have set up a shell company in Bermuda to reduce their tax bill. According to BBC reporting on the topic: 'Ithaca Energy set up a "shell" company in the tax haven of Bermuda in 2012 to purchase its share in a $50m (£38m) North Sea oil production platform. In the leaked papers, Ithaca stated it was "important" to its tax position the company was controlled from Bermuda.'

Bermuda is popular as a home for offshore subsidiaries as they do not tax income or capital gains. The set-up is technically legal under UK law; however, if it is ruled that the company is being run from the UK, not Bermuda, it would nullify any Bermuda tax benefits and potentially lead to a challenge from HMRC. Professor Avi-Yonah told the BBC that:

I think the point is to take the profits that are derived from operations in the North Sea and to funnel them through the Jersey company to Bermuda and then have them sit there as long as you want until the Canadian company wants to have them, and at that point you send them out to Canada and they're tax-exempt in Canada as well because they're treated as dividends...It's perfectly clear. The only reason to have a Bermuda company in there is because Bermuda is a tax haven. I can't see any other reason to have this extra holding company in this structure.

Just how much money there is being lost through these CFCs is unknown, but when the measures were brought in, HMRC calculated that the CFC rule changes would reduce the tax take by £805 million a year by 2016. HMRC released documentation that estimated that multinationals avoided paying £5.8 billion in taxes in 2016, 50 per cent more than government forecasts, and three times higher than the entire government estimates of the benefit fraud bill (£2 billion). That figure does not include losses from the CFC rules under investigation. Since the Conservatives came to power in 2010, Britain has built a corporate tax haven for multinationals that included slashing corporation tax from 28 per cent to 17 per cent and capital gains tax from 28 per cent to 18 per cent, a new favourable tax regime for multinationals with offshore financing subsidiaries, and tax breaks for patent-owning companies. As a result, Britain saw a number of large corporations like Aon, Fiat Industrial, and Starbucks's European operations set up headquarters in the UK with a small number of staff in order to take advantage of these tax laws. Fossil fuel companies benefitted from the VAT cut from 20 per cent to 5 per cent on petrol, gas, and coal, on top of tax breaks that save them some £280 million a year. In 2012, Osborne granted a £3 billion allowance for drilling around the Shetlands. The environmental audit committee estimated that the nuclear industry is the beneficiary of £2.3 billion per year in subsidies. There are laws set to come into place in January 2019 requiring all member states to have anti-tax avoidance rules governing CFCs on the statute book. These measures and crackdowns are part of a lengthy EU campaign to fight corporate and multinational tax evasion and Britain is not the only company facing challenges to their tax structures.

Back in 2015, Britain rejected plans announced by Brussels to combat 'industrial-scale tax avoidance by the world's biggest multinationals'. The common tax regulations would have clamped down on offshoring and removed many of the elements of Britain's competitive tax advantages over the other EU member states. The Treasury at the time declined to give reasons for their rejection of the plans, but issued this statement:

'Direct taxation is a matter for EU countries, and any direct taxation matters require unanimity across all EU countries. We're fully involved in international discussions on tax issues and have consistently supported global measures, through the EU, G20 and OECD, which will strengthen international rules to prevent corporate tax avoidance.'

In 2015, Conservative, UKIP, and DUP MEPs also voted against EU plans to crack down on corporate tax dodging, by making companies report where they make their profits and pay taxes. The plan included a requirement for all member states to agree on a common EU position for the definition of tax havens and for co-ordinated penalties to be imposed upon countries or territories across the world that are uncooperative in tackling tax evasion. It also called for a blacklist to be drawn up of these countries and, perhaps most importantly, it calls for the member states to:

'equip their competent authorities to carry out rigorous and thorough investigations, and put forward sanctions such as suspending or revoking the banking or advisory licences of financial institutions, accountants, law firms or other financial advisors if it has been proven that they have assisted in tax fraud...'

In 2013, Cameron personally wrote to the then President of the European Council, Herman Van Rompuy, to prevent offshore trusts from being dragged into an EU-wide crackdown on tax avoidance requesting that trusts should not automatically be subject to the same transparency requirements as companies. The EU had planned to increase transparency on the dealings of offshore bodies by publishing a central register of their ultimate owners but, in a letter unearthed by the Financial Times, Cameron said:

'It is clearly important we recognise the important differences between companies and trusts...This means that the solution for addressing the potential misuse of companies – such as central public registries – may well not be appropriate generally.'

Rather than holding trusts to the same standards as companies by forcing them to make their owners publicly known, the prime minister argued that the EU should ask the Organisation for Cooperation and Development and the G20 to agree on a global framework for transparency agreements. However, despite these protests, the EU has now moved forward with these plans, and the new rules came into force in 2019.

The UK doesn't just help these companies out by blocking legislation, it actively protects their corporate donors. Lycamobile was investigated by the French authorities for tax fraud and money laundering, but the Conservatives refused to sanction a raid on the company headquarters to seize evidence for their investigation. They were also happy to continue taking donations from Lycamobile. The official response from HMRC in March 2017 noted that Lycamobile is 'a large multinational company' with 'vast assets at their disposal' and would be 'extremely unlikely to agree to having their premises searched'. It went on to cite that 'they are the biggest corporate donor to the Conservative party led by Prime Minister Theresa May and donated 1.25m Euros to the Prince Charles Trust in 2012'.

The Isle of Man government gave out more than $1 billion in tax refunds on the import of hundreds of private jets into Europe. Jet owners were allowed to claim back 100 per cent VAT refunds on the basis that their jets were part of leasing businesses, where they permanently rented the jet to themselves. The Isle of Man does not tax company profits. Jim Mellon of Leave.EU ran a bar through an Isle of Man company, Calabrese Holdings Ltd, to help minimize his tax liability. Lord Ashcroft, the billionaire Conservative donor, former party treasurer, and patriotic Brexiteer, has advocated for businesses to simply up and move to Malta after Brexit. Ashcroft, an outspoken critic of EU integration of tax policy, moved a lot of his companies and tax arrangements to Belize in the early 1990s. Whilst there he successfully lobbied the government to enable corporations and wealthy individuals to set up secret trusts there to hold money or assets in exchange for an annual registration fee. Ashcroft, who is worth £1.35 billion (ninety-fifth on the 2017 Sunday Times Rich List), donated £5.1 million between 2003 and 2008 to the Conservatives through his firm Bearwood Corporate Services and £500,000 to Theresa May's 2017 campaign. These donations were investigated but no law was found to have been broken. He runs his own polling company as well as the website ConservativeHome, a right-wing blog aimed at grassroots party members. He was turned down for a peerage in 1999 and then again in 2000 because of his tax arrangements and was granted the honour after vowing to relocate to the UK. However, by 2010 he was still taking advantage of his offshore tax arrangements, but after much outrage, he promised to abandon his non-domicile tax status after a 2010 law made it illegal for him to sit in parliament. He resigned his seat in the Lords in 2015 but retained the peerage.

His Bermuda-based Punta Gorda Trust was created in 2000, just after he became a peer, and a leaked financial statement recorded it as having assets of $450.4 million (£341 million) in 2006. He avoided millions in capital gains tax by selling shares immediately before and after his time as a peer. A week after he announced his resignation from the House of Lords in March 2015 he sold shares worth £11.2m. If he had still been sitting in parliament, he would have been required to pay capital gains tax on any profits from the sale. Ashcroft has offered up Malta as a possible destination for 'ambitious' UK firms who want access to Europe post-Brexit. In an article on ConservativeHome, he said: 'As a hard-nosed, self-made businessman, I believe that Malta represents the best destination for ambitious UK firms that must have a post-Brexit presence in the European Union.' Malta is often referred to as Europe's 'Pirate base for tax'.

For the free-market disciples of Britain, the intellectual and political heirs to the Mont Pelerin Society, Brexit presents the perfect opportunity to unleash the true power of the market on Britain. Brexit was not a triumph for the working classes, those who have been trodden on since Thatcher. It was a triumph for the cheerleaders of Thatcher who could now finish what she started by turning Britain into a free-market haven once they slip the shackles of Europe. If they manage to negotiate and pass the hard Brexit they desire, we are almost guaranteed to suffer the now-familiar 'shock treatment'. At the time of writing, Brexit is far from a certainty, but if the vote is overturned, the Friedmanites that dominate British politics will bide their time and await the next sufficiently destabilizing crisis, natural or engineered. When the time comes, we will be sold the stories of the economic miracles around the world that have benefitted so much from Chicago School economics. Yet, in reality, the models we will follow are countries that have been ravaged by the greed and corruption of politicians and multinationals. Every time the 'bitter medicine' of the shock doctrine is prescribed what follows is an affront to democracy. The policies are not implemented because of their widespread popular support. The only way to put the Chicago School ideas into practice is by finding a population sufficiently destabilized by war, financial crisis, or natural disaster. The Hayek trifecta of privatization of state assets, tax cuts for the wealthy, and the lowering of trade barriers is always accompanied by brutal policies of repression, excessive police violence, spikes in wealth inequality, poverty, and the creation of a wealthy class of billionaires profiting from it all. The Thatcher revolution kicked off the neo-liberal domination of Britain to a backdrop of war and police brutality towards the unions. Cameron and Osborne assaulted the working class of Britain with their brutal austerity regime. Now the free-marketeers fill the highest offices in the land and will take any opportunity to turn Britain into the Singapore of Europe. The NHS will be privatized, environmental regulations and workers' rights will be scrapped, and globalization will continue unabetted. As is always the case with neo-liberalism, the worst off will bear the economic hardships whilst the wealthiest reap the rewards.

9. The Establishment Civil War

You may be wondering why I have arrived at the final chapter without having mentioned the very title of my book. To help best explain my overarching point I felt that the story should be peeled back in layers, beginning with the loss of our data and concluding with disaster capitalism. For Owen Paterson, the EU referendum was the modern equivalent of the English Civil War. The war ended with the beheading of Charles I and the exile of his son Charles II. Lacey Baldwin Smith, author of This Realm of England, 1399 to 1688, said of the conflict, 'the words populous, rich, and rebellious seemed to go hand in hand'; a phrase that is difficult not to compare to the billionaire Brexiteers fighting back against the liberal elite. The country was similarly divided in the 1400s, then over the issue of the monarchy. The Royalists or 'Cavaliers' enjoyed widespread support in the countryside, the shires, and areas of the north and west of England, whilst the supporters of parliament were centred in cities and economically developed areas. Paterson hosted weekly Eurosceptic, cross-party meet-ups after PMQs on a Wednesday in the lead up to the referendum, unironically under the watch of his portrait of Charles I.[81] The English Civil War saw the removal of the head of state, in every sense of the word; Brexit has seen the heads of two prime ministers roll (metaphorically in this case) and the loss of our collective minds. Farage said after the referendum, 'Brexit was the first brick that was knocked out of the establishment.'

Brexit is nothing more than an Establishment Civil War; a fight between two factions of the modern ruling class. The current political consensus was built slowly in Britain over the past 40 years. First came the outriders, a host of campaigners, political extremists, journalists, and academics, all determined to overthrow the post-war consensus of government intervention in the economy and replace it with free-market capitalism. They built a new consensus which Owen Jones in 'The Establishment' described as an amalgamation of 'institutions and ideas that legitimize and protect the concentration of wealth and power in the very few hands'. Just as free-market capitalism or neo-liberalism (however you wish to define it) has spread through every institution of power in Britain, so too has it circled the globe, always facilitated by shock and chaos. Often this is applied in countries beginning to come into their own, with great capacity for positive growth and change. The recipe is simple, shock and reform. As the 'Shock Doctrine' has been slowly applied around the globe, the Chicago Boys and the corporate world have become the new rulers of the global economy. The project that began at the Mont Pelerin Society has transformed the modern world. From its bloody origins in Indonesia, Brazil, Chile, and Bolivia, neo-liberalism has become the accepted wisdom of Western governments, financial institutions, and even the IMF (which is now stacked with Chicago Boys) and the World Bank.

In China through the 1980s, the Communist Party began a project that would ape the Chilean model, combining free-market capitalism with an authoritarian government. In 1983 Deng Xiaoping opened the country up to foreign investment, reduced workers protections, and formed a 400,000 strong 'People's Armed Police' to prosecute the 'economic crimes' of striking or protesting. Faced with widespread resistance by 1988, Deng reversed some of the price controls that had caused unemployment and inequality to sky-rocket. That's when Milton Friedman paid them a visit. He reiterated the 'importance of privatization, free markets, and of liberalizing at one fell stroke', praising the initial reforms, but urging them to go much further. The anger at this programme of reform culminated in the massacre of Tiananmen Square, where peaceful student protestors were fired on and assaulted by soldiers. Somewhere between 2000 and 7000 were killed and around 40,000 were arrested. Factory workers were executed or imprisoned for daring to think they could stand in the face of the neo-liberal crusade. Days later Deng reaffirmed his commitment to the reform programme, which was to be more radical than ever before. The state was opened up to foreign investment and the children of the Communist Party officials grew fabulously wealthy (90 per cent of China's billionaires were children of Party officials by 2006) as they bought up state companies at rock-bottom prices. The democratization of ownership and the introduction of the free market did nothing to change the political hierarchy. The same people were still in power, except now they enjoyed a much higher standard of living courtesy of the free market. Outside the party, workers were exploited by multinationals as China became the sweatshop of the world, populated by workers who had the deaths in Tiananmen Square still fresh in their memory.

When the authoritarian communist regime collapsed in Poland, the grassroots left-wing party Solidarity swept to power, only to find the country paralyzed by debts of $40 billion and inflation at 600 per cent. They were too pre-occupied with avoiding economic meltdown to roll out the post-communist economy they had promised, replete with work-owned factories and a transition away from a centrally-managed, state-run economy. Jeffrey Sachs, by now being hailed as the 'Indiana Jones of Economics', persuaded Solidarity to agree to his shock therapy in exchange for IMF debt relief. He pushed for the sale of state mines, shipyards, and factories and the elimination of price controls overnight. Sachs predicted that the shock therapy would result in 'momentary dislocations', but the economy would quickly stabilize. Capital markets, a stock exchange, and a new currency were married with massive budget cuts 'as fast as possible and all at once'. Halina Bortnowska, a human rights activist, commented at the time, 'you can no longer expect people to act in their own best interests when they're so disoriented they don't know – or no longer care – what those interests are'. The Polish finance minister dubbed it a period of 'extraordinary politics' in which the rules and conventions of normal politics, based in consultation, discussion, and debate, were no longer applicable. You enter a democracy free zone. Shock therapy in Poland caused a 2-year depression, a 30 per cent reduction in industrial production, and unemployment hit 25 per cent by 1993. By 2003, 59 per cent of Poles were living below the poverty line (compared to just 15 per cent under communism).

In 1989, Francis Fukuyama declared that we were witnessing 'an unabashed victory of economic and political liberalism' and 'the endpoint of mankind's ideological evolution'. Free-market capitalism had won. Communism was collapsing and there was no ideological opposition to challenge the Chicago School hegemony. A year later, the World Bank and the IMF unveiled the Washington Consensus. It was to be the new template for free-market capitalism, the latest version of 'the Brick'. As communism collapsed and Mikhail Gorbachev took charge of the crumbling Soviet Union, he declared that he would find a 'third way' between capitalism and communism. His reforms were welcomed by the open arms of the West. The policies of 'glasnost' (openness) and 'perestroika' (restructuring) had allowed Russia to move towards a great democratization. They now had an elected parliament, president, local councils, a free press, and were moving towards a Scandinavian-style social democracy. Gorbachev won the Nobel Peace Prize for his work in 1990. When he arrived at the July 1991 G7 Summit, that all seemed to be for nothing. He was told bluntly that the Soviet Union had to embrace radical shock therapy, just as Poland had done a year earlier. John Major, George H.W. Bush, and the Canadian and Japanese prime ministers told him that Russia would have to follow the Poland model on an accelerated timetable. This was not to be as easy as in China. Democratic forces had been unleashed in Russia that would not be easily suppressed and which threatened to bring a halt to the Chicago Boys blueprint being demanded of the Russian president. An article in The Economist urged Gorbachev to model himself on their favourite Latin American dictator and dish out 'the Pinochet approach to liberal economics'. Gorbachev sent tanks to surround the new Russian parliament and the demonstrators led by the Russian president, Boris Yeltsin. Yeltsin allied himself with two other Soviet republics, signalling the breakup of the Soviet Union; in the words of political scientist Stephen Cohen, 'the only country most Russians had ever known', and forcing Gorbachev's resignation. Later that year, Yeltsin went to the Russian parliament in 1991 to ask for a one-year period in which he could rule by decree. He promised to solve the economic crisis gripping Russia and return the country to good health. He assembled a team of Russian economists celebrated as 'the Chicago Boys' in the Russian press and the 'Young Reformers' in the West. They were preparing to enact shock therapy on the Russian population.

The Russian president wanted Jeffrey Sachs, who was inside the Kremlin on the day the Soviet Union collapsed, to secure the same IMF relief that he had arranged in Poland. Sachs told him if he subscribed the now-familiar model of privatization, he could arrange for IMF aid. Yeltsin unveiled his shock therapy just a week after Gorbachev's resignation for maximum effect. Whilst the country was still reeling from the dissolution of the biggest empire in the world, he lifted price controls and began a fire sale of the 225,000 state-owned companies. In a former Communist country where 67 per cent of the population wanted workers cooperatives to replace state-owned companies, Yeltsin unleashed unfettered Chicago School capitalism. Except in Russia, as in China, multinationals were kept out of the process and the wealthiest businessmen in Russia were elevated to the new class of oligarch. The shock therapy not only enriched a handful of businessmen beyond their wildest dreams, it also pushed tens of millions of Russians into poverty. Opposition to Yeltsin's programme grew quickly. The Constitutional Court ruled it unconstitutional on eight counts and the parliament voted to revoke his special powers. Yeltsin, with the support of Western governments, declared a state of emergency, abolished the constitution, and dissolved the parliament after they voted 636-2 to impeach him. The IMF was threatening to revoke a $1.5 billion loan because they were unhappy with the way the parliament was getting in the way of their agreed reform programme. The US Congress responded to the suspension of democracy by awarding a $2.5 billion aid package. Yeltsin sent in troops to surround the parliament in a 2-week blockade that ended with the bombing of the parliament building he had defended a few years earlier and the massacre of 100 peaceful protestors.

Russia became a war zone, new Wild West. Organized crime was rife, martial law was implemented, and armed police roamed the streets. With the country now reeling from the latest shock, Yeltsin rammed through huge budget cuts, removed price controls on the remaining essentials like bread and milk, and accelerated the sale of state assets. Russian businessmen bought up the state companies at bargain prices and then opened the stock up to foreign investors, sending profits soaring. Norilsk Nickel, whose annual profits reached $1.5 billion, was sold for $170 million and Yukos, which controlled more oil at the time than Kuwait, was sold for $309 million. Some of the oil fields were sold to Russian businessmen funded by loans from the state bank, in a twist that meant the Russian state was directly funding the purchase of their own assets for rock-bottom prices. By the mid-90s, 74 million were living below the poverty line (compared to 2 million under communist rule) and 37 million, a full quarter of the population, were living in conditions described as 'desperate' poverty.

Britain has suffered through three waves of neo-liberalism. Brexit, if it goes ahead, will provide the opportunity for free-marketeers to fulfil their deepest fantasies. Within days of the

Brexit vote, Lynton Crosby (who ran Boris Johnson's first failed leadership bid and his London mayoral campaigns) set up offices in Washington DC. He touted his access to British politicians and his ability to help US corporations shape Brexit. Thatcher began the first wave of neo-liberalism. She used the Falklands War to push through a wave of financial deregulation, brutalize the unions, and sell off huge portions of the state. Blair chose not to rock the boat and challenge the newly established free-market consensus developing amongst the British ruling class, expanding PFI contracts and endorsing the US shock therapy in Iraq. Then came the 2008 crash, enabling the most expansive sale of state assets in history, the slashing of the welfare budget, and cuts to the top-level tax rate, corporation tax, and capital gains tax.

The richest 10 per cent in Britain now own 45 per cent of the wealth. Britain is home to the poorest and richest regions in Northern Europe. There's been a £37 billion drop in welfare spending since 2010, funding a cut in corporate tax rates and the top rate of tax. This was made under the guise of getting our public finances under control. To date, the Conservative Party has ballooned the national debt from around £800 million in 2010 to £2.26 trillion as of October 2019. And for what? A lost decade of wage growth, increased wealth and income inequality, rising homelessness, underfunded public services, and rising private debt. The housing crisis is getting worse, climate change looms over our heads, and student debt is spiralling out of control. The UN has condemned the cruelty of the welfare cuts in Britain, stating that there was no need for the brutality of the regime. Between 2015 and 2020 the poorest third of Britain will be an average of £715 worse off whilst the richest third will be £185 better off. We've outsourced government services to management consultancy firms to the point where one-third of public money goes to unaccountable corporations, allowing money to be siphoned off to offshore shareholders and accountants along the way. A total of 25 out of the 34 private organisations that receive £100 million or more in government contracts operate from offshore havens, 19 of which are situated in countries on the EU tax haven blacklist or grey list. Money goes straight from the government purse to companies run from tax havens without so much as the bat of an eyelid. We're slowly becoming the kind of barbell economy that has afflicted every major Chicago School project, from Chile and Argentina in Latin America, to Poland and Russia in Europe. The middle class is hollowed out and wealth inequality grows unimpeded as those at the top use their resources to get further and further ahead. It's a sad phenomenon that is being made worse by the advance of technology. David Cameron called the free market the 'best imaginable force for improving human wealth and happiness'. Yet each successive wave of neo-liberal consolidation has left the majority of the population worse off, not just in Britain but around the world.

In the book 1984, the main protagonist, Winston, is eventually captured by the Party after having committed numerous real and thought crimes in an attempt to reject the dystopian world that had been built by the Party. Once captured he is tortured beaten, and given electroshock therapy. He asks at one point when they will kill him and his captors respond, once he 'truly loves' Big Brother. At that point, they can kill him. Just as with the 'Shock Doctrine', the goal is to break Winston down so they can be remade upon a blank slate, where 2 + 2 equals 5 if the party wills it so. We've been repeatedly told that we need to lower regulation and cut taxes on the wealthy to help the economy grow. It's the Chicago way. If we want everyone to prosper you shouldn't try to divide the pie differently, you should make the pie bigger. By cutting the taxes of the richest in society we are enabling the wealth creators and then the rewards time to benefit the rest of us. In reality, it is more like a champagne pyramid where the glasses at the top overflow whilst those at the bottom catch the drops. Yet every time a crisis appears we are told that we need more tax cuts, more deregulation, more privatization; the only solution is a more free market. Hungarian author Stephen Vizinczey once wrote, 'All great power has to do to destroy itself is persist in trying to do the impossible.' We're stuck in a closed loop where the only acceptable remedy is more extreme versions of the same programme.

The principles of the free-market ideology have been fully embraced by the ruling elite and passively by huge portions of the population. It's an issue of complexity, much like the EU itself. Would the average person on the street be able to give you a summary of Chicago School economics? It's not meant as slander or an insult; of course people can't. None of us learn that in school and barely any of us need to know for our day-to-day lives. There is an inherent trust that we place in the politicians elected to parliament that they will act in the best interests of the country (or at least what they believe to be the best interests). Corruption and corporatism have put a stop to that. The political class has become intertwined with free-market purists and corporate Britain to the point where the three are all but indistinguishable. There are backers of this ideology in each of the three main parties, offering three shades of neo-liberalism and privatization. Jeremy Corbyn has faced mass opposition from his parliamentary party who still believe in the New Labour model.

The first major division that has emerged in the British ruling class is the role of Europe in our lives. In The Establishment Owen Jones laid out how 'The European Union represents one of the few great schisms to mark the modern Establishment.' To some, it holds the established order in place and provides a bogeyman in elections, but to others it is a project totally at odds with the free market. It places major burdens on governments, ensuring that they must not pollute their country, allow citizens to be ripped off, defrauded, or mistreated by employers or as consumers. It prevents economic growth from springing forth by wrapping governments in red tape. The Establishment Civil War at its heart is about whether Europe helps to entrench the neo-liberal status quo or whether it is a hindrance to the great free-market project. Jones writes:

'Some elite figures – such as Fraser Nelson – believe the EU actually helps to hem in Establishment policies and ideas, neutralising possible threats to them. Others oppose the EU, not because they want to defend British 'sovereignty', but because they believe the EU poses a threat to Establishment mantras.' This is ultimately what this book is trying to say, our politicians (and more specifically the Conservative Party) started a war amongst themselves for ideological reasons. For the establishment, this is little more than a game. Now you might say that this is always how politics has worked, its games and theatre designed simply to keep people in power. Perhaps I'm too idealistic but I believe it's possible for the game to be for the benefit of all (or at least not solely for a small minority). Brexit is an ideological war within the British elite over the best way to maintain and further consolidate their own power. It was sprung upon us by businessmen and disaster capitalists as a way to escape EU regulation of industry and tax havens. US corporations foresee it as a way for them to extend their tendrils into Britain and take advantage of any post-Brexit trade deal to get their hands on the NHS. The war within the Conservative Party exploded out into the country, exposing cultural divisions that few truly acknowledged existed. Whatever the outcome, it will be to the benefit of the richest. The concerns and problems of modern Britain will continue to go unaddressed whilst we remain in this proxy culture war. Behind the anti-PC war on elites live something greater, a population fighting to find a way in the globalized modern Britain. That is nothing to be resented. Yet, instead of fighting back against neo-liberalism as a whole, the ideology that has spent 40 years slowly asset-stripping Britain, we have become embroiled in a war amongst ourselves over our place in the world, both as individuals and as a country. Are things better now or do we want to re-tread our past donning rose-tinted glasses? It's nostalgia vs progressivism, Anywheres vs Somewheres.

Whilst this fight consumes us, there are two certainties. Firstly, that the real problems we face as a nation will go ignored. Income inequality, poverty, climate change, the underfunding of schools and the NHS, the rising cost of living comparative to wages, the housing crisis, the list goes on. Secondly that the stagnation that we continue to experience because of Brexit will cost our economy dearly. Foreign investment is down, companies have begun bleeding out to European locations. Nissan, Jaguar, Land Rover have all either relocated or are scaling down their operations, and that's just the car industry. Uncertainty means we are likely heading for another economic shock regardless of the outcome of Brexit. We all know what the prescription will be – tax cuts, privatization, and lower public spending. We will all suffer the consequences of this Establishment Civil War, left trying to dodge the falling debris as two giants duke it out above. None of the politicians, financial backers, disaster capitalists, or press barons will be negatively affected by the outcome, either way. Those at the top will not suffer the economic consequences of their actions.

Liz Truss (former Chief Secretary to the Treasury), Secretary of State for Trade and International Development at the time of writing, was pressed by Eddie Mair in an interview over comments about the country having to make 'difficult choices' and whether she had been personally affected by the decisions that have been made to implement brutal cuts to the social safety net whilst cutting the top rate of tax. She is visibly amused by the question. She scoffs and questions why he is even asking such ridiculous things. She thinks it inconceivable that she might have been affected by the austerity that her party inflicted upon the country. She wasn't affected, it's ludicrous to think that they would be. She won't be negatively affected on the same scale as the rest of the population in the case of a hard or no-deal Brexit. Our current political landscape is the result of a negligent ruling class whose internal ideological divisions have led us down a road of parliamentary gridlock and nationwide turmoil. The internal split revealed a deep unhappiness amongst the British people with the current status quo. The domination of neo-liberalism is being fundamentally rejected, on an economic, socially, and cultural level.

A smidge over 40 per cent of the electorate chose to vote for Jeremy Corbyn's Labour Party in 2017, despite heavy opposition from the tabloid press and the political establishment. For a man that is now (officially) the most smeared politician in British history, whose personal popularity is dead in a ditch outside his fanbase, that's a lot of votes (and a higher portion of the vote than Tony Blair achieved in 2001 or 2005). A total of 17.4 million people voted to reject the European project and take back control of their lives, to find some semblance of control in a country run by and for the free-marketeers. Corbyn, Farage, Brexit, Trump; they are all rejections of this kind of politics as usual. But unless we can reform our electoral system, this anger will be exploited by bad actors and disaster capitalists. Technology has given politicians the power to understand our behaviour more comprehensively and accurately than any other time in history. This understanding has been and will continue to be weaponized against us in more and more potent ways unless we reject it wholesale right now. Any crisis sufficiently hyped can be used to force through policies that would otherwise be inconceivable. With social media, we are willingly handing over the keys to our collective psyche. Once a party or campaign group understands what provokes hatred, fear, or desperation, in one person, it is simply a matter of scaling that approach across entire populations. Bogeymen can be invented, crises can be exaggerated, and populations can be divided.

Corporate Britain is preparing to lobby the government to deregulate post-Brexit. The Henry VIII powers that have been included in Johnson's 2019 Withdrawal Agreement will enable the government to change vast swathes of the law with little to no scrutiny in parliament. The Chicago School blueprint will be followed once again. Speed is the key, just as with Johnson's Brexit deal, scrutiny and delays only encourage dissent and backlash. Katie Perrior, former director of communications for Prime Minister Theresa May, said lobbyists were preparing to take advantage of the brand-new set of regulations that were set to emerge from the Brexit process. Once separated out from European Law (however long that may take), British law will be open to deregulation that would never have been allowed as a part of the EU and every industry is keen to ensure they get a say in the deregulation of Britain. Perrior commented that, 'Every charity or business is taking this opportunity to lobby for a slight change in something.' The Alliance for Lobbying Transparency puts the UK lobbying bill at roughly £2 billion annually. Do you think they are wasting their money? Remaining in the EU does not curb the problem of corporate greed and influence. There are an estimated 20,000 lobbyists in Brussels, and in 2015 alone, 1.5 billion euros were spent on lobbying.

Within days of getting into office, Trump pushed through the Dakota Access Pipeline and stopped an environmental review of the project. He quickly put in place plans to approve the Keystone XL pipeline rejected by the Obama administration over environmental concerns. He killed Obama's Clean Power Plan and announced plans to expand drilling off the Gulf Coast. Klein accuses Trump and his cabinet of being the final takeover of corporate America, the US government itself:

> Rather than risk the possibility of further progress (and
> further lost profits), this gang of predatory lenders, planet

destabilising polluters, war and security profiteers joined forces to take over the government and protect their ill-gotten wealth. After decades of hawking how to get rich manuals, Donald Trump understands exactly how little needs to be behind the promise if the desperation is deep enough.

This is what we risk unleashing by enabling a hard Brexit. The chaos required for the final corporate takeover of British politics. The purist free-marketeers occupy the front benches of the Conservative Party and they need only chaos to complete their mission. The lobbying industry was filled with ex-New Labour politicians and advisers until quite recently. Now, with some time back in government clocked up, a host of former Tory politicians and advisers have jumped out of the firestorm of contemporary politics and into some private sector lobbying or communications jobs. David Cameron's former director of communications, Craig Oliver, has taken up a post as senior managing director at the US management consultancy firm Teneo, who are marketing a 'Brexit client transition unit' to help clients navigate the mess he played a hand in creating. Former Conservative special advisers Ameet Gill, Paul Stephenson (Vote Leave communications director), and Lizzie Loudon have set up their own PR firm, Hanbury Strategy. Stephenson even credited their early success to the connections to the Brexiteers in government. Having fought on the front lines of the Establishment Civil War, they have retired to make money off the chaos that still engulfs us.

Politics was just the latest frontier of digital transformation. It was only inevitable that the relentless march of technological advancement would conquer the political world as well. Now politicians, campaign groups, foreign governments, and unaccountable corporations have control and access to our personal data, they hold more information on the populations of the world than anyone has ever amassed in the history of the human race. We've given it to them willingly. Now we are the product. An ever-greater understanding of our digital behaviour is marketed to anyone looking to sell a product or idea. A/B testing and RCT experiments mean that every little click is monitored, analysed, processed, and applied in real-time. It's little wonder that information has become the twenty-first century's most valuable resource; data, as they say, is the new oil. It's binary gold, used to exploit us in every way imaginable, preying on our deepest thoughts and fears. It's used to sell over-priced degrees, high-interest loans, and anti-depressants. The technology that is meant to connect and empower us is giving politicians or anyone with sufficient resources the power to divide us.

Social media is toxic, it is not a healthy place for us to have political discussions. Outrage is the biggest driver of interactions, it's why social media algorithms push us towards content that pushes our buttons, and during an election cycle, that tendency is ratcheted up and up. Jordan Peterson sees social media as an amplifier, that magnifies our behaviour, good and bad, and politicians are exploiting these tendencies to divide us. The lax regulation allows them to employ a digital version of the Trump strategy, using outrage to generate attention and flood the digital world with targeted lies. These sites design every single aspect to influence our behaviour, to hook us in for more and more time. The lords of Silicon Valley brought in psychologists and behavioural experts to understand addiction. Dark patterns keep us locked inside social networks, networks that fragment and tribalize society. Filter bubbles, echo chambers, and epistemic bubbles are all amplified by social media, as are their problems. The interconnected world means it is easier to spread misinformation than ever before. Facebook and Twitter have given anyone with enough resources a direct line into the pocket of almost every single person you see walking down the street. Propaganda seeps its way from dark ads, to Facebook timelines, onto the evening news, and into the mouths of journalists and politicians. With the ability to flood the online world with your message without restriction or oversight, you can direct the conversation in the real world. From the day that Boris Johnson was elected as leader of the Conservatives, the party began running over 500 variations on adverts asking people to tell the new prime minister what they wanted to see him working on. Reports from inside Number 10 revealed that Dominic Cummings has set up the UK government website to harvest data from its users. Number 10 has also set up their own data-harvesting site called Get Brexit Done, which asks users for their postcode and helps them identify how their local MP is stopping Brexit.

The press are a key part of the British Establishment. They vilify and cast out anyone who may dare to challenge the status quo, even from within their own ranks. They've used hate-filled anti-EU and anti-immigrant rhetoric for decades, demonizing those at the bottom as 'scroungers' whilst ignoring the successive corporate raids of the British treasury. The UK hands out £100 million annually on working-age benefits, just one-tenth of the cost of bailing out the banks in the wake of the 2008 crash. But why question top-rate tax cuts, tax havens, and privatization, when benefit scroungers and immigrants are the real problem? The mediacracy that holds together our offshore funded foreign press is a major obstacle to a better political environment. The press has played a larger part than most in the destruction of our national debate. Journalism isn't dead. There are still some fantastic outlets doing brilliant investigative work. The Guardian, Private Eye, Buzzfeed Politics, OpenDemocracy, Channel 4 and numerous others are still holding the government to account, but they are swimming against the tide.

The right-wing press may be losing its grip, sales are declining and their smear campaign against Jeremy Corbyn didn't prevent him winning 40 per cent of the vote in 2017. Yet they still influence the national conversation and dominate newspaper sales. The BBC, still the most popular news outlet in Britain and a cherished institution, has tried to hold politicians to account. The complexity of the Brexit process made it difficult for journalists to press politicians for answers and when they did they were accused of being anti-Brexit. The BBC is not pro- or anti-Brexit, but they remain pro-establishment. The BBC Trust and the collection of senior journalists in the corporation are almost entirely made up of former Conservative Party members, all of whom tow the free-market line. The BBC regularly hosts economists and analysts from 55 Tufton Street and allows them to pose as concerned academics from neutral institutions. The bias in the mainstream press has no clearer example than the reaction to the DUP discussions with paramilitary leaders prior to their rejection of Boris Johnson's deal with the EU. They didn't consult union leaders, businesses, local constituents, just members of the UDA and the UVF. Jeremy Corbyn is vilified for his work in the Northern Ireland Peace Process (Mo Mowlam sought his help specifically when the process stalled) and yet the media were silent that the party that had been propping up the Tory majority was consulting directly with paramilitary leaders. It's a shocking double standard.

All this was possible because of our divided country. We are, as David Goodhart illustrates in The Road to Somewhere, seeing the emergence of the new tribes of British politics. The Anywheres and the Somewheres. These new divisions are defined by three characteristics, education, location, and comfort with the modern world. Freedom of movement and unimpeded immigration has been difficult for the majority of the population to accept. No party has successfully managed to reduce the level of immigration coming from the EU until 2016 when the Brexit vote appears to have made a serious dent, though that could be just because of uncertainty over the status of EU nationals. The majority of the population has expressed a desire to reduce immigration and yet no major party was willing to take real action. The Conservatives because they understood the benefits of immigration to the economy and Labour and the Liberal Democrats because they believe in the global village. The Anywheres that occupy parliament and the political system view immigration and free movement as a positive. How could they not when it is a part of their very identity, forged since they uprooted themselves to study at university?

What's more, problems that have been created by successive waves of neo-liberalism; falling wages and over-stretched public services, schools, and hospitals are blamed on immigrants, by politicians and our tabloid press. They couldn't admit that these problems were caused by neo-liberalism and not by immigration, and thus they had no way to combat the anti-immigration rhetoric pushed by the Leave campaign. Peter Mandelson urged David Cameron to offer some form of compromise or relief fund on immigration, but he rejected it, fearing that it may give more fuel to his opposition.

It's not just social media and our economy that are broken, it's our human minds. We all like to imagine ourselves as rational, objective, and honest people. But in reality, we're prejudiced, more impressionable than we think, and often irrational in the face of overwhelming evidence. We can be impulsive, reckless, and even cruel to our fellow human beings. We reach for easy conclusions, ignore truths that hurt us, and perform outstanding mental gymnastics to justify our beliefs and actions. We believe lies the more we hear them, we double down when we're shown evidence that contradicts our worldview, and let the social cost of being wrong cloud our judgement. 'Project Fear' became synonymous with anything negative about leaving the EU. Two simple words that made all the painful consideration of counter-arguments disappear. No need to get bogged down in thoughtful consideration of the pros and cons, when all the cons are just 'Project Fear'. Reality has gone MIA from politics, there is no subjective truth to be had anymore. Iris Murdoch once wrote,

'We live in a fantasy world, a world of illusion. The great task in life is to find reality.' In a review of the now highest-grossing film of all time, Avengers: Endgame, the author for ScreenRant made a quip about the transformation of fictional escapism. They joked that our fantastical escapes from reality on the big screen have changed from simply watching heroes taking on the forces of evil to the Endgame plot where our heroes go back in time to undo what happened in the previous film. The reviewer asks solemnly 'can I do a time heist on my own life?' Perhaps this is where we are now, the present is so terrifying we resort to a desire to retrace the paths of our parents back to when life was simpler. Taking back control was the perfect vague remedy for the cultural erosion and feeling of dislocation that modern Britain is suffering from. It inspired 3 million more people to vote in the Brexit referendum than in the 2015 General Election.

Next we have to turn our eyes to the foreign influence and attempts to subvert British democratic processes. Russia was clearly pro-Brexit, much as they were clearly pro-Trump, though nowhere near as blatantly – we didn't have Boris Johnson or Nigel Farage attempting to alter party policy to be more pro-Russia or fail to believe their own intelligence agencies over ex-KGB agent Vladimir Putin. Despite the best efforts of some MPs we haven't quite managed to produce a politician with quite as little subtlety as Donald Trump. Pro-Brexit Russian-linked bots launched waves of campaigns on Twitter. Russian officials met with the funders of Leave.EU on numerous occasions. First it was one, then it was three, then four, now 11 separate meetings have been confirmed and they were offered business deals involving diamond and gold mines. Now Boris Johnson's administration is blocking a report on Russian interference in the Brexit referendum, but for what exactly is unclear.

SCL has repeatedly popped up in controversial elections around the world. They have used secrecy, bribery, shady electioneering tactics, and digital propaganda across Africa,

Asia, and the Caribbean. Cambridge Analytica and AggregateIQ (for whom they own the intellectual property) were at the centre of a data scandal that allowed the harvesting of personal data of hundreds of millions of people, that was then weaponized to target billions of adverts at swing voters. SCL is embedded in the military establishment of Britain and the US, deploying weapons-grade military psy-ops across the globe. They've now turned the technology on the populace on both sides of the Atlantic, though it will forever remain unclear as to how much of an effect it has had. Brexit was a perfect storm of a disengaged cynical electorate, primed by years of anti-immigrant and anti-Europe sentiment, pushed by a press owned by foreign millionaires and billionaires. In March 2018, The Economist asked:

> Does any of this matter beyond Westminster? If Vote Leave is found to have breached the rules, that will support the notion that Leavers played fast and loose in 2016. Yet Remainers spent a lot more, and benefited from a government leaflet costing £9m that openly backed their cause. On the evidence so far, it is hard to conclude that the 52:48 result was changed by digital marketing, however cleverly done.

Vote Leave has broken Electoral law and evaded investigation at every turn. We cannot allow that to be forgotten, especially if Brexit enables the type of neo-liberal destruction that we have witnessed at home and abroad.

It's easy to feel like we are in the middle of a war. Battle lines were drawn down the middle of the European question. Both sides dug in, slinging insults, lies, and rhetoric dripping in fear and destruction. No single moment better summed up the feeling that the Brexit campaign stirred up than Nigel Farage's declaration that Britain needed to summon their Dunkirk spirit. Brexit is painted as a battle against the evil European bureaucrats, a fight against the EUSSR. It makes it much easier to rally people to your side when you sweep them up on a wave of nostalgia for the time when plucky Britain took on the world's greatest evil and triumphed victoriously against seemingly insurmountable odds and in the face of great hardship. If we won then why can't we win now? We are Great Britain (and Northern Ireland) after all. Not that the world has ever been simple, but the decision to fight against the Nazis was a fairly straightforward one. They were trying to take over Europe and the world by force, abolishing democracy and committing genocide on a terrible scale. The enemy of the people of Britain is no longer so easily defined as a foreign invading force coming to take everything you hold dear, though the rhetoric would have you believe something else. Those that would do the most harm to you sit at the desks of Downing Street, in sky-scraping office blocks, and promise the best of intentions. They hide in plain sight, masquerading as the saviour of British politics, as businessmen offering prosperity, or paid commentators posing as independent academics. It's no longer as simple as hating the enemy across the sea, literally invading your country and attempting to take it by force. Instead, we have to believe in ideals beyond the hatred of a distinct evil. We have to pursue justice, equality (not equity), and truth above all else. Of course, it is easy to sit here and write all this on a page, it's incredibly easy to get preachy from a keyboard (trust me). But to begin with, it's crucial we try to diffuse the war mentality that has come to engulf almost all discussions on Brexit and politics more broadly.

Not long ago, comparisons of the EU to the Soviet Union were the stuff of sweaty diatribes on UKIP web forums. Now they are aped by a foreign secretary who voted to remain. It is symptomatic of a project to pretend that Britain never had pro-EU Conservatives or a pro-European political tradition. It is the systematic erasure of remain from the national story. The new Tory orthodoxy casts EU membership as an aberration, an alien thing imposed by a few citizens of nowhere on a captive people who prayed in secret for deliverance, then rose up to take back control. That isn't how 48 per cent of voters, 16.1 million people, saw it. But it takes an effort to keep hold of the memory. The past 2 years have felt like a vast exercise in gaslighting, the method of psychological coercion that involves subtly undermining people's confidence in what is real until they begin to question their own judgement. Thus have the parameters of sanity in the debate shifted. The norms have moved so far that any deal starts to look like a victory for common sense over extremism. Today's political maps don't even mark the spot where realistic accounts of Britain's European interests used to appear.

Electoral Reform

In the process of researching this book, I came across countless authors who conclude their book with a laundry list of fixes for the problems that they have highlighted. Sometimes that may come in the form of a manifesto for change to be adopted by political parties or a wish list of policies that would lead us to a better future. Most of these policies and ideas to change the world will require us to vote in a party who has a genuine desire to help out the people of Britain. A genuine politician may be rare, but I do believe they exist (I couldn't write this book if I wasn't still optimistic that things can improve). The biggest problem with this kind of list is that most of the ideas are often pipedreams, a picture of the road to utopia, but ultimately unachievable. I believe that to truly induce a change in this country you have to first address our electoral system.

Electoral reform is a fairly broad topic and can encompass a multitude of different areas. I believe Britain needs a more robust Electoral Commission, one with greater scope for oversight and power to levy punishments, stronger laws that govern social media and digital advertising (even if that means banning political advertising altogether until we can figure out how to better regulate political ad content). Dark ads need to be banned and elections should ideally be publicly funded. One of the fastest ways to stop money influencing the decisions of politicians is to stop them from being beholden to it. Andrew Yang, an entrepreneur who ran for the 2020 Democratic nomination for president, talked frequently about introducing the idea of 'democracy dollars', where each voter is given a certain number of credits (or 'democracy dollars') to give to a party or candidate. Those credits are then exchanged by the recipient for a portion of publicly allocated funds. It gives everyone, regardless of income or location, the ability to contribute to the party they feel represents their views. This doesn't mean that the business world will have no influence, of course, their views will still be heard, but it means they no longer have advantageous leverage over parties beholden to their donors. That also means barring MPs from holding second, third, and fourth jobs. Whether that is as a paid newspaper columnist (Boris Johnson was paid £250,000 a year for his Telegraph column prior to his election as party leader) or board members for large corporations (George Osborne was paid £650,000 a year whilst still a backbencher for one day of work per week at BlackRock, the world's largest fund manager). They cannot be impartial and committed to doing the best work for their constituents whilst receiving such vast sums of money from private corporations. Most crucial in this electoral reform package is the removal of FPTP as a voting system. FPTP means that any vote that is not cast for the winning party in a constituency is wasted, it becomes worthless. How can that be a system meant to empower people? In a tight three-way race in a marginal constituency, it's conceivable that 70 per cent of the vote might not count for anything. It also helps to entrench the two-party system. Just as binary referendums leave us more open to manipulation, so too does the two-party system. It enables opportunistic politicians to divide us, based on an 'us vs them' mentality that plays on humans' natural tribalism. By switching to some form of proportional representation (PR) we are likely to see a more pluralistic political representation and parties making more effort to engage with voters. Fear of the alternative is much more difficult to sell when there are multiple alternatives.

A more representative parliament would also, in theory, reduce the feeling that the views of parliament are not reflective of those of the population. The two-party system now seems to be cracking under the weight of Brexit and could give way to a much more diverse selection of parties and opinions. Yet without proportional representation, we cannot expect that selection to be truly representative of the people and if the party system splits us into smaller factions, FPTP will almost certainly mean an even less representative government than we have right now. In a PR voting system, it becomes much more difficult for politicians to boil down an election to a handful of wedge issues that they have identified.

My proposed package of electoral reforms also includes automatic voter registration. If we can give every person in the UK a national insurance number, we can make them all eligible to vote without hindrance. There is even a case to be made for compulsory voting, as they have in Australia. Though it should be noted that this is considered a violation of your right to choose whether to vote or not by some. At the very least polling day should be a national holiday, without question, and those who are still required to work should be given ample time to vote. There is no excuse for erecting barriers to maximum turnout and representation in a democracy. In the Brexit referendum, turnout was 72.2 per cent of eligible voters. That means more than one in every four people didn't feel they wanted to or were able to have a say in what could be the single most consequential vote in modern British history. A turnout of 72.2 per cent is remarkably high as well, figures for general elections have been trending downward since the 1980s. Just 66 per cent of voters turned out in the 2015 election, though that did increase to 69 per cent in 2017. Throughout the 1970s and 1980s turnout was consistently in the 70-80 per cent range or higher. We also need to reform and strengthen press oversight. That does not mean curtailing freedom of speech, it means holding papers more accountable for what they print. We need to enforce anti-trust laws, end foreign and offshore ownership, and find a way to create an independent regulator that ensures press accountability.

The other plea I want to make to readers of this book, get informed and get involved. It is not enough to disapprove of the way in which Britain is being asset-stripped, you have to do something about it. Knock on some doors at the next election, take some time to inform your friends and family, back politicians that work in your interests, not their own. If you can, spare some money for quality journalism, it's more important now than ever.

We need to embrace vision and imagination for the future of the country. I am still an optimist. As much as my friends like to tell me I complain a lot, I still believe in the possibility of a Britain that truly works for everyone. Though there is no official proof, Winston Churchill is rumoured to have once said, 'The best argument against democracy is a five-minute conversation with the average voter.' I'm slightly more optimistic. I believe that with a more level playing field, a robust press, and a fair electoral system, humans have enough intuition to choose options that will empower rather than diminish them and stop the corporate takeover of Britain and the wider world. Remove money and corporate influence from politics and I believe anything is possible. The rejections of the status quo in the form of Trump and Brexit validate that for me, they show people understand that the neo-liberalism consensus must be broken.

Today's politicians are seriously lacking in a vision. The Conservative Party runs every election as an exercise in fear harvesting. Every campaign has been dominated by economic fear-mongering; the 2010 GE, 2015 GE, Scottish Independence referendum, AV referendum, Brexit referendum, and the 2017 GE. As much as they preach the attraction of free-market capitalism, they focus far more on the peril of choosing the more radical option. Only in the Brexit campaign have they failed to use fear to drive voters to the polls, though 2017 showed that these tactics are becoming increasingly less salient. At times I'll flick through my Twitter feed or turn on Question Time and see the same arguments playing out over and over and over. Specificity has still not arrived at the negotiating table. Something that often strikes me is that Leavers and Remainers almost seem to speak in different languages. For Remain voters, they believe in the European ideals of co-operation and camaraderie across one continent and many fear the consequences of a Tory Brexit, consciously or unconsciously fearing the free-market purity that we discussed in the last chapter. For Brexit voters, there is a fear of what the EU is imposing on us, that Britain is being slowly eroded by the creep of European expansion and stealth federalization. The loss of sovereignty, the lack of control over their own world, and the sense of dislocation in a rapidly evolving society. Dialogue cannot exist between these two groups of people without a common language.

People used to be motivated to vote by the vision of a better future, but as big data has shown that fear drives voting more effectively than hope, politicians have been drawn to this style of campaigning. FPTP makes this more effective, as long as you can sufficiently vilify the alternative, people will abstain or reluctantly vote for you, that's why the press machine is so crucial to the maintenance of the status quo. Aside from Brexit, all the campaigns we mentioned above have seen the majority of the press on the same side as the Conservative establishment. Their co-operation has ensured the status quo remained untouched until they were no longer fighting the same battle. Hillary Clinton lost because she was unable to articulate a positive vision for the future that combatted Trump's bluster and wild promises, she was happy with the status quo. In her mind America was already great, it just needed a few little tweaks. In the same way, the free-market Anywheres who occupy the upper echelons of politics see no reason to upset the status quo. It's why many of them pushed so hard against Brexit, they have done well in the current set up, so why rock the boat? Cameron had nothing positive to offer us as a vision for Britain during the referendum, just more of the same. It is only natural that a large crisis is followed by periods of sweeping reform. The post-war era saw the creation of the NHS, the welfare state, and the rebuilding of Britain. Yet, the last major crisis in the form of the 2008 crash saw few positive reforms. The 2008 crash was heralded as the last gasp of the dying capitalist ideology. The Occupy movement was filled with optimism about the future, it was the moment to seize upon and take back control of the global economy from the multinationals who now dictate to governments around the world. Instead, it was used by the Chicago School believers to implement the brutal austerity regime, cut taxes, and sell off the British state. Sometimes it can be difficult to feel outraged at the sale of public assets, especially at cut prices. Why should we care? We don't feel a real sense of ownership or pride towards our public services (save except for the NHS and perhaps Royal Mail). We need to think of our public assets as belonging to all of us, there to provide a public good and not simply to drive profits. Your taxes, your parents' taxes, perhaps even your grandparents' taxes paid for these institutions. They were built on the backs of our collective labours and should not be so willingly and flippantly auctioned off in the name of a quick buck.

Neo-liberalism is so hated by the British public that Boris Johnson has masqueraded himself as a form of economic nationalist, almost in a Bannon-esque style. Though this is not surprising given that Bannon has been intermittently advising the new PM. Empty spending promises are echoed time and again as if Johnson has a vision to invest in the country, when the reality is that, if he is given a chance, he will enable a corporate race to the bottom on standards and regulations. Let none of my condemnation of the use of divisive politics dispel from the fact I believe that we, as a country, need to have a discussion about the trade-offs of immigration, the impact of freedom of movement, and whether we want to be a part of that. The Brexit campaign spoke to the people who felt their unease at the rising level of immigration to Britain hadn't been addressed and that will continue until their concerns are at the very least discussed openly. The problem with populists like Trump or Farage is that they aren't providing any real solutions to the problems they are speaking about, they are exploiting divisions, not addressing them. Abraham Lincoln once said, 'Elections belong to the people. It's their decision. If they decide to turn their back on the fire and burn their behinds, then they will just have to sit on their blisters.' It's an attitude shared by some Remain voters now. Exasperated by the inability of Brexiteers to heed their warnings of the consequences of Brexit, some have become almost vindictive. But what we will get is not what we are being promised. The dreams of sunny Brexit uplands will give way to more of the same, except without the constraints of European legislation.

I've already spoken about how Brexit has become a battle for the soul of Britain, but the results will not address the problems that caused the vote in the first place. If anything, they will further deepen the divides as the grievances of the working-class Brexit voters go ignored in favour of corporate deregulation and more globalization. The human impact of Brexit is readily dismissed by Brexit politicians and commentators of all shades. Every single forecast made by the treasury shows us to be worse off in the case of leaving the EU. That in itself is not an argument against Brexit. Voters are more than capable of voting for their own economic hardship in exchange for something greater, but I would wager that most voters believe that the government will do everything in its power to mitigate harmful effects, to ensure the smoothest and least chaotic exit from the EU. Again the reality is the complete antithesis, with neo-liberalism, the chaos is the point. As we have seen, without chaos, you cannot force through the next wave of privatization and deregulation.

In 1984, Winston learns of the plan of Big Brother that enables them to maintain power. It's not unlike the 'Shock Doctrine'. The idea of perpetual war enables them to keep the population subdued, the control of the press and means of information keep the populace in the dark, and the struggle to exist day-to-day in the poverty-stricken streets keeps the proles focused on survival:

> The war is not meant to be won, it is meant to be continuous. Hierarchical society is only possible on the basis of poverty and ignorance. This new version is the past and no different past can ever have existed. In principle, the war effort is always planned to keep society on the brink of starvation. The war is waged by the ruling group against its own subjects and its object is not the victory over either Eurasia or East Asia, but to keep the very structure of society intact.

This is the reality we now inhabit. Albeit less extreme. The Establishment are true believers in the free market. Friedman's ideas are now the accepted logic of politicians, journalists, civil servants, and academics. They intertwine with the desires of corporate Britain and three waves of neo-liberal shock therapy have enabled the asset-stripping of the country's wealth. The rapid globalization of Britain and trouble with integrating a burgeoning immigrant population, whilst stripping away the social safety net, means we have lost our sense of shared community. It's what Klein describes in 'No Is Not Enough' as, 'Something we humans need for our well-being, and for which we never cease to long: community, connection, a sense of mission larger than our immediate and atomised desires.' Corporate sale of a lifestyle, an idea, rather than a product itself has increased as we have lost our communities. They sold us something we all yearn for, something to which we belong, a tribe, whether that was Apple users, Porsche drivers, or Tropicana drinkers. An article in The Economist from October 2018 suggested that we currently inhabit 'a political world dominated by fantasy and wish fulfilment'. 'Voodoo politics' promised Brexit would take us back to an age where we were strong, where we were certain of our place at the top of the world order. Back to when everything made sense. The modern world induces the form of psychological dislocation that accompanied shock therapy (economic and physical) and politicians and corporations will continue to expose that fraught frame of mind to accept more and more shocks. Brexit is the ultimate expression of this. A divided population was exposed to unbridled digital warfare and caused the biggest political earthquake of modern times. Now the disaster capitalists are attempting to use Brexit to slice up what remains of the British state and turn the country into a low-regulation tax haven. The NHS will be carved up and sold off, pollution standards will be lowered, and the free-market crusade that began in Britain with Thatcher will be completed.

Hope is not yet lost. If we reform our electoral system effectively, we can ensure that the government begins working for its population again and not just their donors. Tim Shipman suggested in All Out War that 'politicians had found a big old pot of electoral mandate and they were going to use it to paint any picture they damn well pleased'. We cannot allow an unaccountable voting system to continue to entrench the status quo by letting politicians off the hook for practising 'Voodoo politics'. The choice is still ours to make. If we continue to enable free-market disaster capitalism, it will never cease in its pursuit of profit. Democracy, protest, and international borders do not stop the greed of capital. There is only one route out of this dire situation. Elect politicians who work for everyone and that starts with reforming our voting system.

Final Thoughts

There are countless reasons I could give to want to stay in the EU, all of which you could quite easily write off as some project fear propaganda or romanticized millennial rubbish. To me, one of the most inspiring pieces of film or television I have seen on the topic came in the form of an HSBC advert called 'Global Citizen'. It glorifies the global nature of Britain, its relationship with Europe and its place in the world as a country that has been constantly defined and redefined with each new wave of people from around the world, be they Germans, Belgians, West Indians, Pakistanis, Irish, Eastern Europeans, Asians, or South Americans – Britain is almost uniquely built on a melting pot not seen since early-twentieth century America. The transcript for the advert reads as follows:

> We start the day with a Colombian, a Guatemalan, or a piping-hot Costa Rican and a Danish to go.
> We drive German, German, Japanese, German, and we ride Taiwanese.
> We watch American movies on Korean tablets and struggle with Swedish flat packs.
> Our heroes hail from Chile, Argentina, Brazil, and often Belgium.
> We eat Chinese, Italian, Indian, and go Dutch.
> Some of our best friends are Mexican, Siberian, Hungarian, and French.
> We live on a wonderful little lump of land in the middle of the sea but we are not an island, we are part of something far, far bigger.

When I went to find the video, I hoped that perhaps the YouTube comments section may be filled with at least the occasional hopeful remark, but alas I was mistaken. The entire comments section was filled with accusations of HSBC 'shilling' for globalists, that it was simply Remainer propaganda, that this was simply designed to brainwash us, forget about our own culture, and move us towards a new world order with a one world government.

I can see the pitfalls of the ad, it preys on feelings of patriotism, national pride, and those of us who enjoy our amalgamation of cultures into something truly unique. It celebrates our integration with the world, but the critiques of it miss the point (not that I really expected to find great insight in the YouTube comments section). We can pretend that we are leaving Europe, to become a truly 'global Britain', but we cannot escape the fact that Europe has (and will likely continue to be) our closest neighbour culturally, economically, and geographically. We cannot pretend that Europe doesn't exist and, save for some sort of cataclysmic severance of the tectonic plates, we will always be a part of it.

Acknowledgements

This book would have been impossible without a number of close friends. I want to thank Jamie, Sam, Thomas, and Chris for listening to my mad ramblings over the past year. I'd like to thank my Mum for her patience and encouragement in helping prepare the manuscript for submission. I was truly inspired by some of the amazing books I read in the process of writing and researching. Books by Naomi Klein, Owen Jones, Jamie Bartlett, Tim Shipman, and David Goodhart were crucial in helping my understanding and shaping my arguments. Reporting done by Carole Cadwalladr at The Guardian, by OpenDemocracy, and by DeSmog UK piqued my interest in the story to begin with and without their tireless work, writing this book would have been impossible.

References

1   (Bartlett, 2018)
2   (Bartlett, 2018)
3   (Shipman, 2016)
4   (Shipman, 2016)
5   (Jones, 2014)
6   (Bartlett, 2018)
7   (Bartlett, 2018)
8   (Bartlett, 2018)
9   (Bartlett, 2018)
10 (Bartlett, 2018)
11 (Stephens-Davidowitz, 2018)
12 (Stephens-Davidowitz, 2018)
13 (Shipman, 2016)
14 (Bartlett, 2018)
15 (Bartlett, 2018)
16 (Syed, 2015)
17 (Syed, 2015)
18 (Syed, 2015)
19 (Syed, 2015)
20 (Syed, 2015)
21 (Shipman, 2016)
22 (Shipman, 2016)
23 (Shipman, 2016)
24 (Sunday Times (London) August 6, 2000)
25 The Independent (London) August 6, 2000
26 The Age (Melbourne, Australia) August 7, 2000 Monday Late Edition SECTION: NEWS; International News; Pg. 9
27 The Independent (London) August 6, 2000, Sunday SECTION: FOREIGN NEWS; Pg. 17
28 Sunday Times (London) August 6, 2000
29 (Jones, 2014)

30   (Bartlett, 2018)
31   (Bennett, 2016)
32   (Bennett, 2016)
33   (Bennett, 2016)
34   (Bennett, 2016)
35   (Shipman, 2016)
36   (Shipman, 2016)
37   (Shipman, 2016)
38   (Shipman, 2016)
39   (Bartlett, 2018)
40   (Bartlett, 2018)
41   (Bartlett, 2018)
42   (Shipman, 2016)
43   (Bennett, 2016)
44   (Sumpter, 2018)
45   (Shipman, 2016)
46   (Bennett, 2016)
47   (Bennett, 2016)
48   (Bennett, 2016)
49   (Bennett, 2016)
50   (Bennett, 2016)
51   (Bennett, 2016)
52   (Bennett, 2016)
53   (Bennett, 2016)
54   (Shipman, 2016)
55   (Bennett, 2016)
56   (Shipman, 2016)
57   (Shipman, 2016)
58   (Klein, 2017)
59   (Shipman, 2016)
60   (Bennett, 2016)
61   (Shipman, 2016)
62   (Meek, 2015)
63   (Klein, 2017)

64 (Klein, 2007)
65 (Klein, 2017)
66 (Klein, 2007)
67 (Klein, 2017)
68 (Klein, 2007)
69 (Klein, 2007)
70 (Klein, 2017)
71 (Klein, 2017)
72 (Klein, 2017)
73 (Lowenstein, 2015)
74 (Jones, 2014)
75 (Jones, 2014)
76 (Jones, 2014)
77 (Jones, 2014)
78 (Klein, 2017)
79 (Bennett, 2016)
80 (Jones, 2014)
81 (Klein, 2007)

CULTURE, SOCIETY & POLITICS

The modern world is at an impasse. Disasters scroll across our smartphone screens and we're invited to like, follow or upvote, but critical thinking is harder and harder to find. Rather than connecting us in common struggle and debate, the internet has sped up and deepened a long-standing process of alienation and atomization. Zer0 Books wants to work against this trend. With critical theory as our jumping off point, we aim to publish books that make our readers uncomfortable. We want to move beyond received opinions.

Zer0 Books is on the left and wants to reinvent the left. We are sick of the injustice, the suffering, and the stupidity that defines both our political and cultural world, and we aim to find a new foundation for a new struggle.

If this book has helped you to clarify an idea, solve a problem or extend your knowledge, you may want to check out our online content as well. Look for Zer0 Books: Advancing Conversations in the iTunes directory and for our Zer0 Books YouTube channel.

Popular videos include:

Žižek and the Double Blackmain

The Intellectual Dark Web is a Bad Sign

Can there be an Anti-SJW Left?

Answering Jordan Peterson on Marxism

Follow us on Facebook
at https://www.facebook.com/ZeroBooks and Twitter at https://twitter.com/Zer0Books

Bestsellers from Zer0 Books include:

Give Them An Argument
Logic for the Left
Ben Burgis
Many serious leftists have learned to distrust talk of logic. This is
a serious mistake.
Paperback: 978-1-78904-210-8 ebook: 978-1-78904-211-5

Poor but Sexy
Culture Clashes in Europe East and West
Agata Pyzik
How the East stayed East and the West stayed West.
Paperback: 978-1-78099-394-2 ebook: 978-1-78099-395-9

An Anthropology of Nothing in Particular
Martin Demant Frederiksen
A journey into the social lives of meaninglessness.
Paperback: 978-1-78535-699-5 ebook: 978-1-78535-700-8

In the Dust of This Planet
Horror of Philosophy vol. 1
Eugene Thacker
In the first of a series of three books on the Horror of Philosophy,
In the Dust of This Planet offers the genre of horror as a way of
thinking about the unthinkable.
Paperback: 978-1-84694-676-9 ebook: 978-1-78099-010-1

The End of Oulipo?
An Attempt to Exhaust a Movement
Lauren Elkin, Veronica Esposito
Paperback: 978-1-78099-655-4 ebook: 978-1-78099-656-1

Capitalist Realism
Is There No Alternative?
Mark Fisher
An analysis of the ways in which capitalism has presented itself
as the only realistic political-economic system.
Paperback: 978-1-84694-317-1 ebook: 978-1-78099-734-6

Rebel Rebel
Chris O'Leary
David Bowie: every single song. Everything you want to know,
everything you didn't know.
Paperback: 978-1-78099-244-0 ebook: 978-1-78099-713-1

Kill All Normies
Angela Nagle
Online culture wars from 4chan and Tumblr to Trump.
Paperback: 978-1- 78535-543-1 ebook: 978-1-78535-544-8

Cartographies of the Absolute
Alberto Toscano, Jeff Kinkle
An aesthetics of the economy for the twenty-first century.
Paperback: 978-1-78099-275-4 ebook: 978-1-78279-973-3

Malign Velocities
Accelerationism and Capitalism
Benjamin Noys
Long listed for the Bread and Roses Prize 2015, *Malign Velocities*
argues against the need for speed, tracking acceleration
as the symptom of the ongoing crises of capitalism.
Paperback: 978-1-78279-300-7 ebook: 978-1-78279-299-4

Meat Market
Female Flesh under Capitalism
Laurie Penny
A feminist dissection of women's bodies as the fleshy fulcrum of
capitalist cannibalism, whereby women are both consumers and
consumed.
Paperback: 978-1-84694-521-2 ebook: 978-1-84694-782-7

Babbling Corpse
Vaporwave and the Commodification of Ghosts
Grafton Tanner
Paperback: 978-1-78279-759-3 ebook: 978-1-78279-760-9

New Work New Culture
Work we want and a culture that strengthens us
Frithjoff Bergmann
A serious alternative for mankind and the planet.
Paperback: 978-1-78904-064-7 ebook: 978-1-78904-065-4

Romeo and Juliet in Palestine
Teaching Under Occupation
Tom Sperlinger
Life in the West Bank, the nature of pedagogy and the role of a
university under occupation.
Paperback: 978-1-78279-637-4 ebook: 978-1-78279-636-7

Ghosts of My Life
Writings on Depression, Hauntology and Lost Futures
Mark Fisher
Paperback: 978-1-78099-226-6 ebook: 978-1-78279-624-4

Sweetening the Pill
or How We Got Hooked on Hormonal Birth Control
Holly Grigg-Spall
Has contraception liberated or oppressed women?
Sweetening the Pill breaks the silence on the dark side of hormonal
contraception.
Paperback: 978-1-78099-607-3 ebook: 978-1-78099-608-0

Why Are We The Good Guys?
Reclaiming your Mind from the Delusions of Propaganda
David Cromwell
A provocative challenge to the standard ideology that Western
power is a benevolent force in the world.
Paperback: 978-1-78099-365-2 ebook: 978-1-78099-366-9

The Writing on the Wall
On the Decomposition of Capitalism and its Critics
Anselm Jappe, Alastair Hemmens
A new approach to the meaning of social emancipation.
Paperback: 978-1-78535-581-3 ebook: 978-1-78535-582-0

Enjoying It
Candy Crush and Capitalism
Alfie Bown
A study of enjoyment and of the enjoyment of studying. Bown asks what enjoyment says about us and what we say about enjoyment, and why.
Paperback: 978-1-78535-155-6 ebook: 978-1-78535-156-3

Color, Facture, Art and Design
Iona Singh
This materialist definition of fine-art develops guidelines for architecture, design, cultural-studies and ultimately social change.
Paperback: 978-1-78099-629-5 ebook: 978-1-78099-630-1

Neglected or Misunderstood
The Radical Feminism of Shulamith Firestone
Victoria Margree
An interrogation of issues surrounding gender, biology, sexuality, work and technology, and the ways in which our imaginations continue to be in thrall to ideologies of maternity and the nuclear family.
Paperback: 978-1-78535-539-4 ebook: 978-1-78535-540-0

How to Dismantle the NHS in 10 Easy Steps (Second Edition)
Youssef El-Gingihy
The story of how your NHS was sold off and why you will have to buy private health insurance soon. A new expanded second edition with chapters on junior doctors' strikes and government blueprints for US-style healthcare.
Paperback: 978-1-78904-178-1 ebook: 978-1-78904-179-8

Digesting Recipes
The Art of Culinary Notation
Susannah Worth
A recipe is an instruction, the imperative tone of the expert, but
this constraint can offer its own kind of potential. A recipe need
not be a domestic trap but might instead offer escape – something
to fantasise about or aspire to.
Paperback: 978-1-78279-860-6 ebook: 978-1-78279-859-0

Most titles are published in paperback and as an ebook.
Paperbacks are available in traditional bookshops. Both print and
ebook formats are available online.
Follow us on Facebook
at https://www.facebook.com/ZeroBooks
and Twitter at https://twitter.com/Zer0Books